ZAGAT®

Best of
London

LOCAL EDITORS
Malika Dalamal, Sholto Douglas-Home,
Jeremy Hazlehurst and Susan Kessler
STAFF EDITORS
Donna Marino Wilkins with Troy Segal

Published and distributed by
Zagat Survey, LLC
4 Columbus Circle
New York, NY 10019
T: 212.977.6000
E: bestoflondon@zagat.com
www.zagat.com

ACKNOWLEDGMENTS

We thank Deborah Bennett,
Karen Bonham, Caroline Clegg,
Claire Coleman, Ricki Conway,
Alex, Louis and Tallula Douglas-
Home, Rosanne Johnston, Larry
Kessler, Le Cordon Bleu
(London), Pamela and Michael
Lester, Leuka 2000, Margaret
Levin, Missy Modell, Anne
Semmes, Alexandra Spezzotti,
Peter Vogl, Susan and Jeffrey
Weingarten, as well as the
following members of our staff:
Chris Miragliotta (editorial
project manager), Amy Cao
(editorial assistant), Sean
Beachell, Maryanne Bertollo,
Sandy Cheng, Reni Chin, Larry
Cohn, Bill Corsello, Deirdre
Donovan, Caitlin Eichelberger,
Alison Flick, Jeff Freier, Shelley
Gallagher, Randi Gollin, Caroline
Hatchett, Karen Hudes, Roy
Jacob, Natalie Lebert, Mike Liao,
Allison Lynn, Dave Makulec,
Rachel McConlogue, Andre
Pilette, Josh Rogers, Becky
Ruthenburg, Robert Seixas, Kelly
Stewart, Kilolo Strobert, Liz
Borod Wright, Sharon Yates
and Kyle Zolner.

The reviews published in this guide
are based on public opinion
surveys, with numerical ratings
reflecting the average scores given
by all survey participants who voted
on each establishment and text
based on direct quotes from, or fair
paraphrasings of, participants'
comments. Phone numbers,
addresses and other factual
information were correct to the best
of our knowledge when published in
this guide; any subsequent changes
may not be reflected.

Contents

Ratings & Symbols

Ratings and Reviews

All **ratings** throughout this guide are on a scale of 0 to 30 as follows:

0 – **9**   poor to fair
10 – **15**   fair to good
16 – **19**   good to very good
20 – **25**   very good to excellent
26 – **30**   extraordinary to perfection
     ∇   low response | less reliable

Ratings apply to the key aspects of the category covered (Dining, Shopping, Attractions, etc.). See the Ratings & Symbols key in each section.

Cost is covered differently in each category, as noted in the Ratings & Symbols keys. Costs are indicated in British pounds.

Surveyor comments are shown in quotation marks within reviews.

Symbols

Z   Zagat Top Spot (highest ratings, popularity and importance)
●   serves after 11 PM
S   closed on Sunday
M   closed on Monday
⊄   no credit cards accepted

See also the Ratings & Symbols key in each section.

Index

All establishments are listed alphabetically, with their page number, in the Alphabetical Index at the back of the book.

Maps

Index maps show establishments with the highest ratings in those areas.

About This Survey

Here are the results of our first **Best of London Survey,** covering 1,306 of the city's finest restaurants, nightspots, shops and attractions as rated by 7,822 surveyors. We've also included leading hotels as rated by avid travelers. Like all our guides, it's based on the collective opinions of thousands of savvy consumers and is designed to help locals and visitors alike make smart choices about where to spend their time and money.

WHO PARTICIPATED: Of the 7,822 participants, 44% are women, 56% men; the breakdown by age is 13% in their 20s; 29%, 30s; 22%, 40s; 19%, 50s; and 17%, 60s or above. Collectively they bring a vast amount of experience and knowledge to this Survey (their comments are shown in quotation marks within the reviews). We sincerely thank each of these participants – this book is really "theirs."

HELPFUL LISTS: Whether you're looking to celebrate or keep things simple, our lists can help you find exactly the right place. See the Most Popular and Top Ratings lists on pages 8-12, as well as the tips and lists that begin each section: Dining (pages 14-20); Nightlife (pages 80-82); Shopping (pages 118-121); Attractions (pages 172-173) and Hotels (pages 194-195). We've also provided detailed neighbourhood maps (pages 285-290) and 14 handy indexes.

OUR EDITORS: Special thanks go to our local editors: Malika Dalamal, a fashion and shopping writer who has written for *Elle, L'Officiel,* Net-A-Porter.com, *The Daily Telegraph* and *The Daily Mail;* Sholto Douglas-Home, a London restaurant critic for over 15 years and an international marketing executive; Jeremy Hazlehurst, the Diary Editor at *City AM;* and Susan Kessler, a cookbook author and consultant for numerous lifestyle publications in the U.K. and U.S.

ABOUT ZAGAT: This marks our 29th year reporting on the shared experiences of consumers like you. What started in 1979 as a hobby involving 200 of our friends has come a long way. Today we have over 300,000 surveyors and now cover dining, entertaining, golf, hotels, movies, music, nightlife, resorts, shopping, spas, theatre and tourist attractions worldwide.

SHARE YOUR OPINION: We invite you to join any of our upcoming surveys – just register at **zagat.com,** where you can rate and review establishments year-round. Each participant will receive a free copy of the resulting guide when published.

AVAILABILITY: Zagat guides are available in all major bookstores, by subscription at **zagat.com** and for use on a wide range of mobile devices via **Zagat To Go** or **zagat.mobi.**

FEEDBACK: There is always room for improvement, thus we invite your comments and suggestions about any aspect of our performance. Just contact us at bestoflondon@zagat.com.

New York, NY
24 October, 2007

Nina and Tim Zagat

What's New

Travel to London is booming, with the city welcoming a record 15.2 million overseas visitors in 2006. The largest increase came from Europe, up 11.6% to 9.6 million, and, despite a weak American dollar, from the U.S., up 5.2% to 2.4 million.

PLEASED TO BE PUFFLESS: The British government banned smoking in restaurants and bars this past summer (a policy endorsed by 93% of Zagat surveyors). Close to one in three respondents say they'll now eat out more than before and almost one in two will hit a nightlife venue more frequently.

PARTY ON: Our London surveyors clearly enjoy their nightlife. On average, they go out 2.3 times per week and order an average 3.6 drinks – slightly more than those famous New York partyers, who average 2 nights and 3.2 drinks. Plus they're spending a whopping 44 pounds per outing, excluding dinner. This Survey's Most Popular bar is the high-end Claridge's in Mayfair, whilst the spot that earned the Top Appeal score is Soho's lounge Milk and Honey (sister to the NYC outpost), which boasts a members-only floor.

CHANGING OF THE GUARD: Über-restaurateur Sir Terence Conran spun off his stable of eateries into a new company, D&D London, and has refreshed some ageing hipsters as well as opened new ones (South Bank's Skylon). Meanwhile, our surveyors rated Chez Bruce in Wandsworth No. 1 for Food, knocking out Chelsea's Gordon Ramsay.

ROOM AT THE INN: Room rates, which were already expensive, have risen since last year. As noted above, that hasn't hampered tourism, but it may help ex- plain a hotel building boom. The most significant new entrant in the lodging scene is the Financial District's Hyatt-managed Great Eastern Hotel, while on the boutique side, the Haymarket debuted in the Theatre District. Luxury-lovers are watching two posh bastions: Covent Garden's Savoy, which closes for a redo in December, and Mayfair's Connaught, which reopens after a renovation around the same time.

BIG VS. SMALL: It's no shock that our Survey's Most Popular store is the beloved Harrods, but 55% of our surveyors prefer to shop in small boutiques. They voted apparelmaker Loro Piana (Knightsbridge and Mayfair) No. 1 for Quality and awarded two Mayfair jewellers No. 1 spots: Harry Winston for Display and Asprey for Service. Of course, antiquing is always popular, as a walk down Portobello Road and Church Street will confirm.

STANDARDS TO ATTRACT: Keeping England's 6,000 visitor attractions up to snuff is the goal of an initiative by the national tourism agency, VisitBritain, which hopes to institute a Code of Practice to ensure quality. Indeed, high standards are de rigueur for this Survey's Most Popular Attraction – the British Museum – which earns the No. 1 ranking for Appeal as well.

New York, NY
24 October, 2007

Donna Marino Wilkins

A London Primer

With a population of 7.7 million, London is one of the world's truly great cities, with an incredible range of peoples and cultures that's reflected in its diversity of restaurants, nightlife and activities.

WHEN TO VISIT: Since almost all of London's attractions are open year-round, it's never a bad time to visit. Although the weather is most pleasant during the peak season from June to September, crowds are thicker and prices higher. You'll often find better deals in November, January and February. Any time of year, the weather can be unpredictable, with bouts of rain and cold, so keep an umbrella handy. When timing your trip, you may want to take advantage of (or avoid) annual events, including sales and holidays. Public holidays include 1st January, Good Friday, Easter Monday, May Day, the last Monday in May, the last Monday in August, 25th December and 26th December. Be aware that most attractions and shops close Christmas Day, and many are also closed 24th December, 1st January and Good Friday, so make plans accordingly.

FROM HERE TO THERE: London's public transportation is usually the best way to get around. Buses are the cheapest option, operating regularly from 7 AM to midnight. The Tube (or Underground) is the second cheapest option, offering 12 colour-coded lines. Pick up a Travelcard good for one, three or seven days if you plan to ride frequently. One-day, off-peak passes (good from 9:30 AM–4:30 AM) start at £6.60 for adults, and they can be used for Tubes, most buses and railways. Children under 11 travel free during these times. Taxis are plentiful, but a minimum fare of £2.20 is applied at all times. The metre calculates the fare based on the time of day, distance travelled and taxi speed. To hail one, just wave when you see the illuminated yellow light above the windscreen.

MONEY MATTERS: The British currency is based on the pound (or 'quid') consisting of 100 pence. Exchange rates fluctuate daily, but the pound has been generally strong, which means that almost everything in London will feel very expensive to most visitors from abroad. It's favourable to wait until you're in town to exchange money or to withdraw local currency from your account via the ubiquitous ATMs. A service charge of 10 to 15% is often already included in the bill. If there is no charge included (be sure to check), add 10 to 15%. There's usually no tipping in pubs, but bar staff at more upscale establishments do expect one (10% is standard). Tip taxi drivers and hairdressers at least 10%.

LINE UP: Brits can be rigid about queueing, or standing in line, so be patient and do the same, or you may risk a scolding. You'll also want to stand to the right on escalators, keeping the left clear for passing, and stand aside at arriving trains in order to let departing passengers off.

TELEPHONE TIPS: If you have a serious emergency, dial 999 (or 112) to be connected to fire, police or ambulance. If you're calling abroad from London, dial 00 before the country code. For calls to London from outside the country, dial the country code (44) and the complete phone number, removing the first 0 from the local code.

Dining

Each surveyor has been asked to name his or her five favourite places. This list reflects their choices.

1. Wagamama
2. Nobu London
3. Ivy, The
4. Gordon Ramsay/68 Royal
5. J. Sheekey
6. Wolseley, The
7. Gordon Ramsay/Claridge's
8. Le Gavroche
9. Rules
10. Zuma
11. Hakkasan
12. Square, The
13. Gaucho Grill
14. Zafferano
15. Le Caprice
16. Pétrus
17. Amaya
18. Yauatcha
19. Pizza Express
20. Tamarind
21. Locanda Locatelli
22. Asia de Cuba
23. Le Manoir/Quat'Saisons
24. Savoy Grill*
25. Belgo
26. Chez Bruce
27. Capital Rest.
28. Fat Duck
29. Royal China
30. L'Atelier/Robuchon
31. River Café
32. Busaba Eathai
33. Maze
34. Cinnamon Club
35. Carluccio's
36. Nobu Berkeley St.
37. Galvin Bistrot
38. Cipriani
39. Bibendum
40. St. John

TOP FOOD RATINGS

Ratings are to the left of names. List excludes places with low votes.

28
- Chez Bruce
- Gordon Ramsay/68 Royal
- Hunan
- Le Manoir/Quat'Saisons
- Square, The
- Pétrus
- Pied à Terre

27
- La Trompette
- Le Gavroche
- River Café
- Fat Duck
- Nobu London
- Capital Rest.
- Morgan M*
- Waterside Inn
- Enoteca Turi
- Defune
- Rasoi Vineet Bhatia*

26
- L'Atelier/Robuchon
- Roussillon
- Zuma
- Theo Randall
- Assaggi
- Miyama
- Foliage
- Café Japan
- Club Gascon*
- Mosimann's (club)
- Nobu Berkeley St.
- Umu
- Tom Aikens
- Jin Kichi
- Aubergine
- Zafferano
- Nahm

25
- Gordon Ramsay/Claridge's
- Quirinale
- Clarke's

* Indicates a tie with establishment above

Nightlife

MOST POPULAR

Each surveyor has been asked to name his or her five favourite places.
This list reflects their choices.

1. Claridge's Bar
2. Milk & Honey
3. Nobu Berkeley St.
4. Fifth Floor
5. Dorchester Bar
6. Rivoli Bar
7. Library
8. e&o
9. Belgo
10. All Bar One
11. Sketch
12. Chinawhite
13. Annabel's (club)
14. American Bar
15. Slug and Lettuce*
16. Pitcher & Piano
17. Tiger Tiger*
18. Grenadier
19. Smollensky's
20. O'Neill's
21. Absolut Icebar
22. Cuckoo Club
23. Boujis
24. Ronnie Scott's
25. Café de Paris
26. Dukes Hotel Bar
27. Fabric*
28. End, The
29. Long Bar*
30. Tup*
31. Waxy O'Connor's*
32. Yauatcha*
33. Ling Ling
34. Smiths/Smithfield
35. Holly Bush
36. Mocotó*
37. G-A-Y
38. Café Boheme
39. Comedy Store*
40. Whisky Bar*

TOP APPEAL RATINGS

Ratings are to the left of names. List excludes places with low votes.

27	Milk & Honey
26	Ling Ling
25	Ronnie Scott's
	Claridge's Bar
	Holly Bush
	Loungelover*
	Rivoli Bar
24	Annabel's (club)
	Nobu Berkeley St.
	End, The
	Dukes Hotel Bar
	Ye Olde Cheshire
	Yauatcha
	Grenadier
	Dorchester Bar
23	Spaniard's Inn
	Heaven
	Whisky Bar*
	Absolut Ice Bar
	Cuckoo Club

Library
Gordon's
Vertigo 42*
Cow

22	American Bar
	Engineer
	Light Bar
	Fabric
	Bleeding Heart Tavern
	Cork & Bottle*
	All Star Lanes
	Prospect Whitby*
	e&o
	Sketch
	Chinawhite
	Purple Bar
	Sherlock Holmes
	Mocotó
	Jerusalem
	Boujis

Shopping

Each surveyor has been asked to name his or her five favourite places. This list reflects their choices.

1. Harrods
2. Selfridges
3. Fortnum & Mason
4. Harvey Nichols
5. Marks & Spencer
6. Liberty
7. John Lewis
8. Topshop*
9. Boots
10. Hamleys
11. Peter Jones
12. Burberry
13. Victoria & Albert Museum*
14. Tate Modern
15. Gieves & Hawkes
16. Conran Shop, The
17. Thomas Pink
18. Zara*
19. Molton Brown
20. Monsoon
21. National Portrait Gallery
22. SPACE.NK apothecary
23. Muji
24. Smythson of Bond Street
25. Asprey
26. Prada
27. H & M
28. Habitat
29. Neal's Yard Remedies*
30. Accessorize
31. Brioni*
32. Jo Malone
33. Penhaligon's
34. Abercrombie & Fitch
35. Body Shop, The
36. Kiehl's
37. Gap
38. Chanel
39. Hermes
40. Tod's*

TOP QUALITY RATINGS

Ratings are to the left of names. List excludes places with low votes.

29
- Loro Piana
- Brioni
- Chanel
- Asprey
- Manolo Blahnik
- Harry Winston
- Hermes

28
- Thomas Goode
- Jimmy Choo
- Christian Louboutin
- Garrard
- Giorgio Armani
- Ermenegildo Zegna
- Dunhill
- Prada*
- Smythson of Bond Street
- Bottega Veneta

27
- Louis Vuitton
- Cartier
- N.Peal
- Church's
- Penhaligon's
- Issey Miyake
- Salvatore Ferragamo
- Fortnum & Mason
- Browns
- MaxMara
- Anne Fontaine
- Tod's
- Alberta Ferretti
- Vivienne Westwood
- Valentino

26
- Tiffany & Co.
- Fendi
- Fratelli Rossetti*
- Kiehl's
- Harvey Nichols
- Jo Malone*
- Burberry
- Gucci

Attractions

MOST POPULAR

Each surveyor has been asked to name his or her five favourite places. This list reflects their choices.

1. British Museum
2. Tower of London
3. Buckingham Palace
4. London Eye
5. National Gallery*
6. Tate Modern
7. Westminster Abbey
8. Windsor Castle
9. Victoria and Albert Museum
10. Hampton Court Palace
11. St. Paul's Cathedral
12. Imperial War Museum
13. Hyde Park
14. National Theatre
15. Covent Garden
16. Shakespeare's Globe
17. Houses of Parliament
18. National Portrait Gallery
19. Borough Market
20. Portobello Market

TOP APPEAL RATINGS

Ratings are to the left of names. List excludes places with low votes.

28 British Museum
Westminster Abbey
Tower of London
National Gallery
Windsor Castle
Hampton Court Palace
Houses of Parliament
Royal Botanic Gardens, Kew

27 St. Paul's Cathedral
Churchill Museum
Imperial War Museum

Buckingham Palace
Courtauld Institute
   Galleries
Victoria and Albert
   Museum

26 Shakespeare's Globe
National Portrait Gallery
Regent's Park
Science Museum
Tate Britain
Borough Market

Hotels

MOST POPULAR

Each surveyor has been asked to name his or her five favourite places. This list reflects their choices.

1. Claridge's
2. Lanesborough
3. Savoy, A Fairmont Hotel*
4. Connaught, The
5. Ritz, The
6. Dorchester, The
7. Four Seasons
8. Sheraton Park Tower
9. Mandarin Oriental
10. Berkeley, The

TOP OVERALL RATINGS

Ratings, shown to the left of names, are the average of the hotel's scores for Rooms, Service, Dining and Facilities. List excludes places with low votes.

26 Lanesborough
25 Claridge's
24 Four Seasons Canary Wharf
   Dorchester, The
   Connaught, The

   Ritz, The
   Goring, The
   Mandarin Oriental
   Four Seasons
23 47 Park Street

DINING

Dining

A revolution in gourmet dining has made London an exciting culinary destination. An array of cuisines – from the traditional English fare at pubs to a plethora of ethnic eats to fine dining via star chefs such as Gordon Ramsay and Bruce Poole – means the capital can be a serious food-lovers' paradise.

CHECK-OUT COUNTER: Eating out in London is generally expensive. The average cost of a meal went up 3% to £39 over last year, and 74% of our surveyors say they're spending more than they did back in 2005. When the bill arrives, look at it carefully – sometimes the service charge (10–15%) or a cover charge is already added. Don't mistakenly tip twice. Check to see if a prix fixe includes VAT (Value Added Tax) as well.

TIMING IS EVERYTHING: Many restaurants offer two set-price menus, one for dinner and one for lunch. If you eat your main meal early, you can sample the cuisine of some of this town's best chefs for a fraction of the evening cost. Whilst restaurants keep varied hours, lunch is usually available from noon until 2 PM and dinner from 7:30 until about 10 PM, though more are staying open later or offering pre-theatre specials. Many restaurants are closed on Sunday and for a few days around Christmas.

PUB GRUB: For the most characteristic British drinking and dining, the classic pub is the choice. If possible, avoid eating from 1–2 PM when the crush of office workers heads out for lunch. Over the past decade, the rise of the gastropub has elevated the variety and quality of pub cuisine. Some of the best are this Survey's Top Gastropub, Waterloo's Anchor & Hope and Anglesea Arms in Shepherd's Bush.

FISH 'N' CHIP CHAMPS: One of England's most famous dishes, fish 'n' chips has been a popular takeaway food in London from at least the mid-19th century and today can be found everywhere from the modest 'chippy' shops to pubs and restaurants. The deep-fried fish and accompanying fried potatoes, with salt and vinegar added, were traditionally sold wrapped in newspaper. For the best samples, head to popular places like Finchley's Two Brothers Fish, Sweetings in the City or Bloomsbury's North Sea.

A SPOT OF TEA: Another great British institution is afternoon tea. The speciality of grand hotels, it usually includes a selection of fine teas served with finger sandwiches (cucumbers, smoked salmon) along with pastries, cakes, crumpets and scones with clotted cream. The traditional time for tea is 4 PM, but most places serve it between 3 and 5 PM. The fanciest afternoon tea services, such as the one at the Ritz, have a dress code, require advance reservations and are fairly expensive.

Key Newcomers

There's always a new flavour of the month on London's busy restaurant scene. Below is our take on some of the past year's most notable arrivals.

Acorn House	Hoxton Grille
Albion, The	Kobe Jones
Atami	L'Atelier/Robuchon
Bacchus	Magdalen
Barnes Grill	Mews of Mayfair
Barrafina	Mocotó
Benja	Narrow, The
Bouga	Olivomare
Bumpkin	Raviolo
Burlington Club	Rhodes W1 Rest.
Butcher & Grill	Rist. Semplice
C Garden	1707 Wine Bar
Chelsea Brass.	Skylon
Club, The	Spread Eagle
Cookbook Cafe	St. Alban
Dinings	St. Germain
Empress of India	Suka
Fat Badger	Tamarai
Forge, The	Theo Randall
Great Queen St.	Tom's Kitchen
Haiku	Trinity
Hat & Feathers	Via Condotti
Hawksmoor	Wallace, The
High Road Brass.	XO

Coming up later this year, lauded Shropshire destination **Hibiscus** is relocating to smart Mayfair digs; Dulwich will be welcoming **The Rosendale,** a gastropub; and Tony Kitous dishes up another North African experience with **Kenza** in the City. The bandwagon of Big-Name ventures rolls on: the peripatetic Gordon Ramsay is planning more pubs, along with a separate grill for his Maze in Mayfair; Tom Aikens opens seafooder **Tom's Place** in Chelsea; and Rowley Leigh debuts **Le Café des Anglais** in the Whiteleys shopping centre. There are hot happenings in hotels too: chef extraordinaire Alain Ducasse's fine-dining restaurant for The Dorchester and Richard Corrigan's eatery, earmarked for a spring 2008 arrival in the revamped Grosvenor House.

Top Food Ratings

Ratings are to the left of names. Lists exclude places with low votes.

BY CUISINE

ASIAN

23	Eight Over Eight
22	e&o
	Asia de Cuba
	Great Eastern
21	Cocoon

BRITISH (MODERN)

28	Chez Bruce
25	Clarke's
	St. John
24	Glasshouse, The
	Gravetye Manor

BRITISH (TRAD.)

24	ffiona's
	Wilton's
	Dorchester/The Grill
	Bentley's
	Mark's Club (club)

CHINESE

28	Hunan
25	Yauatcha
	Kai Mayfair
24	Hakkasan
	Royal China Club

CHOPHOUSES

24	Rib Room
23	Rules
	Sophie's Steak
22	Gaucho Grill
	Guinea Grill

ECLECTIC

26	Mosimann's (club)
24	Lanes
22	Michael Moore
	Banquette
	Providores, The

EUROPEAN (MODERN)

27	La Trompette
	Fat Duck
26	Foliage
25	Gordon Ramsay/Claridge's
24	Arbutus

FISH 'N' CHIPS

24	Two Brothers Fish

	Sweetings
23	North Sea

FRENCH (BISTRO)

24	Galvin Bistrot
23	Le Café du Marché
22	Racine
	Bibendum Oyster
	La Poule au Pot

FRENCH (CLASSIC)

27	Le Gavroche
	Waterside Inn
24	L'Oranger
23	French Horn
22	Oslo Court

FRENCH (NEW)

28	Gordon Ramsay/68 Royal
	Le Manoir/Quat'Saisons
	Square, The
	Pétrus
	Pied à Terre

INDIAN

27	Rasoi Vineet Bhatia
25	Quilon
	Amaya
	Tamarind
	Zaika

ITALIAN

27	River Café
	Enoteca Turi
26	Theo Randall
	Assaggi
	Zafferano

JAPANESE

27	Nobu London
	Defune
26	Zuma
	Miyama
	Café Japan

LEBANESE

24	Ishbilia
22	Al Waha
	Al Hamra
	Fairuz
	Al Sultan

MEDITERRANEAN

25 Moro
24 Ottolenghi
23 Fifteen
22 Pescatori
Baker & Spice

PIZZA

24 Osteria Basilico
23 Delfino
Il Bordello*
Buona Sera
Oliveto

SEAFOOD

25 J. Sheekey
24 Wilton's
Bentley's
Sweetings
23 Le Suquet

SPANISH

24 Cambio de Tercio
23 El Pirata
Fino
22 Tapas Brindisa
Salt Yard

THAI

26 Nahm
23 Patara
22 Churchill Arms
21 Busaba Eathai
20 Blue Elephant

VEGETARIAN

27 Morgan M
26 Roussillon
25 Gate, The
24 Food for Thought
Rasa

BY SPECIAL FEATURE

BREAKFAST
(other than hotels)

24 Cinnamon Club
23 Ladurée
21 Wolseley, The

BRUNCH

25 Clarke's
24 Le Caprice
22 Lundum's
Providores, The
19 Tom's Kitchen

CHEESE BOARDS

28 Chez Bruce
Gordon Ramsay/68 Royal
Square, The
Pétrus
26 Tom Aikens

CHILD-FRIENDLY

27 River Café
26 Zuma
21 La Famiglia

COMMUNAL TABLES

24 La Fromagerie
Ottolenghi
Food for Thought
22 Baker & Spice
21 Busaba Eathai

HOTEL DINING

28 Le Manoir/Quat'Saisons

Pétrus
(The Berkeley)
27 Nobu London
(Metropolitan Hotel)
Capital
Waterside Inn

LATE NIGHT

26 L'Atelier/Robuchon
25 Roka
24 Hakkasan
23 Ivy, The

MEET FOR A DRINK

26 Zuma
L'Atelier/Robuchon
Nobu Berkeley St.
25 Moro
24 Hakkasan

NEWCOMERS (RATED)

26 L'Atelier/Robuchon
Theo Randall
22 Mews of Mayfair
21 St. Alban
Bacchus

OUTDOOR

27 River Café
25 Ledbury, The
22 Santini
La Poule au Pot
Le Pont de la Tour

PEOPLE-WATCHING

- 27 Nobu London
- 26 Zuma
- 25 Maze
- 21 Wolseley, The
- 20 Cipriani

PRIVATE CLUBS

- 26 Mosimann's
- 24 Harry's Bar
- Morton's
- Mark's Club
- 22 Annabel's

ROOM WITH A VIEW

- 27 Waterside Inn
- 26 Foliage
- 24 Ubon
- 23 Rhodes 24
- 22 Le Pont de la Tour

SMALL PLATES

- 28 Hunan
- 26 Club Gascon
- 25 Amaya
- Maze
- 24 Le Cercle

TASTING MENU

- 28 Gordon Ramsay/68 Royal Square, The
- 27 Fat Duck
- 26 Zuma
- Tom Aikens

TEA SERVICE
(other than hotels)

- 25 Yauatcha
- 24 La Fromagerie
- 23 Ladurée
- 21 Wolseley, The

THEATRELAND

- 26 L'Atelier/Robuchon
- 25 J. Sheekey
- 23 Richard Corrigan
- Ivy, The
- 21 St. Alban

WINNING WINE LISTS

- 28 Gordon Ramsay/68 Royal Square, The
- Pétrus
- 26 Tom Aikens
- 25 Greenhouse, The

BY LOCATION

BELGRAVIA

- 28 Pétrus
- 26 Mosimann's (club)
- Zafferano
- Nahm
- 25 Amaya

BLOOMSBURY

- 24 Hakkasan
- 23 North Sea
- Malabar Junction
- 22 Cigala
- 21 Busaba Eathai

CANARY WHARF

- 24 Quadrato
- Ubon
- Royal China
- 22 Gaucho Grill

CHELSEA

- 28 Gordon Ramsay/68 Royal
- 27 Rasoi Vineet Bhatia
- 26 Tom Aikens
- Aubergine
- 25 Ziani

CHISWICK

- 27 La Trompette
- 21 Gourmet Burger
- 20 High Road Brass.

CITY

- 25 Haz
- 24 Sweetings
- 23 Rhodes 24
- Vivat Bacchus
- Café Spice Namasté

COVENT GARDEN

- 26 L'Atelier/Robuchon
- 25 J. Sheekey
- 24 Food for Thought
- Savoy Grill
- Clos Maggiore

FITZROVIA

- 28 Pied à Terre
- 25 Latium
- Roka
- 24 Rasa
- 23 Sardo

ISLINGTON

27	Morgan M
24	Ottolenghi
	Rasa
20	Pasha
19	Wagamama

KENSINGTON

25	Clarke's
	Zaika
24	ffiona's
	Locanda Ottoemezzo
22	Koi

KNIGHTSBRIDGE

27	Capital Rest.
26	Zuma
	Foliage
24	Ishbilia
	Park, The

MARYLEBONE

27	Defune
25	Locanda Locatelli
	Orrery
24	La Fromagerie
	Galvin Bistrot

MAYFAIR

28	Square, The
27	Le Gavroche
	Nobu London
26	Theo Randall
	Miyama

NOTTING HILL

26	Assaggi
25	Ledbury, The
24	Ottolenghi
	Notting Hill Brass.
	Books for Cooks

PICCADILLY

24	Yoshino
	Bentley's
22	Gaucho Grill
	1707 Wine Bar
21	St. Alban

SHOREDITCH/ SPITALFIELDS/ HOXTON

23	Fifteen
	Viet Hoa
22	St. John Bread/Wine
	Eyre Brothers
	Great Eastern

SMITHFIELD

26	Club Gascon
25	St. John
23	Le Café du Marché

SOHO

25	Yauatcha
24	Alastair Little
	Arbutus
23	Red Fort
	Richard Corrigan

SOUTH KENSINGTON

24	L'Etranger
	Star of India
	Cambio de Tercio
	Bibendum
23	Patara

ST. JAMES'S

24	L'Oranger
	Wilton's
	Le Caprice
23	Ritz, The
22	Green's

Top Decor Ratings

Ratings are to the left of names.

29	Les Trois Garçons
27	Cliveden House
	Ritz
	Gravetye Manor
	Sketch/Lecture Rm.
	Archipelago
	Le Manoir/Quat'Saisons
	Taman Gang
26	Sketch/Gallery
	Lanesborough

	Mosimann's (club)
	Waterside Inn
	Wolseley, The
25	Pétrus
	Wallace, The
	Momo
	Home House (club)
	La Porte des Indes*
	Rhodes 24*
	Hakkasan

Top Service Ratings

Ratings are to the left of names.

28	Gordon Ramsay/68 Royal		Foliage
			Fat Duck
27	Lanes	25	Roussillon
	Waterside Inn		French Horn
26	Le Manoir/Quat'Saisons		Chez Bruce
	Le Gavroche		Dorchester/The Grill
	Square, The		Mosimann's (club)
	Quadrato		Quirinale
	Mark's Club (club)		Oslo Court
	Pétrus		George (club)
	Capital Rest.		

Best Buys

1. Food for Thought
2. Leon
3. Books for Cooks
4. Churchill Arms
5. Little Bay
6. Mildreds
7. Tokyo Diner
8. Jenny Lo's Tea
9. New Tayyabs
10. Gourmet Burger
11. Ed's Easy Diner
12. Lucky 7
13. Wagamama
14. Patisserie Valerie
15. Le Pain Quotidien
16. Pepper Tree
17. Chelsea Bun
18. Babes 'n' Burgers
19. La Porchetta
20. Mandalay

Dining

Abingdon, The *European*   22 | 18 | 21 | £34

Kensington | 54 Abingdon Rd., W8 (Earl's Ct./High St. Kensington) | 020-7937 3339 | fax 7795 6388 | www.theabingdonrestaurant.com
"Essentially a gastropub, but the quality of food and lovely room feel more like a restaurant" attest admirers of this "buzzy", "cosy" "gem a stone's throw away from Kensington High Street", with an "inventive, dependable" Modern European menu that "changes regularly" and "smiling", "knowledgeable staff"; "comfy couches" and "big, red dinerlike booths add massively to the charm."

NEW Acorn House Ⓢ *British*   ▽ 19 | 19 | 15 | £35

King's Cross | 69 Swinton St., WC1 (King's Cross) | 020-7812 1842 | www.acornhouserestaurant.com
"The standard-bearer for ecological eateries" – with carbon-neutral paint on the walls and biodegradable takeaway packaging – this "welcome addition to King's Cross" from a co-founder of Fifteen boasts "lovely ambience in a modern setting"; whilst "the care put into the Modern British food" is appreciated, the deli-counter may be preferable, given the "slightly chaotic service."

Alastair Little ●Ⓢ *British*   24 | 15 | 21 | £49

Soho | 49 Frith St., W1 (Leicester Sq./Tottenham Court Rd.) | 020-7734 5183 | fax 7734 5206
"Despite the name, Juliet Peston does the cooking" – and most feel she "has maintained the high standard" set by this Soho stalwart in the '80s; if a few feel this Modern Brit is "resting on good will from days gone by" – the dining room definitely "needs a thorough refresh" – the "adorable service" and "intimate atmosphere" still attract an "arty crowd, especially later in the evening."

NEW Albion, The *British*   – | – | – | M

Islington | 10 Thornhill Rd., N1 (Angel) | 020-7607 7450 | www.the-albion.co.uk
This country-style Georgian pub in the middle of Islington – feted for its impressive 450-sq.-meter garden with fruit trees and clinging wisteria – has received a sympathetic refurb after being taken over by

	FOOD	DECOR	SERVICE	COST

chef Richard Turner (ex Automat); the midpriced Traditional British menu features classics such as shepherd's pie and bubble and squeak, with BBQ and spit roasts prepared outside in the summer.

Al Hamra ◗ *Lebanese*   22 | 14 | 18 | £34

Mayfair | 31-33 Shepherd Mkt., W1 (Green Park) | 020-7493 1954 | fax 7493 1044 | www.alhamrarestaurant.co.uk

"Popular with Middle Eastern plutocrats, cosmocrats" and "well-heeled" locals, this Shepherd Market Lebanese offers "delectable" fare, including a "tempting assortment of mezze"; even if service is "somewhat abrupt" and the "setting ordinary", it's often "bustling" at the "particularly nice" pavement tables; P.S. whilst it's "akin to eating in a cafeteria", the Brasserie across the street has lower prices and French charcuterie.

Alloro ⓩ *Italian*   22 | 17 | 22 | £50

Mayfair | 19-20 Dover St., W1 (Green Park) | 020-7495 4768 | fax 7629 5348

"Great for business or a glam date", this "polished act" in Mayfair boasts "accomplished" Italian *cucina* that's "delicious in its simplicity", supported by "helpful, unobtrusive staff"; just be advised that the food and, especially, the "wines can be pricey."

Alounak ◗ *Persian*   23 | 15 | 16 | £22

Westbourne Grove | 44 Westbourne Grove, W2 (Bayswater/Royal Oak) | 020-7229 4158 | fax 7792 1219
Olympia | 10 Russell Gdns., W14 (Olympia) | 020-7603 1130

The "tight quarters" and "no-frills" decor notwithstanding, patrons proclaim this a "pleasant Persian" pair, primarily on account of the "awesome", "melt-in-your-mouth" cooking at "reasonable prices"; "bring your own wine" and "expect to wait an eternity for a table", whether in Westbourne Grove or Olympia.

Al Sultan *Lebanese*   22 | 15 | 20 | £33

Mayfair | 51-52 Hertford St., W1 (Green Park) | 020-7408 1155 | fax 7408 1113 | www.alsultan.co.uk

Despite its 22 years, this "pleasant surprise" is "less well known than many other Lebanese, but is preferable" for its "attentive service" and "authentic", "consistently delicious" cooking; some connoisseurs claim it's "not cheap for Middle Eastern fare – guess you pay for the location" in Shepherd Market.

Al Waha ◗ *Lebanese*   22 | 16 | 20 | £31

Bayswater | 75 Westbourne Grove, W2 (Bayswater/Queensway) | 020-7229 0806 | www.waha-uk.com

"Contemporary interpretations of Lebanese cuisine" that "pack a punch", along with "homely service", draw followers to this small Westbourne Grove eatery; it's "not much to look at" and "gets tight on a busy evening", but "they do a nicely presented delivery service."

ⓩ Amaya ◗ *Indian*   25 | 24 | 21 | £52

Belgravia | 15-19 Halkin Arcade, Motcomb St., SW1 (Knightsbridge) | 020-7823 1166 | fax 7259 6464 | www.realindianfood.com

"As Nobu is to Japanese, this is to Indian" gush groupies of this "glitzy" Belgravia eatery – "low lighting and candles everywhere" – whose "tasty" small plates and "curries with class" make "a refreshing departure from the usual"; some pout the "pricey" "portions are small", but

most of the "manicured clientele" maintain this colony of the Chutney Mary empire is "a serious find in London's high-end food stakes."

Anchor & Hope *British*
24 | 15 | 18 | £33

Waterloo | 36 The Cut, SE1 (Southwark/Waterloo) | 0871-075 7279

"If you must go to a gastropub, then this is the one" maintain mavens of this "busy" Modern Brit in Waterloo, whose "hearty food in hefty portions" is ideal "to share family-style"; although the "no-bookings policy is a killer" ("best arrive early"), "it's worth the wait at the bar, in the street, anywhere"; N.B. they do take reservations for Sunday lunch.

Andrew Edmunds *European*
22 | 19 | 21 | £37

Soho | 46 Lexington St., W1 (Oxford Circus/Piccadilly Circus) | 020-7437 5708

"Most would walk past and ignore" this "hidden" "Soho diehard" – pity, because they'd miss a "rustic ambience" with "lots of romantic candles" ("perfect for a second date"), a "daily changing", "great-value" Modern European menu of "simple dishes that's complemented by an extensive wine list" and "staff who know how to please"; in short, a "fantastic cubbyhole", even if it can "feel a little claustrophobic."

Anglesea Arms *British*
23 | 19 | 15 | £29

Shepherd's Bush | 35 Wingate Rd., W6 (Goldhawk Rd./Ravenscourt Park) | 020-8749 1291 | fax 8749 1254

"Shepherd's Bush should rejoice" that it has this "relaxed" gastropub, a "mainstay" for Modern British fare that's "cooked to perfection"; "the excellence of the food is not matched in the service" – "the waits can be eternal" – but with "big leather sofas, an open fire" and "offbeat", mismatched chairs, it's "a fantastic place to while away an afternoon."

Annabel's ●Ⓩ *British/French*
22 | 24 | 25 | £75

Private club; inquiries: 020-7629 1096

The "ultimate London private club", this 45-year-old Berkeley Square landmark "is cool again", offering an "exclusive, elusive" combo of "divine people-watching", "glamourous" atmosphere and "top-notch service"; sure, it's "vvvvvery expensive" "for drinks, dancing" and decent Classic French–British cuisine, "but remember, you get what you pay for" at this "perfectly mah-velous" place.

Arbutus *European*
24 | 17 | 18 | £42

Soho | 63-64 Frith St., W1 (Leicester Sq./Tottenham Court Rd.) | 020-7734 4545 | www.arbutusrestaurant.co.uk

"If you can ignore the rather drab, noisy room" and "patchy service", you too may "join the crowd raving about" this "welcome addition to the Soho scene"; accolades accrue for Modern European cuisine that "dazzles in the mouth" and is "decently priced" ("especially given the location"), and for a "super wine list that encourages experimentation", as most "bottles are available in 250 ml carafes"; N.B. its Mayfair offshoot, Wild Honey, opened post-Survey.

Archipelago Ⓩ *Eclectic*
21 | 27 | 22 | £49

Fitzrovia | 110 Whitfield St., W1 (Goodge St./Warren St.) | 020-7383 3346 | fax 7383 7181

Those who "like to experiment" when they eat – think "locusts, chocolate-covered scorpions and kangaroo" – find this "very, very

odd" Fiztrovian Eclectic with "exotic jungle decor" and "dark", "romantic" ambience is "always an amazing experience"; but it's "atrociously expensive" too, leading sceptics to suggest, "less insects, more chef-ing please."

Asia de Cuba ● Asian/Cuban   22 | 23 | 19 | £52

Covent Garden | St. Martins Lane Hotel | 45 St. Martin's Ln., WC2 (Leicester Sq.) | 020-7300 5588 | fax 7300 5540 | www.chinagrillmanagement.com

Still "swank, sleek and happening several years after its opening", this Theatreland haunt serves "creative" "Cuban classics with an Oriental twist" in "jumbo portions" – "so order less than you might think"; some tut it's "tired", with "service not up to the price mark"; but the "models and mega-stars" keep it so "loud" "you can't hear yourself think – or taste"; P.S. "don't wear white, you might blend into the background."

Assaggi ⑤ Italian   26 | 15 | 23 | £53

Notting Hill | 39 Chepstow Pl., 1st fl., W2 (Notting Hill Gate) | 020-7792 5501 | fax 0870-051 2923

The "mood is set by the exuberant maitre d' who explains the menu with gusto and passion" at this "exquisite Italian" in a "homely", albeit "spartan", room "above a pub" in Notting Hill; the "simple, rustic" dishes are "magnificently executed" and "beautifully served" – all of which explains why it's so "very hard to get a table."

NEW Atami Restaurant & Bar ⑤ Japanese   ▽ 24 | 20 | 19 | £43

Westminster | 37 Monck St., SW1 (St. James's Park) | 020-7222 2218 | www.atami-restaurant.com

"In a neighbourhood where good places are sparse", this "fantastic new addition" to Westminster (hence, a few "MPs from Parliament nearby") is a "design-led Japanese" displaying "originality and class" in both the "sleek" decor and cuisine – "inventive dishes, plus your staple sushi"; the "courteous service" is "a bit slow", however.

Aubergine ⑤ French   26 | 20 | 24 | £71

Chelsea | 11 Park Walk, SW10 (Gloucester Rd./ South Kensington) | 020-7352 3449 | fax 7351 1770 | www.auberginerestaurant.co.uk

From its low-key "side street location" in Chelsea, this "quaint place subtly exerts its culinary clout" through chef William Drabble's "seductive" New French food – the "pièce de résistance is the degustation menu" – "executed with style" and served by "attentive, yet unobtrusive" staff; a few malcontents "expect more for this kind of cash", but most maintain this is "a model for how haute cuisine should be conducted"; P.S. the lunch prix fixe is a relative "bargain."

Babes 'n' Burgers Hamburgers   17 | 11 | 13 | £15

Notting Hill | 275 Portobello Rd., W11 (Ladbroke Grove) | 020-7229 2704 | fax 7792 5670 | www.babesnburgers.com

"Packed with visitors to Portobello Market, families and locals (weekends are bit of a nightmare)", this "little place" specialises in "made-from-scratch" organic hamburgers and staff who are "great with babies"; numerous salads and non–red meat alternatives make it "good for veggie" or fat-avoiding friends too.

DINING

	FOOD	DECOR	SERVICE	COST

NEW Bacchus ⑤ *Eclectic* — 21 | 16 | 21 | £46
Hoxton | 177 Hoxton St., N1 (Old St.) | 020-7613 0477 | fax 7100 1704 |
www.bacchus-restaurant.co.uk
"Fine dining in a casual gastropub setting" summarises this Eclectic,
whose "bold, dashing" dishes "are more hit than miss" and staff are
"friendly without being overbearing"; the vaguely "'70s-influenced decor can look pretty basic", and the Hoxton location downright "fright-
ening", but most will bacchus up when we say this novice is "worth the
effort to get to."

Baker & Spice *Mediterranean* — 22 | 16 | 15 | £22
Belgravia | 54-56 Elizabeth St., SW1 (Sloane Sq./Victoria) | 020-7730 3033 |
fax 7730 3188
Kilburn | 75 Salusbury Rd., NW6 (Queens Park) | 020-7604 3636 |
fax 7604 3646
NEW St. John's Wood | 20 Clifton Rd., W9 (Warwick Ave.) |
020-7266 1122 | fax 7266 3535
Chelsea | 47 Denyer St., SW3 (Knightsbridge/South Kensington) |
020-7589 4734 | fax 7823 9148
www.bakerandspice.com
Yes, the "prices are mind-boggling", but they really have some of "the
best pastries, baked goods" and Med savouries at these "brilliant"
"bespoke delis" around town; if the "service seems variable" and the
communal tables "cramped", remember these are "mainly takeaway
places" – and besides, "sometimes you [just] need a pricey cookie."

Baltic ❶ *Polish* — 21 | 21 | 19 | £39
Southwark | 74 Blackfriars Rd., SE1 (Southwark) | 020-7928 1111 |
fax 7928 8487 | www.balticrestaurant.co.uk
"Hidden away where you least expect it" in a "cavernous" 1850s
coach-builders workshop, this "boisterous" but "stylish" "Southwark
stalwart" supplies "rib-sticking" Polish fare in "generous portions",
plus "killer *wodkas*" "to work through whilst waiting for the food"; best
of all, there's "no shock when the bill arrives."

Banquette *Eclectic* — 22 | 21 | 20 | £47
Covent Garden | Savoy Hotel | The Strand, WC2 (Covent Garden/
Embankment) | 020-7420 2392 | fax 7592 1601 | www.gordonramsey.com
"It's the Savoy, so you can't really go wrong here" at this discreet (remember it "if you're having an affair") Eclectic eatery say those enamoured by the "comfortable ambience" and "carefully prepared" "mixed
bag of a menu"; whilst it's "perfect for a quick bite", however, some are
"left scratching our heads at the cost"; N.B. due to close in late 2007
during the hotel's renovation.

NEW Barnes Grill *British* — – | – | – | E
Barnes | 2-3 Rocks Ln., SW13 (Barnes Bridge B.R.) | 020-8878 4488 |
fax 8878 5922 | www.awtrestaurants.com
The latest in chef-entrepreneur Antony Worrall Thompson's grills gal-
axy (Kew Grill, Notting Grill), this Barnes Britisher specialises in – you
guessed it – grilled steaks (there's also chicken and fish, but it's really
"not for non-meat eaters") in a hunting-lodge setting that combines
cushions of "purple, reds and pinks with brown leather and animal
heads"; though "staff are very friendly", that doesn't mollify many for
the "enormous bill."

	FOOD	DECOR	SERVICE	COST

NEW Barrafina 🛇 *Spanish* ▽ 24 | 19 | 21 | £34

Soho | 54 Frith St., W1 (Leicester Sq./Piccadilly Circus) | 020-7813 8016 | www.barrafina.co.uk

It's just 23 stools surrounding an L-shaped bar, but "Fino's younger brother" is a "beacon of Spanish gastronomic excellence", attracting a "cool, understated crowd" with "excellent Barcelona-quality tapas" ("the highest form of snacking"), "knowledgeable staff" and a "great sherry" selection; but "you can't book", so "be prepared to queue" at this "great addition to the Soho scene."

Bar Shu ⏺ *Chinese* 22 | 17 | 16 | £36

Soho | 28 Frith St., W1 (Leicester Sq./Tottenham Court Rd.) | 020-7287 8822 | fax 7287 8858 | www.bar-shu.co.uk

"Hot, hot, hot in more ways than one", this "smart" Soho site is a rare Szechuan specialist in town, preparing "authentic", "unusual dishes covered in vibrant red chilli" that makes them "fiery like a dragon, and refreshingly so"; although "surprisingly brusque service lets it down", most agree this "tongue-tingling" spot is "a cut above."

Belgo *Belgian* 19 | 16 | 17 | £24

Covent Garden | 50 Earlham St., WC2 (Covent Garden) | 020-7813 2233 | fax 7209 3212

Chalk Farm | 72 Chalk Farm Rd., NW1 (Chalk Farm) | 020-7267 0718 | fax 7284 4842

www.belgo-restaurants.com

It's "like dining in a 1980s music video" at this communal-table, "chaotic", "cavernous" Covent Garden and Chalk Farm pair where staff dressed as "Trappist monks serve hearty Belgian fare", "mainly mussels" and frites ("anything else, skip it") – along with a "mind-boggling beer list" of brews; "although a bit 'fast-food' in its feel" and "upscale frat scene" in its ambience, it's "perfect for an early dinner" from 5–6:30 PM, when the price equals the time of your order (Earlham Street only).

Benares *Indian* 23 | 23 | 20 | £53

Mayfair | 12A Berkeley Square Hse., Berkeley Sq., W1 (Green Park) | 020-7629 8886 | fax 7499 2430 | www.benaresrestaurant.com

Its "lush decor" – "beautifully modern with classical touches" – is the first sign there's something different about this "edgy Indian" in Berkeley Square; chef-patron Atul Kochhar's "menu seems limited at first, but every dish is outstanding", "always pushing the envelope"; a few fusspots protest the "pushy staff", but still, this "sleek" establishment stays "busy with business types" who can afford to bear the "nose-bleeding prices."

NEW Benja 🛇 *Thai* – | – | – | E

Soho | 17 Beak St., W1 (Oxford Circus/Piccadilly Circus) | 020-7287 0555 | fax 7287 0056

Its name means 'five' and the quintet theme runs throughout this three-storey elegant Soho newcomer, from the five taste sensations (sweet, spicy, sour, bitter and salty) of its "pricey but very good" traditional Thai fare to the five colours (red, black, green, turquoise and yellow) in its "great" decor, which includes wall-mounted ceramic flying fish and carved lotus.

	FOOD	DECOR	SERVICE	COST

Bentley's *British/Seafood* | 24 | 19 | 21 | £49 |

Piccadilly | 11-15 Swallow St., W1 (Piccadilly Circus) | 020-7734 4756 | fax 7758 4140 | www.bentleys.org

Now "under the sway of respected chef Richard Corrigan, this strictly British seafood house has enhanced its past reputation" for "fish that's sublime"; diners can go for the "lively" "outstanding oyster bar" ("one of the best options after-theatre") or "ambrosial Dover sole" in the more "intimate" upstairs; "not cheap", but "a plus for the London scene."

Bibendum *French* | 24 | 23 | 22 | £57 |

South Kensington | Michelin Hse. | 81 Fulham Rd., SW3 (South Kensington) | 020-7581 5817 | fax 7823 7925 | www.bibendum.co.uk

21 years on, it's "still a hit" say fans of this "stylish" New French in the "whimsical Michelin building" (the tyre company's "old U.K. HQ"), where the "innovative" fare is "a feast for the eyes and palate", aided by "delightful service"; the bellicose blow a gasket at the "eye-popping prices", but most declare they could "die in bliss" here.

Bibendum Oyster Bar *French/Seafood* | 22 | 21 | 19 | £39 |

South Kensington | Michelin Hse. | 81 Fulham Rd., SW3 (South Kensington) | 020-7589 1480 | fax 7823 7925 | www.bibendum.co.uk

"How amusing to sit in an old garage and eat oysters" at this "lively" Brompton Cross bistro where a display of "fabulous winkles, shrimp and lobster" forms the backbone of the "good, cold" French menu; whilst "pricey", it's still a "cheaper way to visit this wonderful landmark" – the 1911 Michelin building – than the restaurant upstairs.

Bleeding Heart ⊠ *French* | 22 | 20 | 20 | £44 |

Farringdon | 4 Bleeding Heart Yard, off Greville St., EC1 (Farringdon) | 020-7242 8238 | fax 7831 1402

Bleeding Heart Tavern ⊠ *British*

Farringdon | 19 Greville St., EC1 (Farringdon) | 020-7404 0333 | fax 7831 1402
www.bleedingheart.co.uk

"A bit off the beaten track" in a "historic" Farringdon courtyard, this venue is actually "a collection of great spots": a "cosy" bistro with "cute Swiss log cabin decor" and a more "fancy" "atmospheric downstairs" restaurant, both serving "wholesome, satisfying" New French fare and "well-priced wines"; then there's the informal Tavern on Greville Street, "good for Traditional British soul food and a pint."

Blue Elephant ● *Thai* | 20 | 25 | 19 | £44 |

Fulham | 4-6 Fulham Broadway, SW6 (Fulham Broadway) | 020-7385 6595 | fax 7386 7665 | www.blueelephant.com

"Koi carp, bridges", "beautiful plants and streams in the middle of Fulham" – "the decor never ceases to surprise" at this "exotic tropical jungle"; true, the "traditional Thai food", though "nice", "would be one-third of the price without all the razzamatazz", and the "staff in military-style outfits" "can be slow"; still, whilst "weird and wacky, it works."

Bombay Brasserie ● *Indian* | 22 | 22 | 19 | £37 |

South Kensington | Courtfield Rd., SW7 (Gloucester Rd.) | 020-7370 4040 | fax 7835 1669 | www.bombaybrasserielondon.com

For a "high-end Indian fix" with "that Merchant-Ivory feeling", this slightly pricey South Ken stalwart remains "a classic" choice where

diners can "dig deep into the exotic menu, or play it safe"; foes feel the "service is somewhat uptight" and the decor "tired" – but the latter at least is slated for a post-Survey refurb.

Books for Cooks ⑤Ⓜ *Eclectic*   24 | 21 | 21 | £18

Notting Hill | 4 Blenheim Crescent, W11 (Ladbroke Grove/ Notting Hill Gate) | 020-7221 1992 | fax 7221 1517 | www.booksforcooks.com

"An iconic destination for serious cooks", this "teeny tiny" cafe "located at the back of a unique bookshop" off Ladbroke Grove features "wildly exciting", "experimental" Eclectic meals (one choice per day), using recipes "taken from featured cookbooks"; it's "the biggest bargain in town – but don't tell anyone, it's busy enough."

ⓃⒺⓌ Bouga *Moroccan*   – | – | – | M

Muswell Hill | 1 Park Rd., N8 (Archway) | 020-8348 5609

"A fun addition to buzzy Crouch End", this newcomer dishes up all the predictable Moroccan mainstays, plus "great cocktails" and weekend belly dancers, amidst the candlelit contours of an Old Marrakech setting.

Boxwood Café ● *British*   21 | 20 | 21 | £59

Belgravia | Berkeley Hotel | Wilton Pl., SW1 (Knightsbridge) | 020-7235 1010 | fax 7235 1011 | www.gordonramsay.com

Strictly speaking, this "stylish", "buzzy" Gordon Ramsay–owned eatery is "not a cafe at all" attest fans who fall for the "imaginative" takes on Modern British "comfort food" (like "the heavenly veal and foie gras burger") and "attentive-without-being-starchy service"; admittedly, whilst "cheaper than other Ramsay [venues], it's not cheap at all", and hostiles huff it "has a hotel-restaurant feel about it" too (well, it *is* in the Berkeley).

Brown's Hotel - The Grill *British*   22 | 24 | 25 | £56

Mayfair | Brown's Hotel | Albemarle St., W1 (Green Park) | 020-7518 4060 | fax 7493 9381 | www.brownshotel.com

"After the recent renovation", this newly "chic", slightly modernised Mayfair hotel grill is "as good a treat in haute cuisine as ever", with a "delicious", "classic" British bill of fare – "even the [carving] trolley" – and "professional" service; naturally nostalgists note it's "lost its old charm" and is "too much like a typical hotel" (i.e. "expensive" "for what you get"), but devotees declare it's "destined to be a classic" again; P.S. you "must book" the "ultimate English experience" – afternoon tea in the lounge.

ⓃⒺⓌ Bumpkin ● *British*   21 | 20 | 20 | £37

Notting Hill | 209 Westbourne Park Rd., W11 (Westbourne Park) | 020-7243 9818 | www.bumpkinuk.com

For a "hearty" British "country meal with a twist of London hippiness thrown in", try this triparte "newcomer to Notting Hill"; "each level has something to offer": a "lively, fresh, ground-floor" brasserie ("be ready to wait" as you can't book in advance, except on Sunday), a more "romantic" restaurant upstairs and finally, "don't miss the [for-hire] whisky lounges on the top floor"; "the staff welcome you like they've known you for years" – and indeed, "you won't want to leave."

	FOOD	DECOR	SERVICE	COST

Buona Sera ● *Italian*
| | 23 | 19 | 20 | £28 |

Battersea | 22-26 Northcote Rd., SW11 (Clapham Junction B.R.) | 020-7228 9925 | fax 7228 1114
Chelsea | 289A King's Rd., SW3 (Sloane Sq.) | 020-7352 8827 | fax 7352 8827

The "innovative" setting of bunk bed–style tables "is a brilliant way to make the most of the limited floor space (makes dropping your fork a bit of a hazard, though)" at these Chelsea and Battersea Italians; "family-friendly at weekends", but "equally good for a night out with the girls", their "excellent selection of pizza and pasta" "never disappoints" as long as you "don't expect fireworks."

NEW Burlington Club ●⚅ *Spanish*
| | – | – | – | E |

Mayfair | 12 New Burlington St., W1 (Oxford Circus/Piccadilly Circus) | 020-7734 0233 | fax 3102 3071 | www.burlingtonclub.com

Mayfair mavens bask in the Basque bites, served amidst decor of coloured lights and whimsical furniture, of this new small-plates place; a few feel it's "expensive for tiny tapas – better to come later", when it becomes a bar/lounge featuring fresh juice cocktails.

Busaba Eathai *Thai*
| | 21 | 19 | 16 | £21 |

Bloomsbury | 22 Store St., WC1 (Goodge St.) | 020-7299 7900 | fax 7299 7909
Marylebone | 8-13 Bird St., W1 (Bond St.) | 020-7518 8080 | fax 7518 8088
Soho | 106-110 Wardour St., W1 (Piccadilly Circus/Tottenham Court Rd.) | 020-7255 8686

If you "are not put off by the queues outside" (which do "move quickly") and "don't mind the informal communal seating" ("which can either be fun or annoying"), this "funky", "fast and furious" Thai trio is "fantastic to go to alone or bring friends and share" "exotic" edibles that "won't break the bank"; "service is swift", but often "unfriendly."

NEW Butcher & Grill, The *British*
| | ▽ 15 | 15 | 16 | £36 |

Battersea | 39-41 Parkgate Rd., SW11 (Sloane Sq.) | 020-7924 3999 | fax 7223 7979 | www.thebutcherandgrill.com

The former Café Rouge site backing onto a tranquil Battersea dock has been transformed into a "cheerful" eatery with a "decent" Traditional British menu (though "inconsistently sized portions" can make it "a bit pricey"); staff are "well-meaning", even if some "can't remember what is on or off the menu"; P.S. there's also a "good in-house" butcher's shop.

Café Japan Ⓜ *Japanese*
| | 26 | 10 | 19 | £28 |

Golders Green | 626 Finchley Rd., NW11 (Golders Green) | 020-8455 6854 | fax 8455 6854

"What a top-flight Japanese is doing" in this "hole-in-the-wall setting" "in Golders Green is anyone's guess", but the "legend lives on" for "spectacular sushi" and "the best grilled fish"; just remember to "get there early, as tables go quickly" and there are no reservations; N.B. a cash-only lunch is served weekends.

Café Spice Namasté ⚅ *Indian*
| | 23 | 16 | 18 | £33 |

City | 16 Prescot St., E1 (Aldgate/Tower Hill) | 020-7488 9242 | fax 7488 9339 | www.cafespice.co.uk

Chef-patron "Cyrus Todiwala is a genius", and it shows in the "inventive Indian food" cooked at his colourful place "near Tower Hill" (admittedly

"out-of-the-way unless you're in the City"); more controversial is the setting, a strongly hued "warehouse" that reminds one reviewer of "an '80s Mexican chain restaurant, best suited to large groups."

Caldesi 🖪 *Italian*   22 | 17 | 20 | £40

Marylebone | 15-17 Marylebone Ln., W1 (Bond St.) | 020-7935 9226 | fax 7935 9228 | www.caldesi.com

Dining at this "intimate" trattoria is "pretty close to being back in Tuscany", thanks to cuisine that offers "a true taste of traditional" fare, an "assured welcome" ("if you're a regular") and ambience that's as "good for a celebration as for a quiet dinner for two"; if some quibble it's the "kind of place you can't find fault with until you see the price", most maintain it's "one of Marylebone's best-kept secrets."

Cambio de Tercio ● *Spanish*   24 | 17 | 19 | £42

South Kensington | 163 Old Brompton Rd., SW5 (Gloucester Rd./ South Kensington) | 020-7244 8970 | fax 7373 8817 | www.cambiodetercio.co.uk

"The crowd, the food, the pace" - it all adds up to "a truly Spanish experience" at this "absolute must-go" in South Ken with an "innovative" Iberian menu (including "the best roast baby pig in town"), "dramatic" yellow-and-red decor and "quite helpful" - if sometimes "rushed" - staff; just "don't look at what they're delivering to other tables, or you'll order too much."

Canteen *British*   22 | 19 | 19 | £29

Spitalfields | 2 Crispin Pl., E1 (Liverpool St.) | 0845-686 1122 | fax 0845-686 1144

NEW **South Bank** | Royal Festival Hall | Belvedere Rd., SE1 (Waterloo) www.canteen.co.uk

"Just what London needs more of" cry converts to this "buzzy" Brit set in a "modern canteen (surprise)"-style room and serving "gourmet interpretations of classic dishes" "at the right price"; "fast service" ensures the communal benches turn quickly, but "get a booth if possible" to "watch as crowds mull past" Spitalfields Market; P.S. those who had "fingers crossed that it expands" should rejoice: a Royal Festival Hall offshoot opened in June 2007.

🖪 Capital Restaurant, The *French*   27 | 22 | 26 | £75

Knightsbridge | Capital Hotel | 22-24 Basil St., SW3 (Knightsbridge) | 020-7591 1202 | fax 7225 0011 | www.capitalhotel.co.uk

"A tiny piece of heaven in the middle of Knightsbridge" is how "discerning diners" view this "serene", "understated" hotel New French that "gives one the impression of eating in a rich relative's dining room"; provided by near-"perfect", "pukka service", chef Eric Chavot's cuisine is "a real treat" "not to be missed" - even if it does require "a second mortgage" on the *maison*; all told, a capital experience, though perhaps "not for the young and hip."

Carluccio's Caffe *Italian*   17 | 15 | 15 | £24

Bloomsbury | 8 Market Pl., W1 (Oxford Circus) | 020-7636 2228 | fax 7636 9650
Marylebone | 3-5 Barrett St., W1 (Bond St.) | 020-7935 5927 | fax 7487 5436
Marylebone | St. Christopher's Pl., W1 (Bond St.) | 020-7935 5927
Mayfair | Fenwick | 63 New Bond St., downstairs, W1 (Bond St.) | 020-7629 0699 | fax 7493 0069

(continued)

Carluccio's Caffe

Canary Wharf | Reuters Plaza | 2 Nash Ct., E14 (Canary Wharf) | 020-7719 1749 | fax 7513 1197

Smithfield | 12 West Smithfield, EC1 (Farringdon) | 020-7329 5904 | fax 7248 5981

Islington | 305-307 Upper St., N1 (Angel) | 020-7359 8167 | fax 7354 9196

Fulham | 236 Fulham Rd., SW10 (Fulham Broadway) | 020-7376 5960 | fax 7376 3698

Putney | Putney Wharf, SW15 (Putney Bridge) | 020-8789 0591 | fax 8789 8360

Hammersmith | 5-6 The Green, W5 (Ealing Broadway) | 020-8566 4458 | fax 8840 8566

www.carluccios.com

"Packed from morning to night", chef-owner Antonio "Carluccio's empire" of "casual", "comfy" cafes – "one of the foodie success stories of the new century" – offers an "affordable" experience of "quick and easy [eating], based on tried and tested" Italian recipes; it's "a great formula", the "chainy atmosphere" with "a little chaos thrown in" notwithstanding; P.S. another "big plus is the deli to pick up food for home."

NEW C Garden *Italian*   ▽ 18 | 18 | 19 | £41

Chelsea | 119 Sydney St., SW3 (Sloane Sq./South Kensington) | 020-7352 2718 | www.cgarden.co.uk

After an "ownership change and refurbishment" of the site that was "formerly the Chelsea stalwart Dan's", this yellow-hued yearling, a "charming" cousin to Carpaccio, attracts a "clubby clientele" with "good Italian cooking" from a kitchen and staff that are "trying very hard"; the "outside garden is a dining treat and bonus" – when it's sunny, "the only way to pack more in it would be with olive oil."

Chapter Two *European*   24 | 15 | 22 | £38

Blackheath | 43-45 Montpelier Vale, SE3 (Blackheath B.R.) | 020-8333 2666 | fax 8355 8399 | www.chaptersrestaurants.co.uk

"Has never failed to delight me" gush lovers of this "reliable and reasonably priced" Blackheath haute cuisine haven whose "excellent" Modern European meals are served by staff that are "attentive, yet relaxed enough to leave you to it"; "the room lacks a bit of soul though."

NEW Chelsea Brasserie *French*   16 | 15 | 15 | £40

Chelsea | Sloane Square Hotel | 7-12 Sloane Sq., SW1 (Sloane Sq.) | 020-7881 5999 | www.sloanesquarehotel.co.uk

"Right on Sloane Square", a revamped hotel has reopened to reveal this "Paris brasserie-esque" place, featuring a "sinful" menu that lets Francophiles get their "raclette fix"; but *hélas*, pessimists find it "pretentious in extremis", with "dull decor", "prices that must reflect their high rent and waiters you need a bullhorn to flag down."

Chelsea Bun ❿ *British*   18 | 9 | 16 | £16

Chelsea | Limerstone St., SW10 (Earl's Ct./Sloane Sq.) | 020-7352 3635 | fax 7376 5158 | www.chelseabun.co.uk

"Chelsea residents' idea of a working men's caff", this "terrific greasy spoon" is "the place to go to" if you "have a craving" for "that perfect hung-over breakfast" and other, "so fatty good" Traditional British dishes; "but be prepared to wait for a table" at weekends.

	FOOD	DECOR	SERVICE	COST

Cheyne Walk Brasserie *French*   23 | 22 | 20 | £49

Chelsea | 50 Cheyne Walk, SW3 (Sloane Sq./South Kensington) | 020-7376 8787 | fax 7376 5878 | www.cheynewalkbrasserie.com

"One of the better French brasseries – certainly one of the friendliest" is how converts characterise this Chelsea Embankment "grand, cosy local", with a huge "open fire grill adding to the splendid atmosphere" as it cooks those "classic", "simple" yet "excellent" meats; although it's on the "pricey" side, "booking's advised well in advance"; P.S. don't forget to "retire for a nightcap" to the "dream bar upstairs."

☑ Chez Bruce *British*   28 | 21 | 25 | £57

Wandsworth | 2 Bellevue Rd., SW17 (Balham B.R./ Wandsworth Common B.R.) | 020-8672 0114 | fax 8767 6648 | www.chezbruce.co.uk

"Simply no restaurant can match the quality for the quid" of this "Wandsworth wonder", which has knocked off Gordon Ramsay as London's No. 1 for Food with its "reliably fantastic", "flawlessly executed" Modern British cuisine; "everything [else] about it is class" too – "knowledgeable" but "never intrusive" staff, "the extensive wine list and possibly the largest selection of cheese in town"; the "cosy" room can be "cramped", but really, "the only problem is getting a reservation" ("even for long-term customers").

Chez Gérard *French*   18 | 17 | 17 | £37

Covent Garden | Opera Terrace, The Market | 45 E. Terrace, 1st fl., WC2 (Covent Garden) | 020-7379 0666 | fax 7497 9060 ◐

Holborn | 119 Chancery Ln., WC2 (Chancery Ln.) | 020-7405 0290 | fax 7242 2649 ⓢ

Mayfair | 31 Dover St., W1 (Green Park) | 020-7499 8171 | fax 7491 3818 ⓢ

Victoria | Thistle Hotel | 101 Buckingham Palace Rd., SW1 (Victoria) | 020-7868 6249 | fax 7976 6073

Fitzrovia | 8 Charlotte St., W1 (Goodge St./Tottenham Court Rd.) | 020-7636 4975 | fax 7637 4564 ◐

City | 1 Watling St., EC4 (Mansion House/St. Paul's) | 020-7213 0540 | fax 7213 0541 ⓢ

City | 14 Trinity Sq., EC3 (Tower Hill) | 020-7480 5500 | fax 7480 5588 ⓢ

City | 64 Bishopsgate, EC2 (Bank/Liverpool St.) | 020-7588 1200 | fax 7588 1122 ⓢ

Waterloo | 9 Belvedere Rd., SE1 (Waterloo) | 020-7202 8470 | fax 7202 8474 www.santeonline.co.uk

These "unpretentious" "Parisian brasserie–style" places in "prime locations" around town – including "a unique spot overlooking Covent Garden" – have been "reliable for years", with their "reassuringly familiar" (some say "factory"-like) menu of steak frites and such; but some suffer from "scatterbrain service", and whilst "everything seems good value, you're surprised that the bill is quite so big."

Chez Kristof ◐ *French*   22 | 19 | 16 | £40

Hammersmith | 111 Hammersmith Grove, W6 (Hammersmith) | 020-8741 1177 | fax 8846 3750 | www.chezkristof.co.uk

"Holding up in an odd area" in Hammersmith, this tightly packed "neighbourhood-style brasserie" is cited for Classic French fare that's "full of flavour" (pity the "staff can appear bored"); all also agree the "outside tables are a treat in summer", plus there's "plenty to keep you interested" in the next-door deli, especially the "wonderful breakfast."

Churchill Arms *Thai*
22 | 17 | 15 | £15

Notting Hill | 119 Kensington Church St., W8 (High St. Kensington/ Notting Hill Gate) | 020-7727 4242 | www.fullers.co.uk

It's "a bizarre mix" – "perfect" "pub with an authentic Thai restaurant attached" – but it "somehow works" at this flower-bedecked "favourite" in Notting Hill; annoyances include the need to book and "service that shoos you out the door", citing the "one-hour table rule", but the "tremendous value" makes it "worth a trip out of the way to savour."

Chutney Mary ● *Indian*
23 | 22 | 21 | £43

Chelsea | 535 King's Rd., SW10 (Fulham Broadway) | 020-7351 3113 | fax 7351 7694 | www.realindianfood.com

Whilst it's long been London's "epicentre of Indian cuisine", a recently "revamped menu (out with the Anglo-Indian, in with zesty [regional]) has blown new wind into the slightly sagging sails of this Chelsea mainstay"; some snap it "strays too far from its heritage", but most salute this "ever-evolving" "slick operation"; when reserving, regulars advise "always try for the conservatory" (vs. the "dark", candlelit main room).

Cigala *Spanish*
22 | 17 | 19 | £35

Bloomsbury | 54 Lamb's Conduit St., WC1 (Holborn/Russell Sq.) | 020-7405 1717 | fax 7242 9949 | www.cigala.co.uk

"A real find in the neighbourhood" near the British Museum, this often "overlooked" "Iberian eatery" offers up "delicious peasant food", along with an "amazing selection of sherries" and "ports to accompany" the meal; "friendly staff" provide a "relaxing atmosphere."

Cinnamon Club ⊠ *Indian*
24 | 24 | 22 | £49

Westminster | Old Westminster Library | 30-32 Great Smith St., SW1 (Westminster) | 020-7222 2555 | fax 7222 1333 | www.cinnamonclub.com

"Enter and you believe the British still rule India" at this "upmarket" Westminster venue, whose "magnificent library setting serves as counterpoint to the unusual Indian cuisine" ("East meets West in a sensible kind of way"); the "zinging" fare is "not for the faint-walleted", and service ranges from "responsive" to "intermittently indifferent", but it's still packed with the "political 'in' crowd" from breakfast to dinner.

Cipriani ● *Italian*
20 | 21 | 19 | £69

Mayfair | 25 Davies St., W1 (Bond St.) | 020-7399 0500 | fax 7399 0501 | www.cipriani.com

"A people-watching place if ever there was one", this "lively" "London edition" of the Cipriani chain sees "celebs, socialites and wannabes congregate" ("more plastic than in Legoland") to enjoy "fresh food true to its Italian roots"; this is "not a place to be adventurous with your palate", and it may be "the worst value for money in Mayfair", but for "entertainment" appeal alone, many think "the experience is worth it."

Clarke's ⊠ *British*
25 | 18 | 24 | £58

Kensington | 124 Kensington Church St., W8 (Notting Hill Gate) | 020-7221 9225 | fax 7229 4564 | www.sallyclarke.com

After almost a quarter-century, Sally Clarke's Kensington corner continues to be "consistently classy" "without the fuss often associated with high-end" places; her Modern British menus – now "with a choice of entrees" – are "still fresh" and "fabulous", the "service exceptional" and the "atmosphere pleasant" (if you "sit upstairs"); the "limited"

number of offerings "aren't for everybody", but overall, this is possibly "the most reliable restaurant in London."

⧉ Cliveden House *French/Mediterranean* `24` `27` `25` `£82`

Taplow | Cliveden House Hotel | Berkshire | 01628 668561 | fax 01628 661837 | www.clivedenhouse.co.uk

Live in the "grand manner in a grand manor" at this "gorgeous" Berkshire hotel – "part of history" as the Astor family's former country house; there is "fantastic" Med cuisine in the subterranean Waldo's, whilst the upstairs "Terrace has a view" "that never ends", "decor right out of *Pride and Prejudice*" and "good, if not great" New French fare; although it's all "so expensive", most say the "atmosphere and setting are worth it" – oh, and being "treated like royalty"; N.B. Waldo's is closed Sunday–Monday.

Clos Maggiore ⧉ *French* `24` `24` `23` `£45`

Covent Garden | 33 King St., WC2 (Covent Garden/Leicester Sq.) | 020-7379 9696 | fax 7379 6767 | www.maggiores.uk.com

"Escape into a small world of intimate perfection" at this "romantic Theatreland" address, "almost Eden-like" with its "beautiful inner courtyard" ("a cloistered garden" with fireplace); the "exquisite" New French cuisine, "enormous wine list" and "superb service" mean that "reservations can take a Herculean effort" (the savvy suggest going in the early evening as a "respite from the crowds").

🆕 Club Bar & Dining, The ⧉ *Eclectic* `–` `–` `–` `E`

Soho | 21-22 Warwick St., W1 (Oxford Circus/Piccadilly Circus) | 020-7734 1002 | www.theclubbaranddining.co.uk

Exposed brickwork and Gothic touches (candelabras, mirrors, etc.) set the tone at this new Soho venue in The Sugar Club's former premises; the quirky Eclectic menu stretches from toasted sandwiches and burgers to caviar and whole roast piglets, served from a narrow open kitchen; downstairs, there's a dark, sultry lounge.

Club Gascon ⧉ *French* `26` `21` `22` `£62`

Smithfield | 57 W. Smithfield, EC1 (Barbican/Farringdon) | 020-7796 0600 | fax 7796 0601 | www.clubgascon.com

"Never has the phrase 'quality over quantity' been more true" than with the "well-constructed", "exquisitely presented" small plates offered at this "charming Gallic experience" in an old Smithfield tea house; featuring "foie gras more ways than most people have had hot dinners", backed by an "excellent Gascon wine list", it's "perfect for a business or a romantic dinner (no small feat)"; "the bill piles up quickly", but "you won't remember what it cost, only how nice it was to be there."

Cocoon ❶⧉ *Pan-Asian* `21` `24` `17` `£55`

Piccadilly | 65 Regent St., W1 (Piccadilly Circus) | 020-7494 7600 | www.cocoon-restaurants.com

"The cocoon theme is carried throughout" this "seriously cool" Piccadilly Pan-Asian, and whilst the "great bar scene" dominates the "*Stingray*-like retro surroundings", there's "surprisingly good (given its trendiness)" fusion fare to be had, especially at the "funky sushi" bar; on the downside, the "bill leaves something to be desired" and the staff seem "gorgeously disinterested."

	FOOD	DECOR	SERVICE	COST

NEW Cookbook Cafe *European* | - | - | - | M |

Mayfair | InterContinental Park Ln. | 1 Hamilton Pl., W1 (Hyde Park Corner) | 020-7409 3131 | fax 7493 3476 | www.cookbookcafe.co.uk

Following the major revamp of the InterContinental Park Lane, the new everyday dining room (separate from Theo Randall's upscale eatery) lives up to its name with recipe tastings, cookery classes and bookshelf-lined decor; the Modern European menu includes four daily specials prepared to order at an open station in the middle of the floor.

Cow Dining Room, The *British* | 21 | 16 | 17 | £35 |

Notting Hill | 89 Westbourne Park Rd., W2 (Westbourne Park) | 020-7221 0021 | fax 7727 8687 | www.thecowlondon.co.uk

"Holy cow" cry converts to this Notting Hill eatery, which despite its name "serves such fresh seafood" "you'll eat yourself silly" ("portions aren't stingy", either); the bar specialises in "lovely oysters" and "old authentic pubby atmosphere" but is "crowded all the time", whilst "dining upstairs" in the Modern Brit restaurant "is more civilised, albeit a bit boring"; expect "iffy service" at each.

Da Mario ● *Italian* | 22 | 16 | 19 | £27 |

Kensington | 15 Gloucester Rd., SW7 (Gloucester Rd.) | 020-7584 9078 | fax 7823 9026 | www.damario.co.uk

"Reported to have been Princess Diana's favourite pizzeria", this "casual place in an upscale area" of Kensington attracts a "regular clientele who appreciate the homestyle atmosphere" and "strong vibrant flavours" of the "crisp, thin-crust pizzas" and other dishes on the meat-free Italian menu.

Z Defune *Japanese* | 27 | 16 | 20 | £63 |

Marylebone | 34 George St., W1 (Baker St./Bond St.) | 020-7935 8311 | fax 7487 3762

There are those who "refuse to have sushi anywhere else" than this "serene", "friendly" Marylebone Japanese, maintaining its "marvellous, freshest" victuals are "perfect in size and consistency"; "you'll be shocked how much you're spending", especially since the "decor's nothing fancy", but "if you have an expense account, give it a try."

Delfino Z *Italian* | 23 | 16 | 19 | £26 |

Mayfair | 121A Mount St., W1 (Bond St.) | 020-7499 1256 | fax 7493 4460 | www.finos.co.uk

A "well-priced" Italian "menu for everyone" with "probably the best pizza in London", "quick service" and "buzzy atmosphere" – "what more can one ask for from a Mayfair local?" – well, perhaps a little legroom ("tables cramped").

NEW Dinings Z *Japanese* | - | - | - | M |

Marylebone | 22 Harcourt St., W1 (Edgware Rd.) | 020-7723 0666 | fax 7723 3222

Behind a demure terrace facade in Marylebone, this tiny Japanese offers a setting as simple as they come, with a grey stone floor and basic wooden partitions and furniture; what distinguishes the place (run by chef-patron Tomonari Chiba, who made his name at Nobu) is a competitively priced menu that majors on sushi and sashimi and varied tapas-style plates, helpfully split into hot and cold choices.

Don, The ⬛ *European*
| 22 | 20 | 21 | £48 |

City | The Courtyard | 20 St. Swithins Ln., EC4 (Bank/Cannon St.) | 020-7626 2606 | fax 7626 2616 | www.thedonrestaurant.co.uk

"Consistently packed with the great and the good from the City" – it's "one of the better places open for dinner" *and* lunch – this Modern European is "hard to find, but easy to like", with "consistently high" but "not overpriced" cuisine, "unstuffy, atmospheric" premises and "staff that are a credit to the place"; there's a "good bistro downstairs" in the vaulted cellar too; P.S. the wine list includes an "interesting selection of sherries" and ports – in homage to the 1798 building's past as Sandeman's warehouse.

Dorchester Hotel - The Grill *British*
| 24 | 24 | 25 | £67 |

Mayfair | Dorchester Hotel | 53 Park Ln., W1 (Hyde Park Corner/Marble Arch) | 020-7629 8888 | fax 7317 6464 | www.dorchesterhotel.com

"Feel like a Lord" in the "aristocratic surroundings" of the Dorchester's "timeless" dining room with its dramatic Scottish-themed mural and decor; new chef Aiden Byrne's "refined" fare is "superb" "for classic English roast beef, salmon", etc., backed up by "marvellous staff" and a "great wine expert"; ok, it's "old-fashioned, but who cares" – this is a "special-occasion place you won't regret opening your wallet for."

e&o *Pan-Asian*
| 22 | 20 | 18 | £43 |

Notting Hill | 14 Blenheim Crescent, W11 (Ladbroke Grove) | 020-7229 5454 | fax 7229 5522 | www.eando.nu

"You are bound to see someone from [the pages of] *Hello!* or *OK* walk in the door" of this Notting Hill hipster, still a scene after seven years thanks to its "lively" vibe and "creative", "though pricey" Pan-Asian dishes; if cynics say the cuisine's "excellent&original no more" (been "overtaken by more adventurous players"), the majority maintain if the place "weren't so cramped and overflowing with customers, it'd be flawless."

Ed's Easy Diner *Hamburgers*
| 15 | 15 | 16 | £16 |

Covent Garden | 15 Great Newport St., WC2 (Covent Garden) | 020-7836 0271 | fax 7836 3230

Piccadilly | London Trocadero Ctr. | 19 Rupert St., W1 (Piccadilly Circus) | 020-7287 1951 | fax 7287 6998

Soho | 12 Moor St., W1 (Leicester Sq./Tottenham Court Rd.) | 020-7439 1955 | fax 7494 0173
www.edseasydiner.co.uk

"If you want the feeling of a great ol' American diner" with "juicy", "old-fashioned burgers" and "legendary milkshakes" that are "easy on the wallet, if not the waist", try this retro trio around town (the Chelsea branch is gone); but the uneasy tremble it's "getting tired", comparing the hamburgers to "thin hockey pucks on a bun."

Eight Over Eight *Pan-Asian*
| 23 | 20 | 19 | £43 |

Chelsea | 392 King's Rd., SW3 (Sloane Sq.) | 020-7349 9934 | fax 7351 5157 | www.rickerrestaurants.com

This "sister of e&o" is "one of the best picks on King's Road" – a "fabulous hot spot" with "great people-watching" and "creative" Pan-Asian cuisine in which "flavours, colours and delightful surprises abound"; a few feel the minimalist Asian "decor doesn't score", but "young professionals" hail it as a "hip" option "for a date, drink or dinner with friends."

El Pirata ●☒ *Spanish* | 23 | 17 | 20 | £32 |

Mayfair | 5-6 Down St., W1 (Green Park/Hyde Park Corner) |
020-7491 3810 | fax 7491 0853 | www.elpirata.co.uk

"Hidden in a restaurant-free part of Mayfair", this "swinging" Spaniard
"fills up quickly", as "everyone loves" "some of the tastiest tapas
around", a "fantastic wine list" and "warm, friendly" servers; "not too
pricey", it's "great for large groups", even if "the number of people
crammed in can make the place hot."

NEW Empress of India *British* | - | - | - | M |

Hackney | 130 Lauriston Rd., E9 (Bethnal Green) | 020-8533 5123 |
www.theempressofindia.com

With "stunning decor" that includes a "wonderful antique mirror",
huge shell chandeliers and wallpaper scenes of the Raj, this Victoria
Park gastropub evokes colonial India; the all-day Modern Brit menu
takes a more gamey tone, with signatures such as haunch of venison
and mallard carved tableside.

☑ Enoteca Turi ☒ *Italian* | 27 | 19 | 23 | £47 |

Putney | 28 Putney High St., SW15 (Putney Bridge) | 020-8785 4449 |
fax 8780 5409 | www.enotecaturi.com

"We have to keep reminding ourselves this is just across the Thames,
not in the hills in Tuscany" say fans of this rustic ristorante that's "just
about the best Italian in London" (and "the best in Putney by far"); the
fare "never fails to impress" and there's "a phenomenal wine list too";
"tables are too close", but "personal attention from the owner and his
wife ensures" a "pleasant evening."

Eyre Brothers ☒ *Portuguese/Spanish* | 22 | 19 | 21 | £40 |

Shoreditch | 70 Leonard St., EC2 (Old St.) | 020-7613 5346 | fax 7739 8199 |
www.eyrebrothers.co.uk

There's "always a warm welcome and a kitchen that can produce some
fine Spanish-Portuguese food" at this "sleek yet comfortable"
Shoreditch eatery from the eponymous Eyres; it's a "good choice if you
want something slightly different", though it "can get pricey."

Fairuz *Lebanese* | 22 | 16 | 19 | £31 |

Marylebone | 3 Blandford St., W1 (Baker St./Bond St.) | 020-7486 8108 |
fax 7935 8581
Bayswater | 27 Westbourne Grove, W2 (Bayswater/Queensway) |
020-7243 8444 | fax 7243 8777 ●
www.fairuz.uk.com

Those lusting for Lebanese fare find it "easy to pop into" this "casual"
yellow-hued duo (separately owned) in Marylebone and Bayswater
for "enormous portions" of "well-executed basics", all served up
by "fun" staff.

NEW Fat Badger, The *British* | ▽ 15 | 17 | 14 | £23 |

Notting Hill | 310 Portobello Rd., W10 (Ladbroke Grove/Westbourne Park) |
020-8969 4500 | www.thefatbadger.com

It's early days for this Portobello Road newcomer that offers a "relaxed
atmosphere, with comfy couches and big windows to see the world
passing"; the Modern Brit menu offers some "surprisingly good" pub
grub (and the "edgy neighbourhood crowd makes the food cooler");
pity the "pretty staff" seem "utterly uninterested in serving."

	FOOD	DECOR	SERVICE	COST

☑ Fat Duck, The Ⓜ *European* `27` `22` `26` `£118`

Bray | High St., Berkshire | 01628 580333 | www.fatduck.co.uk
Chef-owner Heston Blumenthal allows his "imagination to run wild" on the "sensational, sensual" and "sublime" Modern European menu at this "now classic" Bray cottage; even "the waiters seem to enjoy working" here and serving such mainstays of "molecular gastronomy" as snail porridge and Douglas fir purée; it may be "too complicated for more than once a year", "you need a fat wallet to pay for it" and the one-hour "drive from London is a drag", but "for the brave" it's "a culinary journey" worth taking.

ffiona's Ⓜ *British* `24` `20` `22` `£36`

Kensington | 51 Kensington Church St., W8 (High St. Kensington/Notting Hill Gate) | 020-7937 4152 | www.ffionas.com
Owner Ffiona Reid-Owen "continues to be the star of the show" – "chatting to you at the table" – at this "rustic", "candlelit" dinner-only Kensingtonian that "feels like someone's home"; the "simple, yet tasty", Traditional British "comfort food" is pretty "ffabulous" too.

Fifteen *Mediterranean* `23` `18` `21` `£54`

Hoxton | 15 Westland Pl., N1 (Old St.) | 0871-330 1515 | fax 020-7251 2749 | www.fifteenrestaurant.com
"Six years on, the fuss around Jamie Oliver's charity-program restaurant still hasn't died down" – and why not, as it remains a "refreshing" option in Hoxton, provided you "put yourself in the hands of the chefs-in-training and enjoy the ride"; they'll offer you "innovative" Med cuisine that's "awesome" (even if it's "not a bargain") in either the "casual trattoria" or the "trendy, but relaxing" dining room; service is a bit "spotty", but "charming" overall.

Fino Ⓩ *Spanish* `23` `19` `20` `£47`

Fitzrovia | 33 Charlotte St., W1 (Goodge St./Tottenham Court Rd.) | 020-7813 8010 | fax 7813 8011 | www.finorestaurant.com
"Truly excellent tapas" take you on a "culinary trip through Spain" at this "hip", "high-quality" and "highly priced" Fitzrovian; if the basement digs are "disappointing", the staff are "knowledgeable" and there's a "great" all-Iberian wine list – though "with such good house wine, why run your finger any lower" down?

Flaneur *European* `22` `20` `15` `£31`

Farringdon | 41 Farringdon Rd., EC1 (Farringdon) | 020-7404 4422 | fax 7831 4532 | www.flaneur.com
"Sitting among the aisles of a posh supermarket and eating exceptional food is an experience" at this "surprising find in an otherwise dull part of Farringdon Road"; "using ingredients from the shop", the "healthy" Modern European menu changes daily, but "be prepared for laissez-faire service"; P.S. naturally, it's "a great place to pick up some treats after the meal."

Foliage *European/French* `26` `23` `26` `£71`

Knightsbridge | Mandarin Oriental Hyde Park | 66 Knightsbridge, SW1 (Knightsbridge) | 020-7201 3723 | fax 7235 2001 | www.mandarinoriental.com
"Beautiful in every respect" maintain admirers of the Mandarin Oriental's dining room where "culinary wizard Chris Staines" pro-

duces Classic French–Modern European cuisine "with vision, zest and skill", served by "gracious staff" in Adam Tihany–designed premises ("light, with big windows"); though the "cost is equal to trans-Atlantic airfare", "it's worth every posh penny"; P.S. "ask for a window table" to savour the "splendid view of Hyde Park."

Food for Thought ⊘ *Vegetarian* | 24 | 10 | 16 | £10 |

Covent Garden | 31 Neal St., WC2 (Covent Garden) | 020-7836 9072

"Get to know your neighbours over enormous portions" of "hearty vegetarian fare" at this Covent Garden "cramped cellar where table-sharing is compulsory at peak times"; the "innovative recipes are nowhere near the traditional view of veggie" – and "so good you wouldn't know they're healthy", for both body and bank account (this is London's Top Best Buy).

NEW Forge, The ● *European* | – | – | – | E |

Covent Garden | 14 Garrick St., WC2 (Covent Garden/Leicester Sq.) | 020-7379 1432 | fax 020-7379-1530 | www.theforgerestaurant.co.uk

Sibling of stalwarts Le Café du Jardin and Le Deuxième, this "welcome" Covent Garden novice takes over the erstwhile L'Estaminet space to offer seafood-centric Modern European fare in an uncluttered, exposed-brick setting; pluses include a lengthy wine list (more than 500 labels!) and a cosy basement bar serving an edited menu; even though the staff are "reactive rather than proactive", they offer "attention when needed."

Four Seasons Chinese ● *Chinese* | 22 | 7 | 11 | £23 |

Bayswater | 84 Queensway, W2 (Bayswater) | 020-7229 4320 | fax 7229 4320

"Everyone orders the justly famous roast duck" at this "hugely popular" Queensway Chinese, which "offers some of the most authentic food in London" – and at "low prices" to boot; just "be prepared for substandard service" and to "get there before 6 PM or you'll wait" as "they don't take reservations."

French Horn *French* | 23 | 21 | 25 | £61 |

Sonning | French Horn Hotel | Berkshire | 01189 692204 | fax 01189 442210 | www.thefrenchhorn.co.uk

In a "dreamy location by the river" Thames, this Sonning family-run 19th-century inn an hour outside London is "worth the trip" for "lovely" Classic French cuisine (including "duck roasted right in front of you over an open fire"), an "excellent wine cellar" and "comforting" service; even if it "just falls short" of its "fancy prices", it's "great for impressing."

Fung Shing ● *Chinese* | 22 | 13 | 18 | £31 |

Chinatown | 15 Lisle St., WC2 (Leicester Sq.) | 020-7437 1539 | fax 7743 0284 | www.fungshing.co.uk

"Divine seasonal specials", "unusual foods like eel done well" and "authentic" Cantonese standards served by "smiling waiters" have made this Chinatown veteran a "family favourite" for decades; it's also "great for pre- or post-theatre dining" even if the "tired" setting "looks like the set from a bad Peter Sellers movie."

	FOOD	DECOR	SERVICE	COST

Galvin at Windows Restaurant & Bar *French* | 22 | 23 | 21 | £65 |

Mayfair | Hilton Park Ln. | 22 Park Ln., W1 (Hyde Park Corner) | 020-7208 4021 | www.hilton.co.uk

"Bag a table by the window for the most amazing views" (like "the Queen's garden") at this "sleek, minimalist" venue atop the Hilton on Park Lane; but if the weather is obstructive, "not to worry as the food will more than make up for it" – "subtle" New French dishes, "superbly executed"; perhaps cousin Galvin Bistrot de Luxe has "better food at better value", but this one remains "a place for the power wallets to impress."

Galvin Bistrot de Luxe *French* | 24 | 20 | 20 | £44 |

Marylebone | 66 Baker St., W1 (Baker St.) | 020-7935 4007 | fax 7486 1735 | www.galvinbistrotdeluxe.co.uk

On otherwise bleak Baker Street, there's "a real bistro in London" at last – the Galvin brothers' highly hyped "gem" with its "superb atmosphere", "robust" "French cuisine as it used to be" and a "fine wine list"; if the "knowledgeable" service can be "painfully slow", it fails to deter the "good mix of people" – from a "mature crowd" to more "boisterous" types – who have "nothing but superlatives for this place."

Gate, The Ⓢ *Vegetarian* | 25 | 16 | 22 | £30 |

Hammersmith | 51 Queen Caroline St., W6 (Hammersmith) | 020-8748 6932 | www.thegate.tv

"In an atmosphere that will bring you back to days spent in student cafes" (i.e. "not posh"), this "magnificent vegetarian" "behind the Apollo Theatre" has an "inventive" menu that "proves that food without meat isn't bland or boring" – and could "make even the biggest carnivore think" about converting.

Z Gaucho Grill *Argentinean/Chophouse* | 22 | 18 | 18 | £41 |

Holborn | 125-126 Chancery Ln., WC2 (Chancery Ln.) | 020-7242 7727 | fax 7242 7723 Ⓢ

Piccadilly | 25 Swallow St., W1 (Piccadilly Circus) | 020-7734 4040 | fax 7734 1076 ●

Broadgate | 5 Finsbury Ave., EC2 (Liverpool St.) | 020-7256 6877 | fax 7795 2075

City | 1 Bell Inn Yard, EC3 (Bank/Monument) | 020-7626 5180 | fax 7626 5181

Canary Wharf | 29 Westferry Circus, E14 (Canary Wharf) | 020-7987 9494 | fax 7987 9292

Hampstead | 64 Heath St., NW3 (Hampstead) | 020-7431 8222 | fax 7431 3714 ●

Chelsea | 89 Sloane Ave., SW3 (South Kensington) | 020-7584 9901 | fax 7584 0045

NEW Richmond | The Towpath | Richmond Riverside, TW10 (Richmond) | 020-8948 4030 | fax 8948 2945

www.gaucho-grill.com

"Feel like a cowboy in the Pampas" amidst the "masculine atmosphere" of these "loud" Latin Americans with "cheeky waitresses" and trademark cow-hide chairs ("uncomfortable if wearing sheer hosiery"); a few find it "formulaic", advising "enter only with a fat wallet", but "if you're a lover of divine bovine", you'll "get your fill of Argentinean beef" you "can cut with a butter knife" here.

	FOOD	DECOR	SERVICE	COST

George ⑤ *European*   22 | 24 | 25 | £68

Private club; inquiries: 020-7491 4433

With a "perfect combination of sophistication and casual style", this "exclusive", "glamourous dining club" in Mayfair attracts a "swish crowd" with an "unfussy" Modern European menu that "suits all tastes" and "willing service"; it's "expensive, but worth every pence"; P.S. don't forget the "fantastic bar downstairs."

Glasshouse, The *British*   24 | 20 | 23 | £55

Richmond | 14 Station Parade, TW9 (Kew Gdns.) | 020-8940 6777 | fax 8940 3833 | www.glasshouserestaurant.co.uk

In an area "known almost exclusively for its wonderful botanical garden", this Kew "jewel" provides a "virtual tour de force of gastronomic delights" on its seasonally oriented Modern British menu, served in a "light, airy" room by "courteous" staff; it suffers from "strange acoustics" – all that namesake glass – but basically is "another winner from the Chez Bruce family."

ⓩ Gordon Ramsay at Claridge's *European*   25 | 24 | 24 | £89

Mayfair | Claridge's Hotel | 45 Brook St., W1 (Bond St.) | 020-7499 0099 | fax 7499 3099 | www.gordonramsay.com

"His kitchen might be hell, but the food is heavenly" at TV star/chef Gordon Ramsay's "art deco fantasy" ("red drapes, swirly light fixtures") in Claridge's, where the team led by exec toque Mark Sargeant is "inspired to deliver" "ever-so-imaginative" Modern European "refined classics" with "old-world charm"; sure, it's a "budget-buster" and, some believe, "a bit of a let-down lately", but most hail it as a "heady wonderland experience"; P.S. "lunch provides 80 percent of the experience at 20 percent of the cost."

ⓩ Gordon Ramsay at 68 Royal Hospital Rd. ⑤ *French*   28 | 24 | 28 | £107

Chelsea | 68 Royal Hospital Rd., SW3 (Sloane Sq.) | 020-7352 4441 | fax 7592 1213 | www.gordonramsay.com

"Dine at the altar of the master", Gordon Ramsay – a "superlative experience" for "serious foodies" in "crisp, chic" Chelsea quarters; the "rich and complex", "hellishly good" New French cuisine is ferried by "suave staff", who deliver "royal treatment" that remains London's No. 1 for Service (manager Jean-Claude Breton "deserves to be as famous as Gordon"); it's "eye-wateringly expensive" – perhaps one reason why it was edged out as No. 1 for Food this year – but all in all, Ramsay's "flagship is sailing high."

Goring Dining Room *British*   23 | 23 | 24 | £57

Victoria | Goring Hotel | 15 Beeston Pl., SW1 (Victoria) | 020-7396 9000 | fax 7834 4393 | www.goringhotel.co.uk

Exuding an "old-world elegance with a touch of modern humour" (don't miss the whimsical crystal chandeliers), this "peaceful" dining room nestled in Victoria's Goring Hotel offers "no glitz – just fabulous" "Traditional hearty British food" matched by very "courteous service"; although it attracts a "mature clientele", it's "not fuddy-duddy" by any means, especially when it comes to the "plentiful, delicious tea."

Gourmet Burger Kitchen *Hamburgers* (aka GBK)

| 21 | 12 | 14 | £15 |

NEW **Covent Garden** | 13-14 Maiden Ln., WC2 (Covent Garden) | 020-7240 9617 | fax 7240 3908
Hampstead | 200 Haverstock Hill, Belsize Park, NW3 (Belsize Park) | 020-7443 5335 | fax 7443 5339
Hampstead | 331 West End Ln., NW6 (West Hampstead) | 020-7794 5455 | fax 7794 4401
Battersea | 44 Northcote Rd., SW11 (Clapham Junction B.R.) | 020-7228 3309 | fax 7978 6122
Fulham | 49 Fulham Broadway, SW6 (Fulham Broadway) | 020-7381 4242 | fax 7381 3222
Putney | 333 Putney Bridge Rd., SW15 (Putney Bridge) | 020-8789 1199 | fax 8780 1953
Richmond | 15-17 Hill Rise, TW10 (Richmond) | 020-8940 5440 | fax 8940 5772
Wimbledon | 88 The Broadway, SW19 (Wimbledon) | 020-8540 3300 | fax 8543 1947
Bayswater | 50 Westbourne Grove, W2 (Bayswater/Royal Oak) | 020-7243 4344 | fax 7243 4234
Chiswick | 131 Chiswick High Rd., W4 (Turnham Green) | 020-8995 4548 | fax 8995 4572
www.gbkinfo.com
Additional locations throughout the London area
"Gargantuan burgers" ("your mouth hurts from having to open so wide") with "adventurous" toppings are what make these fast-fooders such "favourites"; whilst "staff could be a little more proactive", this "happening" chain is "excellent value" and "great for families", especially as "they'll make adjustments to suit" dietary demands.

☑ Gravetye Manor *British*

| 24 | 27 | 25 | £66 |

East Grinstead | Gravetye Manor | Vowels Ln., West Sussex | 01342 810567 | fax 01342 810080 | www.gravetyemanor.co.uk
"Oozing charm and graciousness" in the Elizabethan style, this "marvellous country hotel" in Sussex ("close to Gatwick") is "perfectly set up for a weekend getaway"; an "inventive" Modern British menu uses "ingredients raised on the estate" – even the "water from their deep well is delicious" – and is "worth the journey" (but "do stay overnight").

Great Eastern Dining Room ☒ *Asian*

| 22 | 18 | 19 | £41 |

Shoreditch | 54-56 Great Eastern St., EC2 (Liverpool St./Old St.) | 020-7613 4545 | fax 7613 4137 | www.greateasterndining.co.uk
"Cool", "stylish" and "lively", this 10-year-old "sister of e&o" is a "Shoreditch standard"; a new chef has edged the Asian fare up a "delicious" notch, and the "friendly bar staff" are "competent in all the best cocktails"; it's "reasonably priced for the location" too.

NEW Great Queen Street *British*

| - | - | - | E |

Covent Garden | 32 Great Queen St., WC2 (Covent Garden/Holborn) | 020-7242 0622 | fax 7404 9582
Just off Drury Lane, this bohemian newcomer comes courtesy of "people who know their business" (indeed, they're the the Anchor & Hope team); it mixes a "nice" rustic setting – abundant wood and blood-red walls – with "imaginative, seasonal Modern British food" and old-world wine served in glass tumblers; but some scold an "inability to cope with the volumes, which they surely were expecting by now?"

DINING

	FOOD	DECOR	SERVICE	COST

Greenhouse, The Ⓩ *French*

25 | 23 | 24 | £78

Mayfair | 27A Hay's Mews, W1 (Green Park) | 020-7499 3331 | fax 7499 5368 | www.greenhouserestaurant.co.uk

In the "secluded setting" of a "hidden Mayfair mews", this "enchanting" eatery from restaurateur Marlon Abela (Umu, Morton's) is lauded for a "gorgeously prepared" New French menu that "mixes slightly quirky flavours with standard ones", "presented with flair" by service that's "excellent without being stifling"; true, it can be "difficult to get past the price tag", but you could economise with the wine, as the "simply stunning" list contains "both full and half-bottles."

Green's *British/Seafood*

22 | 20 | 21 | £55

St. James's | 36 Duke St., SW1 (Green Park/Piccadilly Circus) | 020-7930 4566 | fax 7930 2958 | www.greens.org.uk

Within "hushed" St. James's premises "redolent of a gentlemen's club" ("expect lots of old school ties"), this Traditional Brit is a "trusted standby" for "succulent" seafood; a few flinch at the "pretentious atmosphere", advising "dress well if you want to feel at home" here.

Guinea Grill Ⓩ *British/Chophouse*

22 | 17 | 20 | £47

Mayfair | 30 Bruton Pl., W1 (Bond St.) | 020-7499 1210 | fax 7491 1442 | www.theguinea.co.uk

"Just the place for a clubby, macho" meal, this "intimate" "quintessential British establishment" in Mayfair "provides safe harbour" for "well-prepared" chophouse fare – "heavy on steaks" and "amazing steak and kidney pie"; but it's getting "tattered around the edges" and many bemoan the menu prices ("a guinea will buy you nothing here").

NEW Haiku Ⓩ *Pan-Asian*

– | – | – | E

Mayfair | 15 New Burlington Pl., W1 (Oxford Circus) | 020-7494 4777 | www.haikurestaurant.com

This hip new Pan-Asian sits in a cul-de-sac "just off Regent Street, hidden" behind huge wood blinds; it's spread over three dark floors, each with a single-technique kitchen that produces raw, steamed or sizzling fare; there's also a "bar area for the 'been-shopping-on-Bond-Street-and-my-Choos-are-killing-me' crowd."

Ⓩ Hakkasan ● *Chinese*

24 | 25 | 19 | £57

Bloomsbury | 8 Hanway Pl., W1 (Tottenham Court Rd.) | 020-7927 7000 | fax 7907 1889

So "legendary" that "reservations are traded on the futures market", this "sophisticated" seven-year-old is a "standard-setter" for "sumptuous boudoir decor" (carved out of "a converted underground car park" in Bloomsbury), "equally seductive cocktails" and "inventive, delectable" Chinese fusion fare; despite being "abuzz with noise", "outrageous prices" and "staff that think they're too sexy for their jobs", there "couldn't be a cooler" place "to chill out."

Halepi ● *Greek*

24 | 11 | 18 | £29

Bayswater | 18 Leinster Terrace, W2 (Lancaster Gate/Queensway) | 020-7262 1070 | fax 7262 2630

The space may be the "closest thing to a Greek fishing boat this side of the Channel", but this "old-fashioned, family-run" Hellenic makes a "wonderfully hospitable" haven; Bayswater boosters say bring an appetite, as the "consistently high-standard" fare "just keeps coming."

	FOOD	DECOR	SERVICE	COST

Hard Rock Cafe ● *American*

13 | 19 | 15 | £24

Piccadilly | 150 Old Park Ln., W1 (Green Park/Hyde Park Corner) | 020-7629 0382 | fax 7629 8702 | www.hardrock.com

"Everything you'd expect from a Hard Rock Cafe" is at the Hyde Park Corner branch – "the original, with the coolest decor of them all" ("see Lennon's handwritten songs"); cuisinewise, you also "know what you're getting" – "run-of-the-mill American staples" served by "bored staff" with a side of "unbearable noise"; but if you don't mind "tourist-trap" prices, "get your T-shirt, have the burger and move on."

Harry's Bar ●⚫ *Italian*

24 | 24 | 25 | £73

Private club; inquiries: 020-7408 0844

"The 'in' spot if you want to see anyone of importance", this "lively" private dining club in Mayfair exudes the "luxury of a past era", with a rich Northern Italian "menu that always surprises", "brilliant staff" dressed "like indulgent matrons" and "lots of space nearby for your car and driver"; in short, "a special treat" "worth every ridiculous cost."

NEW Hat & Feathers ⚫ *European*

- | - | - | M

Clerkenwell | 2 Clerkenwell Rd., EC1 (Barbican) | 020-7490 2244

"Love the lively bar, love the quiet and elegant upstairs, love the food" gush impressed fans of this new Clerkenwell Modern European, a characterful 1870 boozer revamped with Victorian faux gas lights, large mirrors and gold-leaf cornicing; a "spartan wine list is the only complaint."

NEW Hawksmoor *Chophouse*

▽ 28 | 16 | 24 | £44

Shoreditch | 157 Commercial St., E1 (Liverpool St.) | 020-7247 7392 | www.thehawksmoor.com

First have some "delightful cocktails", then onto the real reason for the visit – the steaks, simply the best you can get in London" rave reviewers about this eclectically furnished grill; the grub's "accompanied by delicious sides" and "divine" sundaes, and "friendly, helpful" staff further ensure it's "worth the walk from Liverpool Street tube."

Haz ● *Turkish*

25 | 16 | 20 | £27

City | 9 Cutler St., E1 (Liverpool St.) | 020-7929 7923 | fax 7623 5132

"The best Turkish food in London" – "satisfying", "healthy" and "cooked to order on the open" grill hail habitués of this "popular" haunt; whilst it would "benefit from fewer tables to feel less like a canteen", "the dining experience is much improved in the evening or weekend when the [lunchtime] City folk have departed."

NEW High Road Brasserie *European*

20 | 24 | 19 | £41

Chiswick | High Road Hse. | 162-166 Chiswick High Rd., W4 (Turnham Green) | 020-8742 7474 | www.highroadbrasserie.co.uk

"Once again, Nick Jones [Soho House] has worked his magic", creating a "chic" scene at this "buzzy" blue and brown–toned Chiswick brasserie; there are "fabulous cocktails" and a Modern European "menu that covers a bit of something for everyone" ("better on the grilled meats than more complex dishes" perhaps); stung by "snippy" servers, some wonder "will this star last?", but for now, it's "hard to get a walk-in table."

Hinds Head *British*
| | 23 | 18 | 20 | £41 |

Bray | The High St., Berkshire | 01628 626151 | fax 01628 623394 | www.hindsheadhotel.co.uk

Now "under the co-direction of Heston Blumenthal of The Fat Duck" nearby, this "oldie worldly" Traditional Brit in Bray is worth a heads-up – and in fact "the place to be Sunday lunchtime"; "don't be tricked into thinking it's pub grub – it's Heston's twist on home-cooked treats" (e.g. "to-die-for triple-cooked chips"); "food can be slow coming out of the kitchen", but otherwise, "this vision of a gastropub really works."

Home House ● *British/European*
| | 20 | 25 | 21 | £59 |

Private club; inquiries: 020-7670 2100

The "elegant surroundings of this posh private club" – all high ceilings, crystal chandeliers and silk-padded walls – attract an "über-cool media crowd" to its Portman Square premises; "attentive service" boosts the "expensive" but "surprisingly good" Modern European–British fare, and for that "decadent dining" feeling, "have dessert in a cosy corner of one of the sitting rooms."

NEW Hoxton Grille, The *Eclectic*
| | - | - | - | M |

Shoreditch | Hoxton Hotel | 81 Great Eastern St., EC2 (Old St.) | 020-7739 9111 | www.grillerestaurants.com

A "pretty interior courtyard" is the key feature to this low-profile but hip Hoxton Hotel venue serving "hearty helpings" of "solid" "basic British"-Eclectic eats; pioneering surveyors say it's "good value by London standards", however – as at many novices – "staff are still finding their feet."

☑ Hunan ⓢ *Chinese*
| | 28 | 14 | 22 | £44 |

Pimlico | 51 Pimlico Rd., SW1 (Sloane Sq.) | 020-7730 5712 | fax 7730 8265

The trick is to let chef-owner Mr. Peng "know what you like and it will keep coming" to you at this "fine choice for the Chinese connoisseur" in Pimlico; awed admirers call it "incomparable" for its Hunanese dishes "dependant on the day's market" and delivered in "tasty little bites"; just be prepared to "ignore the cold surroundings" and "remember to say when you are full – otherwise they will keep feeding you!"

Il Bordello *Italian*
| | 23 | 16 | 20 | £33 |

Wapping | 81 Wapping High St., E1 (Wapping) | 020-7481 9950

An "excellent find in Wapping", this "lively" neighborhood trattoria is "always busy", doling out "huge portions" of "pizza, pasta or classic meat dishes" "at a great price"; "friendly Italian waiters enhance the experience."

Il Convivio ⓢ *Italian*
| | 23 | 20 | 22 | £43 |

Belgravia | 143 Ebury St., SW1 (Sloane Sq./Victoria) | 020-7730 4099 | fax 7730 4103 | www.etruscarestaurants.com

"Airy" and "mercifully uncrowded", this "cosmopolitan" Italian "never disappoints" disciples with its "generally delicious, varied menu" served by "attentive, but never intrusive" staff and a "really good sommelier"; "one of the best" of The Boot in Belgravia – but one of the "most expensive" too.

	FOOD	DECOR	SERVICE	COST

Il Portico ●Ⓩ *Italian*

| | 22 | 15 | 23 | £35 |

Kensington | 277 Kensington High St., W8 (High St. Kensington) | 020-7602 6262

"A neighbourhood favourite", "this family-run restaurant makes you feel right at home" cry Kensingtonians who crave its "classic" "savoury, satisfying" Italian dishes and "heartfelt service"; best of all, "the bill still leaves some change for the homemade desserts."

Indigo ● *European*

| | 22 | 22 | 23 | £45 |

Covent Garden | One Aldwych Hotel | 1 Aldwych, WC2 (Charing Cross/Covent Garden) | 020-7300 0400 | fax 7300 1001 | www.onealdwych.com

"Get a table next to the railing and enjoy an unimpaired view of the lobby bar below" at the One Aldwych Hotel's "cool" mezzanine Modern European, serving "substantial" meals "with international flavour to business travellers"; "the decor and setting help justify the price tag", as does "smart, friendly" staff.

Ishbilia *Lebanese*

| | 24 | 12 | 18 | £36 |

Belgravia | 9 William St., SW1 (Knightsbridge) | 020-7235 7788 | fax 7235 7771 ●

Knightsbridge | Harrods | 87-135 Brompton Rd., 2nd fl., SW1 (Knightsbridge) | 020-7893 8598

The "sublime" Lebanese cuisine is "as good as anything in Beirut" at this "wonderful, warm, whimsical" Belgravia "local" (with a Harrods sib), "usually packed" with "tables full of families"; "uninspiring decor" doesn't seem to deter from the "convivial atmosphere" created by "engaging staff."

Ⓩ Ivy, The ● *British/European*

| | 23 | 21 | 23 | £55 |

Covent Garden | 1 West St., WC2 (Leicester Sq.) | 020-7836 4751 | fax 7240 9333 | www.the-ivy.co.uk

Sprinkled with "stars of stage and screen" – "beware the paparazzi when you leave" – "this Theatreland diva is still getting rave reviews and standing-room crowds" thanks to her "energised atmosphere", Modern British–Euro "home-cooked-style food" ("simple", yet "terrific") and "polished service"; critics may cavil "it's become something of a cliché", but even they admit they'd "lie, cheat and steal to get into" this "beyond-trendy cafeteria for celebrities."

Jenny Lo's Tea House Ⓩ⊟ *Chinese*

| | 20 | 9 | 17 | £15 |

Belgravia | 14 Eccleston St., SW1 (Victoria) | 020-7259 0399

Some say "it's more like a takeaway place", but "for people who are comfortable with basic decor and communal tables", this "real jewel" in Belgravia from Ken Lo's daughter, Jenny, offers a "solid experience" of "fresh, quick, healthy" Chinese fare at "great value."

Jin Kichi Ⓜ *Japanese*

| | 26 | 10 | 17 | £34 |

Hampstead | 73 Heath St., NW3 (Hampstead) | 020-7794 6158 | fax 7794 6158 | www.jinkichi.com

Almost every critic calls it "cramped", but "what it lacks in space, it makes up for in quality" at this Hampstead "survivor", an "outstanding" option for a "range of choices" of Japanese cuisine ("the yakitori grill bar is the true star here"); "be sure to book in advance" as it is, unsurprisingly, "hard to get into."

	FOOD	DECOR	SERVICE	COST

Z J. Sheekey ● *Seafood* | 25 | 21 | 23 | £55

Covent Garden | 28-32 St. Martin's Ct., WC2 (Leicester Sq.) | 020-7240 2565 | fax 7497 0891 | www.j-sheekey.co.uk

The "peerless seafood has barely stopped breathing" at this "discreet" Theatreland "bastion" where "the warmly lit, woody interior complements the conviviality"; throw in "unerring service" and a "chance to celeb-spot" amongst all "the thespians after a show", and this "slick outfit" "is "rightly revered", "like her sister, The Ivy."

Kai Mayfair *Chinese* | 25 | 21 | 22 | £56

Mayfair | 65 S. Audley St., W1 (Bond St./Marble Arch) | 020-7493 8988 | fax 7493 1456 | www.kaimayfair.co.uk

Embark on a "dining adventure" at this "delightful spot in quiet Mayfair", whose "Chinese food for grown-ups" takes "the concept of originality to extremes"; the setting – "beautiful", "if a bit corporate" – proves Asian eateries "can be posh", and staff pay "meticulous attention to detail"; sure, it's "crazy expensive", but many maintain it's "the best of its kind."

Khan's of Kensington ● *Indian* | 22 | 13 | 16 | £26

South Kensington | 3 Harrington Rd., SW7 (South Kensington) | 020-7584 4114 | fax 7581 2900

"Inspired food" at a "reasonable price" keeps this South Ken Indian going; but several say it's a "great place to pick up takeaway – then you don't have to deal with the lazy service" and "boring" decor.

Kiku *Japanese* | 24 | 17 | 21 | £44

Mayfair | 17 Half Moon St., W1 (Green Park) | 020-7499 4208 | fax 7409 3359 | www.kikurestaurant.co.uk

"Superb sashimi and sushi" and other "excellent", "traditional" dishes set the scene at this "serene", "proper" "Mayfair Japanese"; aside from the "great-value" set lunches, though, it's "quite expensive."

NEW Kobe Jones *Japanese* | 18 | 16 | 13 | £43

Bloomsbury | St. Giles Hotel | 111A Great Russell St., WC1 (Tottenham Court Rd.) | 020-7300 3250 | fax 7300 3254 | www.kobejones.com.au

"In surroundings that take you East" (lots of red-and-black lacquer and dark wood), this large Bloomsbury neophyte offers "Japanese fusion dishes" (e.g. green-tea salmon, sake-infused trifle) that seem "strange" to some, "interesting" to others; overall, the "food's not as excellent as the prices suggest" – and "staff don't look like they know the place."

Koi *Japanese* | 22 | 18 | 19 | £48

Kensington | 1E Palace Gate, W8 (Gloucester Rd./High St. Kensington) | 020-7581 8778 | fax 7589 2788

For "fantastic teppanyaki" and "decent sushi in Kensington", locals rely on this "pleasant" Japanese adorned with traditional low tables and floor mats; if the "speedy service" is maybe "*too* speedy", at least that makes it ideal "for a quick bite on the way home."

Ladurée *French* | 23 | 21 | 18 | £33

Knightsbridge | Harrods | 87-135 Brompton Rd., ground fl., SW1 (Knightsbridge) | 020-7893 8293 | fax 3155 0112 | www.laduree.com

"Already an institution", this "totally *femme*, frivolous" Harrods outpost of the famed "Parisian patisserie" "gives a feeling of being caught

between *Alice in Wonderland*'s dream and Marie Antoinette's boudoir"; alongside the "decadent" display of "inventive macaroons" and other "sinful" delights, the Classic French menu includes "interesting salads and other fare", making it "perfect for a shopping break" – just "leave the diet at home."

La Famiglia ● *Italian*   21 | 16 | 22 | £41

Chelsea | 7 Langton St., SW10 (Fulham Broadway/Sloane Sq.) | 020-7351 0761 | fax 7351 2409 | www.lafamiglialondon.com

"It's all in the name: a family feeling from the moment you enter" this "humming" World's End 40-year-old that "never seems to lose its hearty enthusiasm" (the room could use "a face-lift", though); the "rustic" Tuscan cuisine is "well executed", even if the menu seems "suspiciously long"; P.S. the "glassed-in back area is fantastic."

La Fromagerie Café *European*   24 | 17 | 15 | £24

Marylebone | 2-4 Moxon St., W1 (Baker St.) | 020-7935 0341 | fax 7935 0341 | www.lafromagerie.co.uk

"Amazingly fresh", "adventurous" and "artery-clogging" Modern European dishes "hit just the right note" at this "crowded eatery at the back" of a "frantic" but "fantastic" *fromagerie* in Marylebone; some snarl "the service is always slow" – unless it's just that the "smell of wonderful cheese wafting through the air makes you so hungry!"

La Genova 🗷 *Italian*   23 | 19 | 24 | £52

Mayfair | 32 N. Audley St., W1 (Bond St.) | 020-7629 5916 | fax 7629 5916 | www.lagenovarestaurant.com

An "old-style, elegant Italian with the owner still very much in charge", "making you feel at home", characterises this "cosy" Mayfair haunt; "the food's always fresh, with a wide variety of options" on the Ligurian-oriented menu; P.S. "walk-ups welcome."

🗷 Lanes *Eclectic*   24 | 24 | 27 | £63

Mayfair | Four Seasons Hotel | Hamilton Pl., W1 (Green Park/ Hyde Park Corner) | 020-7499 0888 | fax 7493 6629 | www.fourseasons.com/london

From its "full English breakfasts" to the "rib roast carved at tableside" at dinner, this all-day Eclectic restaurant on the first floor of the Four Seasons Hotel is a "superb" "sure bet" for "travellers and locals alike"; surveyors smile on service that manages to be both "exemplary" and "down-to-earth for [such] a high-end place", and the marbled, stained-glass room offers "nice views" up Park Lane.

Lanesborough Conservatory *Eclectic*   21 | 26 | 25 | £59

Knightsbridge | The Lanesborough | 1 Lanesborough Pl., SW1 (Hyde Park Corner) | 020-7333 7254 | fax 7259 5606 | www.lanesborough.co.uk

"As picturesque a dining room you'll see" – with "delicate colours, whimsical palms and a hint of the Orient" – the Lanesborough's "bright" conservatory "is still a top-flight place" for a "splendid teatime fantasy" or "romantic dinner dance"; the "refined" Eclectic fare is "quite good", if "underwhelming at hotel prices", but most praise the "prompt, attentive service."

La Porchetta Pizzeria *Pizza*   19 | 13 | 17 | £18

Holborn | 33 Boswell St., WC1 (Holborn) | 020-7242 2434 🗷

(continued)

La Porchetta Pizzeria

Clerkenwell | 84-86 Rosebury Ave., EC1 (Angel) | 020-7837 6060 | fax 7837 6200

Muswell Hill | 265 Muswell Hill Broadway, N10 (Highgate) | 020-8883 1500 ◗

Islington | 141-142 Upper St., N1 (Angel/Highbury & Islington) | 020-7288 2488 ◗

Stoke Newington | 147 Stroud Green Rd., N4 (Finsbury Park) | 020-7281 2892 | fax 7837 6200 ◗

Possibly "the clangiest, bangiest restaurants on earth" ("could do with improved acoustics"), this chain is "heaving every night" with "young professionals, families and groups celebrating birthdays" over "amazingly cheap" Italian fare, primarily "pizzas bigger than toilet seats."

La Porte des Indes ◗ *Indian*
21 | **25** | **19** | **£43**

Marylebone | 32 Bryanston St., W1 (Marble Arch) | 020-7224 0055 | fax 7224 1144 | www.laportedesindes.com

"Decorated in colonial Raj style, complete with palms and a waterfall", this "splendid"-looking eatery ("from the folks who brought you Blue Elephant") serves "unusual", "upscale", "French-style Indian food"; and even if the "erratic service" "doesn't keep up" all the time, most concede this mammoth near Marble Arch is "perhaps a bit OTT, but it works."

La Poule au Pot *French*
22 | **23** | **20** | **£44**

Pimlico | 231 Ebury St., SW1 (Sloane Sq.) | 020-7730 7763 | fax 7259 9651

It's "hard to beat the seductive atmosphere" at this Pimlico veteran where "calorifically amazing" "cooking as it used to be in rural France" is served with a traditionally "Gallic approach to customer care"; even if "the bill can crank up", it's "worth the splurge", plus there's "perfect summer dining by candlelight on the outside pavement."

Z NEW L'Atelier de Joël Robuchon ◗ *French*
26 | **24** | **24** | **£85**

Covent Garden | 13-15 West St., WC2 (Leicester Sq.) | 020-7010 8600

Z NEW La Cuisine *French*

Covent Garden | L'Atelier de Joël Robuchon | 13-15 West St., WC2 (Leicester Sq.) | 020-7010 8600

Super-chef Joël Robuchon has "hit town with his fantastic creativity" at this "thrilling" Theatreland yearling; there's a "chic" red/black eatery with a "wall of green plants" and counter seating, and up above, a "black and white kitchen"-themed restaurant, La Cuisine, both offering different iterations of "divine *nouvelle cuisine française*"; given the "minuscule mains", it's all too "pricey" and "pretentious" pessimists protest, but "if you really want to impress, this is where to come"; P.S. there's also a "boudoirlike bar" on the top floor.

Latium ☒ *Italian*
25 | **19** | **24** | **£44**

Fitzrovia | 21 Berners St., W1 (Goodge St.) | 020-7323 9123 | fax 7323 3205 | www.latiumrestaurant.com

"They pack them in" to this "real find" in Fitzrovia, where diners are "welcomed professionally", then fed "impeccable Italian dishes", including "various types of ravioli"; though the "tempting wine list can rack up the bill", a "reasonable" meal "can be had with study."

	FOOD	DECOR	SERVICE	COST

☑ La Trompette *European/French* | 27 | 21 | 25 | £51 |

Chiswick | 5-7 Devonshire Rd., W4 (Turnham Green) | 020-8747 1836 | fax 8995 8097 | www.latrompette.co.uk

Surveyors "sound the trumpets" for this "hidden" "blessing for Chiswick locals" (sister of Chez Bruce), an "elegant" venue with "expertly prepared" Modern European–New French cooking, a "wine list to dive into" and "attentive, but not cloying service"; it's "great to impress for business or that second date (may be a bit flashy for a first)."

L'Aventure ☒ *French* | 22 | 20 | 20 | £45 |

St. John's Wood | 3 Blenheim Terrace, NW8 (St. John's Wood) | 020-7624 6232 | fax 7625 5548

This "secluded" St. John's Wood bistro is "like stepping into another, French world" where the classic "fare is cooked to a high standard"; and even if the service swings from "friendly" to "eccentric", all appreciate the "outdoor area for those global-warming nights."

Le Boudin Blanc *French* | 22 | 17 | 20 | £43 |

Mayfair | Shepherd Mkt. | 5 Trebeck St., W1 (Green Park) | 020-7499 3292 | fax 7495 6973 | www.boudinblanc.co.uk

"You forget that it isn't Paris" at this *vrai français in Shepherd Market*", an "authentic bistro" in everything from the "country-style" cuisine to the "crowded" scene; "staff are helpful", but "rushed."

Le Café du Marché ☒ *French* | 23 | 20 | 19 | £43 |

Smithfield | 22 Charterhouse Sq., EC1 (Barbican) | 020-7608 1609 | fax 7251 8575

"Those in-the-know" about this "secluded" Smithfield site applaud its "romantic" feel – "wooden beams" and "soft live music" – as well as its "lovely comfort food" *à la française,* which includes a "cheese trolley that virtually wheels itself to you", so "if you are dieting, go some place else."

☑ Le Caprice ❶ *British/European* | 24 | 21 | 23 | £56 |

St. James's | Arlington Hse. | Arlington St., SW1 (Green Park) | 020-7629 2239 | fax 7493 9040 | www.le-caprice.co.uk

"Still a thrill after all these years" (25, to be exact), this "stellar, star-studded" St. James's "institution" has its "high standards upheld by [director] Jesus Adorno", who oversees the "slick" service and the "never-failing" Modern British–European fare; but the "tables are squeezed-in" and the "dark art deco setting" could be "jazzed up a little."

Le Cercle ☒☒ *French* | 24 | 22 | 19 | £48 |

Chelsea | 1 Wilbraham Pl., SW1 (Sloane Sq.) | 020-7901 9999 | fax 7901 9111 | www.clubgascon.com

"Minimalist on decor, maximalist on the taste buds", this "discreet" ("black dress, dahling") Sloane Square site stars an "unusual" New French menu of "shareable tapas" with a "strong Southwest emphasis"; those "little plates can get expensive", but the prix fixe "lunch is a breathtaking bargain"; P.S. "beg or bribe for a corner booth."

Ledbury, The *French* | 25 | 23 | 24 | £65 |

Notting Hill | 127 Ledbury Rd., W11 (Westbourne Park) | 020-7792 9090 | fax 7792 9191 | www.theledbury.com

After "a stunning debut" in 2005, this "elegant" Notting Hill sister of The Square "continues to please" with "inventive" New French cuisine

	FOOD	DECOR	SERVICE	COST

that, whilst occasionally "over-the-top", hits "orgasmic" levels; "nicely spaced" tables that "strike the perfect balance between buzzy and so loud you can't have a conversation" and "gracious service" add to the appeal; it's even "not as expensive as you think it's going to be", given how "wonderful" it is.

☒ Le Gavroche ☒ *French* | 27 | 24 | 26 | £95 |

Mayfair | 43 Upper Brook St., W1 (Marble Arch) | 020-7408 0881 | fax 7491 4387 | www.le-gavroche.co.uk

"As expensive as it gets, but as fabulous as it can be" sums up Michel Roux Jr.'s "magnificent" Mayfair "bastion" of haute cuisine in a "sumptuous" "snug basement setting with a real sense of exclusivity"; the "*superbe*" kitchen doesn't "miss a beat" and "every detail is attended to" by "exemplary" staff; but modernists mutter "this 1950s rendition of fancy French" "needs updating."

☒ Le Manoir aux Quat'Saisons *French* | 28 | 27 | 26 | £97 |

Great Milton | Le Manoir aux Quat'Saisons Hotel | Church Rd., Oxfordshire | 01844 278881 | fax 01844 278847 | www.manoir.com

"Spectacular in all respects", chef-owner Raymond Blanc's "ethereal" 15th-century manor house in the Cotswolds "never fails to impress", from its "magical setting" – "stunning gardens" in summer, "welcoming fires" in winter – to its "genius" New French cuisine "lovingly prepared" "from perfect ingredients" grown on-site, and complemented by "solicitous, polite service"; so "sell the family silver and book a table" – better yet, book a "wonderful" bedroom and "stay overnight."

Leon *Mediterranean* | 19 | 15 | 16 | £13 |

NEW **Covent Garden** | 73-74 The Strand, WC2 (Covent Garden) | 020-7240 3070 | fax 7240 9988

Knightsbridge | 136 Brompton Rd., SW3 (Knightsbridge) | 020-7589 7330 | fax 7589 7346

NEW **Marylebone** | 275 Regent St., W1 (Oxford Circus)☒ Ⓜ

Soho | 35 Great Marlborough St., W1 (Oxford Circus) | 020-7437 5280

City | 12 Ludgate Circus, EC4 (Blackfriars) | 020-7489 1580 ☒

Spitalfields | 3 Crispin Pl., E1 (Liverpool St.) | 020-7247 4369 | fax 7377 1653 www.leonrestaurants.co.uk

"Who knew healthy food could taste so good?" – those patronising this fast-growing fast-food chain, that's who, with its "natural", "ethical" offerings that include "hearty" Med fare, "super salads" and "wraps that fill the gap", all "in funky atmosphere"; "portions are small" – but isn't that better for you, anyway?

Le Pain Quotidien *Bakery/Belgian* | 19 | 17 | 15 | £18 |

NEW **Marylebone** | 72-75 Marylebone High St., W1 (Baker St./Regent's Park) | 020-7486 6154

Soho | 18 Great Marlborough St., W1 (Oxford Circus/Piccadilly Circus) | 020-7486 6154 | fax 7486 6164

NEW **South Bank** | Royal Festival Hall | Belvedere Rd., SE1 (Waterloo) | 020-7486 6154

NEW **Kensington** | 9 Young St., W8 (Notting Hill Gate) | 020-7486 6154 www.lepainquotidien.com

"You'll never know who you'll meet at the communal tables" of these "rustic" Belgian bakeries that, as "long queues" attest, "make eating bread trendy again"; the "artfully displayed sandwiches" and "amazing pastries" are "enjoyable", the "confused service" "rather annoying."

DINING

	FOOD	DECOR	SERVICE	COST

Le Pont de la Tour ❶ *French/Seafood* | 22 | 23 | 20 | £63

Tower Bridge | Butlers Wharf Bldg. | 36D Shad Thames, SE1 (London Bridge/
Tower Hill) | 020-7403 8403 | fax 7940 1835 | www.lepontdelatour.co.uk
Its "spectacular setting on the Thames", basking "in the reflected light
of Tower Bridge", makes this Classic French a "solid choice for quality
dining"; if pessimists posit the *pont* "feels a little passé", especially
given the "sky-high prices", its "wide choice of seafood" and "deep,
varied wine list" remain "reliable for an all-round special occasion."

L'Escargot ❶⚹ *French* | 22 | 21 | 20 | £48

Soho | 48 Greek St., W1 (Leicester Sq./Tottenham Court Rd.) |
020-7437 6828 | fax 7437 0790 | www.whitestarline.org.uk
"One of Soho's longest-established restaurants" (born 1927), this
"old-school" Classic French remains a "favourite" "for a business dinner" or "pre-theatre option", especially if you sit upstairs in the art-
filled Picasso Room; "cheap it's not", though, and the not-impressed
snap "a snail would beat me in a race to my next visit here."

⚹ Les Trois Garçons ⚹ *French* | 19 | 29 | 21 | £54

Shoreditch | 1 Club Row, E1 (Liverpool St.) | 020-7613 1924 | fax 7012 1236 |
www.lestroisgarcons.com
Its "great kitsch look" of "taxidermy, antiques" and handbags hung
from the ceiling "never fails to amaze guests" at this Shoreditch site,
who've voted it No. 1 for Decor; the "relatively traditional" French food
is "good", but "should be better given how expensive it is" snap
cynics – both kitchen and staff "have delusions of grandeur."

Le Suquet ❶ *French/Seafood* | 23 | 17 | 20 | £46

Chelsea | 104 Draycott Ave., SW3 (South Kensington) | 020-7581 1785 |
fax 7225 0838
With a "1960s French Riviera feel about it" and a "seafood platter that
could feed Napoleon's army", this "raffish bistro" in Brompton Cross is
"always bustling", not least because "they take care of regulars, of which
there are many"; it "may be a tad overpriced", but it's "still a lot of fun."

L'Etranger *French* | 24 | 18 | 21 | £53

South Kensington | 36 Gloucester Rd., SW7 (Gloucester Rd.) |
020-7584 1118 | fax 7584 8886 | www.etranger.co.uk
"Wonderfully inventive" and "stylishly presented", the fare is an "unusual blend" of French with an Asian twist at this "best-kept secret" on
Gloucester Road; some "love the wine list and helpful staff", but they
advise "avoid the back room, as it vibrates from the disco downstairs."

Little Bay ❶ *European/Mediterranean* | 21 | 17 | 20 | £17

Farringdon | 171 Farringdon Rd., EC1 (Farringdon) | 020-7278 1234 |
fax 7278 5368
Kilburn | 228 Belsize Rd., NW6 (Kilburn Park) | 020-7372 4699 |
fax 7223 6131 ▱
Battersea | 228 York Rd., SW11 (Wandsworth Town) | 020-7223 4080 |
fax 7223 6131
Fulham | 140 Wandsworth Bridge Rd., SW6 (Parsons Green) |
020-7751 3133 | fax 7223 6131
www.little-bay.co.uk
"You have to come very early or very late" to this quartet, which "have
been discovered" for their "smiling staff" and uniquely "cheerful" am-

bience (Kilburn boasts "fantastic balcony tables", like a theatre, and Battersea offers "live opera singers"); "diners almost sit on top of each other, but no one complains" because the "super-cheap" Modern European–Med menu with its "constantly changing specials makes cooking at home pointless."

Locanda Locatelli *Italian*

| 25 | 22 | 22 | £64 |

Marylebone | Hyatt Regency London - The Churchill | 8 Seymour St., W1 (Marble Arch) | 020-7935 9088 | fax 7935 1149 | www.locandalocatelli.com

"Leave the family-style for another day – this is the place" for a "posh" experience attest *amici* of Italian "icon Giorgio Locatelli's" "outstanding, inventive" Northern Italian *cucina* in a Portman Square hotel; it's "popular with the glitterati", causing some to sigh "I'm not famous enough to get much service", but nearly everyone else would "eat here often – if it weren't so horrifically expensive."

Locanda Ottoemezzo 🗷 *Italian*

| 24 | 20 | 24 | £42 |

Kensington | 2-4 Thackeray St., W8 (High St. Kensington) | 020-7937 2200 | fax 7937 9871 | www.locandaottoemezzo.co.uk

"A terrific find off High Street Kensington", this "tiny, somewhat cramped" spot with "deep purple and red decor (refreshingly anti-beige!)" and "lots of silver screen" memorabilia on the walls features a "hearty", "exemplary Italian" menu that "never disappoints", even though it's "quite pricey"; "accommodating service" also gets the thumbs-up.

L'Oranger 🗷 *French*

| 24 | 22 | 24 | £66 |

St. James's | 5 St. James's St., SW1 (Green Park) | 020-7839 3774 | fax 7839 4330 | www.loranger.co.uk

"Excelling in the traditional ways without being pretentious", this "discreet" "place for high-powered bankers" in St. James's has "comfortable" "banquettes rather than hard modern edges", and shows "undoubted artistry" on its "high-end" (if "not cutting-edge") Classic French menu and "intelligent wine list"; "incredibly pleasant management and service" ensure "a wonderful experience overall."

Lucky 7 *Hamburgers*

| 20 | 17 | 14 | £18 |

Notting Hill | 127 Westbourne Park Rd., W2 (Royal Oak/Westbourne Park) | 020-7727 6771 | fax 7727 6798 | www.lucky7london.co.uk

It "feels like you're stepping into a small American diner" at Tom Conran's "vintage-y" Notting Hill establishment, which gets "a bit chaotic" (notably "at weekends, given the horrific queues"), but is "great for a burger" and a "filling milkshake"; "you cannot beat it for price" either.

Lundum's *Danish*

| 22 | 24 | 24 | £49 |

South Kensington | 117-119 Old Brompton Rd., SW7 (Gloucester Rd./South Kensington) | 020-7373 7774 | fax 7373 4472 | www.lundums.com

When you need "a change from the standard gastropub", this "family-run" South Ken Scandinavian is "always reliable" for "delicious Danish" cuisine, especially on the "wacky Sunday smorgasbord lunch", "served with flair in congenial surroundings"; small wonder supporters say this "well-kept secret should get out."

	FOOD	DECOR	SERVICE	COST

Made in Italy ❶ *Italian* | 21 | 12 | 13 | £27 |

Chelsea | 249 King's Rd., SW3 (Sloane Sq./South Kensington) | 020-7352 1880

"Bring your sense of humour" to this "frenetic" Chelsea trattoria; "tables are scarce (with nowhere to wait)" and "service is poor", but the "great atmosphere" and "rustic" Italian staples (starring "*delizioso* pizza") make it a "perennial favourite", and "good value" to boot.

NEW Magdalen ⓔ *European* | - | - | - | E |

Borough | 152 Tooley St., SE1 (London Bridge) | 020-7403 1342 | fax 7403 9950 | www.magdalenerestaurant.co.uk

"Pure breeding shows through" – the chef-owner's pedigree includes Anchor & Hope and The Fat Duck – at this "excellent newcomer" near London Bridge; with an "imaginative, well-planned" Modern European menu and elegant cream-and-aubergine decor, it will satisfy either as a "chilled-out, after-work affair or casual weekend venue."

Maggie Jones's *British* | 21 | 21 | 20 | £36 |

Kensington | 6 Old Court Pl., W8 (High St. Kensington) | 020-7937 6462 | fax 7376 0510

"If you're jonesing for Traditional British" food, this Kensington old-timer is "the perfect place", with "hearty meals" to satisfy "Jurassic appetites" ("order chicken and get the whole bird, almost"); its "quirky" "country-kitchen decor" makes a "great gathering place for friends."

Ma Goa *Indian* | 23 | 14 | 22 | £31 |

Fulham | 194 Wandsworth Bridge Rd., SW6 (Parsons Green) | 020-7384 2122 Ⓜ
Putney | 242-244 Upper Richmond Rd., SW15 (East Putney) | 020-8780 1767
www.ma-goa.com

The "innovative" Goan "food's always full of flavour" at these "family-run, with a welcoming feel" Fulham and Putney Indians; "good with children", "courteous staff" compensate for "cramped" environs.

Malabar Junction *Indian* | 23 | 18 | 19 | £25 |

Bloomsbury | 107 Great Russell St., WC1 (Tottenham Court Rd.) | 020-7580 5230 | fax 7436 9942 | www.malabarjunction.com

This "unusual" Indian is one of the "best places to eat around the British Museum", thanks to its "excellent Keralan" menu and "keen service"; the glass-roofed "gazebo setting" with "plants and paintings all around" manages to seem "spacey and cosy at the same time."

Mandalay ⓔ *Burmese* | 23 | 7 | 21 | £19 |

Marylebone | 444 Edgware Rd., W2 (Edgware Rd.) | 020-7258 3696 | fax 7258 3696

"You'll fill your belly and not empty your wallet" at this "low-budget" "basic" Burmese; despite being in a "dodgy" stretch of Edgware Road, it "attracts regulars from all over London" with an "amazing variety" of "delicately prepared dishes, served with genuine friendliness."

Mandarin Kitchen ❶ *Chinese* | 23 | 10 | 14 | £33 |

Bayswater | 14-16 Queensway, W2 (Bayswater/Queensway) | 020-7727 9012 | fax 7727 9468

A "huge menu" with "some of the most unusual seafood outside Hong Kong" ("the lobster noodles are fantastic") makes this "crowded"

	FOOD	DECOR	SERVICE	COST

Queensway Chinese a "must-go place", but there "isn't much decor to speak of" and "surly service" "lets this place down big time."

Mao Tai ◐ Chinese | 22 | 17 | 16 | £36 |

Fulham | 58 New King's Rd., SW6 (Parsons Green) | 020-7731 2520 | fax 7471 8992 | www.maotai.co.uk

"Even on a bad day, it's still good" at this "classy Chinese in Parsons Green" that also serves "respectable", "healthy-looking" Southeast Asian dishes; scores for the "comfortable" decor may not fully reflect a "recent refurb" after a fire in early 2007.

Mark's Club ⊠ British/French | 24 | 23 | 26 | £85 |

Private club; inquiries: 020-7499 2936

"The height of refinement", this "most formal of clubs" in Mayfair is "like dining at a rich friend's house (with lots of staff)"; "superb" Classic French–British "comfort food" and an "impeccable wine list" are supported by "superior" service, and whilst it's "a bit stuffy, that's part of the charm"; "at least you can have a conversation here."

Maze French | 25 | 21 | 23 | £66 |

Mayfair | 10-13 Grosvenor Sq., W1 (Bond St.) | 020-7107 0000 | fax 7107 0001 | www.gordonramsay.com

"The great man goes tapas" at this highly hyped two-year-old in "Gordon Ramsay's stable" in Grosvenor Square, where "creative" Asian-inflected New French small plates make a "fantastic way to sample different flavours without popping buttons"; cynics snap the yellow-beige "decor lacks character" and the "knowledgeable" "service is uneven", but most are "enthusiastic" about this "exciting concept" (just "be prepared to be a-mazed at the cost").

Mediterraneo ◐ Italian | 22 | 16 | 19 | £35 |

Notting Hill | 37 Kensington Park Rd., W11 (Ladbroke Grove) | 020-7792 3131 | fax 7243 3630 | www.mediterraneo-restaurant.co.uk

"The neighbourhood Italian if you live in heaven" gush Notting Hill *amici* of this "crowded" "classic that never changes" its "homely dishes" ("wonderful sea bass") or "accessible service"; "cramped conditions" aside, it's "a good alternative when [nearby sister] Osteria Basilico is booked."

Mela ◐ Indian | 23 | 16 | 19 | £28 |

Covent Garden | 152-156 Shaftesbury Ave., WC2 (Leicester Sq.) | 020-7836 8635 | fax 7379 0527 | www.melarestaurant.co.uk

Take "a tour of India" via the "mélange of regional dishes" offered by this "delectable" subcontinental; "attentive but not pushy" service, a "remarkable value" prix fixe and its location 'twixt Covent Garden and Soho make it perfect "for the pre-theatre set."

NEW Mews of Mayfair British | 22 | 21 | 21 | £50 |

Mayfair | 10-11 Lancashire Ct., New Bond St., W1 (Bond St./Oxford Circus) | 020-7518 9388 | fax 7518 9389 | www.mewsofmayfair.com

"The combination of club, bar and restaurant in one place works" at this "groovy townhouse" "hidden" in a Mayfair mews; the "slinky", "feminine" upstairs dining room ("looks like an upscale department store") has an "innovative" Modern British menu that's "worth the high price" and "slick service"; the casual "scene downstairs" –

reminiscent of a "cosy, ephemeral nymphs' abode" – serves "good snacks", "perfect for both clients and a date."

Michael Moore ●⊠ *Eclectic* — 22 | 17 | 22 | £45

Marylebone | 19 Blandford St., W1 (Baker St./Bond St.) | 020-7224 1898 | fax 7224 0970 | www.michaelmoorerestaurant.com
"Informative chef"-owner Michael Moore "swans around making sure everything is delicious" and "served with justified confidence" at this Marylebone Eclectic that's "cosy", despite being "bare of decoration"; still, a few feel it's "not worth the price", given the "tiny portions (I thought my starter was the amuse-bouche)."

Mildreds ⊠⇗ *Vegetarian* — 22 | 16 | 18 | £18

Soho | 45 Lexington St., W1 (Oxford Circus/Piccadilly Circus) | 020-7439 2392 | fax 7439 2392 | www.mildreds.co.uk
"Even omnivores salivate" at this "funky" Soho vegetarian specialist whose "creative" cuisine "captures a variety of tastes", and whilst cynics cavil that "the quarters are tighter than pressed tofu" – "you may have to share tables on busy nights" – the "inexpensive" cost compensates.

Mirabelle ● *French* — 22 | 21 | 22 | £63

Mayfair | 56 Curzon St., W1 (Green Park) | 020-7499 4636 | fax 7499 5449 | www.whitestarline.org.uk
Restaurateur Marco Pierre White's re-creation of Mayfair's "legendary place from the 1950s" remains an "unashamedly escapist" venue, with a "classy clubbiness" and "sumptuous" "old-school French" fare; but dissenters declare cuisine and staff "quite variable – some nights excellent, others ordinary" – whilst the "dated decor" and "stratospheric prices" are all too constant.

Miyama *Japanese* — 26 | 12 | 20 | £40

Mayfair | 38 Clarges St., W1 (Green Park) | 020-7499 2443 | fax 7491 1569 | www.miyama.co.uk
This "simple little place on a side street" in Mayfair is "a favourite of the Japanese expat community", serving "exquisite", "excellent sushi and sashimi the size of which will break your chopsticks"; "attentive staff" make amends for "decor that could use some work."

NEW Mocotó ⊠ *Brazilian* — 22 | 22 | 19 | £52

Knightsbridge | 145 Knightsbridge, SW1 (Knightsbridge) | 020-7225 2300 | fax 7225 4460 | www.mocoto.co.uk
A "sexy newcomer" to Knightsbridge, this "buzzy" Brazilian is off with a bang, with "big portions" of "robust" dishes and rustic decor of wooden floors and a ceiling composed of tree trunks ("thought I was going to spot some tumbleweed"); even if the "service still has opening pains", the venue already boasts "the feel of someplace that could get too popular."

Momo ● *African* — 19 | 25 | 18 | £44

Piccadilly | 25 Heddon St., W1 (Piccadilly Circus) | 020-7434 4040 | fax 7287 0404 | www.momoresto.com
The "spicy smells" and "sexy, lavish" "decor transform you and set the mood" at this "intoxicating" Piccadilly North African; whilst the menu may "not rank with the heavy hitters in Arabic cuisine", it's still "a little taste of Morocco that's nearer than Marrakech"; P.S. the bar below is "worth a visit, with lively music and hookah den interior."

	FOOD	DECOR	SERVICE	COST

☑ Morgan M ⓜ *French* | 27 | 17 | 22 | £60 |

Islington | 489 Liverpool Rd., N7 (Highbury & Islington) | 020-7609 3560 | fax 8292 5699 | www.morganm.com

"A real mecca for food lovers", "dedicated chef"-owner Morgan Meunier's "hidden gem" offers Islingtonians "the rare pleasure of an eponymous restaurant with the namesake firmly in control"; the experience involves "delectable" New French fare (including an "outstanding vegetarian" tasting menu), "quirky amuse-bouches and entremets", plus "staff who are trained to please"; P.S. the "refurbishment provides a better", more formal setting.

Moro ☒ *Mediterranean* | 25 | 18 | 20 | £40 |

Clerkenwell | 34-36 Exmouth Mkt., EC1 (Angel/Farringdon) | 020-7833 8336 | fax 7833 9338 | www.moro.co.uk

"The oohs and ahhs of eating" the "exotic" Med cuisine – "bursting with flavour" and "true to the Moorish spirit" – add to the "deafening noise" at this Exmouth Market eatery ("the harsh interior" doesn't help); even if staff are "not always able to keep up with the crowds", the place is "great for a gaggle of girls or a fun night with clients."

Morton's ☒ *French* | 24 | 22 | 22 | £65 |

Private club; inquiries: 020-7518 2982

There's "something a bit special" about this "discreet, private" club with a "wonderful view over Berkeley Square"; a "quiet, elegant" dining room serves "delectable" New French food with multitudes of "waiters at your beck and call", whilst the downstairs bar features a "stunning" wall that changes colour; small wonder some "would kill for a membership" here.

Mosimann's ☒ *Eclectic* | 26 | 26 | 25 | £78 |

Private club; inquiries: 020-7235 9625

"Civilised beyond civilisation as it is today", this Belgravia club offers "a supreme dining experience from start to finish"; within the "dazzling", "dramatic space" (a 19th-century former church) with "many enchanting [private] rooms", guests experience "masterful" Eclectic cooking, "world-class wines" and "interactive but not intrusive waiters"; the "only downside is you need to have a member take you."

Nahm *Thai* | 26 | 20 | 23 | £59 |

Belgravia | Halkin Hotel | 5 Halkin St., SW1 (Hyde Park Corner) | 020-7333 1234 | fax 7333 1100 | www.nahm.como.bz

"If you are a fan of Thai cuisine" – and "your bank account is sufficient" – you'll find the "intricate" menu at this Belgravia hotel eatery "extraordinarily interesting" and even "inspiring"; some call the marble-floored, "minimalist" "decor cold, but warm, pleasant servers" make this a "good special-occasion restaurant."

NEW Narrow, The *British* | - | - | - | M |

Limehouse | 44 Narrow St., E14 (Limehouse) | 020-7592 7950 | www.gordonramsay.com

Gordon Ramsay's first foray into "reasonably priced" pub dining debuts after a revamp of a characterful old dockmaster's house, set dramatically "by the river" in Limehouse; it's already "packed" with people praising the punchy Traditional British fare ("fork-tender, flavoursome pig cheeks", "heavenly egg custard") served in a simply appointed dining room; "service is friendly, but a bit slow."

	FOOD	DECOR	SERVICE	COST

New Tayyabs ● *Pakistani*

| | 24 | 12 | 14 | £16 |

Whitechapel | 83-89 Fieldgate St., E1 (Aldgate/Whitechapel) | 020-7247 6400 | fax 7377 1257 | www.tayyabs.co.uk

"The length of the queues is testimony" to the "true-to-tradition Pakistani" cooking at this "anarchic restaurant" in "edgy" Whitechapel; given the "grubby decor" and "ultrafast" service, it's "not the place for a quiet, intimate meal", but you can't beat the "unbelievably cheap" bill (boosted by "BYO booze").

Nobu Berkeley St. *Japanese/Peruvian*

| | 26 | 21 | 20 | £68 |

Mayfair | 15 Berkeley St., W1 (Green Park) | 020-7290 9222 | fax 7290 9223 | www.noburestaurants.com

There's always "quite a scene going on" at the Nobu empire's number-two Mayfair outpost – "hipper than the one at the Met" – where celebrities and "hedge-fund zillionaires come to play", whether it be in the "brilliant bar" or "bright dining room upstairs"; supporters still swoon over "sushi like you've never tasted before" and the Japanese-Peruvian cuisine that's "divine", if "extremely expensive"; however, the "rush 'em in, rush 'em out policy is not appreciated."

☒ Nobu London *Japanese/Peruvian*

| | 27 | 20 | 21 | £70 |

Mayfair | Metropolitan Hotel | 19 Old Park Ln., W1 (Hyde Park Corner) | 020-7447 4747 | fax 7447 4749 | www.noburestaurants.com

Even after 10 years, Nobu Matsuhisa's "sizzling" Old Park Lane "flagship is firing on all cylinders", with an "exotically marvellous" Japanese-Peruvian menu ("sushi-lovers' heaven") that "exceeds expectations"; ok, the "stark" decor "could do with a splash of paint", the "efficient service sometimes looks harassed" and "booking a table takes creativity"; but few deny this "celestial" spot – rammed with "A- through C-list celebs" – is "definitely a treat, especially if someone else drops the credit card."

North Sea ☒ *Seafood*

| | 23 | 11 | 19 | £20 |

Bloomsbury | 7-8 Leigh St., WC1 (King's Cross/Russell Sq.) | 020-7387 5892 | fax 7388 9770

With "decor to laugh at" and "local clientele to add colour", this "wonderfully old-fashioned, sit-down fish 'n' chips" shop is "worth finding" because – despite its "off-the-beaten-path" Bloomsbury address – it offers some of the "best-priced", "delectable" seafood in town.

Notting Hill Brasserie *European*

| | 24 | 23 | 21 | £51 |

Notting Hill | 92 Kensington Park Rd., W11 (Notting Hill Gate) | 020-7229 4481 | fax 7221 1246

In a "gem of a location" in Notting Hill, this "relaxing", "romantic" eatery ("nicely spaced tables", "sophisticated decor" with "piano player [for] an added touch") fans the flames with an "inventive Modern European menu and inspired wine list", "all delivered at modest prices" given its "special-occasion" status; "professional service" completes the picture at this "well-kept secret."

Oliveto *Italian*

| | 23 | 14 | 18 | £32 |

Belgravia | 49 Elizabeth St., SW1 (Sloane Sq./Victoria) | 020-7730 0074 | fax 7823 5377

"Huge thin-crust pizzas with creative toppings" and other "dependably delicious", "authentic Sardinian" dishes, "served with warmth

and knowledge", pull "the posh set" to this "convivial" if "cramped" and "noisy" Belgravia Italian.

NEW Olivomare ⑤ *Italian/Seafood* | - | - | - | E |

Belgravia | 10 Lower Belgrave St., SW1 (Victoria) | 020-7730 9022
This new Belgravia offshoot from the Olivo/Oliveto team is set in bright, gleaming premises where, apart from one wall bedecked with fishy modern artwork, everywhere is pristine white, including a quirky fishnet over one of the windows; the sophisticated Sardinian seafood menu is not long, but offers a wide selection of species.

1 Lombard Street ⑤ *French* | 22 | 20 | 21 | £55 |

City | 1 Lombard St., EC3 (Bank) | 020-7929 6611 | fax 7929 6622 | www.1lombardstreet.com
"Check out the who's who in finance" at this "civilised" City dweller that boasts "the Bank of England as a neighbour" (is that why they "feel they can charge a lot"?) and a New French menu with "plenty of choice", presented by staff who "love to serve", albeit at a "snail-like" pace; if it's "not as much fun as the Brasserie" up front, its "central location is in its favour."

One-O-One *French/Seafood* | 23 | - | 20 | £65 |

Knightsbridge | Sheraton Park Tower | 101 William St., SW1 (Knightsbridge) | 020-7290 7101 | fax 7201 7884 | www.onemansfish.com
"Delectable" fish with "a fresh twist", served by "accomplished staff", is "the hallmark" of this "oh-so-pricey" New French in Knightsbridge; after a "three-month overhaul" post-Survey, it was slated to unveil an opulent new look and a selection of small plates in mid-summer 2007.

Original Lahore Kebab House ● *Pakistani* | 24 | 6 | 15 | £17 |

Whitechapel | 2-10 Umberston St., E1 (Aldgate East/Whitechapel) | 020-7481 9737 | fax 7488 1300
Highgate | 148-150 Brent St., NW4 (Hendon Central) | 020-8203 6904
"Crowded unlike everywhere else in the neighbourhood", this Whitechapel "curry caff" "with creaky stairs and well-trodden carpet" is a "fail safe for scrumptious tandoori grub" (like "legendary lamb chops") and other "amazing Pakistani" edibles; "value is guaranteed" as there's "no corkage charge for drinks" (both it and its smaller Hendon Central sibling are BYO).

Orrery *French* | 25 | 23 | 23 | £65 |

Marylebone | 55 Marylebone High St., W1 (Baker St./Regent's Park) | 020-7616 8000 | fax 7616 8080 | www.orreryrestaurant.co.uk
Flooded in natural light, this "spacious" Marylebone New French offers a "serene setting" for "understated, yet refined" and "tantalising" tasting menus – culminating in a "divine cheese tray" – "served by professional", if slightly "stiff" staff; ornery souls may sniff it's "not life-changing", and you definitely "feel the money flying from your wallet", but it's "worth every penny" for most.

Oslo Court ⑤ *French* | 22 | 15 | 25 | £49 |

St. John's Wood | Charlbert St., off Prince Albert Rd., NW8 (St. John's Wood) | 020-7722 8795 | fax 7586 7695
"Whatever you desire, they can serve" at this St. John's Wood "'70s time warp" where they "welcome you into their family" with "massive portions" of "uncomplicated" Classic French dishes; sure, some "can't

figure out why it's always packed" as it's "comforting, not exciting (like kissing your grandmother)", but the pleased plead "please God, it never changes"; P.S. there's "no chance of refusing a pudding."

Osteria Basilico ● *Italian* | 24 | 18 | 18 | £34 |

Notting Hill | 29 Kensington Park Rd., W11 (Ladbroke Grove/ Notting Hill Gate) | 020-7727 9957 | fax 7229 7980 | www.osteriabasilico.co.uk

"Don't even think about just turning up" at this "Notting Hill classic" as it's "impossible to get a table" thanks to Italian cuisine (like "perfect pizzas") that "has stayed consistently great through the years"; even the "brusque" staff and "occasional chaotic moment just adds to the atmosphere"; P.S. the summer terrace "makes for great people-watching."

Ottolenghi *Mediterranean* | 24 | 17 | 16 | £24 |

Islington | 287 Upper St., N1 (Angel) | 020-7288 1454 | fax 7704 1456
Notting Hill | 63 Ledbury Rd., W11 (Notting Hill Gate) | 020-7727 1121
www.ottolenghi.co.uk

"Just walking past the window makes the mouth water" at these Med deli/cafes in Notting Hill and Islington whose "original", "sensational food and cakes" can be eaten at "one big round table" or "easily taken home"; they're "quite pricey though", and some wonder "do you have to be grumpy to work here?"

Painted Heron, The *Indian* | 22 | 19 | 21 | £42 |

Chelsea | 112 Cheyne Walk, SW10 (Sloane Sq.) | 020-7351 5232 | fax 7351 5213 | www.thepaintedheron.com

The "strange name belies" the "imaginative dishes" "suitable for an educated palate" at this "upmarket" "modern" Indian on Chelsea Embankment ("hard to find"); add in "friendly service" and it's clear why it's "not to be missed" – just "better be sure you can stand those spices."

Papillon ● *French* | 23 | 22 | 22 | £52 |

South Kensington | 96 Draycott Ave., SW3 (South Kensington) | 020-7225 2555 | www.papillonchelsea.co.uk

"Classy and formal, but still with a neighbourhood feel", this "addition to the Brompton Cross restaurant scene" has made a "superb start" say fans of Soren Jessen's "plush" bistro where an "inventive" "Classic French menu is presented and served well" by "non-snooty servers"; "whilst expensive", it leaves you "without feeling ripped off."

Park, The *Pan-Asian* | 24 | 24 | 25 | £57 |

Knightsbridge | Mandarin Oriental Hyde Park | 66 Knightsbridge, SW1 (Knightsbridge) | 020-7201 3722 | fax 7235 2001 | www.mandarinoriental.com/london

There's "a brilliant view of Hyde Park" at this "gem hidden in an impersonal room" in the Mandarin Oriental; fans fall for the "fabulous service" and the "excellent new menu" of Pan-Asian shared plates that "deliver good food at an acceptable price for the neighbourhood" – and it's "even better when the wine is included", as on the weekday prix fixe lunch.

Pasha *Moroccan* | 20 | 16 | 17 | £34 |

Islington | 301 Upper St., N1 (Angel/Highbury & Islington) | 020-7226 1454 | fax 7226 1617

Despite "bare-bones service and decor" (the latter was being revamped post-Survey), diners "come out having enjoyed a relaxing"

time at this "calming" Upper Street Turk with "well-spaced tables" and "carefully prepared dishes, notable for their lightness."

Pasha ● *Moroccan*

18 | 25 | 17 | £43

South Kensington | 1 Gloucester Rd., SW7 (Gloucester Rd.) | 020-7589 7969 | fax 7581 9996 | www.pasha-restaurant.co.uk

"In a neighbourhood lacking ambience restaurants", the "romantic" "Aladdin's cave atmosphere" of this South Ken Moroccan is like a "jump to Marrakech"; "don't expect to be bowled over by the food – it's average, and so's the service" – but there are "beautiful" belly dancers.

Passione ⊠ *Italian*

23 | 15 | 20 | £48

Fitzrovia | 10 Charlotte St., W1 (Goodge St.) | 020-7636 2833 | fax 7636 2889 | www.passione.co.uk

"Eating here is always a pleasure" proclaim patrons passionate about this "Italian with a big heart" (despite "tight quarters") "in the middle of Fitzrovia"; some are "surprised at how expensive everything is", but the "fantastic food" and "willing-to-go-the-extra-mile service" "are worth it"; P.S. tip: "upstairs is more private and rarely full."

Patara *Thai*

23 | 19 | 20 | £38

Knightsbridge | 9 Beauchamp Pl., SW3 (Knightsbridge/South Kensington) | 020-7581 8820 | fax 7581 2155

Mayfair | 3-7 Maddox St., W1 (Oxford Circus) | 020-7499 6008 | fax 7499 6007

Soho | 15 Greek St., W1 (Leicester Sq./Tottenham Court Rd.) | 020-7437 1071 | fax 7437 1089

South Kensington | 181 Fulham Rd., SW3 (South Kensington) | 020-7351 5692 | fax 7351 5692

www.patarathailand.com

The menu offers "a myriad of spices to greet the palate" at this "busy, buzzy" quartet with "modern yet charming ambience"; true, they're "not cheap, but they're worth the money since the food has an edge and taste that ordinary Thais don't have" – and "gracious" service to boot.

Patisserie Valerie *French*

20 | 14 | 15 | £17

Belgravia | 17 Motcomb St., SW1 (Knightsbridge) | 020-7245 6161 | fax 7245 6161

Covent Garden | 8 Russell St., WC2 (Covent Garden) | 020-7240 0064 | fax 7240 0064

Knightsbridge | 215 Brompton Rd., SW3 (Knightsbridge) | 020-7823 9971 | fax 7589 4993

Knightsbridge | 32-44 Hans Crescent, SW1 (Knightsbridge) | 020-7590 0905

Marylebone | 105 Marylebone High St., W1 (Baker St./Bond St.) | 020-7935 6240 | fax 7935 6543

Piccadilly | 162 Piccadilly, W1 (Green Park) | 020-7491 1717

Soho | 44 Old Compton St., W1 (Leicester Sq.) | 020-7437 3466 | fax 7734 6133

City | The Pavillion Bldg. | Bishops Sq., 37 Brushfield St., E1 (Liverpool St.) | 020-7247 4906

Chelsea | 81 Duke of York Sq., King's Rd., SW3 (Sloane Sq.) | 020-7730 7094 | fax 7730 7094

Kensington | 27 Kensington Church St., W8 (High St. Kensington) | 020-7937 9574 | fax 7937 9574

www.patisserie-valerie.co.uk

"Humming with contented customers", this "time-honoured" chain is "a treat any time of day" for "homemade goodies in a classic French

bistro manner" – though some "skip the food and go straight for" the counter-displayed confections ("calories and cholesterol, but oh so good!"); despite "crowded" digs and "service that could use an energy infusion", it's still a "sweet stop."

Patterson's 🖻 European | 22 | 20 | 21 | £53

Mayfair | 4 Mill St., W1 (Oxford Circus) | 020-7499 1308 | fax 7491 2122 | www.pattersonsrestaurant.co.uk

This "delightful" Mayfair Modern European offers a "good, all-round" package of "well-executed" fare (the "deceptively small portions do fill you up"), "efficient service" and ambience that "can get noisy but not bothersome"; on the flip side, "it's not particularly good value", aside from the "exceptional specials" and prix fixes.

Pearl French | 24 | 22 | 23 | £56

Holborn | Renaissance Chancery Court Hotel | 252 High Holborn, WC1 (Holborn) | 020-7829 7000 | fax 7829 9889 | www.pearl-restaurant.com

The "plush, seriously well-designed" interior of this "white marbled" Holborn hotel dining room is the canvas for chef Jun Tanaka's "original, carefully crafted" New French menu, served by "exceptional staff"; cynics claim it's "just not that memorable", given that "the price is high", but supporters insist it's "great for splashing out."

Pepper Tree Thai | 19 | 11 | 14 | £16

Clapham | 19 Clapham Common S. Side, SW4 (Clapham Common) | 020-7622 1758 | fax 7720 7531 | www.thepeppertree.co.uk

"You may need to recalibrate the idea of cheap and cheerful" after checking out this Clapham Common Thai, with its combination of "really tasty" "decent portions" and little prices; however, the "noisy" digs and communal tables make it a "great stop to get the evening going", "rather than a romantic meal for two."

Pescatori 🖻 Mediterranean | 22 | 16 | 21 | £44

Mayfair | 11 Dover St., W1 (Green Park) | 020-7493 2652 | fax 7499 3180
Fitzrovia | 57 Charlotte St., W1 (Goodge St.) | 020-7580 3289 | fax 7580 0539
www.pescatori.co.uk

"Innovatively, expertly prepared fish" is the mainstay of the Med menu at this Mayfair and Fitzrovia pair, a family-run "reliable house of fins"; habitués also hail the "homely feel" and "lovely service."

⛆ Pétrus 🖻 French | 28 | 25 | 26 | £95

Belgravia | Berkeley Hotel | Wilton Pl., SW1 (Hyde Park Corner) | 020-7235 1200 | www.gordonramsay.com

"Luxuriate in Marcus Wareing's sublime creations" – the epitome of New French "cooking at its most cutting edge", backed by "wines that live up to the name" – at this "beautiful" Belgravia venue where "utterly professional" staff "provide tip-top service"; perhaps it's un peu "pretentious", with "eye-popping prices", but it's also "everything a modern fine-dining institution should be" – "so pick a special occasion, forget the cost and book it."

Phoenix Palace ◑ Chinese | 23 | 17 | 15 | £27

Marylebone | 3-5 Glentworth St., NW1 (Baker St.) | 020-7486 3515
For "upmarket, relaxed Chinese dining away from the hustle and bustle of Chinatown", this Marylebone Cantonese offers "a place to ex-

periment with confidence" from a "comprehensive menu"; "reasonable prices" compensate for "hit-and-miss service."

☑ Pied à Terre ☒ *French* | 28 | 22 | 25 | £82

Fitzrovia | 34 Charlotte St., W1 (Goodge St.) | 020-7636 1178 | fax 7916 1171 | www.pied-a-terre.co.uk

"Hats off to chef Shane Osborne for the culinary masterpieces" he creates at this "small" but "stunning" New French in Fitzrovia; from the "star wine list" to the "extremely knowledgeable servers", it has "everything you could possibly want in a restaurant" (except perhaps the decor – "chic, but nothing eye-grabbing"), and so it's "worth the prices" – "you'll pay for the *pied,* but you'll leave *la terre* for *le ciel!*"

Pig's Ear *British/French* | 22 | 19 | 19 | £33

Chelsea | 35 Old Church St., SW3 (Sloane Sq.) | 020-7352 2908 | fax 7352 9321 | www.thepigsear.co.uk

"Well, maybe you *can* make a silk purse from a pig's ear" quip those enamoured by this "fabulous little gastropub" in Chelsea; diners can have an "adult" drink at the "trendy" bar or head upstairs for "correctly priced" New French–Traditional British cuisine; "the biggest problem is its success: it's impossible to get a table at a normal time."

☑ Pizza Express *Pizza* | 17 | 13 | 15 | £18

Covent Garden | 9-12 Bow St., WC2 (Covent Garden) | 020-7240 3443 | fax 7497 0131 ☾

Knightsbridge | 7 Beauchamp Pl., SW3 (Knightsbridge) | 020-7589 2355 | fax 7589 5159 ☾

Soho | 29 Wardour St., W1 (Leicester Sq./Piccadilly Circus) | 020-7437 7215 | fax 7494 2582

Blackfriars | 125 Alban Gate, London Wall, EC2 (Moorgate/St. Paul's) | 020-7600 8880 | fax 7600 8128

Battersea | 46-54 Battersea Bridge Rd., SW11 (Earl's Ct./Sloane Sq.) | 020-7924 2774

Chelsea | The Pheasantry | 152-154 King's Rd., SW3 (Sloane Sq.) | 020-7351 5031 | fax 7349 9844

Fulham | 363 Fulham Rd., SW10 (Fulham Broadway) | 020-7352 5300 ☾

Fulham | 895-896 Fulham Rd., SW6 (Parsons Green) | 020-7731 3117 | fax 7371 7884 ☾

Kensington | 35 Earl's Court Rd., W8 (Earl's Ct.) | 020-7937 0761 ☾

Notting Hill | 137 Notting Hill Gate, W11 (Notting Hill Gate) | 020-7229 6000 ☾

www.pizzaexpress.com

Additional locations throughout the London area

"Perfect for a casual bite" of "decent pizza" and other Italian staples served "without fuss", this "good value" chain around town "sets the standard for reliability"; aside from the "huge variety of their premises", they offer "no surprises – but that's a good thing."

Providores, The/Tapa Room *Eclectic* | 22 | 16 | 17 | £39

Marylebone | 109 Marylebone High St., W1 (Baker St./Bond St.) | 020-7935 6175 | fax 7935 6877 | www.theprovidores.co.uk

"Wacky, highly imaginative" Eclectic edibles, matched with "extremely nice New Zealand wines", make for a merry time at this Marylebone fusion specialist ("Austral-Asian?") that offers "two dining options": the "always busy", "tight" Tapa Room where you "stand in line to get a table", and Providores, the "serene upstairs" ("more

lonely", but you can book); "too bad" about the "frankly bland" decor and "slow staff."

Quadrato *Italian*

24 | 22 | 26 | £51

Canary Wharf | Four Seasons Canary Wharf | 46 Westferry Circus, E14 (Canary Wharf) | 020-7510 1857 | fax 7510 1998 | www.fourseasons.com

"Customers are treated like kings and queens" – typical "Four Seasons-quality" treatment – at this smart, airy eatery where an "open kitchen provides a stage to watch" the creation of "superb" "regional Italian specials"; whilst some sigh about the slightly "soul-less" "setting just off the lobby", few deny it's the "best bet for a high-end lunch in Canary Wharf."

Quilon *Indian*

25 | 19 | 21 | £41

Victoria | Crowne Plaza London St. James Hotel | 41 Buckingham Gate, SW1 (St. James's Park/Victoria) | 020-7821 1899 | fax 7828 5802 | www.quilon.co.uk

"In its own way, great" say those familiar with this "modern"-looking Indian in a "corporate" hotel south of St. James's Park; it's applauded for "amazing" Keralan cooking that's "true to the region" – though "quite pricey" compared to more standard subcontinental sites.

Quirinale ⊠ *Italian*

25 | 20 | 25 | £47

Westminster | 1 Great Peter St., SW1 (Westminster) | 020-7222 7080 | fax 7233 3080 | www.quirinale.co.uk

"Combining an elegant simplicity with high-quality service", this "Westminster favourite gets the vote" – as well as attracts "the occasional MP" – for "divine" Italian cooking "plus the best selection of cheeses"; although the "comfortable" cream-coloured setting can be "a bit quiet", the "intimate" basement makes it feel "like a club."

Racine *French*

22 | 18 | 21 | £46

Knightsbridge | 239 Brompton Rd., SW3 (Knightsbridge/South Kensington) | 020-7584 4477 | fax 7584 4900

"A haute-bistro that never fails" applaud *amis* of this "busy" Knightsbridge haunt where "the ambience is authentic", down to the "tables close together"; the "hearty" French fare is "a joy" and staff "have the formula for making one feel at home", despite "prices that seem high."

Rasa *Indian*

24 | 17 | 20 | £31

Mayfair | 6 Dering St., W1 (Bond St./Oxford Circus) | 020-7629 1346 | fax 7637 0224 ⊠
Fitzrovia | 5 Charlotte St., W1 (Tottenham Court Rd.) | 020-7637 0222 | fax 7637 0224
Islington | Holiday Inn King's Cross | 1 King's Cross Rd., WC1 (Farringdon/King's Cross) | 020-7833 9787 ⊠
Stoke Newington | 55 Stoke Newington Church St., N16 (Stoke Newington B.R.) | 020-7249 0344 | fax 7637 0224 ◐
www.rasarestaurants.com

"Complex, perfumed" Keralan dishes "will change how you see Indian food" at this "expanding chain"; whilst their menus differ, all offer "superb vegetarian specialities" – some venues are completely veggie – at "reasonable prices", in digs that are "a cross between a handmade hippie joint and upscale" subcontinental.

	FOOD	DECOR	SERVICE	COST

⊠ Rasoi Vineet Bhatia ⑤ *Indian* — 27 | 19 | 23 | £65

Chelsea | 10 Lincoln St., SW3 (Sloane Sq.) | 020-7225 1881 | fax 7581 0220 | www.vineetbhatia.com

With an "exquisite Indian" menu of "dishes that tempt and surprise", chef-owner Vineet Bhatia's "charming" Chelsea townhouse (recently given a light refurb) is "always a pleasure", smoothed along by "superb service"; if a few flinch at the "high-end prices", even they are "entertained" by this "epicurean delight."

NEW Raviolo *Italian* — – | – | – | M

Balham | 1 Balham Station Rd., SW12 (Balham) | 020-8772 0433 | fax 8675 6167 | www.raviolo.co.uk

"Well-located" opposite Balham Station, this "excellent newcomer" offers low-priced "Italian tucker" emphasising the eponymous "ravioli, and lots of it!"; communal tables with bench seating and menus that double as place mats complete the picture of this "cheerful" neighbourhood trattoria.

Red Fort *Indian* — 23 | 21 | 20 | £42

Soho | 77 Dean St., W1 (Oxford Circus/Tottenham Court Rd.) | 020-7437 2525 | fax 7434 0721 | www.redfort.co.uk

This "sophisticated", "swish" Soho subcontinental satisfies supporters – including Tony Blair – with regional cuisine "with interesting twists", red-toned "modern decor" and "service with a smile"; some grumble about being "rushed out for the next sitting", but even "people who swear they'd never eat Indian food beg to go back."

Rhodes Twenty Four ⑤ *British* — 23 | 25 | 23 | £59

City | Tower 42 | 25 Old Broad St., 24th fl., EC2 (Bank St./Liverpool St.) | 020-7877 7703 | fax 7877 7725 | www.rhodes24.co.uk

For "power eating at its best" – with a "spectacular" Pan-London "view thrown in" – chef Gary "Rhodes can always be counted on" at this "airport lounge"-like aerie in a City skyscraper ("security at the building entrance reminds you of a visit to MI5"); the "blessedly short menu" offers a "nouvelle take on Traditional British food", and "service is attentive" – though "mainly to those dining on expenses" some say; it's "not in the same class" as other "expensive" venues, but "the location is the saving grace."

Rhodes W1 Restaurant ⑤Ⓜ *British* — – | – | – | VE

Marylebone | Cumberland Hotel | Great Cumberland Place, W1 (Marble Arch) | 020-7479-3737 | fax 7479 3888 | www.rhodesw1.com

The combination of chef Gary Rhodes' sophisticated Modern British menu (including a small-plates offering) and designer Kelly Hoppen's glammed-up decor (dominated by weeping willow–like beaded chandeliers) creates a dramatic setting for this swanky new venue that sits alongside the toque's eponymous Brasserie in the Cumberland Hotel (though it has its own entrance on Bryanston Street).

Rib Room, The *British/Chophouse* — 24 | 21 | 22 | £63

Belgravia | Jumeirah Carlton Tower Hotel | 2 Cadogan Pl., SW1 (Knightsbridge/Sloane Sq.) | 020-7858 7053 | fax 7823 1708 | www.jumeirahcarltontower.com

A "private-club atmosphere" (all "dark wood, brass and leather") "makes a great business destination" out of this Traditional Brit in

| | FOOD | DECOR | SERVICE | COST |

Belgravia; it might cost "an arm and a leg, but is worth it" for "some of the best beef dishes in London"; "service is excellent if they know you."

Richard Corrigan at Lindsay House 🗹 *British/Irish*

| 23 | 19 | 20 | £71 |

Soho | 21 Romilly St., W1 (Leicester Sq./Piccadilly Circus) | 020-7439 0450 | fax 7437 7349 | www.lindsayhouse.co.uk

Far "from the maddening crowds of Soho", this "quirky", "cosy" townhouse sets the scene for Richard Corrigan's "Irish-inspired dishes", plus some "amazing" Modern British ones; the experience can be "variable" – "as the restaurant fills, the kitchen is overwhelmed, and service suffers" – but most smile on this "serendipitous find."

NEW Ristorante Semplice 🗹 *Italian*

| – | – | – | E |

Mayfair | 10 Blenheim St., W1 (Bond St.) | 020-7495 1509

With its luxe but "tasteful" decor of polished ebony and gold walls, leather seats and a Murano chandelier, it's hard to believe this Mayfair space used to house a fish 'n' chip shop; now a Northern Italian calls it home, with rich and richly priced dishes "of great promise."

🗹 Ritz, The *British/French*

| 23 | 27 | 25 | £71 |

St. James's | Ritz Hotel | 150 Piccadilly, W1 (Green Park) | 020-7300 2370 | fax 7300 2375 | www.theritzlondon.com

"Formality at its finest" reigns at the Ritz Hotel dining room, a "romantic", "regal reminder of a bygone era", complete with a "high level of white-tie service" and highly "enjoyable" Traditional British–Classic French cuisine; a few whisper the "food quality doesn't match the price and fuss", but who else offers the "vintage experience of dinner dances" at weekends – or "the tea of all teas" in the adjacent Palm Court?

🗹 River Café *Italian*

| 27 | 22 | 24 | £63 |

Hammersmith | Thames Wharf | Rainville Rd., W6 (Hammersmith) | 020-7386 4200 | fax 7386 4201 | www.rivercafe.co.uk

Boasting "joyful" "unfussy dishes that showcase exquisite ingredients to beautiful effect", this Italian "evergreen" "never fails to delight", even after 20-plus years; "decor and ambience display a similar lack of pretension, and the informally clad staff clearly enjoy working here"; yes, the Thames-side Hammersmith "location is a problem", but it's "so worth the trip" – especially if you can "sit on the terrace."

Roka ● *Japanese*

| 25 | 20 | 19 | £54 |

Fitzrovia | 37 Charlotte St., W1 (Goodge St./Tottenham Court Rd.) | 020-7580 6464 | fax 7580 0220 | www.rokarestaurant.com

"Zuma's little sister" in Charlotte Street – a "sexy", "sophisticated room of pale wood and glass" – is "notable in its own right", with a "fantastic robata grill" ("see the chefs at work") and "positively sublime" Japanese dishes at "high prices when everything is so tempting"; "haphazard service" irks some, but all "love lounging in the Shochu" bar downstairs with its "deceptively dangerous cocktails."

Roussillon 🗹 *French*

| 26 | 23 | 25 | £72 |

Pimlico | 16 St. Barnabas St., SW1 (Sloane Sq./Victoria) | 020-7730 5550 | fax 7824 8617 | www.roussillon.co.uk

"Deserves to be better known than it is" say fans of this "quiet" Pimlico place with a pleasantly "informal" feel ("like walking into someone's

lounge"); but there's nothing casual about chef/co-owner Alexis Gauthier's "creative" New French cooking that "emphasises vegetables"; with perks like "pampering" service and a "fabulous wine list with one of the smartest sommeliers", it's "worth going on a special occasion."

Royal China *Chinese* | 24 | 16 | 16 | £30 |

Marylebone | 24-26 Baker St., W1 (Baker St.) | 020-7487 4688 | fax 7935 7893
Canary Wharf | 30 Westferry Circus, E14 (Canary Wharf) | 020-7719 0888 | fax 7719 0889
St. John's Wood | 68 Queen's Grove, NW8 (St. John's Wood) | 020-7586 4280 | fax 7722 4750
NEW Fulham | 805 Fulham Rd., SW6 (Parsons Green) | 020-7731 0081 | fax 7384 2998
Bayswater | 13 Queensway, W2 (Queensway) | 020-7221 2535 | fax 7792 5752
www.royalchinagroup.co.uk
"Dim sum as it's meant to be – fast, fabulous" and "freshly prepared" – makes this "crowded" quintet a "real nosher's paradise"; there are also "excellent Cantonese" mains, and "all for a reasonable price", so it's "worth putting up with surly service", "slightly Joan Collins–style black and gold decor" and "about a million other people."

Royal China Club *Chinese* | 24 | 18 | 20 | £44 |

Marylebone | 40-42 Baker St., W1 (Baker St.) | 020-7486 3898 | fax 7486 6977 | www.royalchinaclub.co.uk
"A more refined sister to the Royal China venues", this Chinese "a little off the beaten path on Baker Street" offers "unusual dim sum" "without the queue" and "sparkling" seafood dishes (diners can pick their fish from the tanks on display); "polite service" is appreciated.

☑ Rules ❶ *British/Chophouse* | 23 | 25 | 22 | £51 |

Covent Garden | 35 Maiden Ln., WC2 (Covent Garden) | 020-7836 5314 | fax 7497 1081 | www.rules.co.uk
"Britannia rules" at this 1798 "classic" in Covent Garden, where "classic gentlemen's club decor, with fireplaces and a stags head on the wall" (imagine "Watson and Holmes sitting at the next table") create a "warm, gracious setting" for "delightfully no-nonsense" Traditional British fare ("focused on game") that's "a bit pricey", but "always a treat"; yes, it's "a tourist mecca", and "service can be slow, but we don't care", 'cos there's "nothing like it anywhere in London."

Sakura *Japanese* | 23 | 9 | 12 | £27 |

Mayfair | 9 Hanover St., W1 (Oxford Circus) | 020-7629 2961
"It can be very busy and pretty noisy, but the sushi is fresh, good" and "unbeatable for the price" at this "shabby" "authentic Japanese dive" near Oxford Circus; "you have to wait too long to get in, but service is lightning fast once you get seated."

Salloos ❶☑ *Pakistani* | 23 | 16 | 20 | £45 |

Belgravia | 62-64 Kinnerton St., SW1 (Hyde Park Corner/Knightsbridge) | 020-7235 4444
For over 30 years, this "terrific, upscale Pakistani on an easy-to-miss side street" in Belgravia has been known for "spicy" "northwestern frontier cuisine at its best"; though this family-run venue's "no bargain", the "passionate service" makes it feel "like eating at your grandmother's."

	FOOD	DECOR	SERVICE	COST

Salt Yard 🗷 *European*

| | 22 | 15 | 19 | £35 |

Fitzrovia | 54 Goodge St., W1 (Goodge St.) | 020-7637 0657 | fax 7580 7435 | www.saltyard.co.uk

"Not for the faint-of-hearing", this Fitzrovian establishment spread over two "very busy" floors places "an emphasis on tapas" ("oh, those courgette flowers!") that "elevates the concept to a new level"; there are also "reasonably priced" Modern Euro mains served by "accommodating staff."

Santini *Italian*

| | 22 | 18 | 21 | £52 |

Belgravia | 29 Ebury St., SW1 (Victoria) | 020-7730 4094 | fax 7730 0544 | www.santini-restaurant.com

In the "foodie desert that is Victoria", this "long-time neighbourhood Italian" a stone's throw away delights disciples with its "good, not faddish food" and "beautiful patio" (especially "now the traffic flow has been changed"); but cynics find it an "overpriced, overhectic" venue, with "service that's efficient, but could be more amiable."

Sardo 🗷 *Italian*

| | 23 | 15 | 20 | £45 |

Fitzrovia | 45 Grafton Way, W1 (Warren St.) | 020-7387 2521 | fax 7387 2559 | www.sardo-restaurant.com

"Luscious Sardinian cuisine", "authentic and imaginative", sets apart this "lively" "neighbourhood Italian" in Fitzrovia; the "small" surroundings can be "claustrophobic", but all appreciate "polite staff" and a "wine list full of affordable choices" from The Boot.

Savoy Grill *British*

| | 24 | 24 | 24 | £61 |

Covent Garden | Savoy Hotel | The Strand, WC2 (Charing Cross) | 020-7592 1600 | fax 7592 1601 | www.gordonramsay.com

Whilst the Savoy's closure for renovation in late 2007 looms large, there's still time to sample its "sumptuous", art deco–styled dining room where Marcus Wareing's "top-drawer" Modern British fare and "silky smooth", "savvy service" "make one want to fight for Queen and country"; if a few rebels baulk at the "stuffy undercurrent" and "über-expensive" prices, patriots are pleased with this power brokers' haunt.

Scalini ● *Italian*

| | 23 | 16 | 20 | £45 |

Chelsea | 1-3 Walton St., SW3 (Knightsbridge/South Kensington) | 020-7225 2301 | fax 7581 4224

Aged 20, this trattoria "around the corner from Harrods" remains one of "the buzzing-est Italians" around, with "great celebrity-spotting" and "plenty of eye-candy" squeezed "sardine-style" into seats; the "old-style" food's "as good as ever", if "a bit overpriced"; but what irks most are the "acoustically appalling" digs that "badly need an update."

NEW Scott's *Seafood*

| | 22 | 23 | 19 | £63 |

Mayfair | 20 Mount St., W1 (Bond St.) | 020-7495 7309 | fax 7629 5457 | www.scotts-restaurant.com

It's "fabulous to have this veteran back, and oh, so much better" after the "striking refurb" given it by "the same ownership" as The Ivy; the Mayfair premises now boast a "chic" oak-panelled look and "flavoursome" fish and game, plus a "magnificent oyster bar"; only, staff are "not yet up to scratch for the prices."

DINING

	FOOD	DECOR	SERVICE	COST

NEW 1707 Wine Bar *British* | 22 | 21 | 22 | £30

Piccadilly | Fortnum & Mason | 181 Piccadilly, W1 (Piccadilly Circus) | 020-7734 8040 | fax 7437 3278 | www.fortnumandmason.co.uk
"Well done, Fortnum's, for entering the 21st century with such style" – in the shape of this "classy" new David Collins–designed wine bar (named for F&M's year of birth), which makes the most of the retailer's "wonderful wine selection"; it's supported by Traditional British snacks prepared in the Piccadilly premises' adjacent Food Halls – so "where can you go wrong?"

Signor Sassi ●⧄ *Italian* | 22 | 17 | 20 | £48

Knightsbridge | 14 Knightsbridge Green, SW1 (Knightsbridge) | 020-7584 2277 | fax 7225 3953
It's "fun to watch the waiters" "sing to the diners" at this "always full and noisy" Knightsbridge trattoria; whilst the "nothing-too-fancy" Italian *cucina* is "not cheap", it's "well executed"; P.S. "is what you want not on the menu? – no problem, they'll make it for you!"

Sketch – The Gallery ⧄ *European* | 19 | 26 | 18 | £61

Mayfair | 9 Conduit St., W1 (Oxford Circus) | 0870-777 4488 | fax 7629 1698 | www.sketch.uk.com
"Eat among art and beautiful people" at this "funky" Mayfair spot that morphs from art gallery to "dramatic" dining room at night, with videos and music – oh, and you "must check out the [egglike] bathroom pods"; some suggest "if the decor were less 'out there', people would notice the wildly creative Modern European food" is "surprisingly good"; still, most "diners are there to be seen"; speaking of seeing, "where's the waiter?"

Ⓩ Sketch – | 21 | 27 | 23 | £95
The Lecture Room & Library ⧄Ⓜ *European*

Mayfair | 9 Conduit St., W1 (Oxford Circus) | 0870-777 4488 | fax 7629 1684 | www.sketch.uk.com
"Big, comfortable armchairs envelop you as you talk in hushed tones" at this "magnificent" Mayfair spot, "one of the most luxurious in London" ("the crystal bathrooms are a dream"); the "inspired" Modern European menu is "expensive", but it needs to be to "cover the costs of producing such complicated" – some say "fussy" – dishes; all's brought by "agreeable staff"; P.S. downstairs is The Parlour, "a great place for tea."

NEW Skylon *European* | - | - | - | E

South Bank | Royal Festival Hall | Belvedere Rd., SE1 (Waterloo) | 020-7654 7800 | www.skylonrestaurant.co.uk
Named after an iconic attraction from the 1951 Festival of Britain, this newcomer in the revamped Royal Festival Hall offers a dramatic panoramic view across the Thames; a casual, hardwood-floored grill and smarter, retro-looking restaurant – both serving different incarnations of a Modern European menu from chef Helena Puolakka (ex Fifth Floor) – act as stylish bookends to an airy cocktail bar.

Sophie's | 23 | 18 | 19 | £33
Steakhouse & Bar ● *American/Chophouse*

Chelsea | 311-313 Fulham Rd., SW10 (South Kensington) | 020-7352 0088 | fax 7349 9776 | www.sophiessteakhouse.com
This "boisterous local hangout for the Fulham Road set" is "perpetually packed" with "young Sloanes" who rave about the British "crack-

ing bits of meat" ("great steaks" to you and me) and the "excellent desserts" ("ask for the banoffee pie"); the "no-booking policy means it's a no-no for big groups", but the waits make for a "buzzing bar scene"; P.S. the "American-style weekend brunches" are "more relaxed."

NEW Spread Eagle French ▽ 21 | 21 | 16 | £54

Greenwich | 1-2 Stockwell St., SE10 (Greenwich) | 020-8853 2333 | fax 8293 1024 | www.spreadeaglerestaurant.com

There's been a restaurant on this Greenwich site for over 350 years, and some say the "recent reinvention" has brought these "cranky old dining rooms" "up to West End standards" with exclusively prix fixe menus and local "artwork that's well worth a little look"; still, loyalists lament the fare "has lost its true French flair."

☑ Square, The French 28 | 24 | 26 | £87

Mayfair | 6-10 Bruton St., W1 (Bond St./Green Park) | 020-7495 7100 | fax 7495 7150 | www.squarerestaurant.com

"Fantastic food", "faultless service", "my favourite" fawn fans of this "grown-up", "elegant eatery off Bond Street" that maintains its edge with an "inventive take on Classic French" food, a "gigantic wine list" and "understated" decor that has gotten "warmer after a makeover"; "though the set lunch is reasonable, it's expensive for dinner" – "bring your Black Amex" – but it may be "the best all-rounder in London."

NEW St. Alban ❶ European 21 | 18 | 23 | £51

Piccadilly | 4-12 Regent St., SW1 (Piccadilly Circus) | 020-7499 8558 | www.stalban.net

"Cool, sophisticated" and "celebrity-filled", this Modern European is "the latest Jeremy King/Chris Corbin outlet" (think The Wolseley); "charming, unobtrusive" staff serve up "robust" "culinary combinations" like "sublime slow-roasted pig"; and whilst the "grammar school cafeteria meets airport lounge" decor isn't to everyone's taste, most feel the "promise is high" at this Piccadilly premises.

Star of India ❶ Indian 24 | 18 | 20 | £33

South Kensington | 154 Old Brompton Rd., SW5 (Gloucester Rd./ South Kensington) | 020-7373 2901 | fax 7373 5664

Serving up "delicious" "Indian comfort food" (plus "some surprises") to the "denizens of Brompton", this "old faithful" is "up and running again" after a "long-overdue refit"; the now-"fresh interior" and "family-type service" keep fans flocking back.

NEW St. Germain ❶ French ▽ 21 | 18 | 20 | £34

Farringdon | 89-90 Turnmill St., EC1 (Farringdon) | 020-7336 0949 | fax 7336 0948 | www.stgermain.info

Set in a 19th-century print house, this spacious, "seriously nice" newcomer to the Farringdon foodie scene is already luring a "lively crowd in the evenings" with "French brasserie–style comfort food", served in a monochrome mod "open space" of black-and-white checkerboard floors, striped walls and hanging lamps.

St. John ☒ British 25 | 16 | 20 | £48

Smithfield | 26 St. John St., EC1 (Farringdon) | 020-7251 0848 | fax 7251 4090 | www.stjohnrestaurant.com

"Eating a pig's eyeball was never so much fun" swear supporters of this "snout-to-tail" Smithfield Modern Brit, "after 14 years still

trendsetting" in its use of animal "innards in all their glory"; some beef that the "bare-white" "dreary decor" detracts, but the only moan of most is that "the best 'bits' often sell out quickly."

St. John Bread & Wine British

22 | 17 | 20 | £34

Spitalfields | 94-96 Commercial St., E1 (Liverpool St.) | 020-7251 0848 | fax 7247 8924 | www.stjohnbreadandwine.com

The "less formal" ("still more art crowd than suits, thank God") Spitalfields "offshoot of St. John" has a smaller menu well-suited to "wine-soaked lunches"; expect "tasty English cuisine" in the same vein as its parent with lots of "funny animal bits" and "wonderful bread"; the "open kitchen and bakery add to the noise, but also the charm."

NEW Suka ◐ Malaysian

- | - | - | VE

Fitzrovia | Sanderson Hotel | 50 Berners St., W1 (Oxford Circus/Goodge St.) | 020-7300 1444 | fax 7300 1488 | www.morganshotelgroup.com

Collaborating with acclaimed NYC chef Zak Pelaccio, Fitzrovia's Sanderson Hotel has replaced Spoon with this high-priced Malaysian, whose elevated tables are illuminated by low-slung ceiling lights; sharing and grazing is encouraged by the well-spiced menu with Western influences, which is also served on the calming, pond-filled terrace.

Sweetings ⊠ British/Seafood

24 | 18 | 19 | £40

City | 39 Queen Victoria St., EC4 (Mansion House) | 020-7248 3062

It's weekday lunch only at this "noisy" City Traditional Brit that's served fish ("baked, frilled, poached" or battered) for more than a century; the "democratic 'no-bookings' policy is as refreshing as the Guinness" and means you're likely to find yourself queuing "with all the jolly regulars who already know what they are going to order" from the predominantly piscatorial menu.

Taman Gang ◐⊠ Pan-Asian

22 | 27 | 17 | £56

Mayfair | 141 Park Ln., W1 (Marble Arch) | 020-7518 3160 | fax 7518 3161 | www.tamangang.co.uk

Under new management and, at time of writing, considering a renovation, this "beautiful Thai temple" complete with "carved stone, votives and orchids" "looks more like a spa than a restaurant"; Park Lane princesses and trendy gang members swing by for "amazing" cocktails and "somewhat overpriced" but "interesting Pan-Asian dishes."

NEW Tamarai ◐⊠ Pan-Asian

- | - | - | E

Covent Garden | 167 Drury Ln., WC2 (Covent Garden/Holborn) | 020-7831 9399 | www.tamarai.co.uk

"Dark", "chic and glossy", this "sexy Pan-Asian" that's just come to Covent Garden seems more like a "buzzy nightclub or bar" than "a proper restaurant"; "interesting fusions" pepper the menu, which can be too hot to handle ("the spice nearly required a fire extinguisher"), but fortunately an "extensive cocktail list" and "excellent wine" are on tap to douse any flames.

⊠ Tamarind ◐ Indian

25 | 21 | 23 | £52

Mayfair | 20 Queen St., W1 (Green Park) | 020-7629 3561 | fax 7499 5034 | www.tamarindrestaurant.com

"Deservedly popular" for over a decade, this "regal" Mayfair "milestone" "serves the who's who" with "nouvelle Indian" fare; highly

"helpful waiters" will guide you through the "wonderfully spiced", simultaneously "earthy and ephemeral dal dishes"; but you better "not mind spending the rupees" – a typical "takeaway curry house this is not."

Tapas Brindisa ⚅ *Spanish*   22 | 14 | 16 | £28

Borough | Borough Mkt. | 18-20 Southwark St., SE1 (London Bridge) | 020-7357 8880 | www.brindisa.com

It's "always busy" at this "Borough favourite" crammed with a "convivial after-work crowd" seeking Spanish delights like "distinctly delectable Tempranillo" to wash down the "amazing goat cheese with honey"; a few curse the casa for its "cramped interior" and no-bookings policy, which means "wait times can be long."

NEW Theo Randall at The InterContinental *Italian*   26 | 21 | 24 | £57

Mayfair | InterContinental Park Ln. | 1 Hamilton Pl., W1 (Hyde Park Corner) | 020-7318 8747 | www.theorandall.com

Although it's still "unknown to many", this newly renovated hotel restaurant is "a change for the positive at Hyde Park Corner"; the "wonderful", "innovative Italian food" is "in the tradition of the River Café" (the ex-home of the eponymous chef), and is served by "genial" staff; only the room – "slick" but "somewhat sterile" – sets some back.

Timo ⚅ *Italian*   22 | 17 | 18 | £49

Kensington | 343 Kensington High St., W8 (High St. Kensington) | 020-7603 3888 | fax 7603 8111 | www.timorestaurant.net

Perhaps "the best-kept secret in Kensington" confide locals about this "rather modern Italian" with "absolutely delicous" "pasta, mains and wines", provided by charmingly "casual service"; "though you'd never be deluded you're in Tuscany, it delivers where it matters most – the belly."

Tokyo Diner ◑ *Japanese*   20 | 13 | 19 | £17

Chinatown | 2 Newport Pl., WC2 (Leicester Sq.) | 020-7287 8777 | fax 7434 1415 | www.tokyodiner.com

"Near Leicester Square", this "cheap" "micro-cafe" offers "tasty, no-frills Japanese" fare to a "young, trendy" crowd that create a "casual, chattery atmosphere"; the "canteen-y feel", "closely packed tables and low ceilings" encourage swift turnover but, for a place with a "no-tipping policy", service is surprisingly "courteous."

Tom Aikens ⚅ *French*   26 | 22 | 24 | £83

Chelsea | 43 Elystan St., SW3 (South Kensington) | 020-7584 2003 | fax 7584 2001 | www.tomaikens.co.uk

The "most imaginative food on the planet" enthuse "the shirt-sleeved expense-account crowd" enamoured by the "creative pairings" (both food and wine) offered in "huge portions" by "elegant servers" at this Chelsea New French; critics cavil it's "self-consciously clever" cooking "from the chemistry-set school of cuisine", and views on the monochrome decor range from "austere" to "smart"; either way, "eating here is a true experience"; P.S. the tasting menu is "the way to go."

NEW Tom's Kitchen ◑ *British*   19 | 17 | 14 | £40

Chelsea | 27 Cale St., SW3 (South Kensington) | 020-7349 0202 | www.tomskitchen.co.uk

"Brilliant" vs. "disappointing": commentators clash over what Chelsea-ites cheekily call Tom Aikens' new "ego pub venture", a

"buzzing refectory-style" Modern Brit whose "cramped" "communal seating" means you "really get to know your fellow diners"; supporters salute the "über-quality", "simple food done very well" – "but not at these prices" snap sceptics, who also slam the "diffident staff"; even if "it's not as great as you'd expect from this great chef", "trying to get a table is [already] tricky."

Toto's *Italian*

| 24 | 19 | 22 | £51 |

Chelsea | Walton Hse. | Walton St. at Lennox Garden Mews, SW3 (Knightsbridge) | 020-7589 2062 | fax 7581 9668

Hellraisers should head elsewhere – this is "one of the quieter Italian restaurants" around – but for "elegant, classy" dining, this out-of-the-way Chelsea site remains a "favourite"; an "older crowd" "linger" by the 17th-century fireplace or "lovely" garden, deliberating over delicacies like "divine squid ink pasta" with "outgoing staff."

NEW Trinity *European*

| ▽ 24 | 21 | 21 | £43 |

Clapham | 4 The Polygon, SW4 (Clapham Common) | 020-7622 1199 | fax 7622 1166 | www.trinityrestaurant.co.uk

"Clapham-based foodies can get a fix close to home" at this "fine-dining newcomer" from chef-owner Adam Byatt (fondly remembered for Thyme); within the beige-toned, "relaxed space", he serves an "imaginative and well-executed" Modern European menu paired with "great midrange wines"; but what's "absolutely brilliant" is the "absolute-bargain lunch – three courses for £18."

Truc Vert *French*

| 22 | 15 | 16 | £30 |

Mayfair | 42 N. Audley St., W1 (Bond St.) | 020-7491 9988 | fax 7491 7717

"If you can't get to the south of France straight away", this "quaint" Mayfair cafe is a "pleasant place for a simple breakfast"; at lunch it's "packed with embassy workers" tucking into "solid bistro fare" or grabbing something from the "spot-on", on-site deli.

Tsunami *Japanese*

| 24 | 18 | 16 | £39 |

Clapham | 5-7 Voltaire Rd., SW4 (Clapham North) | 020-7978 1610 | fax 7978 1591

A wave of praise washes over this minimalist Japanese for its "fantastic sushi" that's "reasonably priced" if you "go before 7 PM" (20 percent off); the "slightly odd nightclub-style decor" is due for a revamp as we write, and Claphamites hope the "variable service" gets a makeover too.

Two Brothers Fish ⓈⓂ *Seafood*

| 24 | 12 | 16 | £24 |

Finchley | 297-303 Regent's Park Rd., N3 (Finchley Central) | 020-8346 0469 | fax 8343 1978 | www.twobrothers.co.uk

You "might have to queue" at this "unpretentious" Finchley fish 'n' chippery that's been frying up a storm for over 15 years; it's "heavily patronised by regulars" who don't care that decor is "basic" but are reeled in by "fresh, clean-tasting" fish (fried, grilled or baked) "made with loving hands."

Ubon by Nobu Ⓢ *Japanese/Peruvian*

| 24 | 20 | 19 | £60 |

Canary Wharf | 34 Westferry Circus, E14 (Canary Wharf) | 020-7719 7800 | fax 7719 7801 | www.noburestaurants.com

This "Docklands take on Nobu" serves the signature "sophisticated, well-executed" Japanese-Peruvian fare, is quite "bookable" (unlike its

FOOD | DECOR | SERVICE | COST

"Mayfair cousins") and boasts "spectacular" river views; but cynics say a "Nobu by any other name" is a bit "like going out with David Beckham's sister" – in particular, the "brusque, impatient" "service is a real letdown" – and "it's surely expensive", not that the "wall-to-wall" "city-traders clientele" seem to care.

Umu 🛇 *Japanese*   26 | 25 | 23 | £81
Mayfair | 14-16 Bruton Pl., W1 (Bond St.) | 020-7499 8881 | www.umurestaurant.com

"It always feels special" at this "stylish" Mayfair specialist in kaiseki (traditional Japanese tasting menus); devotees drool over the "delicate" dishes, especially the "exquisite experience" of "fish that still tastes of the sea", served with "finesse" "within a sombre, well-appointed room"; even the few who "don't get the hype", calling it "really overpriced", admit it's a "perfect" "place to impress."

Vama ⚫ *Indian*   24 | 16 | 19 | £40
Chelsea | 438 King's Rd., SW10 (Sloane Sq.) | 020-7565 8500 | fax 7565 8501 | www.vama.co.uk

A few feel it's being "outshone by newer haute Indians", but most still thrill to the "knock-your-socks-off renditions of Punjabi standards" – a "vibrant symphony of curry and spice" – at this "chic" subcontinental that's "expensive but worth it"; the outer Chelsea location is "a drag, but they offer" a delivery service.

Veeraswamy *Indian*   22 | 20 | 21 | £43
Mayfair | Victory Hse. | 99-101 Regent St., W1 (Piccadilly Circus) | 020-7734 1401 | fax 7439 8434 | www.realindianfood.com

For eight decades, this "granddaddy of Indian establishments" in Mayfair has been tickling taste buds with its "creative fare", "competently presented" in a vaguely Jazz Era "fantasyland of the Raj" environment; however, unless you go for the "great value" set menu, remember it's "fancy schmancy" – and "priced accordingly."

NEW Via Condotti 🛇 *Italian*   ∇ 18 | 17 | 19 | £43
Mayfair | 23 Conduit St., W1 (Oxford Circus) | 020-7493 7050 | fax 7409 7985 | www.viacondotti.co.uk

Opinion is split on this Italian "addition to the Mayfair scene"; some reviewers reckon its "accomplished seasonal cooking" and "affordable set menus" make "you really think you're in Rome", whilst naysayers needle that it's "overpriced" for "nothing special."

Viet Hoa ⚫ *Vietnamese*   23 | 9 | 15 | £18
Shoreditch | 70-72 Kingsland Rd., E2 (Old St.) | 020-7729 8293

After a morning spent "gallery-hopping 'round Hoxton Square, those in need of a "cheap and cheerful" culinary experience make a beeline for this "authentic Vietnamese cafe"; "you can't go wrong", given the "marvellous flavours" at prices almost lower than you'd find in Hanoi itself.

Vineyard at Stockcross *British/French*   24 | 21 | 24 | £70
Newbury | Vineyard at Stockcross | Stockcross, Berkshire | 01635 528770 | fax 01635 528398 | www.the-vineyard.co.uk

With 2,000-odd labels on offer, "the wine has always been the star" at this "intoxicating" venue in the Berkshire countryside; but some imbibers insist the Classic French–Modern British "food has caught up

well", "reflecting seasonal specialities on the great-value" prix fixes; all are adamant you should "stay at the adjacent hotel – so no problem sampling the list!"

Vivat Bacchus ⑤ *European*   23 | 18 | 24 | £42

City | 47 Farringdon St., EC4 (Chancery Ln./Farringdon) | 020-7353 2648 | fax 7353 3025 | www.vivatbacchus.co.uk
From Modern European fine dining with an "exceptional" wine list to South African bar snacks and beer, this "unpretentious, friendly" City "power brokers'" "escape" is "well worth discovering"; for those who like to get interactive with their ordering, the "walk-in wine cellars and cheese rooms are a treat."

② Wagamama *Japanese*   19 | 13 | 17 | £17

Bloomsbury | 4A Streatham St., WC1 (Tottenham Court Rd.) | 020-7323 9223 | fax 7323 9224
Covent Garden | 1 Tavistock St., WC2 (Covent Garden) | 020-7836 3330 | fax 7240 8846
Knightsbridge | Harvey Nichols | 109-125 Knightsbridge, SW1 (Knightsbridge) | 020-7201 8000 | fax 7201 8080
Marylebone | 101A Wigmore St., W1 (Bond St.) | 020-7409 0111
Soho | 10A Lexington St., W1 (Oxford Circus/Piccadilly Circus) | 020-7292 0990
Blackfriars | 109 Fleet St., EC4 (Blackfriars/St. Paul's) | 020-7583 7889 ⑤
City | 1A Ropemaker St., EC2 (Moorgate) | 020-7588 2688 ⑤
Camden Town | 11 Jamestown Rd., NW1 (Camden Town) | 020-7428 0800 | fax 7482 4887
Islington | 40 Parkfield St., N1 (Angel) | 020-7226 2664
Kensington | 26A Kensington High St., W8 (High St. Kensington) | 020-7376 1717
www.wagamama.com
Additional locations throughout the London area
Once again London's Most Popular, these Japanese "big space age cafeterias" continue to be "mobbed" with people slurping "bottomless bowls of steaming noodles" and other "delicious, nutritious meals in minutes"; yes, the "service is slipping towards the shambolic", and foes feel they've "outgrown" eating at long communal tables, surrounded by a "gaggle of screaming kids"; but "let's not be snobs about this" – it's "the perfect antidote to an empty stomach and wallet."

NEW Wallace, The *French*   20 | 25 | 16 | £33

Marylebone | Wallace Museum Collection | Hertford Hse., Manchester Sq., W1 (Baker St./Bond St.) | 020-7563 9505 | www.thewallacerestaurant.com
The "secretive location" of this "enclosed courtyard in a museum" "just off busy Oxford Street" creates a "lovely ambience" for "intimate dining"; as dinner is done "only Friday–Saturday", "lunch is the meal" here, though the "generous yet delicate" Classic French food is "wonderful for tea" too; sole downside: the "utterly disorganised service."

② Waterside Inn Ⓜ *French*   27 | 26 | 27 | £96

Bray | Waterside Inn | Ferry Rd., Berkshire | 01628 620691 | fax 01628 784710 | www.waterside-inn.co.uk
"So very romantic" rave venturers to the "gastronomic hamlet" of Bray to visit the Roux *famille*'s "precious" out-of-town offering, aka "Le Gavroche on the Thames"; you're treated to "traditional" but "magnificent" French cuisine, "exemplary service", a "wine list to die for" and

that "spectacular", "serene setting"; so "make the drive, spend the money" – it's "more than worth it" "for that really special occasion."

Wilton's 🅱 *British/Seafood*   24 | 22 | 24 | £66

St. James's | 55 Jermyn St., SW1 (Green Park/Piccadilly Circus) | 020-7629 9955 | fax 7495 6233 | www.wiltons.co.uk

"You can feel the gout seeping up your legs as you cross the threshold" of this "old haunt" in St. James's, where for over 200 years a jacket-clad clientele has consumed "classic" British fare ("remarkable" seafood, "particularly fine" game) under the "starched" gaze of the "superb" staff; some find it "terrifyingly traditional" but the greatest grouse is the cost, which even advocates agree is "expensive – but it keeps out the riffraff."

Ⓩ Wolseley, The ◑ *European*   21 | 26 | 21 | £48

Piccadilly | 160 Piccadilly, W1 (Green Park) | 020-7499 6996 | fax 7499 6888 | www.thewolseley.com

The "wow factor" of its setting – a marble-columned, "grand mittel-Europe brasserie" – makes "everyone feel like the star in the movie of his own life" at this "buzzy" Piccadilly playground; although it's known as a place where the "elite meet to eat", it remains "surprisingly un-stuffy", whether you swing by for a "baronial" breakfast, "impressive" afternoon tea or "divine" dinner.

NEW XO *Pan-Asian*   16 | 18 | 16 | £40

Hampstead | 29 Belsize Ln., NW3 (Belsize Park) | 020-7433 0888 | fax 7794 3474 | www.rickerrestaurants.com

Hampstead hipsters now have their own Will Ricker-backed "see-and-be-seen" Pan-Asian, a green-tinged "carbon copy of e&o"; sceptics say this "pricey" place "doesn't compare to its sister – just not as tasty and service not as good"; nonetheless, punters predict lazy locals will make it "very successful."

Ⓩ Yauatcha ◑ *Chinese*   25 | 22 | 17 | £40

Soho | 15 Broadwick St., W1 (Piccadilly Circus) | 020-7494 8888 | fax 7287 6959

Owner "Alan Yau delivers" with this "sexy" split-level Soho Chinese that attracts a "noisy" crowd of London's "most attractive yuppies"; "interesting" teas and "exquisite" pastries abound in the ground-floor cafe, whilst down the "dark" staircase lies "dim sum as theatre" with "innovative" delicacies like "melt-in-the-mouth venison puffs" washed down with "standout cocktails"; the only "shame" is the "snippy servers'" "conveyor-belt attitude to turning tables."

Yoshino 🅱 *Japanese*   24 | 17 | 18 | £29

Piccadilly | 3 Piccadilly Pl., W1 (Piccadilly Circus) | 020-7287 6622 | fax 7287 1733 | www.yoshino.net

"Tucked away off Piccadilly" "in a little alley", this Japanese is "hard to find but worth the search" for super-"fresh", "beautiful sushi" "at bargain prices" – there's a lunch menu for just £5.80 – especially for "such a central location."

Ⓩ Zafferano *Italian*   26 | 20 | 22 | £59

Belgravia | 15 Lowndes St., SW1 (Knightsbridge) | 020-7235 5800 | fax 7235 1971 | www.zafferanorestaurant.com

"*Bellissima*" bellow believers in this Belgravia venue, for 18 years a "consistently high – very high, in fact" "standard-bearer" for The

Boot's *cucina* ("go around truffle season" or try the "fantastic lobster linguini" anytime); true, tables are "tight" and the "tariffs be high", leading a few to wonder "is it worth it?", but the plethora of celebrities, "local hedge fund mangers and your friendly neighbourhood Russian tycoon dining" here seems to suggest *si*.

Zaika *Indian*

| 25 | 24 | 21 | £47 |

Kensington | 1 Kensington High St., W8 (High St. Kensington) | 020-7795 6533 | fax 7937 8854 | www.zaika-restaurant.co.uk

In between its "creative" "fusion cuisine" (try a "divine chocolate samosa") and its vaulted-ceiling, "ethereal atmosphere, light years from the hustle of Kensington", this "modern" Indian "spoils you for the local" curry house; even so, hostiles huff its "high prices are hard to justify."

Ziani *Italian*

| 25 | 17 | 23 | £38 |

Chelsea | 45 Radnor Walk, SW3 (Sloane Sq.) | 020-7351 5297 | fax 7244 8387 | www.ziani.uk.com

Calf's liver cooked in onions and red wine vinegar and other "wonderful" Venetian specialities supplement the "warm Italian welcome" you get at this "nice little hideaway"; although it can be "cramped" and "rushed on busy nights", it remains "a perennial favourite", "always crowded" with Chelsea locals.

☑ Zuma *Japanese*

| 26 | 24 | 21 | £64 |

Knightsbridge | 5 Raphael St., SW7 (Knightsbridge) | 020-7584 1010 | fax 7584 5005 | www.zumarestaurant.com

If you can breach the "obnoxious reservation system", you too can join the "ultrathin women, middle-aged bankers" "and expense-account types" at this "buzzy to the extreme" Knightsbridge "nouveau Japanese"; ranging from rave-worthy robata to "superb" sushi, the "food's mind-blowing" – and "it's easy to blow a fortune" on it as well; but despite that, and "staff not quite up to" handling the "hot, heaving" scene, this hipster still seems "sensational."

NIGHTLIFE

Nightlife

Europe's largest city is a paradise for partyers who can choose anything from traditional pubs to nightclubs to cool hotel bars to groovy lounges to hopping dance clubs to hip jazz venues – and everything in between.

PUB TIME: Most pubs are open until 11 PM Monday–Saturday and until 10:30 PM on Sundays, although a few have 14-hour licences. The better ones feature a solid range of real ales, a good crowd of locals and tasty food. The classic drink is a pint of bitter, a dark uncarbonated brew, the best of which are pumped by hand in the cellar and served at room temperature.

TIP TIPS: There's generally no tipping in pubs or casual bars, where you can run a tab or pay per drink. You would want to add gratuities at upscale spots with table service, however.

WATCH YOUR WALLET: Designer cocktails with ever-more elaborate ingredients and eye-popping prices are the order of the day in many of the fancier lounges and bars. But just beware the hit on your budget. A cocktail for £10 or more is by no means a rarity. And even pints can set you back £3.50 and up.

MUSIC TO YOUR EARS: From jazz to opera, there's a great concentration of world-class musicians in this city. The best place to hear wonderful classical music is in churches, where performances are usually free. Concerts in historic houses and museums, especially during the City of London Festival in July, are a good bet. And some of the best, and least expensive, alternative music (from folk to blues) is offered free at some pubs.

HIT A HOTEL: Some of the safest bets for upscale intimate drinks are bars in the capital's top hotels. The Most Popular bar in our Survey is Claridge's, and the No. 1 for Service is Dukes Hotel Bar. Other popular hotel watering holes include the Ritz's Rivoli Bar, the Dorchester and the Lanesborough's Library.

Top Appeal Ratings

Ratings are to the left of names. Lists exclude places with low votes.

BY SPECIAL FEATURE

AFTER WORK

26 Ling Ling
24 Ye Olde Cheshire Cheese
23 Gordon's
22 Bleeding Heart Tavern
   Cork & Bottle*

BEER SPECIALISTS

23 Cow
22 Jerusalem Tavern

21 Dove
   George Inn
   Anchor & Hope

COCKTAIL EXPERTS

27 Milk & Honey
26 Ling Ling
25 Claridge's Bar
   Rivoli Bar
24 Annabel's (club)

DANCE CLUBS

24	End
23	Heaven
	Cuckoo Club
22	Fabric
	Chinawhite

DIVES

19	Kick
18	Dog & Duck
17	Comptons of Soho
16	Dublin Castle
15	Chandos

FRAT HOUSE

19	Stringfellows
16	O'Neill's
	Nam Long-Le Shaker
	Tup

GAY BARS

23	Heaven
20	G-A-Y Bar
18	Astoria
17	Comptons of Soho
16	Admiral Duncan

GROWN-UPS

27	Milk & Honey
26	Ling Ling
25	Ronnie Scott's
	Claridge's Bar
24	Annabel's (club)

HOTEL BARS

25	Claridge's Bar

	Rivoli Bar
24	Dukes Hotel Bar
	Dorchester Bar
23	Library

MEAT MARKETS

23	Heaven
22	Chinawhite
	Mocotó
21	Player
	Amika

MUSIC/PERFORMANCE VENUES

18	Astoria
17	Koko
16	93 Feet East
	Dublin Castle
	Madame JoJo's

WINE BARS

23	Gordon's
	Vertigo 42*
22	Bleeding Heart Tavern
	Cork & Bottle*
20	1707

WINE BY THE GLASS

25	Claridge's Bar
24	Annabel's (club)
23	Gordon's
	Cow
22	American Bar

BY LOCATION

BLACKFRIARS

24	Ye Olde Cheshire
18	Corney & Barrow
17	El Vino
16	O'Neill's
	All Bar One

CAMDEN TOWN

22	Engineer
19	Belgo
17	Koko
16	Dublin Castle
	Tup

CITY

23	Vertigo 42
20	Fishmarket

18	Corney & Barrow
17	Balls Brothers
	El Vino

CLERKENWELL

22	Fabric
	Jerusalem Tavern
20	Smiths/Smithfield
19	Kick
15	Turnmills

COVENT GARDEN

24	End
22	American Bar
	Light Bar
19	Coach & Horses
	Belgo

FITZROVIA

26	Ling Ling
22	Purple Bar
20	Long Bar
18	Social
15	Fitzroy Tavern

ISLINGTON

19	Elbow Room
16	Slug & Lettuce
	Tup
15	Pitcher & Piano
14	Bierodrome

MAYFAIR

25	Claridge's Bar
24	Annabel's (club)
	Nobu Berkeley St.
	Dorchester
23	Whisky Bar

PICCADILLY

23	Gordon's
22	Cork & Bottle
	Sherlock Holmes
21	Rockwell
	Waxy O'Connor's

SHOREDITCH

25	Loungelover
19	Elbow Room
	Kick
16	93 Feet East
15	333 Mother Bar

SOHO

27	Milk & Honey
25	Ronnie Scott's
24	Yauatcha
23	Heaven
	Cuckoo Club

Top Decor Ratings

Ratings are to the left of names.

29	Loungelover
26	Ling Ling
	Sketch
25	Milk & Honey
	Yauatcha
24	Rivoli Bar
	Absolut Ice Bar
	Claridge's Bar
23	Library
	Dorchester Bar

	Dukes Hotel Bar
	Nobu Berkeley St
	Mocotó
	Long Bar
	Annabel's (club)
	Purple Bar
22	Ye Olde Cheshire Cheese
	Princess Louise
	Light Bar
	Apartment 195

Top Service Ratings

Ratings are to the left of names.

26	Dukes Hotel Bar
25	Rivoli Bar
	Milk & Honey
24	Claridge's Bar
	Dorchester Bar
23	Library
	Annabel's (club)
	Lab
22	American Bar
21	Whisky Bar
	Sam's Brasserie & Bar

	Gilt Champagne Lounge
	Holly Bush
	Nobu Berkeley St.
20	Rockwell
	Grenadier
	Cork & Bottle
	Red Bar*
	Yauatcha
	Ling Ling
	Ronnie Scott's*
	Ye Olde Chesire Cheese

Nightlife

Ratings & Symbols

Appeal, Decor and **Service** are rated on a 0 to 30 scale.

Cost reflects our surveyors' estimated price of a typical single drink. For places listed without ratings, the price range is:

⌐⅃ below £3   E £6 to £8
M £3 to £5   VE £9 or more

▽ low response | less reliable

Absolut Icebar London   23 | 24 | 18 | £12

Mayfair | belowzero restaurant + lounge | 31-33 Heddon St., W1 (Oxford Circus/Piccadilly Circus) | 020-7478 8910 | www.belowzerolondon.com

"What could be cooler than a bar made out of ice?" wisecrack wits of this "gimmicky" Mayfair experience where boozers don coats and gloves for sub-zero drinking sessions in, as the name suggests, an icy setting (the glasses keep the libations "nice and chilled"); fans chuckle that it's "fun" and "fantastic", but others aver that not only are the drinks "terrifically expensive", but the "novelty melts after a few minutes."

Admiral Duncan   16 | 11 | 17 | £6

Soho | 54 Old Compton St., W1 (Leicester Sq.) | 020-7437 5300

This "divey" "gay stalwart" on Soho's Old Compton Street ("the heart of the gay London universe") prides itself on an atmosphere that's "accepting of men in all shapes and states of repair"; there's "always conversation to be had" (often with an "older crowd reminiscing about the good old days") at this spot that manages to achieve "a delicate combination of good ol' pub and sleazy gay palace."

Ain't Nothin' But   ▽ 15 | 10 | 15 | £6

Soho | 20 Kingly St., W1 (Oxford Circus/Piccadilly Circus) | 020-7287 0514 | www.aintnothinbut.co.uk

You may have to "get there hours before the gigs start to bag a seat" at this "dark" and "dank" Blues venue in Soho that manages to be "hip" and "unpretentious" at the same time; doyens of the Delta "relish the authenticity" from "walls papered with old scores" to the "fantastic" music to the "smokey" environs, but those who come "prepared to stand" wish it weren't "so tiny."

☒ All Bar One   16 | 15 | 15 | £7

Piccadilly | 48 Leicester Sq., WC2 (Leicester Sq.) | 020-7747 9921
Soho | 36-38 Dean St., W1 (Leicester Sq.) | 020-7479 7921
Blackfriars | 103 Cannon St., EC4 (Cannon St.) | 020-7220 9031
City | 15-16 Byward St., EC3 (Tower Hill) | 020-7553 0301
City | 18-20 Appold St., EC2 (Liverpool St.) | 020-7377 9671
Smithfield | 93 Charterhouse St., EC1 (Barbican/Farringdon) | 020-7553 9391
Waterloo | 1-3 Chicheley St., SE1 (Waterloo) | 020-7921 9471
Crouch End | 2-4 The Broadway, N8 (Finsbury Park) | 020-8342 7871
(continued)

(continued)

All Bar One

Chiswick | 197 Chiswick High Rd., W4 (Turnham Green) | 020-8987 8211
Additional locations throughout the London area

"It may be a formula, but it works" shrug fans of this successful chain of "lively" and sometimes "rowdy" bars that attract post-work "yuppies" for "braying and viewing"; still, those who "yawn" with "boredom" over the "bland" decor and dis the "slow service" label these "rusting" relics "minimum-effort money-making machines."

All Star Lanes

22 | 21 | 20 | £7

Bloomsbury | Victoria Hse. | Bloomsbury Pl., WC1 (Holborn) | 020-7025 2676 | www.allstarlanes.co.uk

Aces and amateurs roll into this "mod", "fantastic" Bloomsbury bowling alley whose "great" bar (and "amazing" bourbons) turns any night into a "party"; the "reasonably" priced food "hits the spot", and service is "with a smile", so no wonder folks are "wowed"; P.S. blessedly, you won't find any "screaming children" in these lanes.

☑ American Bar

22 | 21 | 22 | £12

Covent Garden | Savoy Hotel | The Strand, WC2 (Charing Cross) | 020-7836 4343 | www.fairmont.com

"If you've come all the way to London for an American bar" then go straight to Covent Garden's Savoy Hotel for this "legendary" "class act", a "trip to the '20s" that "oozes style and tradition" and where "bar staff know how to do the job properly" and the "camp" piano music "hits a high note"; surely, the experience isn't cheap, but sentiment is summed up in these words: "if I had to go anywhere for my last gin and tonic, this place would be it."

NEW Amika

21 | 21 | 20 | £10

(fka The Settle Down)

South Kensington | Barkers Arcade | 65 High St. Kensington, W8 (High St. Kensington) | 0845-666 5001 | www.amikalondon.com

This "swanky", "very in" South Kensington newcomer crammed with "beautiful people" of the "very young" sort boasts a "fantastic" interior with shiny black walls and chandeliers, and a sound system that's "one of the best in London"; not surprisingly, thanks to its popularity, you'll feel like a "sardine", though most don't mind as long as they're "in the tin with actresses and models."

Anchor & Hope

21 | 16 | 17 | £5

Waterloo | 36 The Cut, SE1 (Southwark/Waterloo) | 0871-075 7279

It may "look like an ordinary pub", but this "popular" ("therefore busy") "little" Waterloo spot by Southwark tube is "raised above the local dross" by "fancy", "fairly adventurous" Modern British platters; a "good choice of beers on tap" makes it "great for after-theatre" if you've been to the Old Vic – just be warned that "they don't take bookings" and it can seem like it's "impossible to get served."

☑ Annabel's

24 | 23 | 23 | £13

Private club; inquiries: 020-7629 1096

"Stuffy English toffs" convene at this "over-the-top-expensive" Berkeley Square "hot spot for the not-so-young" that provides a "discreet" experience even after more than 40 years; devout devotees

have "renewed enthusiasm" for this "sugar-daddy central", thanks to its "younger clientele", adding "nothing in the world comes close to the exclusive atmosphere" even if "has-beens and wannabes" tend to show up.

Apartment 195
21 | 22 | 20 | £9

Chelsea | 195 King's Rd., SW3 (Sloane Sq.) | 020-7351 5195 | www.apartment195.co.uk

Loyalists "love the atmosphere" of this "intimate", "mellow" wine and cocktail bar with "innovative" drinks and a "clever play on a private club theme"; the burnished copper bar is set off by rich damson walls, brown leather sofas, an open fireplace and Victorian bay windows, plus there's an "extremely professional" bar staff; but some who find it "easily forgettable" are turned off by a crowd that has "unsupportably high opinions of itself."

Astoria, The ⊯
18 | 13 | 14 | £7

Soho | 157 Charing Cross Rd., WC2 (Tottenham Court Rd.) | 020-7434 9592 | www.meanfiddler.com

The reputation of this Soho music venue is "based on the bands who've played" there over the years, and the "great location" means that it's still a "steady fave"; true, it falls firmly into the "dive bar" category, and hygienists huff that it's "not the classiest joint", but at least the celebrated "gay nights" mean that it's "an all-time favourite for an old queen."

Balls Brothers
17 | 15 | 17 | £8

Mayfair | 34 Brook St., W1 (Bond St.) | 020-7499 4567
St. James's | 20 St. James's St., SW1 (Green Park) | 020-7321 0882
Victoria | 50 Buckingham Palace Rd., SW1 (Victoria) | 020-7828 4111
City | 11 Blomfield St., EC2 (Liverpool St.) | 020-7588 4643
City | 158 Bishopsgate, EC2 (Liverpool St.) | 020-7426 0567
City | 2 St. Mary-at-Hill, EC3 (Monument) | 020-7626 0321
City | 22 Mark Ln., EC3 (Monument/Tower Hill) | 020-7623 2923
City | 3 King's Arms Yard, EC2 (Bank/Moorgate) | 020-7796 3049
City | 42 Lime St., EC3 (Bank/Monument) | 020-7283 0841
City | Bucklersbury Hse. | Cannon St., EC4 (Bank/Cannon St.) | 020-7248 7557
www.ballsbrothers.co.uk
Additional locations throughout the London area

"Suits" swing over to these City wine bars dispensing a "good" *vins* selections in "faux cellar" quarters; naysayers note the operations are "forgettable" "bores", but most disagree and call the chain "reliable", asking "what's not to love?"

Baltic
20 | 17 | 18 | £7

Southwark | 74 Blackfriars Rd., SE1 (Southwark) | 020-7928 1111 | www.balticrestaurant.co.uk

"One of the few places on the south of the Thames to get a proper drink" assert supporters of this Southwark restaurant, a light and airy postmodern barn whose "small bar area" is a draw due to a "superior selection of vodka", "champagne cocktails" and other "fantastic spirits", all served with "excellent Baltic food" like dumplings and goulash; it's a stroll from the Old Vic, making it a "classy" choice for before or after the theatre.

NEW Bar, The

-	-	-	E

Greenwich | O2 Arena | Peninsula Sq., SE10 (North Greenwich) | 020-7015 1867 | www.theo2.co.uk

Another lounge at the new O2, this American-themed effort is destined to be a pre- and post-gig hot spot with outdoor seating, live music and after-show parties for some of the acts who play the arena; at the bar, which is one of the longest in town, the drinks have a U.S. flavour – think spiced-apple-pie martinis, Sierra Nevada Pale Ale and other beers sourced from Stateside microbreweries.

Bar des Amis

16	14	15	£6

Covent Garden | 11-14 Hanover Pl., WC2 (Covent Garden) | 020-7379 3444 | www.cafedesamis.co.uk

The "friendly" atmosphere at this "meet-up" Covent Garden French bar/eatery appeals to those out after work with *amis* and "colleagues"; late-night hours attract, as do the "good" food and wines (20 by the glass).

NEW Bedford & Strand

-	-	-	M

Covent Garden | 1A Bedford St., WC2 (Charing Cross) | 020-7836 3033 | www.bedford-strand.com

The wooden bar lends an appealing touch to this "gem", a modern bistro just off The Strand; the "great selection" of wines may be the focus, but the modern European food and the "good" beers also help turn it into "a real meeting place" to start an evening in Covent Garden.

Z Belgo

19	17	18	£8

Covent Garden | 50 Earlham St., WC2 (Covent Garden) | 020-7813 2233
Camden Town | 72 Chalk Farm Rd., NW1 (Chalk Farm) | 020-7267 0718
www.belgo-restaurants.com

Habit-ués are hot for this Camden/Covent Garden duo doling out the classic one-two of "wonderful" moules frites and other "good" Belgian nosh accompanied by a "headspinning selection" of "great" brews, all served by waiters in "monk outfits", habits and all; some say the "cavernous" spaces tend to trap sound since they can get "insanely noisy at peak times."

Bierodrome

14	14	13	£4

Holborn | 67 Kingsway, WC2 (Holborn) | 020-7242 7469
Islington | 173-174 Upper St., N1 (Highbury & Islington) | 020-7226 5835
Clapham | 44 Clapham High St., SW4 (Clapham North) | 020-7720 1118
www.belgo-restaurants.com

"When in the mood for beer and conviviality", lovers of Belgian brews head along to these Belgo sisters whose "amazing ales" rule; you'll find the vittles are "good" too, as is the "helpful" service – as long as you can put up with "noise" and "very busy" conditions.

Black Cap, The

13	10	13	£3

Camden Town | 171 Camden High St., NW1 (Camden Town) | 020-7428 2721 | www.theblackcap.com

Though this "funky" "old-style gay club" up in Camden is "a bit shabby" (the building's been around since 1776 – the bunches of mirror balls, nearly as long), most respondents concur that the "late licence", "latest tunes" played by "brilliant DJs", "very good drag acts" and "nice roof terrace" compensate; it "needs to improve in service", but that doesn't stop "rough and ready" locals from keeping it "seriously crowded."

Black Friar, The

| | | | - | - | - | I |

Blackfriars | 174 Queen Victoria St., EC4 (Blackfriars) | 020-7236 5474

You'll find an Edwardian grotto setting with over-the-top art deco stylings at this aptly named bar that's set on the site of the old friary that gives the neighbourhood its name; there's a fat, chortling monk and gargoyles above the door, but inside the drinks are fairly standard.

Bleeding Heart Tavern

| 22 | 19 | 19 | £7 |

Farringdon | 19 Greville St., EC1 (Farringdon) | 020-7404 0333 | www.bleedingheart.co.uk

Those whose tickers race faster for this Farringdon gastropub claim it's "the most romantic spot in the city", while others brand it a "good honest boozer" emitting "old-school appeal" and is about "as pubby as it gets"; all agree the food's "great" and the service "accommodating", adding up to a perfect venue for dinner à deux or for "meeting up with friends."

Bloomsbury Bowling Lanes

| 19 | 15 | 15 | £6 |

Bloomsbury | Tavistock Hotel | Bedford Way, WC1 (Russell Sq.) | 020-7183 1979 | www.bloomsburybowling.com

For pin-bashing beneath the Tavistock Hotel, try this "retro" Bloomsbury bowling alley sporting "lots of kitsch appeal", American diner fare, cinema screens and a karaoke room; it's the place for some good "ol'-fashioned fun", but just "book early" – the lanes "fill up" fast.

Blue Bar, The

| - | - | - | E |

Knightsbridge | The Berkeley | Wilton Pl., SW1 (Hyde Park Corner/Knightsbridge) | 020-7201 1680 | www.the-berkeley.co.uk

Aptly, this intimate, David Collins–designed bar in Knightsbridge's Berkeley hotel is all shades of the namesake hue, with exceptions made for the white onyx bar and black crocodile print leather floors; the classy, highbrow setting is matched with a sophisticated selection of more than 50 whiskies and a specially created Grape and Smoke menu pairing cigars with wines, plus snackers can sample from a menu of savoury and sweet tapas.

Boisdale

| 19 | 19 | 19 | £9 |

Victoria | 15 Eccleston St., SW1 (Victoria) | 020-7730 6922 | www.boisdale.co.uk

"Hyped, but deservedly so" is the deal at this Victoria "watering hole" renowned for its "excellent cigar menu" accompanied by whiskies, wines, "great" jazz and "impressive" servers (they'll "treat you like a king") within a "cosy", "old-school" setting; partiers propose it's "great for networking" with all those "plump bankers" in the house.

Boujis

| 22 | 19 | 17 | £13 |

South Kensington | 43 Thurloe St., SW7 (South Kensington) | 020-7584 2000 | www.boujis.com

Bump up against "royalty", "Eurotrash", "models" and "wannabes" at this "slick" members-only South Ken haunt (made famous from the patronage of William and Harry); fans find the "hardest door in London" the "place to be", while not surprisingly, commoners call it a "cramped dungeon" with "extra attitude" and "braying Sloan Rangers."

	APPEAL	DECOR	SERVICE	COST

Bradley's Spanish Bar
▽ 18 | 14 | 14 | £5

Fitzrovia | 42-44 Hanway St., W1 (Tottenham Court Rd.) | 020-7636 0359
Party like it's 1969 at this "tiny" but "mighty" boozer just north of Oxford Street that offers an antidote to the "plasticated glitz" of the surrounding area; the (vinyl) jukebox of '60s hits has stayed unchanged for 40 years, the "quirky but cool" crowd guarantee a "hilarious night out" and yeah, it's "grimy – and that's exactly why we love it."

NEW Bumpkin
18 | 17 | 18 | £9

Notting Hill | 209 Westbourne Park Rd., W11 (Westbourne Park) | 020-7243 9818 | www.bumpkinuk.com
"Nip in for a pint and a bite" at this "cute", multilevel "country-meets-city" spot purveying British vittles and drinks in the "bad lands of Notting Hill"; those who call it "overhyped" and "overpriced" are out-numbered by fans who walk away smitten by its "charms."

Café Boheme
19 | 18 | 17 | £7

Soho | 13-17 Old Compton St., W1 (Leicester Sq./Tottenham Court Rd.) | 020-7734 0623 | www.cafeboheme.co.uk
"Great Soho people-watching" could be another name for this French bar/brasserie placed in a prime position on Old Compton Street and featuring "fab" breakfasts, a "great jazz brunch" and "reasonable" prices; it earns its bona fides with night owls too: "the best thing is it's open till 3 AM!"

Café de Paris
18 | 19 | 16 | £11

Piccadilly | 3 Coventry St., W1 (Leicester Sq./Piccadilly Circus) | 020-7734 7700 | www.cafedeparis.com
The settings's pure "traditional opulence" while the crowd's "young", "trendy" and "euro" at this "tip-top" (if "rather expensive") classic chandeliered nightclub (dating to 1924) in Leicester Square hosting live blues, rock and house acts; clubbers call it the ideal spot "to start the evening with martinis and finish dancing to disco"; N.B. open Friday and Saturday only.

Chandos, The
15 | 13 | 13 | £4

Westminster | 29 St. Martin's Ln., WC2 (Charing Cross) | 020-7836 1401
"Ye olde English pubbe" in Westminster "caters to tourists", making it "always busy" and sometimes "hard to get a seat" – but that doesn't stop local "students" and "work colleagues" from joining the fray to take advantage of beer (courtesy of the Samuel Smith Brewery) that's "quite reasonably priced for central London"; although it may look "a bit grotty", there's "lots of little nooks" and "comfy sofas" for "a natter with mates" or a "liaison."

Z Chinawhite
22 | 21 | 17 | £13

Soho | 6 Air St., W1 (Piccadilly Circus) | 020-7343 0040 | www.chinawhite.com
A "bling clubbing" Soho "mainstay" that's "harder to get into than Fort Knox", this "exclusive" nightclub may have, for some, been "better years ago", but it's still a "serious" spot and as "trendy" as ever, what with the "happy" "cosmopolitan" crowd and all those "beautiful people" packing the house; old China hands claim that it's "one of the best nightclubs in central London", and if it's "way too expensive", you can capitalize on the "wannabe watching for free."

	APPEAL	DECOR	SERVICE	COST

Cittie of Yorke
▽ 22 | 21 | 18 | £4

City | 22 High Holborn, WC1 (Chancery Ln.) | 020-7242 7670

With its "sawdust floors" and "nooks and crannies" galore, this "huge", mock Tudor pub in the City is, swoon old-schoolers, "the essence of London", where the Sam Smith's ales both signal that it's "cheap and cheerful" and likewise attract "law students" as well as genuine "lawyers"; "fantastic" say fans who conclude it's "worth multiple visits."

☑ Claridge's Bar
25 | 24 | 24 | £12

Mayfair | Claridge's Hotel | 49 Brook St., W1 (Bond St.) | 020-7629 8860 | www.claridges.co.uk

The "place for a smart cocktail in Mayfair", this Survey's Most Popular bar is a "posh" outpost in the Claridge's Hotel where "first-rate" service combines with "elegant", "understated" art deco quarters; "anybody who's anybody" comes to this "old standard", so you'll have to be able to deal well with tabs fit for "hedge-funders."

Coach & Horses
19 | 16 | 16 | £8

Covent Garden | 42 Wellington St., WC2 (Covent Garden) | 020-7240 0553

"Start the night" at this "standard" for Guinness in Covent Garden, a good, old boozer that's a "nice place to mingle" and sample the black stuff; "tourists" make up part of the "busy" scene here – no surprise given that the ales are "cheap"

Coach & Horses
▽ 21 | 14 | 16 | £6

Soho | 29 Greek St., W1 (Leicester Sq.) | 020-7437 5920

Although the "famed publican Norman Balon" is now off his high horse (he retired last year), this "rough and fabulous", "historic dive" remains a Soho fixture; its "local", "down-to-earth" vibe makes it a "great place for meeting friends" (and spotting the journos from the nearby offices of *Private Eye*), but some complain of "grotty loos."

Comedy Store
20 | 13 | 17 | £8

Piccadilly | 1A Oxendon St., SW1 (Piccadilly Circus) | 020-7344 0234 | www.thecomedystore.co.uk

All Piccadilly can hear the "laughs" generated from this classic comedy club whose "intelligent humour" still "packs 'em in" after 28 years; overall, "good nights are guaranteed", but just "buy a ticket" early considering the place's popularity and prime position.

Comptons of Soho
17 | 14 | 15 | £7

Soho | 53-57 Old Compton St., W1 (Piccadillly Circus) | 020-7479 7961 | www.comptons-of-soho.co.uk

"Leather guys and run-of-the-mill queens" along with "black-boot/shaved heads" types are the order of the day at this Soho "gay classic", a "loud" "meat market" that attracts a "slightly older crowd"; there's a "friendly vibe" in the air here, but make no mistake: for the most part, the place "ain't for sissies or twinks."

Cork & Bottle
22 | 18 | 20 | £8

Piccadilly | 44-46 Cranbourn St., WC2 (Leicester Sq.) | 020-7734 7807 | www.donhewitson.com

Discover "hidden treasure amongst all the Leicester Square tourist traps" in the form of this "wonderful" wine bar touted by fans as one

of "London's best" on account of its deep 300-label selection; no surprise, it's packed "wall-to-wall" most of the time, but pros propose patience, and if you can get a seat, it's just the spot to "read the papers while nursing a glass."

Corney & Barrow

| 18 | 18 | 16 | £8 |

Blackfriars | 19 Broadgate Circle, EC2 (Liverpool St.) | 020-7628 1251
City | 1 Leadenhall Pl., EC3 (Bank/Monument) | 020-7621 9201
City | 10 Paternoster Sq., EC4 (St. Paul's) | 020-7618 9520
City | 111 Old Broad St., EC2 (Liverpool St.) | 020-7638 9308
City | 12-14 Mason's Ave., EC2 (Bank/Moorgate) | 020-7726 6030
City | 2B Eastcheap, EC3 (Monument) | 020-7929 3220
City | 3 Fleet Pl., EC4 (St. Paul's) | 020-7329 3141
City | 5 Exchange Sq., EC2 (Liverpool St.) | 020-7628 4367
Canary Wharf | 9 Cabot Sq., E14 (Canary Wharf) | 020-7512 0397
Tower Bridge | 37 Jewry St., EC3 (Aldgate) | 020-7680 8550
www.corney-barrow.co.uk
Additional locations throughout the London area

Loyalists and other "local wildlife" like the "upmarket" vibe, "modern sleek environments" and "reliable" *vins* provided by this chain of wine bars, convenient "standbys" for "after-work" crowds; although the vittles are deemed "very good" and the service pretty "zippy", dispirited sorts say they're "soulless" and some spots "full of networking bankers."

Cow

| 23 | 19 | 18 | £7 |

Bayswater | 89 Westbourne Park Rd., W2 (Westbourne Park) | 020-7221 5400 | www.thecowlondon.co.uk

"Media types, artists" and various moo-vers and shakers flock to this "classic" Bayswater gastropub that, thanks to its "good" food, is equally ideal for those eating on the hoof and for grazers; voters vouch for its "great" atmosphere, plus it offers "outdoor boozing at its best."

Cuckoo Club, The

| 23 | 20 | 18 | £13 |

Soho | Swallow St., W1 (Piccadilly Circus) | 020-7287 4300 | www.thecuckooclub.com

Crowned the "current star of the scene", this glam, "over-the-top" double-decker of a Soho nightclub has become an "amazingly popular" nest for "stars" and their "wannabes"; "beautiful" birdies chirp it's the "best since Boujis."

Cutty Sark Tavern

| 19 | 16 | 13 | £4 |

Greenwich | 4-6 Ballast Quay, SE10 (Cutty Sark DLR) | 020-8858 3146
Sure, it looks a bit "shabby", but things are overall shipshape at this Thames-side veteran pub known for "great" river views and a crowd of "tourists" and "locals"; "good after a day walking in Greenwich" say seadogs who swear it's a "must for Sunday lunch."

Davy's

| 16 | 15 | 16 | £7 |

Covent Garden | 17 The Arches, Villiers St., WC2 (Charing Cross/Embankment) | 020-7930 7737
City | 10 Creed Ln., EC4 (St. Paul's) | 020-7236 5317
City | City Boot | 7 Moorfields High Walk, EC2 (Moorgate) | 020-7588 4766
City | Plantation Pl., Mincing Ln., EC3 (Monument) | 020-7621 9878
Canary Wharf | 31 Fisherman's Walk, E14 (Canary Wharf) | 020-7363 6633
Greenwich | 161 Greenwich High Rd., SE10 (Greenwich) | 020-8858 7204

(continued)

Davy's

Pimlico | Crown Passage, Pall Mall, SW1 (Green Park) | 020-7839 8831
Chiswick | Hand Court, 57 High Holborn, WC1 (Holborn) | 020-7831 8365
www.davy.co.uk
Additional locations throughout the London area

With "sawdust on the floors" and "upturned beer barrels for tables", these spots "try to pretend" they're "old-style pubs" – but the "suits" who habituate them betray the truth: they're "upmarket wine bars"; despite the identity crisis, though, they're "cosy" "fallback venues" for "a bottle of red in the snug in winter" or "a bottle of white in the court-yard in summer" (patios not available in all locations).

De Hems

16 | 13 | 15 | £4

Chinatown | 11 Macclesfield St., W1 (Piccadilly Circus) | 020-7437 2494
"It reminds me of Amsterdam" sigh those who love the "strong" selec-tion of brews at this "real Dutch bar" incongruously placed on the out-skirts of Chinatown; it's "a hot spot for late nights" as one can see by the "lively" crowds that swarm the place; P.S. lowlanders say "Queens Day in April is so much fun."

Dog & Duck

18 | 14 | 17 | £5

Soho | 18 Bateman St., W1 (Tottenham Court Rd.) | 020-7494 0697 | www.mitchellsandbutlers.co.uk
"All types" find their way into this "cosy" boozer sporting original tiles and an unspoiled, old-style ambience; though inside is a sure bet, most opt to "drink outside, where you can savour the delights of Soho."

☑ Dorchester Bar

24 | 23 | 24 | £12

Mayfair | Dorchester Hotel | 53 Park Ln., W1 (Hyde Park Corner) | 020-7629 8888 | www.dorchesterhotel.com
"Posh", "fab" and "sexy" all sum up this plush Mayfair hotel bar, the destination for "A-listers", assorted "beautiful" people and "expense-accounters"; "top-notch" libations are part of the package, as is the discreet ambience (it's the "perfect place to meet for an affair").

Dove

21 | 17 | 15 | £5

Hammersmith | 19 Upper Mall, W6 (Ravenscourt Park) | 020-8748 5405
The "smallest snug" around, this "old" Hammersmith pub "icon" might be off the beaten path, but it's still a "great hideaway" with "lovely" Thames views and "good ales on tap"; "until recently a well-kept secret", it's now gotten "overcrowded."

Dragon

▽ 23 | 18 | 15 | £5

Shoreditch | 5 Leonard St., EC2 (Old St.) | 020-7490 7110
"The East Village comes to London" at this showpiece in Shoreditch, a "funky", arty bar with "comfy" sofas and abundant "charm"; champi-ons cheer the "great" DJs and like the somewhat "hidden" location.

Dublin Castle ⌀

16 | 12 | 15 | £4

Camden Town | 94 Parkway, NW1 (Camden Town) | 020-7485 1773
"Greasy crowds" soak up the "great" suds and live gigs at this "friendly" Camden music venue, the "original" indie music spot for knowledgeable fans; "great" rock 'n' roll is the order of the day, and no-body here seems to care about the "dilapidated" digs.

Duke of Cambridge
▽ 20 | 16 | 17 | £4

Islington | 30 St. Peter's St., N1 (Angel) | 020-7359 3066 | www.sloeberry.co.uk

If you want to have a pint and feel healthy while doing it, head to the first certified organic gastropub, opened 10 years ago in Islington, where the exclusive brews are organic and "taste great"; there's an "amazing" twice-daily changing menu using local, seasonal ingredients and a "relaxed", "old-fashioned-pub" ambience that many "really like", so who cares if this "quite appealing" bar is a little "more expensive" than the norm.

Duke's Head
19 | 16 | 15 | £3

Putney | 8 Lower Richmond Rd., SW15 (Putney Bridge) | 020-8788 2552 | www.dukesheadputney.co.uk

A favourite out in the wilds of Putney, this olde worlde waterside boozer has a "fantastic location" "by the river", especially "if you can find a perch" outdoors; a refurb by Young's has given the Victorian-era pub a new lease on life, with the brewery's own beers along with others on tap; some find it "very buzzy", others "quite chilled out", but all agree that "standing outside" is probably the best place to enjoy this one.

⊠ Dukes Hotel Bar
24 | 23 | 26 | £12

St. James's | Dukes Hotel | 35 St. James's Pl., SW1 (Green Park) | 020-7491 4840 | www.dukeshotel.com

While the "warm welcome" from a "professional staff" that makes you "feel like a lord" earns this "elegant" bar in the Dukes Hotel in St. James's a No. 1 ranking for Service in the London Survey, some clearly visit soley to order "absolutely the best martini in the world"; "take someone you want to impress", especially if they're "over 40", and enjoy an "intimate" evening "on a rainy night when there's a fire in the fireplace", and just ignore those youngsters who yawn it's "riding on its reputation."

⊠ e&o
22 | 20 | 18 | £10

Notting Hill | 14 Blenheim Crescent, W11 (Notting Hill Gate) | 020-7229 5454 | www.eando.co.uk

"Go for the drinks, stay for the crowd" say fans of this "outstanding Notting Hill institution" where the "beautiful people" (and "bankers") go to "see and be seen" in a "trendy", "chic" setting; unfortunately, its popularity makes for a "crowded", sometimes "stifling" atmosphere, but you'll get serious "star-spotting" for your patience.

1802
18 | 14 | 15 | £6

Canary Wharf | Museum of Docklands | No. 1 Warehouse, Hertsmere Rd., West India Quay, E14 (Canary Wharf) | 0870-444 3886 | www.searcys.co.uk

It might be "yuppie central" for some, but for others this Canary Wharf bar set in a "stylish" circa-1802 warehouse is "the best place on the Wharf for a quiet drink"; it's also perhaps "the most expensive", which, sniff snobs, "keeps the riffraff out", but for those who can afford it the "quick bar service" and "great cocktails" mean that it's a destination among the "dime-a-dozen" chain bars in this area; P.S. even better, it's "chock-full-of totty" on weekends.

Elbow Room

19	15	17	£8

Shoreditch | 97-113 Curtain Rd., EC2 (Liverpool St./Old St.) | 020-7613 1316
Islington | 89-91 Chapel Mkt., N1 (Angel) | 020-7278 3244
Notting Hill | 103 Westbourne Grove, W2 (Bayswater) | 020-7221 5211
www.theelbowroom.co.uk

This chain of "cool pool halls" combined with cocktail bars in trendy venues across the capital "still pushes buttons" for cue-jockeys who like to "hang out" and "chill with friends"; while some "explode with life", others have a more "relaxing" vibe", but it's no wonder they tend to attract "trust-fund" types given the "expensive" play.

Electric Ballroom, The ⊄

15	10	10	£4

Camden Town | 184 Camden High St., NW1 (Camden Town) | 020-7485 9007 | www.electricballroom.co.uk

"Get ready to bang your head" at this Camden classic live music club set in a "boogaloo basement" that attracts the local "rock and metal scene"; even if it's a "bit like a dodgy youth club", with its "scruffy", "down and dirty" atmosphere, it's still "worth going for the gigs."

El Vino

17	15	17	£6

Blackfriars | 30 New Bridge St., EC4 (Blackfriars) | 020-7236 4534
Blackfriars | 47 Fleet St., EC4 (Temple) | 020-7353 6786
City | Alban Gate | 125 London Wall, EC2 (Barbican) | 020-7600 6377
City | 6 Martin Ln., EC4 (Monument) | 020-7626 6876
www.elvino.co.uk

Once the haunt of bibulous Fleet Street hacks, you can still "step back into the 19th century" when you head for "after-work drinks" at one of the wine bars in this mini-chain; the area's legal eagles find a "pleasant place to while away the evening" "impressing" others, but a few say the "too City-fied" scene is "a bit poncey" and suggest they're just "living on a reputation."

☑ End, The

24	19	16	£8

Covent Garden | 18 W. Central St., WC1 (Holborn/Tottenham Court Rd.) | 020-7419 9199

"No trip through London nightlife would be complete without visiting" this "dance music classic" in Covent Garden that's co-owned by Mr C of The Shamen; there's a "changing weekly line-up" of top-quality DJs and it's a "fun" choice whether "early or late", but design divas should be warned: "you don't come here for the decor."

Engineer, The

22	20	18	£5

Camden Town | 65 Gloucester Ave., NW1 (Camden Town/Chalk Farm) | 020-7722 0950 | www.the-engineer.com

A boozer-cum-eatery in Primrose Hall, this "über trendy" Camden "hangout" in a 19th-century building "can get pretentious" but it has a "fab garden" in summer (orange trees and lilacs), private party rooms and a "laid-back" setting for "casual" dining on "very good" Modern British fare; overall, fans say it's a "lovely" choice "in a nice area."

Fabric

22	18	15	£9

Clerkenwell | 77A Charterhouse St., EC1 (Farringdon) | 020-7336 8898 | www.fabriclondon.com

With an "amazing sound system" playing the "best music in town" from "trailblazing DJs", this cavernous Clerkenwell superclub with "in-

sane crowds" reminds reviewers of "old-school New York dance clubs"; all sorts of repetitive beats are on offer from "drum and bass" to "trance", so it's "pure heaven for clubbing fanatics"; just be prepared – you may "need a megaphone to order a drink."

🄩 Fifth Floor Bar   19 | 18 | 19 | £11

Knightsbridge | Harvey Nichols | 109-125 Knightsbridge, SW1 (Knightsbridge) | 020-7235 5000 | www.harveynichols.co.uk

If you're looking for a "chic" pit stop to "refuel for more shopping", this "beautiful" bar on the fifth floor of Harvey Nichols in Knightsbridge is a "funky", "flashy" choice with city and park views and "definite electricity" due to the "jet-set young crowd" and the "pickup scene"; though some find it too "loud", "pricey" and just a bit "stale", others feel "lucky to get a seat."

Filthy MacNasty's   ▽ 19 | 15 | 18 | £4
(fka Filthy's Bar & Kitchen)

Islington | 68 Amwell St., EC1 (Angel) | 020-7837 6067 | www.filthymacnastys.com

"I once saw The Pogues in here" muses one fan, and it's hardly surprising as this Islington classic is part-owned by singer Shane McGowan who can often be found soaking up the "good Guinness" with pal Pete Doherty; the back bar hosts free bands, comedy and spoken word including poetry readings and open mike events, but fans say the chance to see a music legend as well as listen to "guaranteed" "great" tunes is why they come.

Fishmarket (Champagne Bar)   20 | 21 | 16 | £11

City | Great Eastern Hotel | Liverpool St., EC2 (Liverpool St.) | 020-7618 7215 | www.london.greateastern.hyatt.com

Champagne socialites savor this "City-like" bubbly bar in the Square Mile's Great Eastern Hotel, reveling in the "amazing" buzz, "beautiful" location and "fantastic" selection of the featured libation; but a few who choose it only for a "celebratory drink" find it too "crowded" with the "after-work" scene, "expensive" and even a bit "clichéd" for regular visits.

Fitzroy Tavern   15 | 10 | 13 | £4

Fitzrovia | 16 Charlotte St., W1 (Goodge St.) | 020-7580 3714

After a few pints in this "old" Victorian "haunt" in Fitzrovia, swiggers swear "the ghosts of George Orwell" and other famous regulars (Dylan Thomas, Augustus John) "come alive"; "another excellent Sam Smith's" place with a full selection of beers from Tadcaster and a "friendly bar staff", it gets points from its large "student clientele" for being "one of the cheapest places in Central London"; just get there early for your "crazy afternoon drink" or after-work shot because "the crowd spills onto the street on sunny evenings."

Flask   21 | 18 | 15 | £4

Highgate | 77 Highgate West Hill, N6 (Archway/Highgate) | 020-8348 7346

An "old-world" atmosphere pervades this "cosy", "friendly" boozer "off the beaten track" in Highgate, where plenty of "nooks and crannies" mean you can settle in comfortably for a spell; in summer, the garden is a "smashing spot for a Pimms" or for a "good range of beer" choices while you "watch the world go by" (grab a "veggie burger from

the barbecue"), and at all times the "sedate" setting is perfect for "the oldies" or for a "quiet" Sunday "recovery."

Flask, The

| 17 | 12 | 12 | £4 |

Hampstead | 14 Flask Walk, NW3 (Hampstead) | 020-7435 4580
This "charming" pub "tucked away off the high street" in Hampstead is "stuck in the last century" say some, but that makes it all the more "atmospheric" and "fun"; "inviting after a walk on the Heath", with a "friendly" ambience, solid beers and "the best Bloody Mary ever", it nonetheless prompts a few to whisper "grungy."

Floridita
(fka Mezzo)

| 21 | 21 | 19 | £9 |

Soho | 100 Wardour St., W1 (Tottenham Court Rd.) | 020-7314 4000 | www.floriditalondon.com
"Dance all night" at "one of the best Latin spots in London" say foot-stomping fans of this "fun and friendly" Soho mega-bar and club from the Conran Group where they drink the "best mojitos in town" and enjoy "fantastic" bands from Havana; you can really "let your hair" down, unless you're a killjoy who finds it just an "expensive" "faux Cubana."

43
(fka Qhew)

| ▽ 19 | 21 | 23 | £8 |

Mayfair | 43 S. Molton St., W1 (Bond St.) | 020-7647 4343 | www.the43club.com
"An oasis of peace" on a quirky side street off the shopping meccas of Oxford and Bond streets, this "eclectic" Mayfair bar sports an interior that feels like the contents of a country house have been rammed into a tiny space, what with all the stag heads, assorted knickknacks, over-stuffed chairs and obscure portraits; service is "the right side of friendly", making it a "good spot" to meet for cocktails and conversation.

Freedom

| 15 | 15 | 12 | £5 |

Soho | 60-66 Wardour St., W1 (Leicester Sq.) | 020-7734 0071
"There's a scarcity of genuine cool polysexual bars" in London, but this Soho mainstay with its "young and trendy", gay and lesbian crowd gets the thumbs-up; "glitzy and chintzy" decor, a "good vibe", "free entry" and "cheap drinks" ensure that it's always busy" (and "you're guranteed to meet some nutters"), but the sheer volume means it's "not a place for conversation."

French House, The

| 19 | 15 | 17 | £5 |

Soho | 49 Dean St., W1 (Leicester Sq./Piccadilly Circus) | 020-7437 2477
The "history" is the draw of this "charming" Soho bar where the Free French holed up during WWII; go for the "irresistible Bastille Day party" or just to "share a bottle of Chablis" before heading upstairs to dine, just don't be surprised if it gets so "crowded" you're either "rammed" out onto the street or stuck in a "drunken conversation"; N.B. the walls are plastered with signed photos of notables.

NEW Galvin at Windows

| – | – | – | E |

Mayfair | Hilton Park Ln. | 22 Park Ln., W1 (Hyde Park Corner) | 020-7208 4021 | www.galvinatwindows.com
With a glam interior evoking the '30s, this restaurant bar on the 28th floor of Mayfair's London Hilton predictably has a spectacular city

view, along with bespoke furnishings, mirrored table surfaces and an Italian Saint Laurent marble bar top; there's a menu of light bites, plus an impressive line-up of classic and modern cocktails.

G-A-Y Bar
| 20 | 15 | 15 | £7 |

Soho | 30 Old Compton St., W1 (Leicester Sq.) | 020-7494 2756 | www.g-a-y.co.uk

"The vibe is still alive" at this "F-A-B" and "camp" club in Soho where "queens" come for "hot young studs and suds"; regulars rave about the "killer" tunes and "video screen", but the real pull may be the live performances from acts like Kylie.

George Inn
| 21 | 17 | 14 | £4 |

Borough | 77 Borough High St., SE1 (Borough/London Bridge) | 020-7407 2056

The National Trust owns this "great old" pub (dating back to the 16th century) set in a cobblestoned Borough courtyard, the oldest surviving galleried coaching inn that serves a "range of beers"; the "beautiful" Tudor-style exterior is best admired from the outdoor garden ("one of the best in London"), and Casanovas confirm it's nice to "cuddle up in the wood-panelled bar" come winter.

NEW Gilt Champagne Lounge
| 21 | 21 | 21 | £13 |

Knightsbridge | Jumeirah Carlton Tower | 1 Cadogan Pl., SW1 (Knightsbridge) | 020-7235 1234 | www.jumeirahcarltontower.com

"All the rich kids" flock to soak up the "upbeat" atmosphere at this champagne lounge within Knightsbridge's Jumeirah Carlton Tower hotel; as you'd expect, the bubblies are "excellent" and the "plush", "beautiful", golden-hued quarters get a thumbs-up – just make sure you have good credit to cover the "expensive" tabs.

Gordon's
| 23 | 20 | 18 | £9 |

Piccadilly | 47 Villiers St., WC2 (Charing Cross/Embankment) | 020-7930 1408 | www.gordonswinebar.com

The "good" *vins* come with a side of "history" when you visit this "dark" basement wine cave in Piccadilly still featuring a "marvelously atmospheric" setting with brick-lined walls, "low ceilings", "wonky furniture" and lots of "nooks and crannies"; there's always a "heavy hum of conversation" – perhaps because the joint's usually "crowded."

Greenwich Union, The
| - | - | - | M |

Greenwich | 56 Royal Hill, SE1 (Greenwich) | 020-8692 6258 | www.greenwichunion.com

"Locally brewed" beer from the Meantime brewery is the "main attraction" at this Greenwich pub where the selection includes IPAs, porters, lagers and stouts; the location on a beautiful Georgian backstreet makes it a favourite with locals and tourists alike, while the "lovely" garden and "relaxed" vibe add to the pull.

Z Grenadier, The
| 24 | 22 | 20 | £8 |

Belgravia | 18 Wilton Row, SW1 (Hyde Park Corner) | 020-7235 3074

Breathless boozers say this "lovely", "cute" venue is the "quintessential British pub", a spot purveying "history" as well as "great" pub food and drinks down a cobblestoned Belgravia mews; tipplers hail the "best Bloody Marys in London", ideal during "Sunday hangovers."

	APPEAL	DECOR	SERVICE	COST

NEW Hawksmoor ▽ 20 | 16 | 21 | £7

Shoreditch | 157 Commercial St., E1 (Liverpool St.) | 020-7247 7392 | www.thehawksmoor.com

Named after the architect who built nearby Christ Church, this Shoreditch gastro-venue offers some of "the best cocktails in London by a country mile" to go with a hearty American selection of "superb" grilled meats; the setting's "Citified", but the sight of drinkers downing libations from "punch bowls" helps keep the vibe down to earth.

Heaven 23 | 21 | 18 | £8

Soho | The Arches, Villiers St., WC2 (Charing Cross/Embankment) | 020-7930 2020 | www.heaven-london.com

"If this is what heaven is like, I can't wait to get there" croon queens who favor this Charing Cross institution, the official "mother church of gay London" that occupies a "huge", "cavernous" space and boasts plenty of "hidden dance floors"; what's more, it's guaranteed to be "jam-packed with boys" every night, so finding a mate shouldn't be too tough.

NEW Hideaway, The – | – | – | M

Islington | 114 Junction Rd., N19 (Archway/Tufnell Park) | 020-7561 0779 | www.thehideawaybar.co.uk

A relaxed neighbourhood bar upstairs and a happening late-night basement club below, this hideaway in Islington draws different sets of fans; Friday and Saturday nights, DJs play an eclectic mix including classics, funk, northern soul and rock until 2 AM, and on Thursdays there's live jazz and acoustic sessions; noshes include stonebaked pizza, burgers and cheese from the reputable La Fromagerie.

⚡ Holly Bush, The 25 | 21 | 21 | £5

Hampstead | 22 Holly Mount, NW3 (Hampstead) | 020-7435 2892

"Tucked away in the heart of Hampstead" dwells this "excellent secret", a "cute" pub that takes you "back 100 years" via wood panelling and "great" ales dispensed from hand pumps; cronies confirm there's cosiness to spare – the venue has "romantic" written all over it.

Hoop & Grapes, The – | – | – | M

Shoreditch | 47 Aldgate High St., EC3 (Aldgate) | 020-7265 5171

Situated in one of the only buildings to survive the Great Fire in 1666, this Aldgate boozer has been pulling 'em through the wonky wooden doors since 1598; despite the pedigree, some say it's little more than an "average City pub", though allies aver the "sausage menu" and "table service" lift it above the usual.

Hoxton Square Bar & Kitchen 19 | 18 | 17 | £5

Hoxton | 2-4 Hoxton Sq., N1 (Old St.) | 020-7613 0709 | www.barworks.com

"Trendy" is the word for this Hoxton hipster haven that manages to be "buzzing, alternative, arty" and "chic" all at once; "fabulous" music means that the "cosy" bar tends to be packed with "up-for-it pretty young things", and dancers dig it for "end-of-the-evening boogies."

100 Club 15 | 12 | 12 | £5

Soho | 100 Oxford St., W1 (Oxford Circus/Tottenham Court Rd.) | 020-7636 0933 | www.the100club.co.uk

The list (The White Stripes, Sex Pistols, The Stones and Muddy Waters) "reads like a who's who of music" marvel fans at the acts that

APPEAL | DECOR | SERVICE | COST

have walked on stage at this "grungy" Oxford Street "dive" and "piece of history" that "hasn't changed much" since 1942; hepcats head for the "modern jazz retro mix" and gigs by boldface modern bands, plus, the place is "centrally located" and right near the main Tubes.

ICA Bar & Cafe
19 | 19 | 15 | £7

Westminster | Institute of Contemporary Arts | The Mall, SW1 (Charing Cross/Piccadilly Circus) | 020-7930 3647 | www.ica.org.uk
A "casual afterthought" tacked onto the Institute for Contemporary Arts in Westminster, this "funky, energetic" spot with a "splendid location" if you love art is a "decent place to drink" or meet "for coffee"; you'll need a museum ticket to enter, as well as a good set of ears, 'cause it gets plenty "crowded" and "noisy" for such a highbrow home.

Jamaica Wine House
∇ 24 | 19 | 20 | £6

City | 12 St. Michael's Alley, EC3 (Bank) | 020-7929 6972 | www.massivepub.com
On the venerable site of London's first coffeehouse (burned down in the Great Fire of London), the Jampot is a "remnant" of the 17th century that "tingles the imagination"; those who've found it "down a cobblestone walk" say it's the "best-kept secret" with "lots of character", a busy post-work scene and an outdoor drinking area.

Jamies
∇ 17 | 18 | 16 | £10

Fitzrovia | 74 Charlotte St., W1 (Goodge St.) | 020-7636 7556
Blackfriars | 119-121 The Minories, EC3 (Tower Hill) | 020-7709 9900
City | 107-112 Leadenhall St., EC3 (Bank) | 020-7626 7226
NEW **City** | 155 Bishopsgate, EC2 (Liverpool St.) | 020-7256 7279
City | 5 Groveland Ct., EC4 (Bank) | 020-7248 5551
Canary Wharf | 28 Westferry Circus, E14 (Canary Wharf) | 020-7536 2861 www.jamiesbars.co.uk
With some of its locations in the City and Canary Wharf, this chain of wine bars will always be "busy with bankers" and their ilk enjoying "decent drink selections" that can be "a cut above" some local competitors, especially when taken "outside on a summer's day" with a view; but bored boozers find "yet another regular chain" that doesn't excite.

Jerusalem Tavern
22 | 20 | 18 | £4

Clerkenwell | 55 Britton St., EC1 (Farringdon) | 020-7490 4281 | www.stpetersbrewery.co.uk
"Everything is perfect" say those who have experienced the "great beers" from the Suffolk-based St Peter's Brewery at this "atmospheric and tiny" Clerkenwell classic; there's a "pretty good crowd" to soak up the "utterly fabulous" "olde worlde" atmos, where you can "feel the history" coming off the frescoed walls, just make sure you get to this "true pub" "early, if you want a seat."

John Snow
12 | 12 | 13 | £3

Soho | 39 Broadwick St., W1 (Oxford Circus) | 020-7437 1344
"A busy, cheerful pub" in Soho with an "unpretentious atmosphere" and a "relaxed" staff, this "rough-and-ready boozer" is always "packed" with locals "spilling onto the street" while enjoying "cheap" Sam Smith's beers; most say it's "a place to hang on a regular basis", but a few fret it's "remarkable only for" its namesake, who discovered that a cholera outbreak started at "the famous waterpump" located right "outside."

	APPEAL	DECOR	SERVICE	COST

Kabaret's Prophecy
| | 16 | 18 | 15 | £9 |

Soho | 16-18 Beak St., W1 (Oxford Circus/Piccadilly Circus) | 020-7439 2229 | www.kabaretsprophecy.com

If you want to spend the evening "ordering Moët", "celeb-spotting" and listening to "'80s music", then this Soho boîte is "not a bad" choice; "wonderful decor" and a "hip crowd" create a "cool" vibe, but an "unimpressed" minority maintain it's simply "overhyped."

Kettners
| | 20 | 20 | 19 | £8 |

Soho | 29 Romilly St., W1 (Leicester Sq.) | 020-7734 6112 | www.pizzaexpress.com/kettners

"An oasis in Soho" where you can easily "lose an afternoon with a lot of bubbles and a friend", this "legendary" champagne bar (founded by Napoleon III's chef in 1867) is an "unpretentious", "classy environment" for a "late-night glass" while listening to live piano as well; the "luxe surroundings" include a "gorgeous" plethora of "chintz couches", but a few say a recent "refurb" put a slight dent in the old "charm."

Kick
| | 19 | 16 | 16 | £4 |

Clerkenwell | 43 Exmouth Mkt., EC1 (Farringdon) | 020-7837 8077
Shoreditch | 127 Shoreditch High St., E1 (Liverpool St./Old St.) | 020-7739 8700
www.cafekick.co.uk

It's all about the "table football" at this duo of bars where the game is played on beachwood French Bonzini tables with cast-iron figurines and World Cup cork balls; "perfect for chilling with friends" over a Portuguese "bock beer" (there's a selection of bottled imports from all over Europe), they're also just the spot to watch "local life" go by at the same time you're "pretending you're somewhere on the continent."

NEW Kitts
| | ▽ 17 | 19 | 14 | £8 |

Chelsea | 7-12 Sloane Sq., SW1 (Sloane Sq.) | 020-7881 5990 | www.kitts-london.com

It may be "very small", but this Chelsea "hot spot" is "well decked" with a curved bronze bar, "really nice" booths and interesting lighting features; an "excellent location" along with "throngs of good-looking, eligible bachelors" means it's "great for the ladies", although chaps looking for love may be disappointed in the amount of competition.

Koko ☞
| | 17 | 17 | 14 | £4 |

Camden Town | 1A Camden High St., NW1 (Mornington Crescent) | 0870-432 5527 | www.koko.uk.com

"Sooo cool" marvel the "rather cute audiences" who've checked out this Camden Town venue, a former theatre that's been restored to "gorgeous" bordello-red-with-gold-trim splendour; "lots of bars and seating areas" surrounding the open pit and stage are "fab" – however, the gigs swing between "great" and "rubbish", and on club nights, sometimes "they let far too many people onto the dance floor."

Lab
| | 21 | 17 | 23 | £8 |

Soho | 12 Old Compton St., W1 (Leicester Sq./Tottenham Court Rd.) | 020-7437 7820 | www.lab-townhouse.com

"From outside, you wouldn't give a penny to this anonymous" Soho bar, "but once you start sipping" the "innovative, inspiring" (and "pricey") cocktails, featuring "creative fresh-fruit muddles", you'll see

why it's already "a classic"; it may be "too cool for school", but the mixologists are as "friendly" as they are "talented", making it a "perfect spot for pre-drinks before hitting the clubs" or to "just chill out on a weeknight."

La Grande Marque

| - | - | - | VE |

City | 47 Ludgate Hill, EC4 (Blackfriars/St. Paul's) | 020-7329 6709
NEW **City** | Temple Library Bldg. | Middle Temple Ln., EC4 (Temple) | 020-7583 5946
www.lagrandemarque.com

Set in what was once a bank on Ludgate Hill and in the Temple Library, these wine bar/restaurants both boast "great decor" in old-world-feeling locales; for the barristers and other City business types who look to them for relaxing after-work vino and champagne tastings accompanied by "exquisite" Modern European nibbles, it "lives up to expectations."

Lamb Tavern

| 17 | 13 | 14 | £4 |

City | Leadenhall Mkt. | 10-12 Leadenhall Mkt., EC3 (Bank/Monument) | 020-7626 2454 | www.thelambtavern.co.uk

A "classic pub in an old classic market", namely the City's Leadenhall Market, a stone's throw from The Monument, this "legend" of a "traditional pub" "has not changed since the '70s", if not longer; the "location" means that it's always "crowded" after work with those from Lloyds and elsewhere, and some say it's really a "man's haunt", but it's still a "legend" worth visiting.

☑ Library, The

| 23 | 23 | 23 | £14 |

Knightsbridge | The Lanesborough | 1 Lanesborough Pl., SW1 (Hyde Park Corner) | 020-7259 5599 | www.lanesborough.co.uk

As "suave and debonair" as its "slick", "upper-class" clientele, this "sumptuous", "clubby" lounge in the Lanesborough hotel in Knightsbridge employs "amazing barmen" and "spot-on waiters" who proffer "every type of whisky", a "yummy wine list" and both classic and "21st-century cocktails"; it's "super for business" meetings, to "impress a new love" or to merely feel "pampered" "away from the hoi polloi" – just "bring buckets of money."

Light Bar

| 22 | 22 | 18 | £11 |

Covent Garden | St. Martins Lane Hotel | 45 St. Martin's Ln., WC2 (Leicester Sq.) | 020-7300 5599 | www.stmartinslane.com

"Cool, hip and happening", this Covent Garden bar in the trendy St. Martins Lane Hotel offers "sophisticated" decor that includes atmospheric lighting in shades of green, orange, pink and violet along with walls full of artist Jean Baptiste Mondino's enormous black-and-white up-close photos of faces; the central location "close to theatres" and the "eye-candy" crowd please many, though simpler sorts snap it's "kinda snobby" and you'll need a "fat purse" for all those "glam" cocktails.

☑ Ling Ling@Hakkasan

| 26 | 26 | 20 | £12 |

Fitzrovia | 8 Hanway Pl., W1 (Tottenham Court Rd.) | 020-7907 1888

The "exquisite, edgy decor" and "eastern-themed cocktails" are hallmarks of this Fitzrovia bar attached to Alan Yau's Chinese restaurant, that's still "*très chic*" after all these years; if you can "fight your way past the bouncers", you'll enter an "underground heaven" where the "stylish crowd" (who keep "one eye on the nearest mirror")

drink "outrageously expensive", yet "gorgeous", cocktails and create an "extraordinary buzz"; it's all a "delightfully sinful" – if "achingly expensive" – experience.

Long Bar at the Sanderson

20 | 23 | 16 | £12

Fitzrovia | Sanderson Hotel | 50 Berners St., W1 (Oxford Circus/Tottenham Court Rd.) | 020-7300 1400 | www.morganshotelgroup.com

The "yummy cocktail menu" might be beside the point at this Philippe Starck-designed light and white Fitzrovia bar in the Sanderson Hotel that "bursts at the seams with a trendy see-and-be-seen crowd"; "lots of models" and other "pretty people" fight with the "nouveau riche" for space at the very long bar (sometimes it's "five-deep"), so hit this one "early"; still, a few cutting-edgers cry the "staff still thinks this is the place to be" but the "celebs are long gone and only the prices remain."

☑ Loungelover

25 | 29 | 19 | £9

Shoreditch | 1 Whitby St., E1 (Liverpool St.) | 020-7012 1234 | www.loungelover.co.uk

It might be "camp as Christmas and proud of it", but this Shoreditch bar behind Les Trois Garcons restaurant has the kind of "funky fabulousness" that lounge lizards who vote it the London Survey's No. 1 for Decor love; "definitely worth the trek" "just for" the "eclectic decor" that features red drapes, surreal artwork and flamboyant sofas, it's also got an "impossibly long" list of "amazing", if "expensive", cocktails; a handful of true hipsters tut over too many "suits", but others just sit back and enjoy the "swishest place in town."

Lowlander

 – | – | – | E

Covent Garden | 36 Drury Ln., WC2 (Covent Garden/Holborn) | 020-7379 7446

NEW **City** | 20 Creechurch Ln., EC3 (Aldgate) | 020-7623 8813
www.lowlander.com

Modelled in the Belgian and Dutch grand-cafe tradition, these City and Covent Garden pub/restaurants serve up "great bites" and "some of the best beer" in the capital, including dozens of low-country treats like Trappists, fruit beers, lambics and more; cheers also to the monthly tasting events and what some consider the "best-looking bar staff" about.

Lucky Voice

 – | – | – | VE

Soho | 52 Poland St., W1 (Oxford Circus/Tottenham Court Rd.) | 020-7439 3660 | www.luckyvoice.co.uk

A rare karaoke bar in Soho, this spot is "good fun" for bashing out tunes – and nine private rooms mean there's no need to be embarrassed for lack of singing prowess; while it's obviously "great for groups" (especially a "birthday" celebration), most "wouldn't go there just for a drink", being that it's so "expensive."

Madame JoJo's

16 | 11 | 14 | £5

Soho | 8-10 Brewer St., W1 (Leicester Sq./Piccadilly Circus) | 020-7734 3040 | www.madamejojos.com

"Tacky" but "always a scream", this "intimate", red-hued "transvestite cabaret"/dance club "right in the middle of things" in Soho draws a "clique-y" "scene" of "youngsters" for "burlesque drag shows", "up-and-coming bands" and DJ nights like the long-running Deep Funk; the decor may "need an update", but it's a "great place to take friends

from overseas" and, despite the fact that some of the "waitresses are transsexuals", lads, it's "not bad for pulling birds either."

NEW Mahiki

18 | 20 | 17 | £9

Mayfair | 1 Dover St., W1 (Green Park) | 020-7493 9529 | www.mahiki.com
Managing to be both "seductive" and "kitschy" at the same time, this "trendy" "bamboo-clad" Hawaiian "tiki lounge" in Mayfair serves tropical drinks "in amusing vessels" like volcanoes and skulls (the owner "certainly knows his rum" – too bad "staff don't match his enthusiasm"); the "concept" attracts a "see-and-be-seen" crowd of "B-list celebs", "Sloanes" and "young royals" – Princes Harry and William and their hangers-on are reported to be regulars.

Market Place

14 | 13 | 13 | £4

Fitzrovia | 11-13 Market Pl., W1 (Oxford Circus) | 020-7079 2020 | www.marketplace-london.com
"Post-work", Fitzrovia "media types" "relax" over the "excellent beer" and "nice cocktails" offered at this "decent" bar, while later in the evening, a "good buzz" permeates thanks to "some great DJs" in the basement (where it "can get busy on Friday nights"); the interior may be "a bit grungy", but its "nice to sit outside in summer."

Market Porter, The

18 | 15 | 16 | £3

South Bank | 9 Stoney St., SE1 (London Bridge) | 020-7407 2495 | www.markettaverns.co.uk
It's "a beer festival" at this "busy, buzzing", "crowded" pub where the crowd "spills out" into Borough Market every afternoon, evening and, believe it or not, morning (it opens at 6 AM for the traders); there's an "excellent range" of "constantly changing" suds – "the best real ale in London" say some – and the Globe Theatre is so close that it's a perennial tourist fave too.

Medcalf

– | – | – | M

Clerkenwell | 40 Exmouth Mkt., EC1 (Angel/Farringdon) | 020-7833 3533 | www.medcalfbar.co.uk
Up on trendy Exmouth Market, this bar attached to a restaurant in a converted turn-of-the-century butcher's shop with food worth ordering can get "busy in the evenings", especially in summer when the crowd overflows to the outdoor tables; it's "good" scruffy-chic "fun" for loyalists who say "you'd be lucky if this was your local."

NEW Mews of Mayfair

19 | 20 | 19 | £10

Mayfair | 10-11 Lancashire Ct., New Bond St., W1 (Bond St./Oxford Circus) | 020-7518 9388 | www.mewsofmayfair.com
"If you want to find a hedge-fund husband", you could do worse than this "trendy and expensive" Mayfair bar "hidden away in one of London's wonderful alleyways" where a "young, professional", "vibrant" crowd settles into leather sofas and Queen Anne chairs beneath an 18th-century chandelier; N.B. a more discreet basement lounge has glass-beaded walls and secluded alcoves.

Z Milk and Honey

27 | 25 | 25 | £9

Soho | 61 Poland St., W1 (Oxford Circus) | 020-7734 0700 | www.mlkhny.com
It looks like a "1920s ocean liner" or your "gran's front room" crossed with an American Prohibition-era "speakeasy", but this "laid-back",

"stylish" "joint" in Soho (sibling to one on NYC's Lower East Side) is a "grown-up place" where you can "have a conversation without raising your voice" – hence its rating as the No. 1 spot for Appeal in this the London Survey; it's hard to find (and open to nonmembers by reservation only until 11 PM), but the ladies love the "rule that prohibits men from approaching women" and unknowns appreciate a staff that "doesn't care if you're rich and famous."

Mint Leaf
18 | 19 | 17 | £7

Piccadilly | Suffolk Pl., SW1 (Piccadilly Circus) | 020-7930 9020 | www.mintleafrestaurant.com

This "sophisticated" and "understated" spot is a "great starting point for a fantastic meal" in the attached Indian restaurant, with a long bar, an extensive cocktail menu and a "seductive atmosphere" perfect for "people who want to be able to hear each other"; predictably, the namesake herb is featured in many of the libations – try the Strawberry Mint Chill that also includes super-premium rum and dried chili.

NEW Mocotó
22 | 23 | 18 | £12

Knightsbridge | 145 Knightsbridge, SW1 (Knightsbridge) | 020-7225 2300 | www.mocoto.co.uk

"The upstairs bar" of this Brazilian restaurant in Knightsbridge "has it all": "fabulous, exotic" cocktails to sip, "good food to nibble on" and "beautiful people to look at"; there's no doubt that it's "trendy", but it's also "friendly", making it "easy to mix" with the "local crowd" ("nice atmosphere for couples" too) – a shame it's also "really expensive."

NEW Montgomery Place
19 | 16 | 17 | £7

Notting Hill | 31 Kensington Park Rd., W11 (Ladbroke Grove) | 020-7792 3921 | www.montgomeryplace.co.uk

"A haven for mature" Notting Hill locals, this "tiny little" retro watering hole serves "fine wines" and old-school cocktails like sazeracs and south side fizzes accompanied by an edited selection of Eclectic bites in a "prototypical" upscale-pub setting; the "great lounge vibe" is ideal "for a date or catching up with friends after dinner", although "it closes too early" (at midnight).

NEW Moose, The
- | - | - | M

Mayfair | 31 Duke St., W1 (Bond St.) | 020-7224 3452 | www.vpmg.net

It's "well worth a visit" to this "fantastic" Mayfair spot right next to Selfridges and designed by Shaun Clarkson as an eccentric, rustic ski-ing lodge (cow hide seats, Nordic murals, antler lights); there's a small ground-floor bar and a much larger basement space with DJs spinning tunes six nights a week, plus a light bites menu offering pizza, nachos and the like.

Morpeth Arms, The
14 | 11 | 15 | £4

Pimlico | 58 Millbank, SW1 (Pimlico) | 020-7834 6442

"Many are the charms at the Arms" say the "art students" and art lovers who stop by this no-frills Pimlico pub, run by Wells and Young's Brewery, after "visiting Tate Britain" (it's the gallery's local, which means "it gets extremely busy"); area workers also assure it's "a wonderful little find" for enjoying "a pint by the riverside" "after a hard day at the office."

Mo*vida

20 | 20 | 14 | £14

Soho | 8-9 Argyll St., W1 (Oxford Circus) | 020-7739 8824 |
www.movida-club.com

"In the bowels of the Palladium theatre", this "outstanding" "retro-chic" nightclub offers a "wittily irreverent take on a French château" and decor that includes almost a thousand lights; the crowd veers from "beautiful Euro types" to "Chelsea kids trying to make an impression" to a preponderance of bridge and tunnel-y "hen parties" on weekends; with the "magnums of Cristal" flowing, though, some sneer the real point of coming is to prove you've got "money."

Mulligans of Mayfair

▽ 19 | 17 | 20 | £5

Mayfair | 13-14 Cork St., W1 (Green Park/Piccadilly Circus) |
020-7409 1370 | www.ballsbrothers.co.uk

This Irish pub might look unprepossessing from the outside, but it serves what some consider the "best Guinness in Mayfair", as it's delivered fresh daily from across the sea along with Strangford Lough oysters; warm tones and a fairly spacious curved bar lend a "classy" air to the "joint", in which a well-heeled after-work crowd can often be found enjoying the craic.

Nam Long-Le Shaker

16 | 15 | 17 | £8

Earl's Court | 159 Old Brompton Rd., SW5 (Gloucester Rd./
South Kensington) | 020-7373 1926

The "exotic" "cocktails can be lethal", especially the notorious "Flaming Ferraris", at this "long-time" Chelsea nightspot/restaurant where "lots of booze" often leads to "stupid behaviour" – which can be "amusing, if you're in the right mindset"; if you're not, you may find yourself sympathising with "harassed staff", even as they "pour drinks into you as fast as your bank balance can empty."

NEW Narrow, The

- | - | - | E

Limehouse | 44 Narrow St., E14 (Limehouse DLR) | 020-7592 7950 |
www.gordonramsay.com

"Nicely done" nod those who've sampled this airy Limehouse gastropub, which was taken over by chef Gordon Ramsay (his first of this type) just before Survey time and simply decorated with muted blues, old fireplaces and bare wood; though a tight selection of Traditional nibbles and entrees may be the main event, the unusual beers on tap intrigue ale-adventurers; P.S. "sit outside and watch the river" on clement days.

93 Feet East

16 | 11 | 12 | £4

Shoreditch | 150 Brick Ln., E1 (Aldgate East/Liverpool St.) | 020-7247 3293 |
www.93feeteast.co.uk

"Funky music and clientele" guarantee the "cool" vibe at this "dingy" drinking hole slap bang in the middle of the Shoreditch scene; the "barbecues in the courtyard" make this a "good summer venue" and a winner for "Friday night outdoor drinks", though scenesters sigh "unfortunately, it's only open till 1 AM" on weekends.

☑ Nobu Berkeley St.

24 | 23 | 21 | £14

Mayfair | 15 Berkeley St., W1 (Green Park) | 020-7290 9222 |
www.noburestaurants.com

"If you get in" to this "velvet-rope" Mayfair bar under the "chic" sushi restaurant, "you've made it!" – just look at the "gorgeous" crowd of

"smartly dressed" "stars" and "posh poseurs"; besides the "eye-candy" clientele, there's "brilliant decor" (the whole place is done up as an ultramod Japanese fantasy forest), and "great" martinis and "unusual sake" conveyed by staff that are "shockingly" "friendly" – of course, it's all "stupidly overpriced", but the "elite" feel it's "worth it."

Old Bank of England

15 | 17 | 13 | £4

Blackfriars | 194 Fleet St., EC4 (Temple) | 020-7430 2255 | www.fullers.co.uk
Set in what once was, indeed, the Bank of England in Blackfriars, this "historic" pub/restaurant is "busy in the early evenings" with "fraternities" of "well-paid" "suits", as it's a good place to "take clients" after "closing a deal"; "citified" it may be, but the "roomy" interior, "small garden area out back" and overall "cheerful" vibe make up for it.

Old Thameside Inn

– | – | – | M

South Bank | Pickfords Wharf | 1 Clink St., SE1 (London Bridge) | 020-7403 4243 | www.mbplc.com
"Watch London from Sir Christopher Wren's lookout" (this is reportedly where he viewed the Great Fire of 1666 as it ravaged the city over the river) at this South Bank pub; today, being slap-bang next to the Golden Hinde and a short stroll from Tate Modern and Borough Market, there's no denying it's "Touristville", but the "good outside area" makes it a decent suds choice for the locals too, especially in summer.

☑ O'Neill's

16 | 14 | 16 | £8

Bloomsbury | 73-77 Euston Rd., NW1 (King's Cross) | 020-7255 9861
Covent Garden | 14 New Row, WC2 (Covent Garden) | 020-7557 9831
Covent Garden | 40 Great Queen St., WC2 (Holborn) | 020-7242 5560
Blackfriars | 31 Houndsditch, EC3 (Liverpool St.) | 020-7397 9841
Blackfriars | 65 Cannon St., EC4 (Cannon St./Mansion House) | 020-7653 9951
City | 64 London Wall, EC2 (Liverpool St./Moorgate) | 020-7786 9231
Highgate | 87 Muswell Hill Broadway, N10 (Highgate) | 020-8883 7382
Earl's Court | 326 Earl's Court Rd., SW5 (Earl's Ct.) | 020-7244 5921
Wandsworth | 66 The Broadway, SW19 (Wimbledon) | 020-8545 9931
Shepherd's Bush | 2 Goldhawk Rd., W12 (Goldhawk Rd./Shepherd's Bush) | 020-8746 1288
www.oneills.co.uk
Additional locations throughout the London area
"Handy and predictable", this chain of "traditional Irish pubs" that specialises in "good beer" and "hearty food" gets "noisy" with "afterwork" "groups" and "crowded when there are matches on TV"; while a few fume they're "tired", "fake" and "best to avoid", others shrug there's "nothing wrong with them for a pint."

Paper

17 | 17 | 12 | £8

Soho | 68 Regent St., W1 (Piccadilly Circus) | 020-7439 7770 | www.paperclublondon.com
Opinion is divided on this "high-profile" Soho nightclub: some claim its "A-list parties" can be "brilliant" with "celebrities" and other "young Hollywood types" lounging on the leather sofas and keeping eyes on each other via the mirrored walls; those who don't "have access to the VIP area", however, call the crowd "cheesy" and the space "too crowded", further griping of "extremely rude" staff and "outrageously expensive" tabs.

Perseverance, The

▽ 15 | 12 | 17 | £5

Bloomsbury | 63 Lambs Conduit St., WC1 (Russell Sq.) | 020-7405 8278
"Avoiding" the "trend of making every pub into a bar", this "average" Bloomsbury venue – which sports "shabby" flock wallpaper and deer heads – encourages local legal eagles to "skive from the office", especially "in the summer" when they can "sit outside"; during "peak" evening hours, it's often "crowded" with a "noisy" "young crowd."

☑ Pitcher & Piano

15 | 14 | 16 | £7

Holborn | 42 Kingsway, WC2 (Holborn) | 020-7404 8510
Soho | 69 Dean St., W1 (Tottenham Court Rd.) | 020-7434 3585
City | 200 Bishopsgate, EC2 (Liverpool St.) | 020-7929 5914
City | 28 Cornhill, EC3 (Bank) | 020-7929 3989
Tower Bridge | The Arches, 9 Crutched Friars, EC3 (Tower Hill) | 020-7480 6818
Islington | 68 Upper St., N1 (Angel) | 020-7704 9974
Fulham | 871 Fulham Rd., SW6 (Parsons Green) | 020-7736 3910
Richmond | 11 Bridge St., TW9 (Richmond) | 020-8332 2524
www.pitcherandpiano.com
Additional locations throughout the London area
A chain that divides reviewers, these outposts are "relaxing", "reasonably priced" spots for the City's "preppy contingent" to "unwind" or watch a "rugby match"; but with such "bland, soulless" decor and "uninspired, expensive drinks", critics cry "if you live in London, why go here?"

Plan B

17 | 16 | 15 | £5

Brixton | 418 Brixton Rd., SW9 (Brixton) | 020-7733 0926 | www.plan-brixton.co.uk
A "relaxed and funky atmosphere" and a "great Saturday night crowd" make this Brixton dance club and bar "well worth a visit"; DJs spin an "excellent playlist" from hip-hop to soul to disco to "trance and hard house", all for a "trendy" crowd sipping creative cocktails; even if a few say this one "needs more staff", it comes "well recommended."

Player, The

21 | 20 | 19 | £8

Soho | 8 Broadwick St., W1 (Oxford Circus/Tottenham Court Rd.) | 020-7494 9125
The drinks are the stars at this "small and funky", below-ground Soho sister bar to Milk and Honey with a "great vibe" and "genuinely passionate" staff that "know what they're doing"; a "sexy crowd" and a "lively atmosphere" lead champions to cheer "this place rocks."

Porterhouse

19 | 18 | 14 | £5

Covent Garden | 21-22 Maiden Ln., WC2 (Covent Garden) | 020-7379 7917 | www.porterhousebrewco.com
The main selling point of this Covent Garden branch of the Irish microbrewery chain is the "superb" selection of stouts, ales and lagers brewed on-site, which can be sampled on a "taster tray"; though it's "vast", the proximity to touristland means it's "busy", so you'll have to "fight your way" into the "nooks and crannies" or "stand outside" in summer.

Princess Louise

20 | 22 | 16 | £5

Bloomsbury | 208 High Holborn, WC1 (Holborn) | 020-7405 8816
Look past the ordinary exterior because this "gem" of a pub in an "otherwise thirsty part of town" (namely just north of Holborn) has a "fan-

tastic", "lovingly maintained" interior of "high Victorian excess" (lots of cut glass and gilt mirrors, decorated tiles and ornate plasterwork); a member of the Sam Smith's chain of pubs, it's "one of London's treasures" with "excellent bitter" along with its "historic" "charm."

Prospect of Whitby
22 | 21 | 19 | £5

Wapping | 57 Wapping Wall, E1 (Wapping) | 020-7481 1095

"Historic appeal" is the draw at this circa-1520 riverside pub in Wapping where the likes of Pepys, Dickens and Henry VIII once pulled back a pint; though some locals still like to spend a "lazy Sunday afternoon" being transported to the "days of yore", others are saddened this "unique" "landmark" has become a "tacky tourist destination."

Purple Bar at the Sanderson
22 | 23 | 18 | £9

Fitzrovia | Sanderson Hotel | 50 Berners St., W1 (Tottenham Court Rd./Oxford Circus) | 020-7300 1444 | www.morganshotelgroup.com

Make sure you "dress sexy or they'll sit you out of sight" at this "sophisticated" Ian Schrager hot spot in Fitrovia's Sanderson Hotel that's done up in a riot of lavenders; "tiny" it may be, but it's also "swish" and so "it" that you might not get in (theoretically, it's for guests or those on a guest list), so when you do, find a spot beneath the purple-etched Venetian mirrors and order the "most expensive martini ever."

Queen's Larder
∇ 18 | 15 | 17 | £5

Bloomsbury | 1 Queen Sq., WC1 (Holborn/Russell Sq.) | 020-7837 5627

"Nothing beats an old queen" rave royalists of this "small" Bloomsbury boozer, another well-preserved Victorian with "atmosphere and style" (downstairs, at least – "upstairs", "it loses" it); though bar staff can swing between "friendly" and "stuck up", there's usually enough "fun" to be had to "impress" out-of-towners.

NEW Raan
- | - | - | M

Greenwich | O2 Arena | 11 Peninsula Sq., SE10 (North Greenwich) | 020-7015 1867 | www.theo2.co.uk

From the folks behind Cinnamon Club comes this Indian-themed bar in the newly revamped gig and exhibition venue O2 (formerly known as the Millennium Dome) in Greenwich; spicy kebabs and other bar snacks are washed down with tropical cocktails in a soothing space boasting lots of greenery and a water feature, plus outdoor seating.

NEW Rake, The
- | - | - | E

Borough | 14A Winchester Walk, SE1 (London Bridge) | 020-7407 0557 | www.utobeer.co.uk

Although it's one of London's smallest pubs – outdoor seating area notwithstanding – this newcomer beside Borough Market proffers an enormous array of beers (over 100 bottled, as well as an ever-changing selection on tap) to quench the thirst of shoppers and local workers; there's no danger of running out either, as it's owned by the same people as the Utobeer shop, so a fresh supply is always nearby.

Red Bar
21 | 20 | 20 | £8

Mayfair | Grosvenor House Hotel | 111 Park Ln., W1 (Marble Arch) | 020-7499 6363

"Successful clientele sipping champagne" and exuding "typical Mayfair upscale charm" are what's to be found at this "popular" bar in

the Grosvenor House, where "great service" and "tasteful" crimson decor help create "thoroughly enjoyable nights"; even those who feel it's all "out of their league" won't hesitate to throw on the finery "when invited."

Revolution
14 | 14 | 11 | £5

Soho | 2 St. Annes Ct., W1 (Piccadilly Circus/Tottenham Court Rd.) | 020-7434 0330
Clapham | 95 Clapham High St., SW4 (Clapham Common) | 020-7720 6642
www.revolution-bars.co.uk

"Vodka, vodka and more vodka" in an "extensive selection" of "flavoured shots" and "sweet concoctions" draw "sociable" crowds to these "spacious", "convenient" "carbon copies" from the national brand; but they're "only useful for getting tanked" in a hurry declare counter-revolutionaries who've been "let down by slow staff", "overcrowding" and "seats and tables invariably covered with spills" one too many times.

☑ Rivoli Bar at the Ritz
25 | 24 | 25 | £15

St. James's | Ritz Hotel | 150 Piccadilly, W1 (Green Park) | 020-7493 8181 | www.theritzlondon.com

"It's the Ritz", so you can expect nothing less than "beautiful people" being "pampered" in "low-lit luxurious fabulousness" out of a "James Bond movie" at this "intimate" St. James's hotel bar; the "glamorous, glitzy" "art deco" decor ("a little Lalique here, a little exotic inlaid wood there") and "spot-on service" add to an experience that's "delightful in every way" – "and the cocktails aren't bad" either; just "be sure to be properly dressed" and "have a full wallet."

Rockwell, The
21 | 21 | 20 | £11

Piccadilly | Trafalgar Hilton | 2 Spring Gdns., SW1 (Charing Cross) | 020-7870 2959 | www.thetrafalgar.hilton.com

"If you're a bourbon drinker", then "you've found heaven" when you wander into this "cool bar" in the Trafalgar Hilton, where a "fantastic array" of "imaginative cocktails" made with "a spectacular selection of whiskies" are the "trendy" quaffs of choice; "a sense of calm" prevails in the "marble, glass and leather"–bedecked space (which is "never too crowded", by the way), making it a "special" place to "escape the chaos of London's crowded streets."

☑ Ronnie Scott's
25 | 21 | 20 | £9

Soho | 47 Frith St., W1 (Leicester Sq.) | 020-7439 0747 | www.ronniescotts.co.uk

"Hot, crowded" "subpar food", "sloppy service" – "none of that matters as soon as you hear the first notes" blown at this "historic" Soho "jazz-lover's mecca" where every act, "famous or not", is "worthy of a listen"; though some still complain that it's "lost a little of its soul" "after a recent refurb" and "the demise of poor Ronnie", most cheer it's "looking good" and remains "one of the coolest places in the world."

☑ Royal Oak, The
- | - | - | ∎

Borough | 44 Tabard St., SE1 (Borough) | 020-7357 7173

This classic neighbourhood corner pub on a backstreet in Borough is owned by the Sussex brewer Harvey's, and stocks a range of their ales along with others; set in a well-preserved Victorian room decorated with pictures of old staff and beer-related knickknacks, it draws a loyal

after-work crowd, plus there's a pleasant dining room upstairs, open Thursday to Saturday evenings and for Sunday lunch; historians and lit lovers will note it's on the street where Chaucer's pilgrims set off on *The Canterbury Tales.*

Salt Whisky Bar and Dining Room   ▽ 17 | 17 | 17 | £8

Marylebone | 82 Seymour St., W2 (Marble Arch) | 020-7402 1155 | www.saltbar.com

Occupying what's "not a predictable location for an upscale drinking destination", this Marylebone "whisky bar" proffers "so much" scotch (the "shelves are lined with bottles"), you'll hardly "know where to begin"; while the interior beckons with "warm black walnut", "candlelight and cool lounge music", some say "the tacky new sign out front and velvet rope ruin it" – which may explain reports that some nights it's "empty but for some people watching football on TV."

Sam's Brasserie & Bar   20 | 19 | 21 | £6

Chiswick | Barley Mow Ctr. | 11 Barley Mow Passage, W4 (Turnham Green) | 020-8987 0555 | www.samsbrasserie.co.uk

Most find this bar attached to the Modern European brasserie from celebrity TV chef Rick Stein a "welcome addition to Chiswick"; if a few feel the "former paper factory" is "too cold", many say it "never disappoints" thanks to a "good atmosphere" bolstered by "to-die-for" cocktails like the "lemon and vanilla martini."

Seven Stars   20 | 18 | 20 | £6

Holborn | 53 Carey St., WC2 (Holborn/Temple) | 020-7242 8521

"In the Ancient Pubs division" ("400 years and counting"), this "low-ceilinged" "barrister's favourite" in Holborn places near the top, as it's "lovely and comfortable" enough to attract "merry groups" that always keep it "packed"; "outstanding character and charm" come via "redoubtable" publican Roxy Beaujolais and her famous cat, Tom Paine, who "wears a chorister's ruff and often relaxes on the bar"; P.S. "great" Traditional British "food in generous proportions" is also offered.

NEW 1707 Wine Bar   20 | 19 | 20 | £7

Piccadilly | Fortnum & Mason | 181 Piccadilly, W1 (Piccadilly Circus) | 020-7734 8040 | www.fortnumandmason.co.uk

Located in the basement of quintessentially quaint Piccadilly department store Fortnum & Mason, this "refined", "typically British" and "newly renovated" (courtesy of David Collins) spot is perfect for "brunch" or refuelling before or after "shopping"; for libations, they serve anything from the wine department with minimal corkage, and the nosh (think "fish 'n' chips" and "highlander eggs") is "yummy" – albeit somewhat "expensive."

Sherlock Holmes   22 | 20 | 19 | £7

Piccadilly | 10 Northumberland St., WC2 (Charing Cross/Embankment) | 020-7930 2644

Although it's miles from the fictional detective's Baker Street home, mystery lovers still find this "small", "funny", "kitschy" pub an "elementary" choice, as it's chockablock with "Sherlock Holmes stuff"; if you're not a traveller, however, Piccadilly locals advise you "paste a sign on your forehead that says 'tourist'" before going so that "you shall fit right in."

	APPEAL	DECOR	SERVICE	COST

Shochu Lounge ▽ 21 | 21 | 18 | £8

Fitzrovia | Roka | 37 Charlotte St., W1 (Goodge St.) | 020-7580 9666 |
www.shochulounge.com

Snuggled below much-fancied Japanese restaurant Roka in Fitzrovia, this
"hip" bar offers long sake and shochu lists as well as "wickedly different"
"cocktails with an Asian spin" that are "gorgeous"; local media sorts
and "wannabe models" keep the "cool" subterranean space – a mishmash of rustic wooden bar, plush red banquettes and industrial
accents – "loud", while the "great snacks" keep the crowd sated.

☑ Sketch 22 | 26 | 18 | £14

Mayfair | 9 Conduit St., W1 (Oxford Circus) | 0870-777 4488 |
www.sketch.uk.com

Somewhere between "baroque surrealism" and "space-age" "outland-
ishness" lies this "opulent" Mayfair bar/restaurant/gallery that's a work
of "modern art" in itself (you "must see" the "strange" pod toilets); here,
a "trendy crowd" of "sybarites" sip "delicious", "overpriced" drinks
amidst works that "inspire" – of course, a contingent of "pretension"-
spotters slag it as only "for those who value style over substance."

NEW Skylon – | – | – | E

South Bank | Royal Festival Hall | Belvedere Rd., SE1 (Waterloo) |
020-7654 7800 | www.skylonrestaurant.co.uk

The new bar in the Royal Festival Hall building on the South Bank, this
comfortable spot is both modern and a celebration of the '50s; there's
a list of retro cocktails (think sidecars, Manhattans and mint juleps),
and a seasonally changing selection of martinis, plus the location
means a view of the bridge and the north bank that's especially
spectacular at night.

☑ Slug and Lettuce 16 | 15 | 16 | £8

Mayfair | 19-20 Hanover St., W1 (Oxford Circus) | 020-7499 0077
Piccadilly | 14 Upper St. Martin's Ln., WC2 (Leicester Sq.) | 020-7379 4880
Soho | 80-82 Wardour St., W1F (Piccadilly Circus) | 020-7437 1400
City | 9 Stoney Ln., E1 (Liverpool St.) | 020-7626 4994
Canary Wharf | 30 S. Colonnade, E14 (Canary Wharf) | 020-7519 1612
Borough | 32-34 Borough High St., SE1 (London Bridge) | 020-7378 9999
South Bank | 5 Chicheley St., SE1 (Waterloo) | 020-7803 4790
Islington | 1 Islington Green, N1 (Angel) | 020-7226 3864
Clapham | 4 St. John's Hill, SW11 (Clapham Junction B.R.) | 020-7924 1322
Fulham | 474-476 Fulham Rd., SW6 (Fulham Broadway) | 020-7385 3209
www.slugandlettuce.co.uk
Additional locations throughout the London area

"Booze aplenty" and a "good reputation" keep this "ubiquitous" "chain
found all over London" "always busy" with "too-young and under-
dressed" types, "recent university leavers", "business" colleagues and
everything in between; though some say its "contemporary" design "predictably lacks character" and decry the "meat-market" atmosphere late
in the evening, it's "as good a place as any for an after-work pint."

Smiths of Smithfield 20 | 18 | 16 | £7

Clerkenwell | 67-77 Charterhouse St., EC1 (Barbican/Farringdon) |
020-7251 7950 | www.smithsofsmithfield.co.uk

"Industrial" design rarely feels as "cosy" as it does at this four-storey
bar/eatery next to the Smithfield meat market in Clerkenwell, where

"leather easy chairs and sofas" prove as "cool" as they are comfy; though some gripe about the "overly aggressive" "City types" that show up during the week, it can be "mellow at the weekend" with crowds of "laid-back hip people"; P.S. hit the roof deck for "amazing views" of the area.

☑ Smollensky's | 17 | 17 | 17 | £10 |

Covent Garden | 105 The Strand, WC2 (Charing Cross/Covent Garden) | 020-7497 2101

Canary Wharf | Canary Wharf | 1 Reuters Plaza, E14 (Canary Wharf) | 020-7719 0101

Tower Bridge | Hermitage Wharf | 22 Wapping High St., E1 (Wapping) | 020-7680 1818

Hammersmith | Bradmore Hse. | Queen Caroline St., W6 (Hammersmith) | 020-8741 8124

www.smollenskys.co.uk

"Decent but not special" seems to be the consensus regarding this "reliable" small chain of American-style bars and grills that are "always very busy", whether with "local business crowds" for weekday "happy hours" or at the weekend with "rowdy, randy" folks "who've had too much to drink"; indeed, those who have no interest in "watching young men and women behaving badly" amidst surroundings that can feel "a bit down at heel" "go elsewhere."

Social, The | 18 | 14 | 16 | £6 |

Fitzrovia | 5 Little Portland St., W1 (Oxford Circus) | 020-7636 4992 | www.thesocial.com

"Good fun" is to be had at this drink-and-eat spot with a "close-to-everything location" just north of Oxford Street in Fitzrovia, where live "music nights" ("often free, so you can't go wrong") and "interesting DJs" make it "feel like a grown-up student bar"; locals also consider it an option for "great cocktails" "after-work or pre-party", which means it "can get very crowded" – some even say "squashed."

☑ Spaniard's Inn | 23 | 20 | 18 | £5 |

Hampstead | Spaniards Rd., NW3 (Hampstead) | 020-8731 6571

Once a staging post for the highwayman Dick Turpin, this "place to chill" by Hampstead Heath is a "historic-feeling" destination "pre- or post"-concerts at Kenwood House or for "a pint on a spring day" in the "fabulous beer garden"; it may be "off the beaten track", but it's "pleasant" enough to justify the "drive" or the "take-your-life-into-your-own-hands" walk "along the highway" from the tube.

Stringfellows | 19 | 17 | 17 | £14 |

Covent Garden | 16-19 Upper St. Martin's Ln., WC2 (Leicester Sq.) | 020-7240 5534

The Wardour

NEW Soho | 201-203 Wardour St., WC2 (Oxford Circus) | 020-7684 2020 | www.stringfellows.com

"Fun and lively", this classic Covent Garden strip club, and its newer Soho sibling, The Wardour, wins many fans who don't mind "spending lots of cash" since it's "always a good value for the money"; even if some say it's "seedy", it "attracts rock stars" and "bankers" so there's "great people-watching" along with "the most famous lap dancers" – just remember "if you're young" you'll fit in better.

	APPEAL	DECOR	SERVICE	COST

Taman Gang
▽ 19 | 22 | 17 | £10

Mayfair | 141 Park Ln., W1 (Marble Arch) | 020-7518 3160 | www.tamangang.co.uk

Sultry lighting, luxe banquettes, carved-limestone walls and Kama Sutra-themed carvings in the loos create the "funky ambience" found at this subterranean Indonesian-themed nightspot/restaurant in Mayfair; the "small bar" and lounge are "great places to hang out" and sample the exotic, albeit "pricey", cocktails, sake and "decent" Pan-Asian nibbles.

Ten Bells, The
19 | 15 | 14 | £4

Spitalfields | 84 Commercial St., E1 (Aldgate East/Liverpool St.) | 020-7366 1721

Have a drink while following "in the footsteps of Jack the Ripper's victims" at this "classic" Spitalfields boozer – it's where the infamous slayer went to pick his prey; though the interior is listed as a landmark, it's "shabby" (at least the "wall tiles are beautiful"), but if you're a "Ripperologist", you'll probably enjoy its "fun" "historic" "character", even if only "for a quick pint" – "hopefully, it won't be your last."

333 Mother Bar
15 | 12 | 13 | £4

Shoreditch | 333 Old St., EC1 (Old St.) | 020-7739 5949 | www.333mother.com

"There's nothing quite like going home with some 333 sludge on your high-heels" reminisce revellers who have indulged in this three-floor "institution" of a Hoxton dive club (it "looks like someone's living room") whose "up-for-it crowd" and "really great DJs" guarantee things'll get "hot and sweaty"; for better or worse, it's "sleazy and scuzzy", but ravers rant it's "the best place to get a drink at 4 AM."

⚡ Tiger Tiger
15 | 15 | 13 | £9

Piccadilly | 29 The Haymarket, SW1 (Piccadilly Circus) | 020-7930 1885 | www.tigertiger.co.uk

"What a zoo!" – this "big, brash" Piccadilly "meat market" is "perennially packed" with "desperate tourists", "large groups of males" who've been "bounced at all the fancy places" and other "young drunk things" "of all ethnicities" "picking each other up"; the "cavernous" space features five distinctly decorated bars, a restaurant and dance club, all playing "different" "loud" music ("mostly hip-hop, R&B and some house"); P.S. "get there before 10" to avoid the cover charge.

Toucan, The
▽ 16 | 13 | 18 | £4

Soho | 19 Carlisle St., W1 (Tottenham Court Rd.) | 020-7437 4123
Fitzrovia | 94 Wimpole St., W1 (Bond St./Oxford Circus) | 020-7499 2440
www.thetoucan.co.uk

This Irish duo in Soho and Fitzrovia is known for serving "excellent Guinness" in environments that are homages to the black stuff; after-workers can often be found enjoying some "good bar snacks", "a drink and a chat" with "friendly staff" that "remember the regulars" – it's just a "shame there isn't much seating" and they "lack in atmosphere."

Trader Vic's
18 | 18 | 18 | £10

Mayfair | Hilton Park Ln. | 22 Park Ln., W1 (Hyde Park Corner) | 020-7208 4113 | www.tradervicslondon.com

"You gotta love the kitsch" at this tiki bar in Mayfair's Hilton on Park Lane, a "worthy outlet" of the original "home of the mai tai" in San

boozer for its "amazing" beers (including a rotating selection of traditional varieties from around the country and Adnams Bitter); "great sandwiches, regular jazz nights", "superb Thursday night quizzes" "and even a cricket team" further make it "worth the effort", as do "welcoming" staff.

❷ Whisky Bar, The
23 | 21 | 21 | £13

Mayfair | Athenaeum Hotel | 116 Piccadilly, W1 (Green Park) | 020-7499 3464 | www.athenaeumhotel.com

"All of the Scottish highlands" are seemingly tucked into this "one small place", the "quiet but elegant", old-school-English bar at the Athenaeum Hotel in Mayfair, which stocks "the best pure single-malt collection" many "have seen" (over 150); but you don't have to be a scotch aficionado to enjoy it, as "educated staff" are on hand to assist in "sipping selections" from the "incredible inventory."

❷ Yauatcha
24 | 25 | 20 | £11

Soho | 15 Broadwick St., W1 (Piccadilly Circus) | 020-7494 8888

Although best known as Alan 'Hakkasan' Yau's "homage to dim sum", this Soho restaurant also hits the spot for "amazing" "premium-priced" cocktails; table service can "perturb" (you're given an "allotted time", and if you linger, they activate "the ejector seat"), so maybe it's best to "chill" at the "dark and mysterious" "basement bar" with the rest of the "hip and trendy" scene-makers.

Ye Olde Cheshire Cheese
24 | 22 | 20 | £6

Blackfriars | 145 Fleet St., EC4 (Blackfriars) | 020-7353 6170

"Yes, it's full of tourists", as well as "lawyers, accountants" and "investment bankers" enjoying inexpensive after-work pints ferried by "friendly bartenders", but this ancient Blackfriars "historical" "time warp" "genuinely deserves the attention"; its labyrinth of "cavernous" rooms, "low-ceilinged" "nooks" ("if you're over 6-ft. tall", watch out!) and "blazing fires" in winter gives it an "olde-worlde feel", and the "food is surprisingly good" too ("try the pies").

Ye Olde Mitre
▽ 26 | 21 | 22 | £5

City | 1 Ely Ct., EC1 (Chancery Ln./Farringdon) | 020-7405 4751

"If you can find" this "quaint" "hidden gem" that's ostensibly in City (ask a "friendly" server why it's technically not), you really "deserve a pint" of the "great beer" – and some famous "toasties" to boot; it "oozes history" (a cherry tree that was once allegedly Elizabeth I's maypole still resides within) and "brims with atmosphere", making it "a must on your pub crawl", but like many spots of this ilk, "tall people should bring a hard hat."

Zebrano
▽ 15 | 14 | 14 | £5

Soho | 14-16 Ganton St., W1 (Oxford Circus) | 020-7287 5267 | www.zebrano-bar.com

Many find this bi-level nightclub, all deep-red with padded walls and animals prints throughout, "superb" "to start or finish off" the evening, thanks in part to decently priced cocktails, a full menu of eats and "hot waitresses"; for others, though, it's just a "dull identikit Soho bar" whose "music could be improved."

SHOPPING

Shopping

With its diverse mix of department stores, hip boutiques, authentic street markets, glossy designer shops and high street retailers, London is arguably the most eclectic shopping capital of the world – and one for all budgets. Modern megastores sit alongside traditional shops that are so established they've become part of the city's cultural heritage, while new and exciting places continue to open. It's all surprisingly easy to navigate if you bear a few things in mind.

EARLY BIRDS GET THE WORM: Although many London stores are fairly traditional in their opening and closing hours, call ahead to confirm. Most boutiques close at either 6 or 6:30 PM weekdays, with late-night hours (until 7 or 8 PM) offered in the West End and Mayfair every Thursday, and in Chelsea and Knightsbridge every Friday. Many are closed on Sundays. But department stores tend to have longer hours during the week and stay open on Sundays. Selfridges, in particular, is a good place to do late-day shopping, as it's open until 9 PM on weekdays.

WEEKEND WARY: Try to avoid shopping in Central London on the weekends – especially around Christmas – as the crowds can be overwhelming, the staff overworked and the queues extremely long. Since the introduction of a congestion charge in this area (requiring vehicles entering to pay £8 a day during the week), many locals save trips to Central London for the weekends. That makes areas like Oxford Street particularly busy on Saturdays and Sundays.

SET YOUR SIGHTS ON SALES: You can pick up fantastic bargains at the end-of-season sales in December/January and June/July, so a shopping-focused trip timed around these dates is likely to be a success. Various newspapers and Web sites publish lists of sales dates – make sure you get there on the first day before the best items are sold and the stores become unbearably messy. The Harrods sale is particularly popular and often launched by a celebrity who opens the doors to waiting crowds. Some shops now hold mid-season promotions as well, so it's worth asking if one is imminent before you make a major purchase.

TAXING TIMES: While the VAT (Value Added Tax) of 17.5% is charged on most consumer goods (with some exceptions), cash-crunched tourists from non-EU countries can reclaim it. Remember to ask for the appropriate forms before you buy.

Top Quality Ratings

Ratings are to the left of names.

BY CATEGORY

ACCESSORIES

28 Smythson of Bond St.
27 Tod's
26 Furla
25 Lulu Guiness

24 Mulberry

CLOTHING: DESIGNER

29 Chanel
Hermes

HAMPSTEAD

- 25 Petit Bateau
- 22 Kurt Geiger
- 21 Nicole Farhi

KENSINGTON

- 25 MAC Cosmetics
- 22 Kurt Geiger
   Diesel
   Russell & Bromley
- 21 Muji

KNIGHTSBRIDGE

- 29 Loro Piana
   Chanel
   Hermes
- 28 Jimmy Choo
   Christian Louboutin

MARYLEBONE

- 25 Neal's Yard Remedies
   L'Artisan Parfumeur
   Selfridges
- 24 Divertimenti
   Mulberry

MAYFAIR

- 29 Loro Piana
   Brioni
   Chanel
   Asprey
   Harry Winston

NOTTING HILL

- 28 Smythson of Bond St.
- 25 Petit Bateau
   Neal's Yard Remedies
   Diane von Furstenberg
- 23 Paul Smith

PICCADILLY

- 27 N.Peal
   Penhaligon's
   Fortnum & Mason
- 26 Burberry
   Kilgour French Stanbury

SOHO

- 27 Church's
- 26 Liberty
- 25 Neal's Yard Remedies
   MAC Cosmetics
   Hamleys

SOUTH KENSINGTON

- 29 Chanel
- 27 Issey Miyake
- 24 Victoria & Albert Museum
- 23 Conran Shop
   Paul Smith

ST. JAMES'S

- 28 Dunhill
- 26 Thomas Pink
- 22 Daks
   Russell & Bromley
- 21 Hackett

WESTBOURNE GROVE

- 27 Anne Fontaine
- 26 SPACE.NK apothecary
- 25 Ballantyne Cashmere
   L'Artisan Parfumeur
- 24 Diptyque

WIMBLEDON

- 25 Diane von Furstenberg
- 22 Matches
- 20 Brora

Top Display Ratings

Ratings are to the left of names.

- 28 Harry Winston
- 27 Cartier
   Asprey
   Chanel
   Loro Piana
   Giorgio Armani
   Jimmy Choo
- 26 Christian Louboutin
   Alexander McQueen
   Penhaligon's

   Thomas Goode
   Prada
   Fortnum & Mason
   Gucci
   Harrods
- 25 Louis Vuitton
   Hermes
   Salvatore Ferragamo
   Bottega Veneta
   Jo Malone

Top Service Ratings

Ratings are to the left of names.

26 Asprey
Harry Winston
Penhaligon's
Brioni

25 Jimmy Choo
Giorgio Armani
Garrard
Church's

24 Cartier
Dunhill

Chanel
Christian Louboutin
Kilgour French Stanbury
Anne Fontaine
Thomas Goode

23 Loro Piana
Salvatore Ferragamo*
Fratelli Rossetti
Manolo Blahnik
Kiehl's

Good Values

Accessorize
American Apparel
Body Shop
Boots
Church's
French Sole
Gap
Gap Kids & Baby Gap
Graham & Green
Habitat
Hackett
H & M
Jigsaw
John Lewis
Kew

Marks & Spencer
Massimo Dutti
Miss Selfridge
Molton Brown
Muji
Neal's Yard Remedies
Office
Primark
Peter Jones
Petit Bateau
Reiss
Russell & Bromley
Topman
Topshop
Uniqlo

Shopping

Ratings & Symbols

Quality, Display and **Service** are rated on a 0 to 30 scale. Newcomers or write-ins are listed without ratings.

Cost reflects our surveyors' estimate of each store's price range.

| $\boxed{I}$ Inexpensive | $\boxed{E}$ Expensive |
| $\boxed{M}$ Moderate | $\boxed{VE}$ Very Expensive |

$\boxtimes$ closed on Sunday $\boxed{M}$ closed on Monday
$\not\oplus$ no credit cards accepted

∇ low response | less reliable

NEW **Abercrombie & Fitch** $\boxed{18}$ $\boxed{22}$ $\boxed{18}$ $\boxed{E}$

Mayfair | 7 Burlington Gdns., W1 (Piccadilly Circus) | 020-7297 9400 | www.abercrombie.com

Already a long-established and "reliable name" in the U.S., this Mayfair branch of an "upscale chainlet" with "beautiful sales people wearing and selling beautiful clothes" was welcomed with cries of "finally" when it opened in London this year; despite the "transatlantic price hike", the "busy" and loud "nightclub-style store" is most popular with "preppy youngsters" in search of "tiny-sized clothes not intended for post-puberty", leaving older potential patrons feeling a bit like "grannies at the disco."

Accessorize $\boxed{16}$ $\boxed{18}$ $\boxed{15}$ $\boxed{I}$

Marylebone | 293 Oxford St., W1 (Bond St.) | 020-7629 0038 | www.accessorize.co.uk
Additional locations throughout the London area

Mothers and daughters alike are drawn to this "cheap but chic" Marylebone flagship of a mega-chain store selling "bright and colourful" accessories arranged in a sweet shop–style display; the "trendy" and "diverse selection" of jewellery, bags, belts, scarves, flip-flops, hats and hairclips will let you "update your look" or "explore your inner fashionista" without "breaking the bank" – just don't expect them to last forever.

Adidas Originals Store $\boxed{21}$ $\boxed{19}$ $\boxed{16}$ $\boxed{M}$

Covent Garden | 9 Earlham St., WC2 (Covent Garden) | 020-7379 4042
Soho | 6 Newburgh St., W1 (Oxford Circus) | 020-7734 9976
Adidas Performance Centre

Marylebone | 415-419 Oxford St., W1 (Bond St.) | 020-7493 1886
www.adidas.com

"If you're into sports clothing", this "classic" trio selling sneakers, T-shirts, tracksuits and other men's and women's athletic apparel is "for you"; the cool minimalist display, however, is lost on some who want "a wider range of international items" to rival the "greater selection and sizes" available in the U.S.; N.B. the Performance Centre also sells sporting goods.

	QUALITY	DISPLAY	SERVICE	COST

Agent Provocateur | | – | – | – | M |

Knightsbridge | 16 Pont Street, SW1 (Knightsbridge) | 020 7235 0229 🗷
Soho | 6 Broadwick Street, W1V (Piccadilly Circus) | 020 7439 0229
City | 5 Royal Exchange, EC3 (Bank) | 020 7623 0229 🗷
Notting Hill | 305 Westbourne Grove, W11 (Notting Hill Gate) |
020 7243 1292 🗷
www.agentprovocateur.com
Be prepared to blush when entering this saucy lingerie shop with four decadent London outlets that sell everything from lacy undies to pink fluffy mules, cheeky costumes, seductive perfumes and naughty toys; the graphic displays and boudoir interior set an over-the-top sexy vibe.

Alberta Ferretti 🗷 | | 27 | 23 | 22 | VE |

Knightsbridge | 205-206 Sloane St., SW1 (Knightsbridge) | 020-7235 2349 |
www.albertaferretti.com
"Feminine, floaty" clothes made for "ladies who want to feel like princesses" are the trademark of this high-fashion designer who manages to keep her "great quality" line timeless and flattering; hit her Knightsbridge boutique "during the twice yearly sales" to avoid high prices or check out her less-expensive diffusion line that's also on the premises.

Alexander McQueen 🗷 | | 26 | 26 | 22 | VE |

Mayfair | 4-5 Old Bond St., W1 (Bond St.) | 020-7355 0080 |
www.alexandermcqueen.com
You never know what to expect from this very British designer, "Vivienne Westwood's Duke" and "a true master" of his art who produces "clever" and "chic" men's and women's collections ranging from sharply tailored cuts in tweeds and tartans to floaty floral evening dresses to provocative leather looks; his über-cool Mayfair boutique feels like a contemporary gallery space with soft lighting, curved lines and whitewashed walls.

All Saints | | – | – | – | E |

Covent Garden | 5 Earlham St., WC2 (Covent Garden) | 020-7379 3749
Covent Garden | 57-59 Long Acre, WC2 (Covent Garden) | 020-7836 0901
Marylebone | 12 Great Portland St., W1 (Great Portland St.) | 020-7323 9222
Soho | 6 Fouberts Pl., W1 (Oxford Circus) | 020-7494 3909
Broadgate | 114 Commercial St., E1 (Liverpool St.) | 020-7392 8098
NEW Islington | 1 Camden Walk, N1 (Angel) | 020-7704 6310
Chelsea | 14 Duke of York Sq., SW3 (Sloane Sq.) | 020-7730 0404
Kensington | 22 Kensington Church St., W8 (High St. Kensington) |
020-7938 4466
www.allsaints.co.uk
For a rock 'n' roll spin on British clothes, this hip and "trendy" men and women's chain is where you will find edgy "street wear" and urban sportswear; music blares in the background as shoppers choose from a selection of popular graphic T-shirts and handcrafted day and formalwear, which most maintain lives up to "a saintly standard."

American Apparel | | 16 | 15 | 17 | M |

Soho | 3-4 Carnaby St., W1 (Oxford Circus) | 020-7734 4477
Shoreditch | 123-125 Curtain Rd., EC2 (Old St.) | 020-7012 1112
NEW Notting Hill | 176 Portobello Rd., W11 (Notting Hill Gate) |
020-7243 8499
www.americanapparel.net
"Great basic" T-shirts, sweatshirts and hoodies in "primary rainbow colours" make this chain "very popular"; there's "nothing unusual or

arresting" in the presentation except for those "dang sexy" "pictures of hot models" on the walls; "affordable prices" and the "non-sweat shop" manufacturing policy are what keep fans coming back for more"; N.B. there's a new offshoot scheduled to open on Kensington High Street this summer.

Andrew Martin 🗷

▽ 23 | 25 | 21 | E

South Kensington | 200 Walton St., SW3 (South Kensington) | 020-7225 5100 | www.andrewmartin.co.uk

It's "where the decorators" shop assert aesthetes about this stylish South Kensington home-furnishings store with classic and modern furniture, lighting, "gorgeous fabrics" and Asian-accented accessories; the fact that it's "full of ideas as well as products" make it a "must-go" for natty nesters as well.

Anne Fontaine

27 | 23 | 24 | E

Mayfair | 30 New Bond St., W1 (Bond St.) | 020-7408 2280 🗷
Chelsea | 14 Sloane St., SW1 (Sloane Sq.) | 020-7838 9210
Fulham | 151 Fulham Rd., SW3 (South Kensington) | 020-7584 7703
Westbourne Grove | 176 Westbourne Grove, W11 (Notting Hill Gate) | 020-7229 8200
www.annefontaine.com

Reviewers call this quartet of "specialised" stores – filled with "beautiful blouses that fit like a glove" – a "white shirt heaven" for "fantastic quality" "classics" in both "simple and dressy" looks; even though "the styles don't change much from season to season", they'll certainly "stand the test of time" making them "well worth the investment."

Anya Hindmarch 🗷

23 | 22 | 19 | E

Knightsbridge | 15-17 Pont St., SW1 (Sloane Sq.) | 020-7838 9177
Notting Hill | 63A Ledbury Rd., W11 (Notting Hill Gate) | 020-7792 4427
www.anyahindmarch.com

Although these Knightsbridge and Notting Hill boutiques offer a seasonal line of clothes and accessories from the namesake British designer, it's the "good quality" handbags that are "stylish" "without being over the top" that are the most sought after items; her custom Be-a-Bag line allows you to supply your own photo to create "unique" "personalized" purses that are "the perfect way to keep your memories in sight" and also make "truly special gifts."

Aquascutum

25 | 20 | 20 | E

Piccadilly | 100 Regent St., W1 (Piccadilly Circus) | 020-7675 8200 | www.aquascutum.co.uk

This Regent Street "British staple" has made a "comeback from the wilderness", transforming itself from a "golden oldie" into a luxury "fashion leader" under a newly appointed design team; shoppers single out the "top-grade raincoats" as an "excellent alternative to Burberry", but there's also a complete line of women and men's modern British classics, which should suit if "you're not looking for something too flashy."

NEW Armani Collezioni

26 | 25 | 21 | VE

Mayfair | 114 New Bond St., W1 (Bond St.) | 020-7491 9888 | www.armani.com

A more casual and less expensive alternative to Giorgio Armani's black label, the well-cut collection at this Mayfair shop will "never go

out of style"; the beautifully "tailored" clothing for both men and women leave loyalists asking "why buy a suit anywhere else?"

☑ Asprey ⊠ — 29 | 27 | 26 | VE

Mayfair | 167 New Bond St., W1 (Bond St.) | 020-7493 6767 | www.asprey.com

Recently "revamped, relaunched and renewed", this "quintessentially British" purveyor of luxury goods dating back to 1781 features "unusual", "well-designed" fine jewellery that "oozes luxury by the stone and pound"; scoring the No. 1 spot for Service in the London Survey, the "beautiful", museumlike "mansion of a store" on Mayfair's smart New Bond Street has "polite and helpful" staff who also help you purchase "everything else you dream of" – silver, china, crystal, leather goods, ready-to-wear and accessories – "at prices only the Saudis can afford."

Ballantyne Cashmere ⊠ — 25 | 17 | 20 | E

Mayfair | 153A New Bond St., W1 (Bond St.) | 020-7495 6184
Westbourne Grove | 303 Westbourne Grove, W11 (Notting Hill Gate) | 020-7792 2563
www.ballantyne.it

"Beautiful", "colourful" cashmere sweaters and accessories for men and women is the name of the game at these Notting Hill and Mayfair specialists; "fine" knitwear doesn't come cheap, but fans feel it's "worth every penny for the quality of the wool and the workmanship."

Bally — 24 | 20 | 19 | E

Mayfair | 116 New Bond St., W1 (Bond St.) | 020-7491 7062 | www.bally.com

"Well-made handbags", "very comfy", "durable" "buttery leather shoes" that "wear like a glove" and ready-to-wear are featured at this "reliable" brand with a Mayfair offshoot; the "clean and uncluttered" display allows shoppers to "see what they like and like what they see", albeit at a price.

Bamford ⊠ — - | - | - | E

Chelsea | 169 Draycott Ave., SW3 (South Kensington) | 020-7589 8729 | www.bamford.co.uk

Bamford & Sons

Chelsea | Old Bank | 31 Sloane Sq., SW1 (Sloane Sq.) | 020-7881 8010
Wimbledon | 32 High St., SW1 (Wimbledon) | 020-8946 1814
Notting Hill | 79-81 Ledbury Rd., W1 (Notting Hill Gate) | 020-7792 9350
www.bamfordandsons.com

Well-heeled gents looking for a high-quality modern take on traditional English style will love these pricey lifestyle stores filled with "beautiful" and luxurious men's and boys' clothing like cashmere sweaters and leather jackets, vintage accessories and grown-up toys and gadgets; N.B. the Draycott Avenue branch is devoted to women's clothing and accessories.

B & B Italia — ▽ 26 | 25 | 19 | VE

South Kensington | 250 Brompton Rd., SW3 (South Kensington) | 020-7591 8111 | www.london.bebitalia.com

Chic, contemporary Italian furniture that "you dream of" is on offer at this stylish but slightly "intimidating" South Kensington store that some say sells the "best sofas in the world", along with other sleek

pieces created in collaboration with prestigious designers; just note that such "great" minimalist looks come with maximum price tags.

NEW Betsey Johnson
20 | 20 | 20 | E

Covent Garden | 4-5 Carriage Hall, 29 Floral St., WC2 (Covent Garden) | 020-7240 6164 | www.betseyjohnson.com

Groupies are "grateful" to have "wild Betsey on U.K. shores" and welcome her new Covent Garden shop featuring bright, glam and girlie dresses and separates made from "great fabrics", along with handbags and accessories; wearing her "fantastically eccentric" clothes means it's unlikely you'll ever end up at "the same event wearing the same outfit as someone else."

Blossom
- | - | - | VE

South Kensington | 164 Walton St., SW3 (South Kensington) | 020-7589 7500 | www.blossommotherandchild.com

Celebs and fashion-conscious yummy-mummies-to-be all flock to this adorable albeit expensive South Kensington shop "that's the place" to go "if you need to look your best with a baby due"; they sell their own brand as well as designer labels in a collection that ranges from loungewear to work clothes and evening dresses; they'll also customize status jeans from the likes of James.

Body Shop, The
20 | 19 | 19 | M

Marylebone | 374 Oxford St., W1 (Bond St.) | 020-7409 7868 | www.bodyshop.co.uk
Additional locations throughout the London area

For 20 years it's been "the green choice for cosmetics" claim "environmentally friendly" fans looking for naturally inspired, "reasonably priced" products for themselves or for "last-minute gifts" at this chain; but some surveyors complain that "the concept is getting stale" and the proliferation of "too many stores these days" is turning it into "the McDonald's" of beauty and bath products.

☑ Boots
20 | 16 | 16 | I

Piccadilly | 44-46 Regent St., W1 (Piccadilly Circus) | 020-7734 6126 | www.boots.com
Additional locations throughout the London area

This "dependable", "inexpensive" and "convenient" chemist chain is "a staple of British life", selling such "an excellent range of products" that reviewers claim "if they don't have it, you don't need it"; most "make a beeline" here to "load up on basics" like their in-house brand cosmetics, toiletries and treatments as well as everything from "pills to perfume", vitamin drinks and body butters, leading proponents to proclaim "may they always be everywhere"; P.S. some branches offer "the best lunch on the run value for money in London."

☑ Bottega Veneta 🖄
28 | 25 | 23 | VE

Knightsbridge | 33 Sloane St., SW1 (Knightsbridge) | 020-7838 9394
Mayfair | 15 Old Bond St., W1 (Green Park) | 020-7629 5598
www.bottegaveneta.co.uk

For low-key, "high-quality" designer leather, this "beyond luxurious" Italian fashion house – found in the super-smart shopping destinations of Old Bond Street and Sloane Street – has become a "modern classic" under creative director Tomas Maier; the signature "baske

| | QUALITY | DISPLAY | SERVICE | COST |

weave pattern" is now just one part of the "excellent selection" of exquisitely crafted bags and shoes, plus there's a sophisticated line of ready-to-wear; no wonder sybarites sigh they "make you want to marry rich"; N.B. the Mayfair store sells accessories only.

☑ Brioni ⑤   29 | 25 | 26 | VE

Mayfair | 32 Bruton St., W1 (Bond St./Green Park) | 020-7491 7700 | www.brioni.it

"Elegant to the nth degree" is this Mayfair shop, an offshoot of "the finest maker and purveyor of Italian suits in the world"; those willing to be "very extravagant" will feel "like 007" in "breathtaking bespoke" and "beautiful" off-the-rack menswear, which shouldn't surprise Bond fans, since present and past actors portraying him, namely Daniel Craig and Pierce Brosnan, have had clothing made here; N.B. there's also a women's collection.

Brora   20 | 17 | 18 | E

Marylebone | 81 Marylebone High St., W1 (Baker St.) | 020-7224 5040
Islington | 186 Upper St., N1 (Highbury & Islington) | 020-7354 4246
Chelsea | 344 King's Rd., SW3 (Sloane Sq.) | 020-7352 3697
Wimbledon | 17 High St., SW19 (Wimbledon) | 020-8971 9146 ⑤ Ⓜ
Notting Hill | 66-68 Ledbury Rd., W11 (Notting Hill Gate) | 020-7229 1515
www.brora.co.uk

Classic Scottish cashmere that's "soft as butter" is available in a "large range of colours" at this chain featuring women's and men's clothing, along with bootees and blankets that make "perfect new baby presents"; pragmatists posit "there may be better quality out there but not typically at this price."

Browns   27 | 21 | 21 | VE

Knightsbridge | 6C Sloane St., SW1 (Knightsbridge) | 020-7514 0040
Mayfair | 23-27 S. Molton St., W1 (Bond St.) | 020-7514 0000 ⑤
Browns Focus ⑤
Mayfair | 38-39 S. Molton St., W1 (Bond St.) | 020-7514 0063
Browns Labels for Less ⑤
Mayfair | 50 S. Molton St., W1 (Bond St.) | 020-7514 0052
www.brownsfashion.com

"The Barneys of London" is what constituents call this "well-edited" men's and womenswear duo on South Molton Street and Knightsbridge; it's "always the first to stock cutting-edge designers a season before they hit the big time", along with the "latest and greatest" from well-known names like Balenciaga and Marc Jacobs, so such an "iconic" "one-stop fashion shop" commands "very high prices"; Browns Focus, across the street from the Mayfair flagship, targets a younger audience, although it can be as "intimidating" as its older sister, while Labels for Less is a "bargain-hunter's paradise."

Bulgari ⑤   ▽ 29 | 28 | 27 | VE

Mayfair | 168-169 New Bond St., W1 (Green Park) | 020-7314 9300 | www.bulgari.com

"Elegance without a hint of arrogance" is how surveyors describe shopping at this highly regarded luxury Italian brand selling fine jewellery, watches, perfumes and leather accessories from a prime Mayfair venue; of course, the very grand looking store with sweeping staircases and high ceilings commands equally elevated prices.

	QUALITY	DISPLAY	SERVICE	COST

Bumpsville
`- | - | - | E`

NEW Chelsea | 317 King's Rd., SW3 (Sloane Sq.) | 020-7795 1700
Notting Hill | 33 Kensington Park Rd., W11 (Notting Hill Gate) |
020-7727 1213
www.bumpsville.com

An uplifting experience for pregnant women awaits at these Notting Hill and Chelsea maternity stores with both comfortable and fashion-forward clothing ranging from retro-looking jersey shirt dresses in seasonal prints to humorous slogan tees; Sprogsville, a cheerful collection of babies' and children's clothing, keeps new mother's coming back even after their nine months are up.

☑ Burberry
`26 | 24 | 22 | VE`

Knightsbridge | 2 Brompton Rd., SW1 (Knightsbridge) | 020-7968 0000
Mayfair | 21-23 New Bond St., W1 (Bond St.) | 020-7968 0000
Piccadilly | 165 Regent St., W1 (Piccadilly Circus) | 020-7968 0000
www.burberry.com

"Nothing says London like Burberry" where the "revived" "iconic" clothing and accessories brand "bridges old class and new sass"; the "trademark trenches" and checks are still there as are hats, bags, scarves and shoes, plus there's the hipper "higher-end Prorsum line"; some sniff at the "getting old", "overexposed" looks and "chilling prices", but most urge "bite the bullet and buy a coat" – "they wear like iron" and will "pay for themselves over the decades that you'll own them."

Canali
`26 | 24 | 21 | E`

Mayfair | 122 New Bond St., W1 (Bond St.) | 020-7499 5605 | www.canali.it

The über-privileged may pronounce it the "poor man's Brioni", but this smart Mayfair shop has its own fancy following for "well-made" Italian menswear and accessories at a "premium price"; the Milanese company, which dates back to 1934, is known for its fine fabrics, tailoring and detailing, like buttons that are made from mother-of-pearl or horn.

☑ Cartier 🗗
`27 | 27 | 24 | VE`

Mayfair | 175-176 New Bond St., W1 (Bond St.) | 020-7408 5700
Mayfair | 40-41 Old Bond St., W1 (Green Park) | 020-7290 5150
NEW City | 1 Royal Exchange Courtyard, EC3 (Bank) | 020-7312 6923
Chelsea | 143-144 Sloane St., SW1 (Sloane Sq.) | 020-7312 6930
www.cartier.com

Devotees declare this "timeless and elegant" French luxury brand – now with four branches in and around London – "the king of jewellers"; it may be "super pricey" but not if you consider the "beautiful" baubles, watches and silver *objets* "investments for life and future generations"; "terrific service" makes the whole experience even more pleasant.

Catimini
`▽ 26 | 23 | 20 | E`

Mayfair | 52A S. Molton St., W1 (Bond St.) | 020-7629 8099
Chelsea | 33C King's Rd., SW3 (Sloane Sq.) | 020-7824 8897
www.catimini.com

There's "wonderful, colourful childrenswear" at these Mayfair and Chelsea shops selling "charming, appropriate" kids' clothes "in contrast to the array of adult copycat" collections often shown elsewhere; the "unique", "exquisite" French designs will make you "proud of your offspring's wardrobe" even if the high price "stops you from being able to go out for a while."

	QUALITY	DISPLAY	SERVICE	COST

Celine 🗷

| | 23 | 21 | 22 | VE |

Mayfair | 160 New Bond St., W1 (Bond St./Green Park) | 020-7297 4999 | www.celine.com

Although some say it hasn't been the same since creative director Michael Kors left in 2004, this "very expensive" French luxury label with an offshoot on Bond Street still has a loyal following; you'll find understated but elegant ready-to-wear, and the accessories line, particularly the leather handbags, is a particular "favourite" among ardent admirers.

🗷 Chanel

| | 29 | 27 | 24 | VE |

Knightsbridge | 167-169 Sloane St., SW1 (Knightsbridge) | 020-7235 6631 🗷
Mayfair | 26 Old Bond St., W1 (Green Park) | 020-7493 5040 🗷
South Kensington | 278-280 Brompton Rd., SW3 (South Kensington) | 020-7581 8620
www.chanel.com

For "ultrachic", timeless style that "never goes out of fashion anywhere", this Karl Lagerfeld–driven über-label encompasses everything from "classic" tweed suits and the little black dress to status accessories like the signature quilted handbags, sunglasses, shoes and cosmetics; while the South Kensington branch caters to a slightly younger customer, the service at all three stores is "unparalleled", leaving satisfied shoppers to comment that the "experience merits the price."

Christian Dior

| | 25 | 25 | 23 | VE |

Knightsbridge | 31 Sloane St., SW1 (Knightsbridge) | 020-7235 1357 | www.dior.com

"Bloody wonderful" is how devotees describe designer John Galliano, "who will be known forever" for injecting his own theatrical and opulent style into this old French label; although some "can't afford anything except a lip gloss" at this "beautiful" Knightsbridge boutique, patricians point out the "excellent, lasting quality" means you will be able to "pass your purchases down to your grandkids."

🗷 Christian Louboutin

| | 28 | 26 | 24 | VE |

Knightsbridge | 23 Motcomb St., SW1 (Knightsbridge) | 020-7245 6510 | www.christianlouboutin.fr

The "gorgeous shoes with red soles" displayed at this Knightsbridge boutique are a "girl's dream" since your "legs look long, lean and beautiful" in them – no wonder they've gone from having a "cult following to mass adoration"; in sum, "it's hard to find a sexier" stiletto, leading most to moan they "wish they could afford as many pairs as Posh Spice."

Church's

| | 27 | 21 | 25 | VE |

Soho | 201 Regent St., W1 (Oxford Circus) | 020-7734 2438 | www.church-footwear.com
Additional locations throughout the London area

"Classic", "solid" and "durable" shoes crafted according to British tradition are featured at this Soho flagship, a favourite with "businessmen" looking for "great" footwear with "no frills" or "over-the-top designs"; the "outstanding quality" makes them "worth every penny" to supporters, who maintain "they might as well be handmade."

	QUALITY	DISPLAY	SERVICE	COST

Claire's Accessories

| 12 | 12 | 11 | I |

Marylebone | 108 Oxford St., W1 (Oxford Circus) | 020-7580 5504 | www.claires.co.uk

Additional locations throughout the London area

"No need to worry about breaking the bank" when you head to this Marylebone branch of an accessories chain aimed at tweens and teens looking "for a quick trinket, hair item", handbag or belt; it's as "cheap as chips" so don't be surprised by the quality of the items or the "messy store" whose motto might well be: "buy, use, toss."

Coco Ribbon

▽ | 16 | 20 | 17 | E |

Notting Hill | 21 Kensington Park Rd., W11 (Ladbroke Grove/ Notting Hill Gate) | 020-7229 4904 | www.cocoribbon.com

Some say if you are looking for "all things frilly and lacy", this Notting Hill store stocks it – from girlie clothing, lingerie (knickers studded with Swarovski crystal) and jewellery to cosmetics and candles; still, while everything is for sale, from the pictures on the walls to the shabby chic-style furniture and crystal chandeliers, more tailored types aren't tempted because "it's hard to find something really compelling" here.

Connolly ⌧

| - | - | - | E |

Mayfair | 41 Conduit St., W1 (Oxford Circus) | 020-7439 2510

Don't be fooled by what some call "bland" designs at this smart Mayfair shop since there's a certain understated, polished style to their top-quality leather goods and accessories, and no flashy logos that distract; they're known for handbags, briefcases and wallets, but they also carry iPod cases, cuff links and sunglasses along with a small selection of clothes and cashmere knitwear.

⌧ Conran Shop, The

| 23 | 24 | 18 | E |

Marylebone | 55 Marylebone High St., W1 (Baker St.) | 020-7723 2223
South Kensington | 81 Fulham Rd., SW3 (South Kensington) | 020-7589 7401
www.conran.com

"The best" of "contemporary U.K. design" can be found at Sir Terrance Conran's "trendy" South Ken and Marylebone stores selling "stylish furniture" and "unique home goods" like "cool cookware"; sure, "good quality" is "expensive, but style matters", so even if you're not buying, it's an "iconic" place to find "inspiration" by "ogling" "the stunning displays."

Daisy & Tom

| 25 | 21 | 18 | E |

Chelsea | 181 King's Rd., SW3 (Sloane Sq.) | 020-7352 5000 | www.daisyandtom.com

A "vast" "one-stop shop" for children's "toys, clothing, furniture", books and baby equipment, this "fun" Chelsea store – with the additional attractions of a full-size carousel and puppet shows – will make you "want to be a kid again"; it's "easy to spend long periods of time here" with offspring who adore everything, but it's also "impossible to escape without buying something."

Daks ⌧

| 22 | 18 | 19 | E |

Mayfair | 10 Old Bond St., W1 (Green Park) | 020-7409 4040
St. James's | 101 Jermyn St., SW1 (Piccadilly Circus) | 020-7839 9980
www.daks.com

Watch this space: with a new head designer announced – namely rising star Giles Deacon – this "quality British" clothing label with

branches in Mayfair (men's and women's clothing and accessories) and St. James's (gents only) seems to be heading for a major shake up; it remains to be seen how the existing fans of this "established" "traditional" store will take to the new look; N.B. the Old Bond Street store has just been completely refurbished.

D & G ⊠ | 22 | 25 | 20 | VE |

Mayfair | 53-55 New Bond St., W1 (Bond St.) | 020-7495 9250 | www.dolcegabbana.it

A younger, funkier and edgier version of the main line Dolce & Gabbana, this "very expensive" Italian label is showcased at a Bond Street boutique with loud rock music blaring in the background, making it feel like a pumping nightclub; provocative looks for men and women – think ripped jeans, corsets and see-through tops – keep sexy supporters wanting to "shop till they drop."

Debenhams | 17 | 15 | 16 | M |

Marylebone | 334-348 Oxford St., W1 (Bond St.) | 0844-561 6161 | www.debenhams.com

Surveyors are split over this "large", "old-fashioned" department store chain with a Marylebone flagship: supporters cite "quality basics" and "a large range" of goods, including men's, women's and children's clothing, home furnishings and electronics at "occasional bargain" prices; but critics counter the "middle-of-the-road" merchandise is "dull", the place is a "complete jumble" and the result is "nothing special" shoppingwise.

Designers Guild | 25 | 22 | 20 | E |

Chelsea | 267-277 King's Rd., SW3 (Sloane Sq.) | 020-7351 5775 | www.designersguild.com

The displays are "never dull" at this "cool" Chelsea interiors, fabric and wallpaper store where you'll need to "put on your sunglasses" as the "fantastic colours" are "bold enough to brighten up the grey London winter"; the "wonderfully innovative" modern designs from Tricia Guild and other names will "inspire you."

Design Museum Shop | 21 | 21 | 17 | M |

South Bank | Shad Thames, SE1 (London Bridge/Tower Hill) | 020-7940 8753 | www.designmuseum.org

At this shop within the South Bank museum, the merchandise ranges from "cool design books" to toys, watches and home accessories by megawatt stars like Tord Boontje, Zaha Hadid and Marc Newson; thank god the "hip" "conversation-starter" stuff is displayed in an "eye-catching" way, especially "considering the name of the museum."

Diane von Furstenberg | 25 | 23 | 21 | E |

🆕 **Wimbledon** | 56 High St., SW19 (Wimbledon) | 020-8944 5995
Notting Hill | 83 Ledbury Rd., W11 (Notting Hill Gate) | 020-7221 1120
www.dvflondon.com

Although the namesake designer makes dresses in a "variety of cuts and colours" that "don't disappoint", it's still her trademark wrap that draws the most attention because "if you have the body" you can just "throw it on and go"; both the Notting Hill and Wimbledon stores carry the complete collection, which includes outerwear, swimwear and accessories.

QUALITY | DISPLAY | SERVICE | COST

Diesel
22 | 21 | 15 | E

Covent Garden | 43 Earlham St., WC2 (Covent Garden) | 020-7497 5543
NEW **Mayfair** | 130 New Bond St., W1 (Bond St.) | 020-7520 7799
Soho | 24 Carnaby St., W1 (Oxford Circus) | 020-7434 3113
Chelsea | 72 King's Rd., SW3 (Sloane Sq.) | 020-7225 3225
Kensington | 38A Kensington High St., W8 (High St. Kensington) |
020-7376 1785
www.diesel.com

With five "intimidatingly trendy" outlets dotted around London, this "fine Italian denim" company lures "urban label lovers" looking for "hip" styles that "fit well" and "look good"; although the "reliable and well-constructed jeans" are what make them "popular with the going out crowd", a few snobs sniff "even my maid has them."

Diptyque
24 | 22 | 23 | E

Westbourne Grove | 195 Westbourne Grove, W11 (Notting Hill Gate) |
020-7727 8673 | www.diptyqueparis.com

Supporters of this Paris-based fragrance house, with over 50 "expensive", "delicious" scents based on nature, single out the "unique candles" that make your "home smell wonderful" and "last forever", but there are also perfumes, bath products and room sprays; the "superb" staff at this Westbourne Grove branch are "knowledgeable, friendly" and "generous with samples."

Disney
18 | 20 | 16 | M

Covent Garden | 9 The Piazza, WC2 (Covent Garden) | 020-7836 5037
Mayfair | 360-366 Oxford St., W1 (Bond St.) | 020-7491 9136
Hammersmith | Broadway Shopping Ctr. | 3 Queen Caroline St., W6
(Hammersmith) | 020-8748 8886
www.disneystore.co.uk

For all things Disney, "look no further" than this trio where you will find a "heavily branded" selection of everything from plush toys, clothing and costumes to stationery and London souvenirs that mouse-mavens maintain make "good inexpensive presents" for the kids; but some sniff that the Covent Garden and Hammersmith stores and displays are so "crowded" it reminds them that "it's a small world after all."

Dispensary, The
- | - | - | E

Soho | 9 Newburgh St., W1 (Oxford Circus) | 020-7287 8145
Notting Hill | 200 Kensington Park Rd., W11 (Notting Hill Gate) |
020-7727 8797
www.thedispensary.net

For almost 20 years, this stalwart has been dispensing "well-made" young designer clothing; the Notting Hill branch features men's labels like Blood & Glitter and sophisticated women's clothing and accessories, while the Soho shop is strictly for chicks, offering "interesting pieces from designers" like Citizens of Humanity.

Diverse
- | - | - | M

Islington | 294 Upper St., N1 (Angel) | 020-7359 8877
Diverse Men
Islington | 286 Upper St., N1 (Angel) | 020-7359 0081
www.diverseclothing.com

Just as the name says, this long-standing Islington boutique stocks a diverse collection of designers, mixing Marc Jacobs and Chloe with

up-and-coming labels, along with a small selection of accessories and shoes – all in a "variety of prices"; further down the road is the menswear store, which some say is among "the best casual retailers in town" for designer jeans and labels like Missoni and Paul Smith.

Divertimenti

| 24 | 20 | 17 | E |

Knightsbridge | 227-229 Brompton Rd., SW3 (Knightsbridge) | 020-7581 8065
Marylebone | 33-34 Marylebone High St., W1 (Baker St.) | 020-7935 0689
www.divertimenti.co.uk

"You get the feeling Nigella Lawson shops here" assert admirers of this Knightsbridge and Marylebone duo for "cooks who love to cook"; you'll find "anything you might want or need to play in your kitchen", from "excellent quality" equipment, gadgets and linens to fine china, crystal and silver; N.B. both branches have small demonstration kitchens and offer cooking classes.

DKNY

| 18 | 17 | 16 | E |

Mayfair | 27 Old Bond St., W1 (Green Park) | 020-7499 6238 | www.dkny.com
Surveyors are split over American designer Donna Karan's younger, more casual and less expensive women's and menswear collection housed in this multilevel glass and aluminium Mayfair store: fans maintain the "au courant fun clothes" are "very popular in England", but the less enthused assert they're "ok, but not something you'd buy for a special occasion", especially given the "rip-off" prices.

Dolce & Gabbana

| – | – | – | VE |

Knightsbridge | 175 Sloane Street, SW1X (Knightsbridge) | 020 7201 0980 🛇
Mayfair | 6-8 New Bond Street, W1S (Green Park) | 020 7659 9000
www.dolcegabbana.com

Worn by the rich, stylish and famous, from Kylie Minogue to Madonna, this stylish Italian brand from the duo of Domenico Dolce and Stefano Gabbana is smartly display in two extravagant stores in Knightsbridge and Mayfair; staples each season include satin corsets, leopard prints, figure-hugging dresses and edgy suits all well-tailored and fashioned from beautiful fabrics.

NEW Donna Karan Collection

| 24 | 21 | 21 | VE |

Mayfair | 46 Conduit St., W1 (Oxford Circus) | 020-7479 7900 | www.donnakaran.com

This "elegant" New York–based designer brings some American chic to women's and men's clothing with "well-cut", "sophisticated" styling that may seem "very expensive" but are "average"-priced "for couture clothing"; the complete collection also includes accessories, hose, fragrance and bedding; post-Survey, the flagship moved from New Bond Street to this landmark townhouse on Conduit Street.

Dover St. Market 🛇

| 24 | 24 | 18 | VE |

Mayfair | 17 Dover St., W1 (Green Park) | 020-7518 0680 | www.doverstreetmarket.com

This "avant-garde" clothing "Narnia for rich people" contains some of the "world's most creative brands" including Azzedine Alaia, Alber Elbaz for Lanvin, Junya Watanabe and Comme des Garçons, whose founder Rei Kawakubo owns the venture; "the wonderfully intimidat-

ing displays" are presented against a "cool" minimalist industrial backdrop of corrugated metal, brick and steel spread over six floors.

Duffer of St. George | 19 | 16 | 14 | E |

Covent Garden | 34 Shorts Gdns., WC2 (Covent Garden) | 020-7836 3722 | www.thedufferofstgeorge.com

This Covent Garden menswear store carries its own brand of "lasts-forever" sportswear, from polo-shirts and T-shirts to hoodies, along with Italian suits, dress shirts and other "cool clothes" at "good value for the money" prices; just beware of the "achingly hip" but "disinterested" staff.

☑ Dunhill | 28 | 24 | 24 | VE |

St. James's | 48 Jermyn St., SW1 (Green Park) | 020-7290 8622 ☒
NEW **Chelsea** | 159 Sloane St., SW1 (Sloane Sq.) | 020-7730 1159
www.dunhill.com

Founded by Alfred Dunhill in 1896, these "top-quality" menswear stores in Chelsea and St. James's "personify English" "gentlemen's style" and are "a great London tradition"; there's a "first-class selection" of bespoke shirts and "jaw droppingly exquisite accessories" like leather goods, luggage and smoking accoutrements, plus colognes – just be sure to "bring all your savings"; N.B. the Jermyn Street branch also boasts a cigar lounge and barber.

Emilio Pucci ☒ | – | – | – | VE |

Knightsbridge | 170 Sloane St., SW1 (Knightsbridge) | 020-7201 8171 | www.emiliopucci.com

This "unmistakably" bold and vibrantly coloured Italian label, now under creative director Matthew Williamson, is as "highly sought after" now by "fashionistas" and celebrities as it was in the '60s; the signature prints at this Knightsbridge offshoot turn up on everything from dresses and bikinis to eyewear and handbags.

Emporio Armani | 23 | 23 | 19 | E |

Knightsbridge | 191 Brompton Rd., SW3 (Knightsbridge) | 020-7823 8818
Mayfair | 51 New Bond St., W1 (Bond St.) | 020-7491 8080
www.emporioarmani.com

Less expensive and more casual than Giorgio's black label but still a "blue-chip brand", this "stylish" men's and women's clothing and accessories line is showcased at these Brompton Road and New Bond Street stores; the "service may not match" the "fashionable" products, but that doesn't keep the collection from being "popular."

Energie | 19 | 20 | 18 | E |

Covent Garden | 47-49 Neal St., WC2 (Covent Garden) | 020-7836 7719
Soho | 31 Great Marlborough St., W1 (Oxford Circus) | 020-7434 3060
Kensington | 42 Kensington High St., W8 (High St. Kensington) | 020-7376 1330
www.energie.it

"Denim that fits like a glove", "original T-shirts" and "hip" jackets, shirts and accessories are on offer at this "stylish" menswear purveyor of an Italian label that's a sibling of Miss Sixty; the result is an "edgy" collection that is "fresh and inspired", but one that won't "break the bank too badly."

	QUALITY	DISPLAY	SERVICE	COST

Erickson Beamon ⊠

— — — M

Belgravia | 38 Elizabeth St., SW1 (Victoria) | 020-7259 0202 | www.ericksonbeamon.com

You'd be forgiven for thinking that you've just walked into a gigantic jewellery box at this small store in Belgravia's Elizabeth Street since it's literally packed full of beautiful bijoux; the two namesake designers – Americans Karen Erickson and Vicki Beamon – are known for their bold, "reasonably priced" costume pieces like chandelier earrings and dramatic chokers that are often inspired by vintage looks.

⊠ Ermenegildo Zegna

28 23 23 VE

Mayfair | 37-38 New Bond St., W1 (Bond St.) | 020-7518 2700 | www.zegna.com

For "perfectly fitted suits" and the "best men's dress shirts" that you could easily "spend a whole month's salary on", the well-heeled hit the Bond Street branch of this "classic" Italian designer label; the tailoring and fabric "quality are amazing", leading loyalists to advise "forget Savile Row and go to Zegna" instead.

Etro ⊠

26 25 22 VE

Mayfair | 14 Old Bond St., W1 (Bond St.) | 020-7495 5767 | www.etro.it

This expensive Italian women's and men's designer label that's known especially for its use of rich colours, fabrics and "gorgeous" trademark paisley prints is "always worth a look"; at its Old Bond Street branch, the dramatic designs turn up on everything from clothing to accessories like handbags and sunglasses.

Fendi ⊠

26 22 22 VE

Knightsbridge | 20-22 Sloane St., SW1 (Knightsbridge) | 020-7838 6280 | www.fendi.com

"There's too much to choose from" wail worshippers of this "beautiful" Italian designer label encompassing "distinctive" men's and women's fashion, furs, leather ("god, handbag heaven") and accessories, plus service is "very attentive" at this Knightsbridge outpost; just remember, *cara*, everything is *caro*.

Fenwick ⊠

22 19 18 E

Mayfair | 63 New Bond St., W1 (Bond St.) | 020-7629 9161 | www.fenwick.co.uk

For a "smaller", "easier to navigate" alternative to the big department stores, this New Bond Street stalwart offers an "interesting" selection of men's and women's clothing, accessories, shoes, cosmetics and housewares all "under one roof"; you can also "grab a spot of lunch" at Carluccio's – "the fun Italian spot in the basement."

Foot Locker

17 14 12 M

Covent Garden | 30-32 Neal St., WC2 (Oxford Circus) | 020-7379 9398
Marylebone | 109 Oxford St., W1 (Tottenham Court Rd.) | 020-7734 5780
Marylebone | 363-367 Oxford St., W1 (Oxford Circus) | 020-7491 4030
Bayswater | Whiteleys Ctr. | 131 Queensway, W2 (Bayswater/Queensway) | 020-7221 3754
www.footlocker-europe.com

It's "a sportsman's heaven" where you'll find "dependable" footwear, including all the "leading brands", for any kind of activity is what supporters say about this chain; but while critics complain about the

"jumbled display", they say that's nothing on the "moody" staff that seem to be either "working there just to get a discount" or "too busy talking to each other" to serve you properly – so try and find the "one employee who actually knows the products."

Formes ▽ 25 | 22 | 25 | E

Covent Garden | 28 Henrietta St., WC2 (Covent Garden) | 020-7240 4777
Mayfair | 33 Brook St., W1 (Bond St.) | 020-7493 2783
Hampstead | 66 Rosslyn Hill, NW3 (Hampstead) | 020-7431 7770
South Kensington | 313 Brompton Rd., SW3 (South Kensington) | 020-7584 3337
www.formes.com

If you "want to dress well while you are pregnant", this quartet of "high-quality" maternity shops that are offshoots of a French chain features a "great selection" of "wonderful styles" that "aren't over the top on pricing"; the staff are also "extremely nice and patient", which helps expectant mothers feel more "relaxed and comfortable."

☒ Fortnum & Mason 27 | 26 | 23 | E

Piccadilly | 181 Piccadilly, W1 (Green Park/Piccadilly Circus) | 020-7734 8040 | www.fortnumandmason.co.uk

"No London trip is complete without a stop" at this 300-year-old "thoroughly British" Piccadilly department store that's known mostly for its "fabled food hall", which is in the midst of an extensive renovation and expansion; the "beautifully displayed" "goodies" include "fragrant teas and coffees", the "best jams", "delicious boxed cookies", chocolates and "amazing cheeses"; you can also "fancy yourself a chum of Bertie Wooster" by "packing (or even purchasing) a picnic hamper"; of course, paying "premium prices " are part of shopping at such an "upper-crust" "grocer to the gentry."

Fratelli Rossetti 26 | 20 | 23 | VE

Knightsbridge | 196 Sloane St., SW1 (Knightsbridge) | 020-7259 6397 | www.rossetti.it

Confused customers "can't understand why everyone isn't wearing" the "classic Italian" shoes sold at this Knightsbridge store; "there's no disputing" that the "high-quality", "beautiful leather" makes for "fashionable" but "comfortable" footwear; N.B. they also sell handbags and small leather goods like wallets.

French Connection 19 | 19 | 16 | M

Marylebone | 396 Oxford St., W1 (Bond St.) | 020-7629 7766 | www.frenchconnection.com
Additional locations throughout the London area

Surveyors are split over this British men's and women's clothing and accessories chain: some "fast and young" fans feel they can find "a good selection" of the "latest frothy" or "edgy fashions" here at this Oxford Street offshoot; but the less enthused assert the collection is "understyled and overpriced", and add they are plain "tired" of that controversial FCUK logo and ad campaign.

French Sole 21 | 17 | 17 | M

Chelsea | 6 Ellis St., SW1 (Sloane Sq.) | 020-7730 3771 | www.frenchsole.com
Ladies looking for "beautiful ballet-style slip-on shoes" in "every colour, fabric and pattern" will find them in this tiny store near Sloane

Square where these "indispensable classics" are both "comfortable and sexy" – especially "the ones that show some toe cleavage"; fans also kick up their heels at the "moderate" prices.

Furla
26	23	22	E

Mayfair | 31 New Bond St., W1 (Bond St.) | 020-7629 9827 Ⓢ
Chelsea | 17 King's Rd., SW3 (Sloane Sq.) | 020-7823 5110
www.furla.com

This "dependable" Italian accessories brand with shops in Mayfair and Chelsea is perfect for those looking for "timeless" "leather products", particularly handbags and shoes, that are "simple" yet "classic"; while the collection "is not cheap, it has all the style of higher priced competitors at more affordable" prices.

Gap
17	16	16	I

Marylebone | 376-384 Oxford St., W1 (Bond St.) | 020-7408 4500 | www.gap.com
Additional locations throughout the London area

Most maintain "you know what you are getting" so "you can't go wrong at this" Bond Street branch of an American chain chock-full of "preppy", "relaxed basics" like T-shirts, sweaters, shorts and jeans; "it's not much different from what you'd find in the States", just "more expensive."

Gap Kids (& Baby Gap)
21	20	17	M

Marylebone | 376-384 Oxford St., W1 (Bond St.) | 020-7408 4500 | www.gapkids.com
Additional locations throughout the London area

If you don't mind "your kid looking like everyone else", this Oxford Street branch of the "colourful and cheerful" chain is the place to find "good quality" "basics" for wee ones that "will last for your second child"; "reasonable" prices and "frequent sales" add to its appeal.

ⓏGarrard Ⓢ
28	25	25	VE

Mayfair | 24 Albemarle St., W1 (Green Park) | 0870-871 8888 | www.garrard.com

As this "impeccable", über-expensive Mayfair company is the British Crown Jeweller, perhaps you best "speak to your bank manager before entering"; dating back to 1735, it's managed to "modernize while keeping its quintessential British roots" by hiring Jade Jagger as creative director to design her own "hip line"; "discreet" staff preside over a luxe setting, with celadon silk-covered walls and leather love seats.

General Trading Company, The
23	24	19	E

Chelsea | 2-6 Symons Street, SW3 (Sloane Sq.) | 020-7730 0411 | www.general-trading.co.uk

For "wedding or hostess gifts", Wasps wend their way to this "Chelsea favourite", a "wonderful place to browse" for "exotic or classic" home accessories; the "tempting" "feast for the eyes" here includes many "unique" items ranging from Asian antiques to modern china.

ⓏGieves & Hawkes
26	21	23	VE

Piccadilly | 1 Savile Row, W1 (Piccadilly Circus) | 020-7434 2001 Ⓢ
Chelsea | 33 Sloane Sq., SW1 (Sloane Sq.) | 020-7730 1777
www.gievesandhawkes.com

If you have to "skimp on food and shelter" to shop at these "traditional" British menswear stores "with an edge" on Savile Row and

QUALITY DISPLAY SERVICE COST

Sloane Square "you'll be glad you did" as "what you buy will hang in your closet long after the final credit card payment has been made"; besides the "prêt a porter" collection, there are "hard-to-resist" "bespoke suits" sold by "gracious and patient" staff.

Gina ⑤   26 | 21 | 20 | VE

Knightsbridge | 189 Sloane St., SW1 (Knightsbridge) | 020-7235 2932
Mayfair | 9 Old Bond St., W1 (Green Park) | 020-7409 7090
www.ginashoes.com

"For the highest heels", "beautiful" "sparkly party shoes" and handbags (many ornamented with crystals), head to these "jewels" in Knightsbridge and Mayfair, where you are "guaranteed to find something" "elegant and stylish" "to match that ball gown or wedding dress"; of course, the "best blingy" accessories are "very expensive."

⑤ Giorgio Armani ⑤   28 | 27 | 25 | VE

Knightsbridge | 37 Sloane St., SW1 (Knightsbridge) | 020-7235 6232 |
www.giorgioarmani.com

"You'll feel stylish just by walking in" to this chic Knightsbridge store where "exquisite, well-cut clothing" by the "original Italian design master" "never disappoints" and is still a favourite with Hollywood A-listers; you might pay a small "fortune" for the ready-to-wear collection, accessories or made-to-measure suits, but "gorgeous" goods and "attentive service" make it worthwhile.

Graham & Green   20 | 18 | 15 | M

Primrose Hill | 164 Regent's Park Rd., NW1 (Chalk Farm) | 020-7586 2960
Chelsea | 340 King's Rd., SW3 (Sloane Sq.) | 020-7352 1919
Notting Hill | 10 Elgin Crescent, W11 (Notting Hill Gate) | 020-7727 9350
Notting Hill | 4 Elgin Crescent, W11 (Notting Hill Gate) | 020-7243 8908
www.grahamandgreen.co.uk

This "tempting" quartet of home-accessories stores "draws you in immediately" with a "quirky" and "eclectic range of urban" goods and gifts sourced from around the world; the "classy and stylish" pieces include Venetian glass mirrors, Moroccan leather poufs and bone-inlay furniture; N.B. the King's Road store also offers clothing and jewellery.

Gucci ⑤   26 | 26 | 22 | VE

Knightsbridge | 18 Sloane St., SW1 (Knightsbridge) | 020-7235 6707
Mayfair | 34 Old Bond St., W1 (Green Park) | 020-7629 2716
City | 9 Royal Exchange, EC3 (Bank) | 020-7623 3626
www.gucci.com

Despite the departure of Tom Ford, this label now under the creative direction of Frida Giannini is still "hip, current and glam" and remains a "must-stop" shop for fashion-forward men and women and "designer handbag junkies"; just remember to bring your "platinum card."

Habitat   20 | 21 | 16 | M

Bloomsbury | 196-199 Tottenham Court Rd., W1 (Tottenham Court Rd.) |
020-7631 3880
NEW **Piccadilly** | 121-123 Regent St., W1 (Piccadilly Circus) |
020-7287 6525
Swiss Cottage | 255 Finchley Rd., NW3 (Swiss Cottage) |
020-7328 3444
Chelsea | 208 King's Rd., SW3 (Sloane Sq.) | 0844-499 1144
Hammersmith | 19-20 Kings Mall, W6 (Hammersmith) | 0844-499 1119

(continued)

Habitat

Kensington | 26-40 Kensington High St., W8 (High St. Kensington) | 020-7795 6055
www.habitat.co.uk

This "old faithful" chain is still "a hip home store" selling "enticing products" like "unusual light fixtures", "trendy glasses and dishes" and "cool" furniture in both modern and traditional styles; "appealing items for urban dwellings" are offered at "reasonable prices", so it's a shame that the staff is so "disinterested."

Hackett

21 | 22 | 20 | E

Covent Garden | 31-32 King St., WC2 (Covent Garden) | 020-7240 2040
Holborn | 20-23 Hatton Hse., EC1 (Holborn) | 020-7405 1767 🗷
Piccadilly | 143-147 Regent St., W1 (Piccadilly Circus) | 020-7494 1855
St. James's | 87 Jermyn St., SW1 (Green Park/Piccadilly Circus) | 020-7930 1300
Broadgate | 117 Bishopsgate, EC2 (Liverpool St.) | 020-7626 7020 🗷
Canary Wharf | 10 Cabot Sq., E14 (Canary Wharf) | 020-7513 0400 🗷
Tower Bridge | 19 Eastcheap, EC3 (Monument) | 020-7626 0707 🗷
Chelsea | 137-138 Sloane St., SW1 (Sloane Sq.) | 020-7730 3331
www.hackett.co.uk

"Good stuff for ruddy good blokes" is the name of the game at this menswear chain selling "traditional" "British staples" with a "unique" updated twist ranging from polo shirts to eveningwear, ascots and the "odd accessory"; while some cite "over-branding", most maintain it's "excellent, especially for the cost."

🔢 Hamleys

25 | 24 | 19 | E

Soho | 188-196 Regent St., W1 (Oxford Circus) | 0870-333 2455 | www.hamleys.com

It might be "cramped", but this world famous Regent Street toy store dating back to 1760 "exudes atmosphere and friendliness"; the "young and young at heart" wander through a "multistorey wonderland" to find "every imaginable" plaything in "every price range", making it a "madhouse" at Christmas that's a "child's dream" and a "parent's nightmare."

H & M

13 | 15 | 12 | I

Bloomsbury | 174-176 Oxford St., W1 (Oxford Circus) | 020-7612 1820
Covent Garden | 27-29 Long Acre, WC2 (Covent Garden) | 020-7395 1250
Knightsbridge | 17-21 Brompton Rd., SW3 (Knightsbridge) | 020-8382 3262
Marylebone | 261-271 Regent St., W1 (Oxford Circus) | 020-7493 4004
Marylebone | 481 Oxford St., W1 (Marble Arch) | 020-7493 8557
Mayfair | 360-366 Oxford St., W1 (Bond St.) | 020-7518 1630
Bayswater | Whiteleys Ctr. | 151 Queensway, W2 (Bayswater/Queensway) | 020-7313 7500
Kensington | 103-111 Kensington High St., W8 (High St. Kensington) | 020-7368 3920
www.hm.com

For "$200 you can get a whole season's wardrobe" at this "cheap and cheerful" "Swedish chain" where – provided you have the "patience" to cope with "the complete chaos in store" – you'll find "inexpensive interpretations of haute couture and basic trends" from the likes of Karl Lagerfeld, Stella McCartney and Madonna; just "don't be too fussy about the quality" as the "surprisingly stylish" clothing is more "wash and toss" than "wash and wear."

	QUALITY	DISPLAY	SERVICE	COST

☒ Harrods
| | 26 | 26 | 22 | VE |

Knightsbridge | 87-135 Brompton Rd., SW1 (Knightsbridge) | 020-7730 1234 | www.harrods.com

Surveyors who vote this enormous Knightsbridge "institution" our London Survey's Most Popular, say it's "part department store, part carnival and part museum" and as much a "cultural experience" as a shopping event; "you can buy anything" from "diamonds to dogs" here, including an "outstanding array" of "cutting-edge" men's and women's fashion and accessories, cosmetics, books and "fabulous" items from the "can't-be-missed food halls"; just "bring money" and beware the "crush of tourists" and "pathetically tacky" tribute to the late Princess Diana and the owner's son, Dodi Al Fayed.

☒ NEW Harry Winston ☒
| | 29 | 28 | 26 | VE |

Mayfair | 171 New Bond St., W1 (Bond St.) | 020-7907 8800 | www.harrywinston.com

"The best jeweller in the world" – favoured by celebrities and the super-rich – finally has a branch in London on Bond Street, where the flawless diamonds, breathtaking stones and elegant watches are so smartly, though "intimidatingly", showcased that our voters deem it the No. 1 for Display among stores in the London Survey; N.B. the top two floors are reserved for private viewings of rare gems.

☒ Harvey Nichols
| | 26 | 24 | 21 | VE |

Knightsbridge | 109-125 Knightsbridge, SW1 (Knightsbridge) | 020-7235 5000 | www.harveynichols.com

Be prepared to do "some serious wallet damage" at this "expensive" but "hip" Knightsbridge department store affectionately known as Harvey Nics; it's "smaller and more manageable than Harrods" although it still has eight floors of the best-quality "trendsetting" clothes and accessories for men and women, along with a cosmopolitan beauty department, food hall and home collection; the fifth floor restaurant is a "great place to have lunch with the girls" or "see and be seen", while the bar is perfect for "post-shopping champagne."

☒ Hermes ☒
| | 29 | 25 | 22 | VE |

Knightsbridge | 199 Sloane St., SW1 (Knightsbridge) | 020-7823 1014
Mayfair | 155 New Bond St., W1 (Bond St.) | 020-7499 8856
NEW | City | 12-13 Royal Exchange, EC3 (Bank) | 020-7626 7794
www.hermes.com

"Conservative" yet "sophisticated" "French style" is showcased at this trio of luxury stores where the "timeless" accessories for both men and women are most popular; "no one touches their quality" when it comes to leather goods, silk scarves, ties, cuff links and the coveted handbags – all of which are "packaged in those wonderful orange boxes"; but reviewers warn that it might help to carry "a Birkin" when shopping here as staff can be a bit "snooty."

Hogan
| | – | – | – | E |

Knightsbridge | 10 Sloane St., SW1 (Knightsbridge) | 020-7245 6363 | www.todsgroup.com

The sportier and "younger sister" of Italian luxury leather goods brand Tod's is showcased at this Knightsbridge store; "high-end" shoes that

are "casual and stylish" as well as understated handbags appeal to those who like their stuff on the subtle rather than flashy side.

Holland & Holland
▽ 28 | 26 | 21 | VE

Mayfair | 31-33 Bruton St., W1 (Green Park) | 020-7499 4411 | www.hollandandholland.com

You will find everything you need for the "perfect" shooting weekend in the "English countryside" at this "top-drawer" Mayfair shop with "monstrous prices"; "sporting enthusiasts" head here for a selection of the finest handcrafted guns and rifles as well as outdoor and safari clothing.

House of Fraser
21 | 17 | 18 | M

Marylebone | 318 Oxford St., W1 (Bond St./Oxford Circus) | 0870-160 7258
Victoria | 101 Victoria St., SW1 (Victoria) | 0870-160 7268
City | 68 King William St., EC4 (Monument) | 0870-160 7274
www.houseoffraser.co.uk

Surveyors are split on this trio of department stores dating back to 1849: supporters say it still "provides the essentials" such as "good quality", "reasonably priced" clothing and cosmetics for "both young and older women" as well as home furnishings like linens; but critics counter it's "a little boring and bland by now."

Hugo Boss
23 | 22 | 21 | E

Chelsea | 35-38 Sloane Sq., SW1 (Sloane Sq.) | 020-7259 1240 | www.hugoboss.com

This new Chelsea boutique devoted to the German designer label is well known for its formal and casual men's clothing and fragrance, but there's also a women's collection featuring "well-fitting trousers" and other pieces that "will last a lifetime"; but even admirers admit it's all "eye-poppingly expensive."

Issey Miyake ⑤
27 | 22 | 21 | E

Mayfair | 52 Conduit St., W1 (Bond St.) | 020-7851 4620
South Kensington | 270 Brompton Rd., SW3 (South Kensington) | 020-7581 3760
www.isseymiyake.com

This cutting-edge Japanese designer with "stark" but "well-organised" stores in Mayfair and South Kensington makes the most of minimalist shapes for both women and men; "great quality" and "creative" construction add up to "original" albeit "expensive" collections.

J & M Davidson
- | - | - | E

Notting Hill | 42 Ledbury Rd., W11 (Notting Hill Gate) | 020-7313 9532 | www.jandmdavidson.com

Located in Notting Hill, this earthy boutique owned by a husband-and-wife design team stocks a collection of their country-chic clothes and accessories that are both "beautiful and unique"; mahogany counters and cowskin rugs are an apt backdrop for handcrafted leather belts, burnished bags and luggage, rugged knitwear and distinctive home items.

Jigsaw
20 | 20 | 19 | M

Mayfair | 126-127 New Bond St., W1 (Bond St.) | 020-7491 4484 | www.jigsaw-online.com
Additional locations throughout the London area

Satisfied shoppers who find that they can "never come out empty handed" love the "affordable" women's "staples" at this New Bond

Street store where the "dependable" collection is a "balance of classic and trendy", from tunics to floral-print dresses; the few who find the clothes "cookie-cutter" confess to only visiting in the hope that they might "see Prince William's on-again-off-again girlfriend, Kate Middleton, working on the shop floor."

Jigsaw Junior ▽ 21 | 19 | 18 | E

Mayfair | 126-127 New Bond St., W1 (Bond St.) | 020-7491 4484
Hampstead | 83 Heath St., NW3 (Hampstead) | 020-7431 0619
Chelsea | The Chapel | 6 Duke of York Sq., SW3 (Sloane Sq.) | 020-7730 4404
South Kensington | 97 Fulham Rd., SW3 (South Kensington) | 020-7823 8915
Westbourne Grove | 190 Westbourne Grove, W11 (Notting Hill Gate) | 020-7229 8654
www.jigsaw-online.com

For "adorable" "mini-versions" of the grown-up women's label, head to this childrenswear chainlet where you will find a "cute" collection of dresses, skirts, party frocks, ballet slippers and accessories that will appeal to both mothers and their daughters; the quality of the clothes is so good that parents posit "they would actually last" if the children "didn't grow out of them so fast."

☑ Jimmy Choo 28 | 27 | 25 | VE

Knightsbridge | 32 Sloane St., SW1 (Knightsbridge) | 020-7823 1051
Mayfair | 27 New Bond St., W1 (Bond St.) | 020-7493 5858 ☒ Ⓜ
www.jimmychoo.com

"They ain't shoes if they ain't Choos" assert admirers of this brand who believe that "every women should own a pair" of these "beautiful" "sexy and stylish" high heels; "it's also hard to find fault" with these "high-class stores" with "high-class service" in Mayfair and Knightsbridge where "everyone who walks through the door is treated as a favoured client."

☑ John Lewis 23 | 19 | 21 | M

Marylebone | 278-306 Oxford St., W1 (Bond St./Oxford Circus) | 020-7629 7711
Finchley | Brent Cross Shopping Ctr., NW4 (Brent Cross/Hendon Central) | 020-8202 6535
www.johnlewis.com

It is not exactly "swish" or "high on glitz and glamour", but this department store with branches on Oxford Street and in Brent Cross is "dependable"; you'll find "anything you think you need" (from "sensible" men's and women's clothing to toys), but surveyors single out housewares, furniture and electronics (with an "excellent warranty policy") as the strongest departments; "knowledgeable staff" and "reasonable prices" add to its practical appeal.

John Smedley 25 | 19 | 20 | E

Mayfair | 24 Brook St., W1 (Bond St.) | 020-7495 2222 |
www.johnsmedley.com

"Top-quality" men's and women's knitwear that strikes the "perfect balance between fashionable and classic" styles is what you'll find at this "expensive" Mayfair purveyor; the focus is on the "softest-money-can-buy" sweaters in cashmere, cotton and merino wool, but they also sell lingerie.

	QUALITY	DISPLAY	SERVICE	COST

Jo Malone
26 | 25 | 23 | E

Mayfair | 23 Brook St., W1 (Bond St.) | 020-7491 9104 🖼
City | 24 Royal Exchange, EC3 (Bank) | 020-7444 1999 🖼
Chelsea | 150 Sloane St., SW1 (Sloane Sq.) | 020-7730 2100
www.jomalone.co.uk

"You'll feel instantly calmer" just walking into any of these three "soothing" shops where you will find "fabulous fragrances, candles" and bath and body products that are "wonderfully displayed" and packaged; Mandarin and Lime Basil are especially popular, but "incredibly friendly and helpful staff" can also "help you personalize your own" scent by layering several of them over each other; "beautiful packaging" also makes the products "fabulous for gifts."

Jones the Bootmaker
20 | 16 | 18 | M

Chelsea | 57-59 King's Rd., SW3 (Sloane Sq.) | 020-7730 1545 |
www.jonesbootmaker.com
Additional locations throughout the London area

"Traditional" chain of men's and women's shoe stores that's popular with young professionals who find the footwear "well-crafted", "hard-wearing" and "reliable"; while the kicks may "not always be fashionable", they do represent "good value for the money."

Joseph
22 | 21 | 17 | E

South Kensington | 77 Fulham Rd., SW3 (South Kensington) |
020-7823 9500 | www.joseph.co.uk
Additional locations throughout the London area

A "mecca of good taste" offering "well-made", "long-lasting" suits, "excellent-fitting trousers", knitwear and other "timeless pieces" that are a must for "stylish" men and women looking for "chic" designs; just don't be put off by the price, which fans reassure is "justified by quality"; N.B. this Fulham Road flagship is ladies' apparel only.

NEW Karen Millen
23 | 23 | 20 | E

Marylebone | 247 Regent St., W1 (Oxford Circus) | 020-7629 1901 |
www.karenmillen.com
Additional locations throughout the London area

"Heaven on the high street for fashionistas" is how enthusiasts describe this chain selling clothes that are "cool" yet "classy" and more "conservative" than its competitors; the "constantly evolving collection of detail-rich wardrobe essentials" includes dresses and suits that are as good "for the office as they are for a blind date."

Kelly Hoppen 🖼 Ⓜ
- | - | - | VE

South Kensington | 175-177 Fulham Rd., SW3 (South Kensington) |
020-7351 1910 | www.kellyhoppen.com

The namesake English interior designer's South Kensington home-furnishings shop sells everything from curtains to fabric, carpets, paints and furniture as well as crystal and cutlery; perhaps a glass of the house's complimentary champagne will make the price tags less painful.

Kenzo
23 | 22 | 17 | E

South Kensington | 70 Sloane Ave., SW3 (South Kensington) |
020-7225 1960 | www.kenzonet.com

"Eye-catching" women's clothes in "startling combinations of reds, turquoises, blacks and greens" will "practically hypnotise" you when

QUALITY DISPLAY SERVICE COST

you enter this luxurious South Kensington store; there's also a men's collection, so with "so many different styles, trends and vibrant colours" to choose from there is sure to "be something for everyone here."

Kew
-	-	-	M

Marylebone | 11-12 James St., W1 (Bond St.) | 020-7495 4646
Chelsea | 124 King's Rd., SW3 (Sloane Sq.) | 020-7823 7304
Bayswater | Whiteleys Ctr. | 151 Queensway, W2 (Bayswater/Queensway) | 020-7229 7609
Kensington | 123C Kensington High St., W8 (High St. Kensington) | 020-7937 8850
www.kew-online.com

A "cheaper" offshoot of High Street's Jigsaw, this affordable British chain of woman's clothing stores is "good for basics" and "cute" "casual" pieces like cardigans, cotton jackets, jeans, T-shirts and accessories; if you want to play it safe, this may be the place, just don't expect to be blown away by cutting-edge designs.

Kiehl's
26	22	23	E

Covent Garden | 29 Monmouth St., WC2 (Covent Garden) | 020-7240 2411
NEW **Chelsea** | 186A King's Rd., SW3 (Sloane Sq.) | 020-7751 5950
www.kiehls.com

This chain's "wonderful" bath and body products in "stylish packaging" might be "twice as expensive" in the Covent Garden and King's Road stores than in the "original New York location", but "the brilliant" goods and "caring service" draw "homesick Americans" and locals "thrilled" they've crossed the pond; P.S. there are "lovely" "free samples."

Kilgour French Stanbury ⊠
26	24	24	VE

Piccadilly | 8 Savile Row, W1 (Piccadilly Circus) | 020-7734 6905 | www.8savilerow.com

The "cutters here are simply genius" rave fans of this Saville Row staple that has, over the years, turned out "fabulous" bespoke suits and shirts classic enough for Cary Grant and "modern" enough for Jude Law; sure, the "slim fits", "expensive" prices and "very British", "trendy" look isn't for everyone, but those who appreciate the "splendid" wear say they're "amongst the best tailors in town."

Koh Samui
-	-	-	E

Covent Garden | 65-67 Monmouth St., WC2 (Covent Garden) | 020-7240 4280

For "young, rich" fashionistas who know Cavalli from Chloe, this eclectic boutique with a mix of labels, including new designers and carefully chosen vintage pieces and accessories, is a "tempting" stop in Covent Garden; expect eye-catching displays arranged by colour.

Kurt Geiger
22	17	17	E

NEW **Marylebone** | 198 Regent St., W1 (Oxford Circus)
Mayfair | 65 S. Molton St., W1 (Bond St.) | 020-7758 8020
Hampstead | 30 Hampstead High St., NW3 (Hampstead) | 020-7794 4290
Chelsea | 33D King's Rd., SW3 (Sloane Sq.) | 020-7901 9041
Kensington | 133 Kensington High St., W8 (High St. Kensington) | 020-7937 3716
www.kurtgeiger.com

For "beautifully crafted" men's and women's shoes, boots and handbags, loyalists head to this "popular local" chain for "trendy" designs under the

store's own label as well as from the likes of Prada and Gucci; although some stores' displays can be a "bit cluttered" and the "busy" staff are often "all over the place", there are "good values" during sales.

Lacoste
21 | 18 | 16 | E

Knightsbridge | 52 Brompton Rd., SW3 (Knightsbridge) | 020-7225 2851
Mayfair | 233 Regent St., W1 (Oxford Circus) | 020-7491 8968
www.lacoste.co.uk

"Who would have thought" this international sportswear brand would be "back in style" and even "considered trendy" after the '80s, when "everyone had at least one" of their crocodile embroidered polo shirts?; loyal fans praise the "quality products" (admitting they're "still wearing shirts they bought 10 years ago"), but they're turned off by a "snobbish" staff that veers toward "unfriendly" on occasion.

L'Artisan Parfumeur
25 | 20 | 19 | E

Marylebone | 36 Marylebone High St., W1 (Baker St.) | 020-7486 3435
City | 4 Royal Exchange, EC3 (Bank) | 020-7623 3131 🗷
Chelsea | 17 Cale St., SW3 (Sloane Sq.) | 020-7352 4196 🗷
Westbourne Grove | 227A Westbourne Grove, W11 (Notting Hill Gate) | 020-7221 2008
www.artisanparfumeur.com

"If you're looking for something special", head to this quartet of "elegant" "artiste's scent stores" to find a "totally unique" fragrance in "lovely packaging"; "sweet" staff point you toward "moderately" priced candles, perfumes, oils and wardrobe and car fragrances in "interesting and exotic blends" inspired by nature.

☑ Liberty
26 | 23 | 22 | E

Soho | Regent St., W1 (Oxford Circus) | 020-7734 1234 | www.liberty.co.uk
An "English retail tradition", this "beautiful bazaarlike" department store set in an "incredible" Tudor mansion on Regent Street combines "old-world charm with new-world prices"; thanks to the "eclectic" range of products – from "fashion-forward" men's and women's clothing from top designers to the Liberty of London brand, to modern furnishings, signature fabrics and bedding – "you can find anything here" say happy hunters, but frugal fans fret that "even the sales are no longer bargains" so just go for "afternoon tea."

Library, The
20 | 19 | 18 | E

South Kensington | 268 Brompton Rd., SW3 (South Kensington) | 020-7589 6569
"It's not what you expect" so don't be fooled by the name – instead of books and silence this trendy South Ken menswear shop with an "informative and helpful staff" is full of "lovely" cutting-edge designer labels accompanied by blaring rock music; it's an "expensive" option that's "too fashionable for staples", however, so if you can't pull off Alexander McQueen or Helmut Lang, it's probably not for you.

Little White Company
23 | 21 | 20 | M

Belgravia | 261 Pavilion Rd., SW1 (Sloane Sq.) | 020-7881 0783
Marylebone | 90 Marylebone High St., W1 (Baker St./Bond St.) | 020-7486 7550
www.thewhitecompany.com

"A one-stop shop" for "irresistible" children's bedding, sleepwear and accessories, these Belgravia and Marylebone offshoots of the larger

White Company are notoriously chaotic at "sale times" but the staff "can't do enough to help" you select "lovely pjs", "well-wearing sheets and towels" and "pretty gifts"; there's "lots of room to move around" the "clean" displays, but if you can't shop in person, there's an "attractive mail order catalogue and Web site."

L.K. Bennett 19 | 19 | 18 | E

Covent Garden | 43 King St., WC2 (Covent Garden) | 020-7379 9890 | www.lkbennett.com
Additional locations throughout the London area

"Pointy shoes and kitten heels" are what you'll find at this "mid-market" chain that, although "lacking imagination", appeals to "prim" types on the lookout for "elegant femininity"; even if some find the styles "predictable", the "colourful", "eye-catching and easy-to-navigate" displays add some pizzazz, just mind the "chorus of no's" when it comes to the "mumsy" clothing collection.

☒ Loro Piana 29 | 27 | 23 | VE

Knightsbridge | 47 Sloane St., SW1 (Sloane Sq.) | 020-7235 3203
Mayfair | 153 New Bond St., W1 (Bond St.) | 020-7499 9300
www.loropiana.com

The "simply wonderful" "high-end" Italian cashmere and "softest wools and leathers" – whether in the form of his-and-hers sweaters, sportswear, baby apparel, accessories or home furnishings – help earn these Mayfair and Knightsbridge shops the No. 1 rating for Quality in the London Survey; it's "like shopping in a museum" sigh awed admirers, although they can't always "justify the breathtaking prices."

☒ Louis Vuitton 27 | 25 | 21 | VE

Knightsbridge | 190-192 Sloane St., SW1 (Knightsbridge) | 020-7399 4050
Mayfair | 17-18 New Bond St., W1 (Green Park) | 020-7399 4050 ☒
City | 6 Royal Exchange, EC3 (Bank) | 020-7399 4050 ☒
www.vuitton.com

The "sophisticated" addresses in Mayfair, Knightsbridge and the City of this "always classy" luxury brand designed by Marc Jacobs are fitting locations for these "fashionable" accessories, particularly the "absolutely stunning" cases and handbags; "eye-catching displays are strategically placed" to seduce and the "excellent" craftsmanship means they'll "last for decades" – all reason enough for the logo-obsessed to ignore both the sometimes "snooty" service and the "ridiculous prices."

Lulu Guiness ☒ 25 | 24 | 21 | E

City | 23 Royal Exchange, EC3 (Bank) | 020-7626 5391
Chelsea | 3 Ellis St., SW1 (Sloane Sq.) | 020-7823 4828
www.luluguiness.com

Fans of this Britsh brand love the "too cute for words" ultra-feminine outposts in the City and Chelsea where the "fun", funky styles are offered up in "lovey creative displays" by a "terrific staff" (the Sloan Square address has a collection of vintage *Vogue* magazines that will "take your breath away"); "refreshing" retro-inspired handbags are "the talk of the town" say fans who gravitate to the adorable flowerpot bag, while walkabouts wander over to the "refreshing" selection of witty shoes, along with costume jewellery, beauty products and accessories.

	QUALITY	DISPLAY	SERVICE	COST

MAC Cosmetics
25 | 24 | 21 | M

Covent Garden | 38 Neal St., WC2 (Covent Garden) | 020-7379 6820
Soho | 28 Foubert's Pl., W1 (Oxford Circus) | 020-7534 9222
Chelsea | 109 King's Rd., SW3 (Sloane Sq.) | 020-7349 0022
Kensington | 28A Kensington Church St., W8 (High St. Kensington) |
020-7937 3738
www.maccosmetics.com

"Every colour under the rainbow sparkles from the tiny perfectly packaged pots" in this quartet of "funky" makeup stores loved by "average girls" and "drag queens" alike; although the "brilliant products" may be "pricey" for some, the "innovative range" along with the "skilled staff" – "friendly", "patient" and happy to give you a "makeover "or "help you try things" – make the whole experience "worth every penny."

NEW Mamas & Papas
21 | 20 | 17 | E

Piccadilly | 256-258 Regent St., W1 (Oxford Circus) | 0870-830 7700 |
www.mamasandpapas.com

The "comprehensive product line" – from strollers to nursery furniture to baby clothes to toys – makes this chain throughout the British Isles a veritable "new parent mecca"; the Regent Street flagship is "one of the best" say fans "easy to find what you're looking for" if you look past the displays of "buggies, buggies everywhere" (the "friendly" staff helps you "test-drive the prams"); sure, it may be for folks that feel "nothing is too costly for your kid", but there is plenty of "value for that money."

Mango
17 | 19 | 15 | I

Covent Garden | 8-12 Neal St., WC2 (Covent Garden) | 020-7240 6099
Marylebone | 233 Oxford St., W1 (Oxford Circus) | 020-7534 3505
Piccadilly | 106-112 Regent St., W1 (Piccadilly Circus) | 020-7434 1384
www.mango.com

If you're looking for "young and trendy" clothes and shoes "to keep your closet fashion-forward" and don't want to "spend a fortune" head to this trio of "stylish" women's apparel stores from the popular Spanish chain where you'll find "fresh", "savvy" and "inexpensive" outfits and accessories, including designer collaborations; but be warned, you may encounter a "messy" display, practically "non-existent" service and maybe even a few "catfights."

Z Manolo Blahnik 🔃
29 | 25 | 23 | VE

Chelsea | 49-51 Old Church St., SW3 (Sloane Sq.) | 020-7352 3863 |
www.manoloblahnik.com

"Every woman should own a pair" of these sexy shoes or sandals – and what better place to buy them than in the "small" Chelsea shop opened by the famous designer in the '70s?; addicts who "bring their platinum card" find "perfection" in high heels here, but others say there might be a "better selection at Bergdorf's in NYC" and are put off by a staff that "aren't too impressive."

NEW Marc Jacobs
23 | 22 | 18 | VE

Mayfair | 24-25 Mount St., W1 (Bond St.) | 020-7907 2515 |
www.marcjacobs.com

Londoners searching for "cute takes on classics" are thrilled by Mayfair's latest Stateside import from the designer whose men's and

| | QUALITY | DISPLAY | SERVICE | COST |

women's apparel is the epitome of NY chic; sure, U.S. tourists tsk "why buy this in London" for "double the price?", but others say the "store location and design are worth stopping by for" even if you can't afford the "extravagant" duds; too bad a few regular folks feel snubbed by the "not so great" service.

Marie-Chantal 🔠

| - | - | - | VE |

South Kensington | 148 Walton St., SW3 (South Kensington) | 020-7838 1111 | www.mariechantal.com

The "ultimate rich baby stores", these elegant South Kensington and Notting Hill boutiques carry "simple, safe and sweet" apparel suitable for the offspring of celebrity clients like Elle MacPherson, Reese Witherspoon and Princess Caroline of Monaco; founded by Crown Princess and über-socialite Marie-Chantal of Greece, a mother of four, the "sweet", comfortable collection strikes some as just "perfect for private school", but "you'll probably pay more for the label than for the originality."

🔠 Marks & Spencer

| 20 | 16 | 16 | M |

Marylebone | 458 Oxford St., W1 (Bond St.) | 020-7935 7954 | www.marksandspencer.com
Additional locations throughout the London area

A long-standing "nationwide chain" of "moderately priced department stores", this brand has "done the British proud for generations"; even if the clothes are a bit "dowdy" (some call them "garments for the middle-aged") and the merchandising "awful", it has one of "the best food halls", "super-soft" undergarments and a "dependable" range of products "from wine to socks, cheese or boots", so even if there's "nothing particularly exceptional", "you get exactly what you expect."

Marni 🔠

| - | - | - | VE |

Knightsbridge | 26 Sloane St., SW1 (Knightsbridge) | 020-7245 9520 | www.marni.com

For luxurious bohemian style clothing and accessories for women, men and kids, head to this "unique" and sleek Knightsbridge store sporting silvery tree-limb fixtures and red accents (there's also a smaller boutique within Selfridges); designer Consuelo Castiglioni presents an "interesting range" of fashions including tunic tops and loose-fitting dresses and coats in rich fabrics.

Massimo Dutti

| 19 | 21 | 17 | M |

Knightsbridge | 71 Brompton Rd., SW3 (Knightsbridge) | 020-7225 4780
Piccadilly | 156 Regent St., W1 (Oxford Circus) | 020-7851 1280
Kensington | 118 Kensington High St., W8 (High St. Kensington) | 020-7361 1840
www.massimodutti.com

The "standard" apparel at this trio of men's and women's clothing shops may "not be the most exciting" and the quality a "bit suspect" ("some items last longer than others"), but it's a "smart" choice for the office given the "classic", yet "up-to-date" styling and "fair" prices; although some find the displays "unexciting", others say they "encourage mixing and matching", just do it yourself since the service varies from "poor" to just "ok."

	QUALITY	DISPLAY	SERVICE	COST

Matches

| | 22 | 18 | 17 | E |

Wimbledon | 34 High St., SW19 (Wimbledon) | 020-8947 8707
Notting Hill | 60-64 Ledbury Rd., W11 (Notting Hill Gate) | 020-7221 0255

Matches Men

Wimbledon | 38-39 High St., SW19 (Wimbledon) | 020-8946 8218
Notting Hill | 60-64 Ledbury Rd., W11 (Notting Hill Gate) | 020-7221 0255

Matches Spy

Wimbledon | 37A High St., SW19 (Wimbledon) | 020-8944 6060
Notting Hill | 85 Ledbury Rd., W11 (Notting Hill Gate) | 020-7221 2334
www.matchesfashion.com

"You'll always find the best pieces of the season", often "ones you can't find elsewhere" say fans of these "enticing" Notting Hill and Wimbledon boutiques that constantly introduce new labels to keep it all cutting-edge; you'll have to come "ready to spend serious dough", whether it's for a pair of Alexander McQueen boots, a Chloe handbag or a MaxMara skirt, and some say service can "either be friendly or snobby" depending, but even so, many "wish they could live here"; N.B. the brand's offshoots include Matches Spy, which sells slightly more casual collections and diffusion lines, and Matches Men.

Matthew Williamson 🗷

| | - | - | - | VE |

Mayfair | 28 Bruton St., W1 (Bond St.) | 020-7629 6200 | www.matthewwilliamson.com

A favourite with A-list celebrities such as Sienna Miller, Kate Moss and Jade Jagger who are often called in to act as his muse, this British designer offers bohemian, hippy-chic clothes in bright colours with embroidery, beading and ethnic influences; the "interesting" Mayfair store decked out in a riot of hot pinks and reds, eclectic furniture and bold wallpaper also carries his line of accessories, perfume and candles, but don't expect much from the sometimes "disinterested" help.

MaxMara 🗷

| | 27 | 22 | 21 | E |

Mayfair | 19-21 Old Bond St., W1 (Green Park) | 020-7499 7902

"If you still have the energy after exhausting your credit card on Bond Street" head to this "trendy" Italian womenswear juggernaut in Mayfair where you'll find a "huge selection" of "well-priced high fashion for city girls" who appreciate "classic" clothes and "impeccable tailoring" that "lasts a lifetime"; the "smiling" staff is "always close by" and "takes pride" in their "attractive displays" of "well-cut" "flawless women's suits", tweed skirts and the "most stylish coats you'll ever find."

Miller Harris 🗷

| | - | - | - | E |

Mayfair | 21 Bruton St., W1 (Green Park) | 020-7629 7750
Notting Hill | 14 Needham Rd., W11 (Notting Hill Gate) | 020-7221 1545
www.millerharris.com

Scent-sters swear by the "best perfumery in London", this Notting Hill and Mayfair duo that proffers "unique" homemade fragrances (salty fig, woody classic, geranium bourbon) and candles in "lovely" black-laquered surroundings; the flagship Bruton Street store has a back library for browsing the options, while a laboratory below the original Needham Road facility is where the concoctions are created; the "helpful" staff win praise, and if you can wait six months, owner Lyn Harris will happily create a personalized perfume just for you.

QUALITY | DISPLAY | SERVICE | COST

Miss Selfridge   18 | 19 | 16 | M

Marylebone | 214 Oxford St., W1 (Oxford Circus) | 020-7927 0188 |
www.missselfridge.co.uk

If you're looking for "trendy, disposable fashion" that's of "better quality" than some others in this category, and you can deal with the "crowds", head for this womenswear chain with "funky", "edgy" and vintage apparel, footwear, accessories and lingerie and "lots of cute uniquely British outfits" mostly for "teens and a bit older"; you may have to "search" a bit and listen to music that's "harsh" on the ears, but you'll find something "not very expensive" that's definitely "worth the effort."

Miss Sixty   20 | 19 | 16 | E

Covent Garden | 39 Neal St., WC2 (Covent Garden) | 020-7836 3789
Soho | 31 Great Marlborough St., W1 (Oxford Circus) | 020-7434 3060
Kensington | 42 Kensington High St., W8 (High St. Kensington) |
020-7376 1330
www.misssixty.com

Originally known for its tight fitting stretch jeans, this Italian chain is now a favourite among "hip and trendy" youngsters who want flesh-baring clubbing clothes and sporty daytime casuals; the trio of London shops also stock other designers including Betsey Johnson, Energie (menswear), Nicole Miller and Stella McCartney, leading more senior shoppers to scoff "if you're 25 or older keep walking."

Miu Miu 🛢   23 | 20 | 19 | E

Mayfair | 123 New Bond St., W1 (Bond St.) | 020-7409 0900 |
www.miumiu.com

"Every girl needs to dream" and Prada's "edgier" sister on New Bond Street is a good place to start; the "cool", "minimalist" layout is perfect for displaying the "quite expensive" Italian designs that "could not be more hip", from super-short minis to super-high heels to super-chic handbags; though service can be "minimal", it is "effective and knowledgeable", which further lulls you into buying more than you can afford.

⧉ Molton Brown   26 | 24 | 21 | E

Mayfair | 227 Regent St., W1 (Oxford Circus) | 020-7493 7319 |
www.moltonbrown.co.uk
Additional locations throughout the London area

Tourists can "take a bit of England home" when they shop at this "heavenly" cosmetics and toiletries chain scattered about London that proffers "quintessentially British" shower gels, hand washes and lotions that'll remind you of five-star "hotels around the world"; the "broad range of products" is a "feast for the senses" – the "rose granati" air freshener is a favourite – and makes either "great presents" or a "lovely" "treat" "for your powder room."

⧉ Monsoon   19 | 20 | 17 | M

Marylebone | 498-500 Oxford St., W1 (Marble Arch) | 020-7491 3004 |
www.monsoon.co.uk
Additional locations throughout the London area

For a "constantly changing" selection of "bright and youthful clothes" that are "rich, vibrant" and often "inspired by Indian prints" this "moderately priced" Oxford Street store is a casualwear "standby" for men, women and children up to 13; although less generous critics complain

| | QUALITY | DISPLAY | SERVICE | COST |

that the name "describes the condition the store is usually in", others have only two words for this popular chain – "love it."

Moschino ⑤   22 | 18 | 17 | E

Mayfair | 28-29 Conduit St., W1 (Oxford Circus) | 020-7318 0555 | www.moschino.it

This fun-loving Italian brand injects some humour into the "stiff English" dress code with the "awesome" women's apparel and accessories found in its Mayfair boutique; expect "bright colours", lots of patterns (polka dots, animal prints), rich fabrics and chic styles all set in "attractive" displays and attended by a staff full of "smiles and advice"; it may be "expensive" to pull off this cutting-edge look, but the quality is so "high" that some would "pay more" if they had to.

Moss Bros   16 | 13 | 17 | M

Covent Garden | 27-28 King St., WC2 (Covent Garden) | 020-7632 9700 | www.mossbros.com
Additional locations throughout the London area

If you are in need of anything for a "black-tie function" at the "last minute" this menswear chain is the "best place" to go; it's "not a bad option for the basics" say fans who find the in-store label along with other reputable designers such as Canali; but those who find "appalling service" and "constant sales" that make it "look cheap" say it now sits somewhere between a "high-class purveyor" and a "discount store."

Muji   21 | 19 | 16 | I

Bloomsbury | 187 Oxford St., W1 (Oxford Circus) | 020-7437 7503
Bloomsbury | 6-17 Tottenham Court Rd., W1 (Tottenham Court Rd.) | 020-7436 1779
Covent Garden | 135 Long Acre, WC2 (Covent Garden) | 020-7379 0820
Soho | 41 Carnaby St., W1 (Oxford Circus) | 020-7287 7323
Chelsea | 118 King's Rd., SW3 (Sloane Sq.) | 020-7823 8688 ⑤ Ⓜ
Bayswater | Whiteleys Ctr. | 151 Queensway, W2 (Bayswater/Queensway) | 020-7792 8283
Kensington | 157 Kensington High St., W8 (High St. Kensington) | 020-7376 2484
www.muji.co.uk

"You'll want one of everything" at this "innovative" Japanese lifestyle chain, and you may just be able to afford it too; from the "best basic" clothing to "excellent stationery", accessories, kitchen goods and "simple and tasteful furniture and houseware", they offer a "cooler" version of "everything you already have" just better designed in "a minimalist Japanese sort of way"; it's just too bad the "nice staff" is "not completely on top of things."

Mulberry   24 | 21 | 20 | E

Knightsbridge | 171-175 Brompton Rd., SW3 (Knightsbridge) | 020-7838 1411 ⑤
Marylebone | 11-12 Gees Ct., W1 (Bond St.) | 020-7493 2546 ⑤
Mayfair | 41-42 New Bond St., W1 (Bond St.) | 020-7491 3900 ⑤
Westbourne Grove | 199 Westbourne Grove, W11 (Notting Hill Gate) | 020-7229 1635
www.mulberry.com

Having recently "reinvented themselves", this "established" luxury brand with four outlets around London "is fast becoming the icon of quality leather goods made in the U.K."; the "decadent" handbags

	QUALITY	DISPLAY	SERVICE	COST

and accessories are perfect examples of "understated elegance", while the "quietly sophisticated clothes" "inspire" even "the more educated fashion shoppers"; "easy on the eyes" displays and service "with a smile" help distract from the prices, which "are not for the fainthearted."

Museum of London
20 | **19** | **18** | **M**

City | London Wall, EC2 (Barbican/St. Paul's) | 0870-444 3851 | www.museumoflondonshop.co.uk

"I spent more time in the shop than I did in the museum" fesses up one visitor to this "lovely" gift store packed with "off-the-beaten-path souvenirs" including a "great selection of everything from books" to "laugh-out-loud" "novelties" to "educational" items; the staff is "interested and involved" and the shelves are "easy to explore", but while the wares are "reasonably priced" for a museum store, one griper grouses that some can be found "cheaper online."

NEW Nanette Lepore
▽ **24** | **25** | **24** | **E**

Westbourne Grove | 206 Westbourne Grove, W11 (Notting Hill Gate) | 020-7221 8889 | www.nanettelepore.com

Perfect for "the banker's wives of Notting Hill" who "love" the feminine retro styles with lots of unique trims, buttons and details that stand out; even if some of the bohemian "locals don't seem so impressed" with the "attitude and service" of this American import, the "beautiful" store itself is hard to dislike, filled with soft colours, pretty chandeliers and girlie touches.

National Portrait Gallery
23 | **21** | **18** | **M**

Westminster | St. Martin's Pl., WC2 (Charing Cross/Leicester Sq.) | 020-7306 0055 | www.npg.org.uk

"A British treasure", this Westminster museum gift shop "for art lovers" features an "excellent selection of art books", "postcards" and "beautiful" journals; the only downside is that – "like many museums in London" – it can "get a little crowded" which is odd "considering there doesn't always seem to be many people in the Gallery."

Neal's Yard Remedies
25 | **19** | **23** | **M**

Covent Garden | 15 Neal's Yard, WC2 (Covent Garden) | 020-7379 7222
Marylebone | 112 Marylebone High St., W1 (Baker St.) | 020-7935 0656
Soho | 12 Foubert's Pl., W1 (Oxford Circus) | 020-7494 9862
Blackheath | 32 Blackheath Vill., SE3 | 020-8318 6655
Borough | 4 Bedale St., SE1 (London Bridge) | 020-7940 1414
Chalk Farm | 68 Chalk Farm Rd., NW1 (Chalk Farm) | 020-7284 2039
Clapham | 6 Northcote Rd., SW11 (Clapham Junction B.R.) | 020-7223 7174
Chelsea | Chelsea Farmers Mkt. | 121 Sydney St., SW3 (Sloane Sq.) | 020-7351 6380
Richmond | 15 King Street, TW9 (Richmond) | 020-8948 9248
Notting Hill | 9 Elgin Crescent, W11 (Notting Hill Gate) | 020-7727 3998
www.nealsyardremedies.com

One of the city's "first stores to sell natural products and essential oils", this "charming" 25-year-old apothecary remains among "the best" thanks to its "simple, elegant scents", "organic" ingredients and "the most helpful staff on the planet"; sure, the "gorgeously packaged" soaps, lotions and "herbal potions" are "pricey", but concensus is that they're still a "good bargain" and "worth the trek."

	QUALITY	DISPLAY	SERVICE	COST

Next
| | 17 | 16 | 15 | I |

Piccadilly | 160 Regent St., W1 (Oxford Circus) | 020-7434 2515 |
www.next.co.uk
Additional locations throughout the London area

A "hit-or-miss" collection of "mass-market" clothing and accessories for
the "everyday girl" and "very British, thirtysomething", "conservative"
dads, as well as for the "toddler set", this chain offers "quick and easy"
outfits that "transition well from work to fun"; but cutting-edgers who
cackle these "dull, dull, dull" duds are "cheap and it shows" shout 'Next!'

Nicole Farhi
| | 21 | 19 | 18 | E |

Covent Garden | 11 Floral St., WC2 (Covent Garden) | 020-7497 8713
Covent Garden | 15 The Piazza, WC2 (Covent Garden) | 020-7240 9983
Knightsbridge | 193 Sloane St., SW1 (Knightsbridge) | 020-7235 0877
Mayfair | 158 New Bond St., W1 (Bond St.) | 020-7499 8368
Hampstead | 27 Hampstead High St., NW3 (Hampstead) | 020-7435 0866
South Kensington | 115 Fulham Rd., SW3 (South Kensington) |
020-7838 0937
Westbourne Grove | 202 Westbourne Grove, W11 (Notting Hill Gate) |
020-7792 6888
www.nicolefarhi.com

You won't find any bold logos or "flashy clothing" at these "not too
trendy and not too conservative" chain stores from the British designer –
instead the "elegant" and "understated" men's and
women's collection is made up mostly of "natural fibers" in soft neu-
tral colours; but a handful of the less-impressed find "fairly indifferent" service and argue that the food at Nicole's, in the basement of the
Bond Street store, is "more interesting than the clothes."

Nicole Farhi Home ⑤
| | - | - | - | VE |

Mayfair | 17 Clifford St., W1 (Bond St.) | 020-7494 9051 |
www.nicolefarhi.com

The "beautifully edited selection of fashionable furniture" at the
British designer's Mayfair store fits perfectly with the laid-back but
luxurious ethos of her namesake fashion label; vintage pieces, modern
elements and one of a kind antiques feel as if they've been plucked out
of a "French country" house while the popular lamps, scented candles
and other accessories draw those with a smaller budget.

Nigel Hall
| | ▽ 20 | 18 | 16 | E |

Covent Garden | 18 Floral St., WC2 (Covent Garden) | 020-7836 8223 |
www.nigelhallmenswear.co.uk

Men who appreciate "excellent value for quality and design" but don't
want to look too "trendy" or like they are "overdoing it" stock up at this
"solid" and sleek Covent Garden menswear shop; the clothing is simple and well-cut (including "shirts that last forever"), featuring subtle
and stylish retro influences from the '50s and '60s.

Niketown London
| | 21 | 23 | 14 | M |

Marylebone | 236 Oxford St., W1 (Oxford Circus) | 020-7612 0800 |
www.nike.com

An "uplifting, bright, loud and energetic" atmosphere pervades this
"very cool, if overwhelming" store that features "new models" of the
brand's trainers "all the time", "high-quality" designs, "in-store activ-
ites" and an "overhead tunnel to bring you your shoes"; some gripe

	QUALITY	DISPLAY	SERVICE	COST

that the selection is "poor compared to in the U.S." and, thanks to "crowds", the Oxford Circus flagship "can't quite cut it servicewise" – yet even those who admit that "it's more of an experience than real shopping" aver: "what can you say? it's Nike."

Nina Campbell 🖂 ·   ▽ 29 | 25 | 24 | E

South Kensington | 9 Walton St., SW3 (South Kensington) | 020-7225 1011 | www.ninacampbell.com

Stylish nesters who "can't afford" to hire designer Campbell to decorate their homes can "pick up some of her amazing accessories" at this very British South Kensington shop, nestled among Walton Street's strip of specialty boutiques, where she sells everything from "lovely home fabrics" to carpets, rugs, antiques, cosmetic bags, glassware and cutlery; some find her style a bit old-fashioned and "staid", but all agree "if you like this stuff, it works."

☑ N.Peal 🖂   27 | 20 | 22 | VE

Piccadilly | 37 Burlington Arcade, W1 (Green Park/Piccadilly Circus) | 020-7493 5376 | www.npeal.com

This is "the place to go for knits with style" say devotees of the Burlington Arcade shop's "very soft", "great quality", "beautifully presented" cashmere in colors "you will never see in the U.S."; the price "will shock", but "when you add up the years" that these sweaters and pashminas last, "it's well worth it."

Office 🖃   17 | 16 | 14 | M

Soho | 16 Carnaby St., W1 (Oxford Circus) | 020-7434 2530 | www.office.co.uk

Additional locations throughout the London area

This "fun and funky" chain "is to a shoe fanatic what chocolate is to a diabetic" rave teens and twentysomethings who favor the shops' "inexpensive trendy" footwear, arrayed in "tempting (too tempting) displays" that are as "colourful as a sweet shop"; the wares are "well made", though some stompers "go through 100 plasters" to break them in, and the "lively" "teenage mutant" staff remains "polite" despite the "crowds."

Oliver Sweeney   - | - | - | VE

Mayfair | 66 New Bond St., W1 (Bond St.) | 020-7355 0387
Broadgate | 133 Middlesex St., E1 (Liverpool St.) | 020-7626 4466
Chelsea | 29 King's Rd., SW3 (Sloane Sq.) | 020-7730 3666
www.oliversweeney.com

Loyal fans laud this British designer's "quality" men's shoes, belts and accessories sold in a trio of London shops as the "best in the world – bar none"; they're handcrafted in Italy using fine leathers so "prices have shot up in recent years", but if you enjoy getting "compliments" on your footwear, these may be worth it.

Original Levi's Store, The   22 | 16 | 15 | M

Covent Garden | 10 Long Acre, WC2 (Covent Garden) | 020-7836 0953
Marylebone | 269 Regent St., W1 (Oxford Circus) | 020-7409 2692
Piccadilly | 174-176 Regent St., W1 (Oxford Circus) | 020-7292 2500
www.levi.com

American shoppers might "cringe at the price compared to home" but Brits sing "jeans glorious jeans" about this "hip and happening" trio of

"the original denim trendsetters"; in addition to the "legendary" "classics" "piled high" on the shelves, expect to find "more options for fashion conscious" buyers without compromising on the "hardwearing quality" – "what else would you expect from Levi's?"

Ozwald Boateng 🖪

| - | - | - | VE |

Mayfair | 9 Vigo St., W1 (Piccadilly Circus) | 020-7437 0620 | www.ozwaldboateng.co.uk

A breath of fresh air on Mayfair's Saville Row, this luxurious designer menswear stop combines British elegance with modern cuts and colours to produce a vibrant ready-to-wear collection as well as shoes, luggage, leather goods, cuff links and ties; with his bespoke couture service, Boateng also creates individualized suits, which leaves the ladies to dream – "if only he made women's clothes, our lives would be complete."

Patrick Cox 🖪

| - | - | - | E |

Chelsea | 129 Sloane St., SW1 (Sloane Sq.) | 020-7730 8886 | www.patrickcox.co.uk

After coming to fame in the '90s, this high-end cobbler is "still going strong", especially now that his intimate and funky Chelsea storefront is selling men's and women's accessories in addition to his fashion-forward, eye-catching footwear; loyal fans "own so many pairs of these shoes that it is scary" but complain about the "generally helpful" yet "snotty at times, which I never appreciate", service.

Paul & Joe

| 22 | 21 | 19 | E |

Covent Garden | 33 Floral St., WC2 (Covent Garden) | 020-7836 3388
Chelsea | 134 Sloane St., SW1 (Sloane Sq.) | 020-7824 8844
South Kensington | 309 Brompton Rd., SW3 (South Kensington) | 020-7589 2684
Notting Hill | 39-41 Ledbury Rd., W11 (Notting Hill Gate) | 020-7243 5510
www.paulandjoe.com

Expect "Parisian clothing with a casual hippie attitude" at this "cute" quartet of stores selling a distinctive collection of clothing for men and women that is fresh, young and anti-conformist; these sparely de-signed boutiques are "reliable" for "finding last minute outfits and accessories" which are quirky and not likely to be "found elsewhere", but penny-pinchers sigh that they're also "a bit expensive."

Paul Smith

| 23 | 22 | 19 | E |

Covent Garden | 40-44 Floral St., WC2 (Covent Garden) | 020-7379 7133
City | 7 Royal Exchange Courtyard, EC3 (Bank) | 020-7626 4778 🖪
Borough | 13 Park St., SE1 (London Bridge) | 020-7403 1678 🖪
South Kensington | 84-86 Sloane Ave., SW3 (South Kensington) | 020-7589 9139
Notting Hill | Westbourne Hse. | 122 Kensington Park Rd., W11 (Notting Hill Gate) | 020-7727 3553 🖪

Paul Smith Jeans

Covent Garden | 9-11 Langley Ct., WC2 (Covent Garden) | 020-7257 8946
www.paulsmith.co.uk

"Cool Britannia" at its best is how sartorial shoppers describe this "true original" men's and womenswear designer whose stores sell "top-notch" "funky" duds featuring "wonderful fabrics and witty flourishes"; the dis-plays are "uncluttered and gorgeous to look at", service is "there when you need it" and prices are "sometimes affordable, often outrageous."

	QUALITY	DISPLAY	SERVICE	COST

Penhaligon's 27 | 26 | 26 | E

Covent Garden | 41 Wellington Rd., WC2 (Covent Garden) | 020-7836 2150
Mayfair | 125 Regent St., W1 (Oxford Circus) | 020-7434 2608
Mayfair | 20A Brook St., W1 (Bond St.) | 020-7493 0002
Piccadilly | 16 Burlington Arcade, W1 (Green Park/Piccadilly Circus) |
020-7629 1416 ☒
City | 8 Royal Exchange, EC3 (Bank) | 020-7283 0711 ☒
Chelsea | 132 King's Rd., SW3 (Sloane Sq.) | 020-7823 9733
www.penhaligons.co.uk

Wonderful "scents selling for reasonable cents" are on offer at this "charming" small chain of "perfumeries" – "the epitome of fine fragrances" – where the dark wood and old-fashioned glass cabinets give the "oozingly British" lairs an "Edwardian England" air; the "upper-crust" "gifts" on display include fragrances, candles and "beautiful smelling soaps and lotions" that are perfect for "your weekend host and hostess."

Pepe Jeans - | - | - | M

Covent Garden | 33 Neal St., WC2 (Covent Garden) | 020-7379 7978
Soho | 42 Carnaby St., W1 (Oxford Circus) | 020-7439 0523
Westbourne Grove | 172 Westbourne Grove, W11 (Notting Hill Gate) |
020-7221 9287
Ladbroke Grove | 309 Portobello Rd., W10 (Ladbroke Grove) |
020-8960 7001 ☒☒
www.pepejeans.com

Aiming to regain the popularity it enjoyed in the '80s, this label has hired Sienna Miller as its face and refurbished its Covent Garden flagship, giving the multilevel space an airy, lofty feel; at all of the outposts you'll find the brand's streetwear-inspired designer denim, plus other edgy, casual togs for men, women and children; N.B. the Ladbroke Grove location is open only on Fridays and Saturdays.

☒ Peter Jones 23 | 19 | 21 | M

Chelsea | Sloane Sq., SW1 (Sloane Sq.) | 020-7730 3434 |
www.peterjones.co.uk

This "essential Sloane Square institution" is every "Chelsea girl's" "reliable standby" for everything from fashion to "top-notch fabrics and soft furnishing, carpets and flooring, electronics, kitchens, personal care products and cosmetics"; there may be "less variety than at sister store John Lewis" but most call this affordable "perfect little department store" a classier and a more "pleasurable" shopping experience – especially the "Sloane Rangers" who consider it their "mother ship."

Petit Bateau 25 | 20 | 19 | E

Mayfair | 62 S. Molton St., W1 (Bond St.) | 020-7491 4498
Hampstead | 19 Hampstead High St., NW3 (Hampstead) | 020-7794 3254
Clapham | 133 Northcote Rd., SW11 (Clapham Common) | 020-7228 7233
Chelsea | 106-108 King's Rd., SW3 (Sloane Sq.) | 020-7838 0818
Notting Hill | 73 Ledbury Rd., W11 (Notting Hill Gate) | 020-7243 6331
www.petit-bateau.com

The chainlet of choice for the "offspring of yummy mummies", these "fashionable" children's clothing purveyors specialize in "beautifully made, simple pieces for newborns and upwards" that are "comfortable" and "durable"; the wares may be "more expensive" than in their native France, but the shopping experience is enhanced by shelves at kids' eye level and the availability of a few styles in women's sizes too.

	QUALITY	DISPLAY	SERVICE	COST

Philip Treacy ⑤

	–	–	–	VE

Knightsbridge | 69 Elizabeth St., SW1 (Sloane Sq./Victoria) | 020-7730 3992 | www.philiptreacy.co.uk

"Oh my, what a hat!" cry devotees of Knightsbrige's haute milliner, whose pricey toppers are perfect for "when you have an audience with the Queen", since they make the wearers "feel like royalty"; Buckingham Palace aside, the sculptural ready-to-wear and bespoke creations at this museumlike boutique have "terrific fits" and are perfect for "going to Ascot" or a wedding.

Pickett ⑤

	24	17	20	E

Piccadilly | 32-33 Burlington Arcade, W1 (Green Park/Piccadilly Circus) | 020-7493 8939

Piccadilly | 41 Burlington Arcade, W1 (Green Park/Piccadilly Circus) | 020-7493 8939

City | 6 Royal Exchange, EC3 (Bank) | 020-7283 7636

Chelsea | 149 Sloane St., SW1 (Sloane Sq.) | 020-7823 5638

www.pickett.co.uk

These four "old-world–style" stores are packed with "wonderful" leather goods, travel accessories, clocks, handbags, photo albums, desk sets, umbrellas, jewellery and jewellery boxes as well as pashminas, scarves and gloves – all "cramped" together in a space that "resembles your quirky aunt's attic"; the quality is "always good" and service comes "with a smile" say fans who label these spots "great places to pick up gifts for everybody."

Poste

	–	–	–	E

Mayfair | 10 S. Molton St., W1 (Bond St.) | 020-7499 8002 | www.office.co.uk

With wares and stores that are more upmarket than sister purveyor Office, this popular men's shoe chain is "a real gem" selling everything from boots to flip-flops and sneakers, culled from designers such as Puma, Paul Smith, Adidas and Y3; jealous women need not despair, a Covent Garden offshoot, Poste Mistress, caters to shoe-loving ladies.

⑦ Prada ⑤

	28	26	22	VE

Knightsbridge | 43-45 Sloane St., SW1 (Knightsbridge) | 020-7235 0008

Mayfair | 16-18 Old Bond St., W1 (Green Park) | 020-7647 5000

www.prada.com

Male and female "fashionistas who love understated elegance" rally around the "minimalist designs", muted colours and beautiful tailoring found in the Mayfair and Knightsbridge outlets of Miuccia Prada's "original Italian brand", selling clothing, accessories and shoes; you'll find "some of the best selection" of the accessories outside Milan, though the experience is more "fun for those with large pocketbooks", and the "sales assistants can be rather snooty"; P.S. Sloane Street has "a wider range of handbags."

Primark

	–	–	–	I

Mayfair | 499-517 Oxford Street, W1 (Marble Arch) | 020-7495 0420 | www.primark.co.uk

It's no wonder that the 70,000-sq.-ft. flagship of this budget fashion chain opened to a stampede of frenzied shoppers – the cheap and cheerful chain has something for everyone from throwaway teenwear to solid basics for inexpensive daywear and pajamas; just make sure to go during the week to avoid the crowds.

	QUALITY	DISPLAY	SERVICE	COST

Pringle of Scotland

| 26 | 20 | 20 | E |

Mayfair | 111-112 New Bond St., W1 (Bond St.) | 020-7297 4580
Chelsea | 141-142 Sloane St., SW1 (Sloane Sq.) | 020-7881 3061 ☒
www.pringlescotland.com

Once known only for its "mass-marketed" "golf course pastel plaids", this "traditional Scottish fashion house" has undergone a "rebirth" and now features "hip" and "chic" "cashmere for the Euro set"; the "jolly good, classic" knitwear at these fashionable Sloane and Bond Street outlets is "indestructible" and makes "great souvenirs", but as you would expect "quality comes with a cost."

Puma

| 22 | 23 | 19 | M |

Soho | 51-55 Carnaby St., W1 (Oxford Circus) | 020-7439 0221 | www.puma.com

Both players and posers hunt down the "newest styles" of "old-school trainers" as well as high-quality activewear – which is also worn by the Italian national football team – at this trendy concept store on Soho's Carnaby Street; the brand's only shop in London, this spot's vibrant decor is based around the label's bounding cat logo.

Ralph Lauren

| 22 | 24 | 18 | E |

Mayfair | 1 New Bond St., W1 (Green Park) | 020-7535 4600
South Kensington | 105-109 Fulham Rd., SW3 (South Kensington) | 020-7590 7990
www.ralphlauren.co.uk

Enthusiasts of this "reliable" American designer laud his "wearable, elegant fashions that last forever" and ability to capture a "sporty", classic and "preppy look" all under one roof; his elegant and "beautiful" Bond Street flagship, where polished hardwood is the prevailing decor element, has a "wonderful selection", and the prices are "somewhat decent" to boot, but service that's "a bit cold" doesn't win any raves; N.B. childrenswear is housed down.

Reiss

| 21 | 19 | 17 | E |

Marylebone | Kent Hse. | 14-17 Market Pl., W1 (Oxford Circus) | 020-7637 9112 | www.reiss.co.uk
Additional locations throughout the London area

"Uptown girls, downtown girls", "sexy secretaries" and "modern", "understated men" stock up at this "good-quality" High Street chain where the "trendy" "yet sassy, classy and sophisticated" clothing is "perfect for glamming it up in the city"; the displays are "easy on the eyes" at the "unencumbered", "spacious" shops, but be aware that "fashion doesn't come cheap" and the service can sometimes be "aloof and lacking."

Rellik ☒Ⓜ

| - | - | - | E |

Ladbroke Grove | 8 Golborne Rd., W10 (Westbourne Park) | 020-8962 0089 | www.relliklondon.co.uk

Don't be surprised to find yourself shopping next to Kate Moss or Penelope Cruz at this bastion of "high-quality and carefully screened" vintage clothes and accessories, most dating from the 1920s through mid-'80s; true masters of their trade, the owners once sold from stalls on nearby Portobello Road, and their collection, displayed on packed racks in the funky storefront, includes eclectic pieces from the likes of Ossie Clark and Vivienne Westwood.

	QUALITY	DISPLAY	SERVICE	COST

River Island

	16	15	13	M

Marylebone | 301-309 Oxford St., W1 (Oxford Circus) | 020-7491 3229 | www.riverisland.com

Additional locations throughout the London area

This affordable "middle-of-the-road" chain is favored by "younger" customers who fawn over the "funky and current" men's and women's clothes, "loud music and hip atmosphere"; but dissenters dis duds that "usually go out of fashion before they wear out" and the "indifferent" salespeople – made up of "fashionable young assistants" – who act so "hassle-free and relaxed" it's as "if they're really on an island."

Rug Company, The

	–	–	–	E

Holland Park | 124 Holland Park Ave., W1 (Holland Park) | 020-7229 5148 | www.therugcompany.info

The walls and floors of this Holland Park emporium are draped with a "stunning range" of "colourful" floor coverings ("the best selection of rugs in London"), including "outstanding and original modern" pieces created and customized by "designers and artists" like Paul Smith, Diane von Furstenberg and Vivienne Westwood; the staff is "helpful" and the goods are of the highest quality thanks to the fact that the textiles are made by hand – but that also means purchases have "long lead times."

Russell & Bromley

	22	19	18	E

NEW **Covent Garden** | 117 Long Acre, WC2 (Covent Garden) | 020-7240 1654
Knightsbridge | 77 Brompton Rd., SW3 (Knightsbridge) | 020-7584 7443
Marylebone | 494-496 Oxford St., W1 (Marble Arch) | 020-7493 3501
Mayfair | 109-110 New Bond St., W1 (Bond St.) | 020-7629 4001
Mayfair | 24-25 New Bond St., W1 (Bond St.) | 020-7629 6903
Mayfair | 395-397 Oxford St., W1 (Bond St.) | 020-7409 2776
St. James's | 95 Jermyn St., SW1 (Green Park/Piccadilly Circus) | 020-7930 5307 ⌂
Chelsea | 64 King's Rd., SW3 (Sloane Sq.) | 020-7584 5445
Kensington | 151-153 Kensington High St., W8 (High St. Kensington) | 020-7938 2643
www.russellandbromley.co.uk

They might "not be Jimmy Choo's", but "there's something for everyone" at this stalwart chain selling "reliable and reasonably priced" shoes you'll wear "for years and years"; if the selection (from "conservative work" to "fun weekend" stompers) is the bonus, the downside, surveyors say, is that the slightly "pushy" sales staff always "tries to sell you a coordinating handbag" from their "fairly dubious" collection.

Salvatore Ferragamo

	27	25	23	VE

Knightsbridge | 207 Sloane St., SW1 (Knightsbridge) | 020-7838 7730
Mayfair | 24 Old Bond St., W1 (Bond St.) | 020-7629 5007
www.salvatoreferragamo.it

"The shoes are a perfect fit" when they come from this family-run Italian luxury brand popular for its accessories and comfortable, chic footwear, including "men's loafers that may last longer than you and never go out of fashion"; the posh Bond Street and Sloane Street stores stock some "different" styles than both Italy and the U.S., but the very same "high quality" remains.

	QUALITY	DISPLAY	SERVICE	COST

Science Museum
20 **19** **16** **M**

South Kensington | Exhibition Rd., SW7 (South Kensington) |
020-7942 4454 | www.sciencemuseum.org.uk

"Geeks" and science freaks love this "informative and educational"
museum gift shop where, thanks to all of the "great gadgetry" for children, "parents are often subjected to blackmail" by their kids; gripers
groan that it shamelessly "capitalizes on the tourist trade" by selling
overpriced "science toys", but most aver that the "brilliant range" of
experiments and "clever", "fun-to-explore" displays will "stimulate
the imagination" of the little ones.

⚡ Selfridges
25 **23** **20** **E**

Marylebone | 400 Oxford St., W1 (Bond St./Marble Arch) | 0800-123 400 |
www.selfridges.com

"After re-hipping itself in the past decade", this "well-organised"
Oxford Street department store has become the "high church for sho-
paholics" in search of "everything from couture and the latest shoes to
books and cosmetics"; the "front windows are a statement in fashion
themselves", but once inside some call the decor "space-agey" – and
warn that the megastore's "dazzling selection" comes "at a price",
plus, at peak times, "finding a sales assistant can be so hard they
should be electronically tagged."

Shellys
15 **14** **15** **M**

Bloomsbury | 159 Oxford St., W1 (Oxford Circus) | 020-7437 5842
Covent Garden | 14-18 Neal St., WC2 (Covent Garden) | 020-7240 3726
Marylebone | 266-270 Regent St., W1 (Oxford Circus) | 020-7478 1730
Chelsea | 124B King's Rd., SW3 (Sloane Sq.) | 020-7581 5537
www.shellys.co.uk

This "trendy" shoe chain with "super-cute designs" is a hit with
teenagers and shoppers looking for disposable "designer knockoffs"
built to last only until the styles change; fans say the lack of quality
is forgivable at these "dirt-cheap prices", but less pardonable is
the spotty service.

Shop at Bluebird, The
- **-** **-** **E**

Chelsea | 350 King's Rd., SW3 (Sloane Sq.) | 020-7351 3873 |
www.theshopatbluebird.com

An "innovative space" on Chelsea's famous King's Road, this shop is
"loaded with European-style" clothing for women as well as an eclectic mix of furniture, books, accessories, children's clothing and
vintage – over 50 designers from around the world are represented in
the frequently changing stock; confused voters find the "weird stuff"
"ridiculously expensive" and are "not keen" on the "unisex changing
area", but others appreciate the "high quality" and "original" concept.

Size?
- **-** **-** **M**

Covent Garden | 37A Neal St., WC2 (Covent Garden) | 020-7379 9768
Soho | 33 Carnaby St., W1 (Oxford Circus) | 020-7287 4016
Ladbroke Grove | 200 Portobello Rd., W11 (Ladbroke Grove) | 020-7792 8494
www.size-online.co.uk

This trio of stores is a great place to find "old-school trainers" like the
recently reissued 1980s Nike Air Max Light, as well as newer stylings
from the big sneaker brands including Adidas, Nike and Puma; a small
selection of unisex T-shirts and hoodies are on offer to complete the

look, but serious sportsmen steer clear, since this cool shop (with faux graffiti on the shoe-lined walls) is strictly for those who want to pose.

✓ Smythson of Bond Street ⑤   28 | 25 | 22 | VE

Mayfair | 40 New Bond St., W1 (Bond St.) | 020-7629 8558
Chelsea | 135 Sloane St., SW1 (Sloane Sq.) | 020-7730 5520
Notting Hill | 214 Westbourne Grove, W11 (Notting Hill Gate) |
020-7243 3527
www.smythson.com

"Elegant and classy" enough to inspire you "to write thank-you cards", these "sublime" stationery boutiques are "so British" that one shopper claims "my accent improved before I left"; the "highest quality" array of papers, diaries, travel wallets and leather goods are so "extraordinarily" expensive that you "need an oligarch to pay for them"; still, most say that this "pure luxury" is "worth the splurge."

Sonia Rykiel ⑤   25 | 21 | 20 | E

Mayfair | 27-29 Brook St., W1 (Bond St.) | 020-7493 5255 |
www.soniarykiel.com

The chic French designer known to some as the "queen of knits" sells fabulous, "flirty" and instantly wearable fashions out of her bright Mayfair boutique; in addition to sweaters and coats, the store stocks a "limited selection" of "top-quality" shoes, handbags and other accessories for "women who know who they are."

SPACE.NK apothecary   26 | 24 | 21 | E

Westbourne Grove | 127-131 Westbourne Grove, W2 (Notting Hill Gate) |
020-7727 8063 | www.spacenk.com
Additional locations throughout the London area

Over 62 brands of "beautifully" presented makeup, skincare, "boutique perfumes" and scented candles are on display at this "modern girl's dream" chain where "hard-to-find European and American" goods share space with the store's own line of bath and home products, making this a great place for gifts – "for oneself!"; the service can be either "polite and expert" or "lukewarm", "depending upon the shift."

Steinberg & Tolkien   23 | 17 | 17 | E

Chelsea | 193 King's Rd., SW3 (Sloane Sq.) | 020-7376 3660

"Dig into the past you wanted" at this "amazing" Chelsea vintage shop "where they know their stuff and charge heftily for it"; you'll find "good-quality" fashion items from all the decades including "shoes, hats, gloves", wedding dresses and "costume jewellery", and even though the store is slightly "cluttered", it's still worth "rummaging for that special vintage find."

Stella McCartney ⑤   22 | 21 | 20 | VE

Mayfair | 30 Bruton St., W1 (Bond St./Green Park) | 020-7518 3100 |
www.stellamccartney.com

At this upscale Mayfair shop, ex-Beatle Paul McCartney's daughter shows off her "trendy, fashionable" creations (including a more casual Adidas line) in a "nice-looking" boutique setting featuring floral wallpaper and a grand staircase; the "impressive collection" of well-tailored womenswear is "cutting-edge" enough "for those wishing to experiment", but "feminine at the same time", and though it all seems "pricey" to some, "that's what you pay for quality."

	QUALITY	DISPLAY	SERVICE	COST

Swarovski
24 | 23 | 19 | E

Bloomsbury | 147 Oxford St., W1 (Tottenham Court Rd.) | 020-7287 9777
Covent Garden | 31 James St., WC2 (Covent Garden) | 020-3077 1000
Knightsbridge | 39-41 Brompton Rd., SW3 (Knightsbridge) | 020-7823 9111
Mayfair | 411 Oxford St., W1 (Bond St.) | 020-7499 4221
Piccadilly | 137-139 Regent St., W1 (Piccadilly Circus) | 020-7434 2500
www.swarovski.com

"Fantastic for magpies" and those who love a bit of "bling with zing", this "eye-catching" quintet uses "clever lighting" to reveal "all of the facets" of their "stunning" Austrian crystal, including figurines, collectibles and home accessories plus "vibrant", "upmarket jewellery" that's "not for the shy or retiring"; "invariably pleasant and helpful" staff are also on hand – and not just to "make sure you don't break anything."

Tanner Krolle
∇ 25 | 24 | 23 | VE

Knightsbridge | 5 Sloane St., SW1 (Knightsbridge) | 020-7823 1688
Piccadilly | 3 Burlington Gdns., W1 (Green Park) | 020-7287 5121 ⑤
www.tannerkrolle.com

"Take out a second mortgage" and head to one of these "stylish" stores in Knightsbridge and Piccadilly, where the selection of "wonderful leather goods" includes everything from "beautifully made handbags", folios and briefcases to iPod holders and women's shoes; the prices may seem "high", but you'll receive "helpful", "knowledgeable" service and a "quality" "product that will last."

Tartine et Chocolat ⑤
∇ 26 | 22 | 19 | E

Mayfair | 66 S. Molton St., W1 (Bond St.) | 020-7629 7233 | www.tartine-et-chocolat.fr

At this Mayfair outlet of a popular French store, the "conservatively" designed childrenswear is so "divine" you'll be hoping your tot never outgrows his or her finery – especially given the "pricey" tabs; still, it's a "fantastic" choice for finding that "beautiful piece for a special occasion" or picking up smart accessories that include shoes, toys, lotions and shampoo.

⒵ Tate Modern
23 | 22 | 19 | M

Southwark | Bankside, SE1 (Southwark/St. Paul's) | 020-7401 5167 | www.tate.org.uk/shop

"Since you can't walk away with the originals", the Tate Modern's "fabulous" museum store might be "the next best thing", offering "cool, funky stuff for the 'artiste' in everyone"; "if you're looking for a certain book, you're sure to find it" within the shop's "extensive" collection, but many are content to simply "peruse" the "eclectic" selection of cards, posters, stationery, housewares "and much, much more."

Ted Baker
24 | 22 | 20 | E

NEW **Covent Garden** | 1-4 Langley Ct., WC2 (Covent Garden) | 020-7497 8862
Covent Garden | 9-10 Floral St., WC2 (Covent Garden) | 020-7836 7808
Mayfair | 245 Regent St., W1 (Oxford Circus) | 020-7493 6251
Canary Wharf | 5 Canada Pl., E14 (Canary Wharf) | 020-7519 6588
Chelsea | 19 Duke of York Sq., SW3 (Sloane Sq.) | 020-7881 0850
www.tedbaker.co.uk

Although this very British chain is best known for its "wonderful" collection of "chic, elegant" menswear (ranging from "classic to trendy"),

	QUALITY	DISPLAY	SERVICE	COST

it also offers a line of women's clothing too; it's "a must whether you're 007 or the average millionaire", but the store's "top-notch", "totally hip" threads – including its signature crease-proof 'endurance' suits – are "still (mostly) wearable by normal people."

Temperley London ☒

| | - | - | - | VE |

Notting Hill | 6-10 Colville Mews, Lonsdale Rd., W11 (Notting Hill Gate) | 020-7229 7957 | www.temperleylondon.com

For boho-chic at its ultimate, head to this whimsical showroom in Notting Hill, where Alice Temperley's feminine, handcrafted designs are delicately crocheted or embellished using embroidery, beading and multilayered printing techniques; for those who can't afford to buy one of her elaborate creations, the store's recently launched accessories line (handbags, sunglasses, wallets) is an affordable alternative.

Theo Fennell ☒

| | - | - | - | VE |

City | 4 Royal Exchange Courtyard, EC3 (Bank) | 020-7623 4380
Chelsea | 169 Fulham Rd., SW3 (South Kensington) | 020-7591 5000
www.theofennell.com

For "cool jewels" that combine sleek elegance with a hint of the traditional, head to either the Chelsea flagship or the City branch of this famed London jeweller, where the "truly wonderful" designs range from rings, necklaces and charms to "excellent" gemstone-studded crosses; in addition to budget-breaking bijoux, the shops also sell sterling silver gifts, including tableware and a playful selection of bottle lids and sleeves.

☑ Thomas Goode ☒

| | 28 | 26 | 24 | VE |

Mayfair | 19 S. Audley St., W1 (Bond St.) | 020-7499 2823 | www.thomasgoode.co.uk

"There's something decadent about this Mayfair boutique" – perhaps it's the "amazing selection" of fine bone china, crystal and silverware that's "displayed as if you were in a Victorian drawing room and not a shop"; a "London institution" since 1827, it creates pieces for the royal family, and although it "reeks of exclusivity", many consider it to be among "the best of the best."

☑ Thomas Pink

| | 26 | 24 | 22 | E |

St. James's | 85 Jermyn St., SW1 (Green Park/Piccadilly Circus) | 020-7930 6364 | www.thomaspink.co.uk

"Always tasteful, never boring", this "superb" British-based chain may have "gone mass market" but it's still "the leader of the shirt pack", proffering "well-made" garments and ties ("the attention to detail is outstanding") with "lots of colour and style"; so "try to ignore the price tag", as this shop is "a must for any man" and – "professional" ladies take note – "one of the few places where the quality of the women's shirts equal that of the men's."

Tiffany & Co. ☒

| | 26 | 25 | 21 | VE |

Mayfair | 25 Old Bond St., W1 (Green Park) | 020-7409 2790
City | 9-11 Royal Exchange Courtyard, EC3 (Bank) | 020-7409 2790
Chelsea | 145 Sloane St., SW1 (Sloane Sq.) | 020-7409 2790
www.tiffany.com/uk

You'll find "excellent quality items that are instant heirlooms" at this "American favourite with something for everyone, from simple ster-

ling silver to huge dripping diamonds"; while some insist New York City's Fifth Avenue flagship has "the best selection", the three London locations are also "wonderful stores" that have "kept up the standards" for "beautiful" jewellery, watches, gifts and accessories.

Tod's ⊠   27 | 23 | 22 | VE

Knightsbridge | 35-36 Sloane St., SW1 (Knightsbridge) | 020-7235 1321
Mayfair | 2-5 Old Bond St., W1 (Green Park) | 020-7493 2237
www.tods.com

"Even if you don't own a car, you'll covet the driving shoes" – they're "the perfect throw-on to walk around London" – available at these "minimalist" Knightsbridge and Mayfair branches of a "classic Italian" brand; it's a "luxury for sure" but "definitely worth the money" for "comfortable", "top-quality" footwear and "fashionable handbags" that "ooze style and class" and are accompanied by "nice, helpful" service.

Tommy Hilfiger   20 | 16 | 15 | E

Knightsbridge | 6 Sloane St., SW1 (Knightsbridge) | 020-7235 2500
NEW **Piccadilly** | 134 Regent St., W1 (Piccadilly Circus) | 020-7287 2843
www.tommy.com

Although many laud the "fashionable gear" featured at these Knightsbridge and Piccadilly outposts of an American casualwear brand, critics claim the label has "lost its luster" in recent years – the "hardwearing, comfortable" clothing "would be great if it were 2002"; though patrons agree that the displays are "well-organised", surveyors are divided on service ("helpful" vs. "lazy") and cost ("reasonable" vs. "expensive").

Topman   14 | 17 | 14 | M

Marylebone | 214 Oxford St., W1 (Oxford Circus) | 020-7636 7700 | www.topman.co.uk

"You'll find plenty of deals and fashion-forward offerings" at the "men's version of Topshop" in Marylebone, where patrons "can pick up some fine basics" or mine for "rather trendy" treasure "without denting a hole in their wallets"; "if you're over 30, be prepared to feel a bit old", as the "hip atmosphere" includes "headache-inducing music" that a few frazzled shoppers say "should be turned down a notch."

⊠ Topshop   17 | 20 | 14 | I

Covent Garden | 32 The Strand, WC2 (Charing Cross) | 020-7839 4144
Marylebone | 214 Oxford St., W1 (Oxford Circus) | 020-7636 7700
Victoria | 18 Cardinal Pl., SW1 (Victoria) | 020-7828 6139
Canary Wharf | 3 Canada Sq., E14 (Canary Wharf) | 020-7512 1996
Kensington | 42-44 Kensington High St., W8 (High St. Kensington) | 020-7938 1242
www.topshop.co.uk

"A staple" for "stylish, affordable" basics, knockoffs and designer/celebrity collaborations, this British-based chain is "always on top of the trends", "somehow managing to satisfy both mothers and daughters" alike with its "fun and funky clothing" and "clublike atmosphere"; "plan to spend the entire day at the Oxford Street flagship" where there's "a good selection of vintage" items and the "shoe department goes on forever."

	QUALITY	DISPLAY	SERVICE	COST

Uniqlo

16 | 14 | 13 | I

Bloomsbury | The Plaza | 120 Oxford St., W1 (Oxford Circus) | 020-7734 5369

Piccadilly | 84-86 Regent St., W1 (Piccadilly Circus) | 020-7434 9688

NEW Kensington | 54-58 Kensington High St., W8 (High St. Kensington) | 020-7376 0054

www.uniqlo.co.uk

Known as "the Gap of Japan", this Asia-based clothing chain now has a trio of London locations, all offering "the good things that [label] implies: quality, subtle design, superb function and value pricing"; though the stores' "simple display" can make you feel "like you're in a warehouse" and there's "not much service", if you're able to snag some "stylish basics" to "mix with your designer items, you win every time."

United Colors of Benetton (aka Benetton)

18 | 18 | 16 | M

Knightsbridge | 23-27 Brompton Rd., SW3 (Knightsbridge) | 020-7591 0925

Marylebone | 255-259 Regent St., W1 (Oxford Circus) | 020-7647 4220

www.benetton.com

At these Knightsbridge and Oxford Circus offshoots of an international chain, the "nice, reliable" basics for men, women and children are characterized by a colourful, "preppy" flair; though "you can find some excellent products", some say the selection is "hit-or-miss", while others who "haven't been here since the 1980s" wonder "do people still shop here?"

Urban Outfitters

16 | 21 | 13 | M

Covent Garden | 42-56 Earlham St., WC2 (Covent Garden) | 020-7759 6390

Marylebone | 200 Oxford St., W1 (Oxford Circus) | 020-7907 0800

Kensington | 36-38 Kensington High St., W8 (High St. Kensington) | 020-7761 1001

www.urbanoutfitters.co.uk

"Why is this store just better in London?" wonder those urbanites unaware that an "infusion of local Brit designers" sets this trio apart from its international brethren; it's "one-stop shopping" at these "eclectic" options where an "imaginative variety" of "funky clothing" ("professionals, look elsewhere") is interspersed with a "mishmash" of accessories, gifts, housewares and more – including items that are "useless but darned funny to have."

Valentino ⊠

27 | 23 | 20 | VE

Knightsbridge | 174 Sloane St., SW1 (Knightsbridge) | 020-7235 5855 | www.valentino.it

At this "posh" boutique in Knightsbridge, one of the top names in Italian haute couture showcases a "stunning range of clothes and shoes" for men and women that are "stylish, versatile" and frequently found on the red carpet; "eye-catching" displays and "personal" service – the "assistants go out of their way" – are an added bonus, and while it all comes at an "expensive cost", "it's Valentino, what do you expect?"

Van Cleef & Arpels ⊠

- | - | - | VE

Mayfair | 9 New Bond St., W1 (Green Park) | 020-7493 0400 | www.vancleef-arpels.com

"It's a pleasure to spend one's hard-earned money" at this Mayfair location of a famed French jeweller, where the collection of art nouveau watches and bijoux is inspired by nature – think butterflies, leaves, lo-

| | QUALITY | DISPLAY | SERVICE | COST |

tuses and flowers; meanwhile, the store itself – it's recently been re-done by the renowned designer Anouska Hempel – offers an environment in which "everyone is treated equally and with respect."

Versace
| | 21 | 21 | 19 | VE |

Knightsbridge | 183-184 Sloane St., SW1 (Knightsbridge) | 020-7259 5700 | www.versace.com

"The name says it all" at this Knightsbridge notch in the belt of a luxury Italian brand, where Donatella Versace has maintained the "stunning quality" of her late brother Gianni's designs, producing "out-of-this-world" pieces that prove "sex sells" – "ooh-la-la!"; the colourful clothing is admittedly "expensive", but the "beautiful shop" comes complete with "nice" staff that make you feel "relaxed and comfortable" as they "help you find a look you'll love."

☒ Victoria & Albert Museum Shop
| | 24 | 22 | 20 | M |

South Kensington | Cromwell Rd., SW7 (South Kensington) | 020-7942 2703 | www.vandashop.com

Featuring a "wonderful mix of items inspired by the museum's collections", this South Kensington shop offers an "unbelievable range of products", from "quirky", "inexpensive trinkets" to "unusual, beautiful and tasteful" jewellery, furniture, textiles, books, crafts, toys and other accessories; in short, it's "one of the best places to buy gifts for friends and family" – just "don't forget [to purchase] a little something for yourself."

Vivienne Westwood
| | 27 | 23 | 20 | E |

Mayfair | 44 Conduit St., W1 (Bond St.) | 020-7439 1109
Mayfair | 6 Davies St., W1 (Bond St.) | 020-7629 3757 ☒

Vivienne Westwood's World's End ☒
Chelsea | 430 King's Rd., SW10 (Sloane Sq.) | 020-7352 6551
www.viviennewestwood.co.uk

Credited with founding the punk style in the '70s, "the empress of fashion" has "lost none of her edge", still filling these three London locations with "wild yet wonderful" clothes, shoes and accessories (including her signature tweeds, tartans and corsets); the merchandise may be "expensive", but those fans who "have been coveting her creations for years" argue that the "brilliant" designs "should be priceless, so we're lucky we can wear them at all."

Warehouse
| | 16 | 14 | 13 | M |

Marylebone | 19-21 Argyll St., W1 (Oxford Circus) | 020-7437 7101 | www.warehousefashion.com
Additional locations throughout the London area

Teenagers and those looking for a bit of "throwaway fashion" will appreciate this "funky" Marylebone link in a British chain, where the "quality basics" and "trendy" womenswear designs "won't max out your credit card"; although there's a "great variety of styles and colours", some patrons are "put off" by "messy", "cluttered" displays and service that's "what you would expect – nothing special."

West Village
| | - | - | - | E |

NEW Covent Garden | 44 Monmouth St., WC2 (Covent Garden) | 020-7240 7835
Chelsea | 315 King's Rd., SW3 (Sloane Sq.) | 020-7349 9199

(continued)

West Village
Notting Hill | 35 Kensington Park Rd., W11 (Notting Hill Gate) | 020-7243 6912
www.thewestvillage.co.uk
Inspired by its namesake hip NYC neighborhood, this funky British chain – now with three London outlets – attracts stylish young women who appreciate the shops' eclectic, candy-coloured collection of denim, vintage styles, accessories and shoes (plus the maternity line, Bumpsville); shoppers can always find "some fabulous designs here", but be forewarned: it can be "pricey."

Whistles
20 | 19 | 17 | M

Marylebone | 12 St. Christopher's Pl., W1 (Bond St.) | 020-7487 4484 |
www.whistles.co.uk
Additional locations throughout the London area
"Attention all readers of British chick lit": this "sweet, sassy and sophisticated" chain is a "reliable" choice for a "variety" of "beautiful, different" Parisian-inspired pieces – suitable for work or "boho needs" – "that will make your wardrobe stand out"; it's all "moderately priced", making this a "treasure chest of a shop" full of "fashion you can afford."

White Company
21 | 20 | 17 | E

Marylebone | 12 Marylebone High St., W1 (Baker St.) | 020-7935 7879
Chelsea | 8 Symons St., SW3 (Sloane Sq.) | 020-7823 5322
www.thewhitecompany.com
Prepare to be "dazzled" by these "whiter than white" home furnishings stores in Chelsea and Marylebone – you'll "need sunglasses" – where a selection of "crisp" bedding and bath linens, "lovely loungewear", rugs, china, glassware and cutlery is displayed in a "minimalist" space that "feels clean" and "inviting"; while some find it "overpriced", most shoppers agree that "the products last well" and are "worth paying that little bit extra" for.

Yves Saint Laurent: Rive Gauche 🗷
▽ 28 | 29 | 20 | VE

Knightsbridge | 171 Sloane St., SW1 (Knightsbridge) | 020-7235 6706
Mayfair | 33 Old Bond St., W1 (Bond St.) | 020-7493 1800
www.ysl.com
Although creative director Tom Ford retired in 2004, this fashionable French brand has continued to produce "elegant", "well-constructed" men's and women's clothing under the care of his replacement, Stefano Pilati; while the Knightsbridge and Mayfair stores are magnets for celebrities (e.g. Sienna Miller, Kate Moss) looking for red-carpet gowns or the next 'it' bag, the shops also sell slightly more affordable perfumes, sunglasses and accessories.

🇿 Zara
17 | 19 | 14 | I

Mayfair | 333 Oxford St., W1 (Bond St.) | 020-7518 1550 | www.zara.com
Additional locations throughout the London area
You'll "always be able to find something" at the Mayfair location of a "reliable" "Spanish fashion staple", where the "inexpensive" women's and men's clothing is "more sophisticated" and the quality "much better" than at similar stores; veering toward the "conservative", the "stylish threads" will have you "covered, from a professional look to a night out with friends"; the only downside: there's "no personalized service."

Noteworthy Antiques Markets

Alfies Antique Market 🛒Ⓜ
Marylebone | 13-25 Church St., NW8 (Marylebone) | 020-7723 6066 |
www.alfiesantiques.com

Camden Market 🛒
Camden Town | Camden High St., NW1 (Camden Town/Chalk Farm) |
www.camdenlock.net

Church Street Market 🛒Ⓜ
Marylebone | Church St., NW1 (Edgware Rd.)

Grays Antique Market 🛒
Mayfair | 58 Davies Street, W1K (Bond St.) | 020-7629 7034 |
www.graysantiques.com

Niche Ⓜ
Kensal Rise | 70 Chamberlayne Rd., NW1 (Kensal Green) |
020-3181 0081

Northcote Road Market 🛒Ⓜ
Clapham | Northcote Rd., SW11 (Clapham Junction B.R.)

Portobello Market 🛒Ⓜ
Notting Hill | Portobello Rd., W11 (Ladbroke Grove/Notting Hill Gate) |
020-7229 8354 | www.portobelloroad.co.uk

Spitalfields Market
Shoreditch | 105A Commercial St., E16 (Aldgate East/Liverpool St.) |
www.visitspitalfields.com

Noteworthy Food Markets

Allens Butchers of Mount St.
Mayfair | 117 Mount St., W1 (Bond St.) | 020-7499 5831

Bluebird Epicerie
Chelsea | 350 King's Rd., SW3 (Sloane Sq.) | 020-7559 1140 |
www.conran.com

Harrods Food Hall
Knightsbridge | 87-136 Brompton Rd., SW1 (Knightsbridge) |
020-7730 1234 | www.harrods.com

Harvey Nichols Food Market
Knightsbridge | 109-125 Knightsbridge, SW1 (Knightsbridge) |
020-7235 5000 | www.harveynichols.com

Hope & Greenwood
Dulwich | 20 N. Cross Rd., SE22 (East Dulwich) | 020-8613 1777 |
www.hopeandgreenwood.co.uk

Hummingbird Bakery
South Kensington | 47 Old Brompton Rd., SW7 (South Kensington) |
020-7584 0055
Notting Hill | 133 Portobello Rd., W11 (Notting Hill Gate) |
020-7229 6446 Ⓜ
www.hummingbirdbakery.com

La Fromagerie
Marylebone | 2-4 Moxon St., W1 (Baker St.) | 020-7935 0341 |
www.lafromagerie.co.uk

L'Artisan du Chocolat ⊠
Chelsea | 89 Lower Sloane St., SW1 (Sloane Sq.) | 020-7824 8365 | www.artisanduchocolat.com

Melt
Notting Hill | 59 Ledbury Rd., W11 (Notting Hill Gate) | 020-7727 5030 | www.meltchocolates.com

Panzer's
St. John's Wood | 13-19 Circus Rd., NW8 (St. John's Wood) | 020-7722 8596 | www.panzers.co.uk

Partridges
Chelsea | 2-5 Duke of York Sq., SW3 (Sloane Sq.) | 020-7730 0651
South Kensington | 17-21 Gloucester Rd., SW7 (Gloucester Rd.) | 020-7581 0535
www.partridges.co.uk

Planet Organic
Bloomsbury | 22 Torrington Pl., WC1 (Goodge St.) | 020-7436 1929
Fulham | 25 Effie Rd., SW6 (Fulham Broadway) | 020-7731 7222
Westbourne Grove | 42 Westbourne Grove, W2 (Bayswater) | 020-7221 7171
www.planetorganic.com

Raoul's Deli
St. John's Wood | 8-10 Clifton Rd., W9 (Maida Vale) | 020-7289 6646 | www.raoulsgourmet.com

Sainsbury's
Swiss Cottage | 241-279 Finchley Rd., NW3 (Swiss Cottage) | 020-7433 1493 | www.sainsbury.co.uk
Additional locations throughout the London area

Selfridges Food Hall
Marylebone | 400 Oxford St., W1A (Bond St./Marble Arch) | 0800-123 400 | www.selfridges.com

Tesco
Kensington | 100 W. Cromwell Rd., W14 (West Kensington) | 0845-6779 388 | www.tesco.com
Additional locations throughout the London area

Tom's
Westbourne Grove | 226 Westbourne Grove, W11 (Notting Hill Gate) | 020-7221 8818

Waitrose
Canary Wharf | 16-19 Canada Pl., E14 (Canary Wharf) | 020-7719 0300 | www.waitrose.com
Additional locations throughout the London area

Whole Foods Market
Kensington | Barkers Bldg. | 63-97 Kensington High St., W8
(High St. Kensington) | 020-7368 4500 | www.wholefoodsmarket.com

ATTRACTIONS

Attractions

It's often said that there's something for everyone in London. Whether you're after museums, art, history, grand squares or relaxing parks, you'll find it within this varied metropolis.

MAP OUT A PLAN: To make the most of your time, figure out an itinerary that suits your interests and visit key sites in the same general area on the same day. Stop at a local British Visitor Centre for free brochures, maps and events calendars before you start. Determine opening and closing times, which can vary by venue (though most are open seven days a week by 10 AM and close between 5:30 and 6:30 PM). Locate the Tube and bus stops nearest your attractions, and purchase a Travelcard if you plan to use public transport frequently.

GET AN OVERVIEW: For first-time visitors, organised tours are a good way to familiarise yourself with the city and its neighbourhoods. Double-decker hop-on, hop-off sightseeing buses may seem touristy, but they provide a solid introduction and often offer passes that allow you to jump the queue at certain attractions. Tickets on these buses are valid for 24 hours so you can choose when, where and how long to spend at each site. Walking tours are also a smart way to gain more in-depth information – and are usually less expensive.

FREE FUN: There's plenty of enjoyment to be had that doesn't cost a pence. Many of the city's best sights are free, from the Houses of Parliament to various art museums such as the British Museum (voted No. 1 for Appeal and the Most Popular in our Survey), the Geffrye, National Gallery, National Portrait Gallery, Tate Britain and Tate Modern. And, many of the most quintessential London spots – the Tower Bridge, Big Ben, Trafalgar Square, the changing of the guards at Buckingham Palace – won't cut into your budget either.

TICKET SAVVY: If you're planning to visit lots of attractions, skip the queues and save money by purchasing a London Pass valid at more than 50 top sites. The passes are sold for one, two, three or six days for a set fee, and also offer discounts on restaurants, theatre and other activities (www.londonpass.com). There are ways to save on some of the higher-priced attractions as well. The London Eye offers 10% discounts on tickets purchased online; Madame Tussauds waxworks museum charges less for visits after 3 PM and even less after 5 PM during the summer; and the London Zoo makes 20% discount coupons available on its Web site.

TAKE A BREAK: If it all gets to be too much, know that you're never far from a park or green space. Hyde Park, Regent's Park and St James's Park offer plenty of respite right in the centre of things, whilst Greenwich Park, about 6 kilometres (4 miles) from the City, has spectacular views over Canary Wharf from the Royal Observatory.

Top Appeal Ratings

Ratings are to the left of names.

BY TYPE

ARTS/PERFORMANCE CENTRES

- 26 Shakespeare's Globe
- 25 Royal Albert Hall
- National Theatre
- 20 Barbican

HISTORIC LANDMARKS

- 28 Tower of London
- Hampton Court Palace
- 27 St. Paul's Cathedral
- Buckingham Palace
- 25 Horse Guards Parade

MUSEUMS

- 28 British Museum
- National Gallery
- 27 Churchill Museum
- Imperial War Museum
- Courtauld Institute

PARKS

- 26 Regent's Park
- St. James's Park
- Hyde Park
- 25 Kensington Gardens
- Hampstead Heath

RELIGIOUS SITES

- 28 Westminster Abbey
- 27 St. Paul's Cathedral
- 26 Westminster Cathedral
- 24 Southwark Cathedral
- 23 Temple Church

SHOPPING CENTRES/MARKETS

- 23 Portobello Market
- Covent Garden
- Jermyn St.
- 22 Spitalfields Market
- 21 Burlington Arcade

BY LOCATION

BOROUGH

- 26 Shakespeare's Globe
- Borough Market
- 24 Southwark Cathedral

CITY

- 28 Tower of London
- 27 St. Paul's Cathedral
- 25 Museum of London

COVENT GARDEN

- 27 Courtauld Institute
- 26 National Portrait Gallery
- 24 Somerset House

MARYLEBONE

- 26 Regent's Park
- 21 Madame Tussauds
- 19 Sherlock Holmes Museum

MAYFAIR

- 26 Hyde Park
- 25 Royal Academy of Arts
- 24 Wellington Museum

SHOREDITCH

- 24 Geffrye Museum
- 22 Spitalfields Market
- 18 Brick Lane

SOUTH BANK

- 26 London Eye
- 25 National Theatre
- 21 London Aquarium

SOUTH KENSINGTON

- 27 Victoria & Albert Museum
- 26 Science Museum
- Natural History Museum

SOUTHWARK

- 27 Imperial War Museum
- 25 Tate Modern
- 16 London Dungeon

WESTMINSTER

- 28 Westminster Abbey
- National Gallery
- Houses of Parliament

Attractions

Ratings & Symbols

Appeal, Facilities and **Service** are rated on a 0 to 30 scale.

Cost reflects the attraction's high-season price range for one adult.

£0 Free
I £5 or less
M £6 to £12

E £13 to £20
VE £21 or more

▽ low response | less reliable

Bank of England, The
19 | 16 | 19 | £0

City | Threadneedle St., EC2 (Bank St.) | 020-7601 5545 | www.bankofengland.co.uk

"Fondle a bar of gold" at this free and "fascinating history of money" in the City where "finance types" and those interested in "how the British empire grew" head for an "old-school" look at currency; audio-visual tours, rotating exhibits and kid-friendly contests (design your own bank notes and money boxes) are "surprisingly fun", but those who find the story of the five-pound note "quite dry" are "not as excited" as they'd hoped; N.B. closed on weekends and bank holidays.

Barbican, The
20 | 21 | 19 | M

City | Silk St., EC2 (Barbican) | 020-7638 4141 | www.barbican.org.uk

This "vast" multi-arts conference and exibition hall "lost in a ghastly area of east London" divides opinions like no other, with fans calling it "what every block of flats aspires to when it grows up" and critics cringing over a "sterile" "monstrosity"; most agree, however, that it's a "top cultural venue" that "has it all" from "theatre to music and film" (there's a concert hall, two theatres, three cinemas, two art galleries, a conservatory and a public lending library on-site); though it's "devilishly hard to find and navigate", a recent interior revamp may have improved things; N.B. the London Symphony Orchestra is based here.

Borough Market
26 | 17 | 20 | £0

Borough | off Borough High St., SE1 (London Bridge) | 020-7407 1002 | www.boroughmarket.org.uk

"Discover what English food really tastes like" at this ancient food market just south of London Bridge, where the "sumptuous" produce, "incredible" "sausage, fish, shrimp, pork, bacon" and "English and French cheese" vie with "jams and baked goods" in a "paradise for foodies"; though it gets "horrifically busy", "brave the crowds" cause it's a "must-do" for lunch or just to "soak up the atmosphere."

Brick Lane
18 | 13 | 15 | £0

Shoreditch | bet. Fournier & Woodseer Sts., E1 (Shoreditch)

"Cool Shoreditch kids" rub shoulders with "Bengali grannies" in this East End area known as Banglatown, where successive waves of immi-

grants have left their stamp (the "Fournier Street mosque" used to be both a church and a synagogue) and foodies can sample the "amazing" Bangladeshi/Indian curry houses that line the streets; you'll get "inexpensive" meals that are "worthy of the trip", "wonderful browsing" opportunities and "great contrasts" – one man's "colourful" is another man's "gritty."

British Library

25 | 25 | 21 | £0

King's Cross | 96 Euston Rd., NW1 (King's Cross) | 020-7412 7332 | www.bl.uk

As you might expect, this King's Cross attraction is "a bibliophile's dream", with "beautiful spaces", "wonderful exhibits", 13 million books and a range of writings on display that's simply "mind-boggling" (from the Magna Carta to a Gutenberg bible to "Paul McCartney's handwritten lyrics for 'Yesterday'"); better still, this "fascinating", "world-class treasure" is one of the capital's "hidden gems" and therefore "not particularly busy."

☑ British Museum, The

28 | 26 | 22 | £0

Holborn | Great Russell St., WC1 (Tottenham Court Rd.) | 020-7323 8000 | www.thebritishmuseum.ac.uk

A "must-see, with good reason", this "world standard" in Holborn that's had an "amazing renovation" is "in a league of its own" say fans who vote it No. 1 for Appeal and Facilities as well as the Most Popular Attraction in the London Survey; those who happily "spend a day here" soaking up exhibits that go "beyond their wildest dreams" find a "bit of something for everybody" – Egyptian artefacts (including mummies), Greek and Roman antiquities, the Rosetta Stone, Assyrian sculptures and the "spectacular" Elgin marbles – and even better, it's free; just remember, it can be overwhelming, so "choose galleries of interest and stick to them", then plan to "revisit every year."

☑ Buckingham Palace

27 | 21 | 18 | M

Westminster | Buckingham Palace, SW1 (Victoria) | 020-7766 7300 | www.royalcollection.org.uk

"If you're in London and don't see" this "iconic" Westminster building – the Queen's residence – "what are you doing here?" ask those who find the "changing of the guards" a "classic" sight, the tour through the "fabulous and opulent private rooms" "wonderful" and the royal family's art collection "amazing"; yes, "tourists are only shown a small part of the palace", but there's still plenty of "pomp and splendour" to inspire "awe."

Burlington Arcade

21 | 17 | 19 | £0

Mayfair | Mayfair, W1 (Green Park/Piccadilly Circus) | 020-7630 1411 | www.burlington-arcade.co.uk

"One of the prettiest shopping arcades in the world" (and Britain's first, opened in 1819), this "old-fashioned mall" off Piccadilly is an "absolutely gorgeous" "reminder of London a hundred years ago"; doormen in Edwardian frock coats, "top hats and white gloves" add to the traditional atmosphere, as does a set of "its own bylaws (no whistling or running) – and beadles to enforce them", but budget-watchers stick to "browsing" and "window shopping", as the stores are "impossibly expensive."

	APPEAL	FACIL.	SERVICE	COST

Camden Market
20 | 13 | 13 | £0

Camden Town | Camden High St., NW1 (Camden Town/Chalk Farm) | www.camdenlock.net

Packed with an "alternative crowd" including "punk rock types with Mohawks and earrings", this "eclectic", "labyrinthine" street market that runs the gamut from "emo T-shirts" to "antiques" to "vintage clothing" to "record stores" "overflowing with treasures" appeals to "teens and twentysomethings" who find just as much "people-watching as shopping"; it's "not for everyone", especially those who find it filled with "cheap trinkets and bad food", but if you do go, arrive "early on the weekends" or you'll get caught "in a crushing mass" of humanity.

Canary Wharf
16 | 20 | 14 | £0

Canary Wharf | access from Canary Wharf tube or DLR stations, E1 (Canary Wharf) | 020-7418 2000 | www.canarywharf.com

A "stylish, modern area" crammed with "shiny monoliths" and "spectacular architecture", this newish East End "commercial" development includes the country's tallest building, the "closest thing to a mall" (full of "top-class shops") and a "delightful Tube station"; although it's "dead on weekends" and some say "there's not enough there to lure tourists", it's "the heart of the new London" and "worth a look."

Carnaby St.
16 | 14 | 14 | £0

Soho | bordered by Beak & Great Marlborough Sts.; Kingly & Marshall Sts., W1 (Oxford Circus) | www.carnaby.co.uk

Former "flower children" "can't miss" a visit to this West End street – once the centre of the Swinging '60s – where "some of the charm still lingers" in the "funky", "quirky" shops; still, many find it's "not what it was back in the day", with too many "tacky souvenirs", "tourists" and "chain stores you have come to know and loathe", claiming it's "so kitschy" now that only "teenagers love it."

Chelsea Physic Garden
21 | 19 | 17 | £0

Chelsea | 66 Royal Hospital Rd., Swan Walk, SW3 (Sloane Sq.) | 020-7352 5646 | www.chelseaphysicgarden.co.uk

Founded in 1673 by the Worshipful Society of Apothecaries, this garden "oasis of calm" is "an easy walk from Chelsea, Belgravia or Pimlico" and features 500 species of mostly medicinal plans; a "small but lovely", "very English" "paradise", it's especially good if you take one of the "guided tours" or "if you can find a spot to perch" on the grass (beware "hordes" on weekends); N.B. open April to October only.

Chinatown
18 | 15 | 13 | £0

Soho | bordered by Lisle St. & Shaftesbury Ave. (inc. Gerrard St.); Wardour St. & Newport Pl., WC2 (Leicester Sq./Piccadilly Circus) | www.chinatown-online.co.uk

There's plenty of "hustle and bustle" in this West End area centered on Gerrard Street, with "Asian grocery stores", dozens of "authentic" shops knocking out Chinese "films and music" and "surprisingly excellent" cuisine (the restaurants are the main attraction); those who are "rather disappointed" it's "so small" compared to other cities' Chinatowns say it's "not very interesting", but others insist the "streets have been rejuvenated" and it's "right next to the Theatre District for great pre-show dining."

	APPEAL	FACIL.	SERVICE	COST

Churchill Museum and Cabinet War Rooms   27 | 25 | 23 | M

Westminster | Clive Steps | King Charles St., SW1 (Westminster) |
020-7930 6961 | www.iwm.org.uk

The "subterranean offices" in Westminster "where Churchill was
based during the blitz" were rediscovered in the '80s exactly how
they'd been left when they were locked up in 1945; the "moving", "engaging and innovative" exhibits – including the prime minister's bed
and the "desk from which he made his speeches" – exude a "tremendous sense of history" so you'll want to "take your time" at this one.

Courtauld Institute Galleries   27 | 22 | 20 | M

Covent Garden | Somerset Hse. | Strand, WC2 (Charing Cross/Temple) |
020-7848 2777 | www.courtauld.ac.uk

"Iconic" works of "19th- and 20th-century art" including Old Masters
and Impressionist and post-Impressionist paintings "chosen with a
connoisseur's eye" make this "outstanding collection" in Covent
Garden a "hidden gem"; it's "off the regular tourist route" in the
Somerset House on the Embankment, but "art-insiders" swear it
"won't wear you down" since it's "small enough not to be overwhelming" but large enough to "house a good collection."

Covent Garden   23 | 19 | 17 | £0

Covent Garden | bordered by Shaftesbury Ave. & Strand;
Charing Cross Rd. & Kingsway, WC2 (Covent Garden/Leicester Sq.) |
www.coventgarden.uk.com

"You'll know why Eliza Doolittle spent so much time here" when you
see the "amazingly charming", "architecturally lovely" piazza, the
weekly antiques and crafts markets, the "street entertainment" including "buskers" and the restored opera house; though doomsdayers
find it "overcommercialized", with too many "American chain stores"
"catering to tourists", the "great people-watching" gets a thumbs-up,
as does the "vibrant" "mayhem on weekends."

Dennis Severs' House   ▽ 27 | 21 | 22 | M

Spitalfields | 18 Folgate St., E1 (Liverpool St.) | 020-7247 4013 |
www.dennissevershouse.co.uk

An "amazing" view of "times past" awaits at this Spitalfields home restored by American artist Dennis Sever to reflect the style of different
eras from the Middle Ages to the early 20th century; the "quirky
"candlelit" tour is "magical", giving visitors an "incredible journey
through the history of London", but you'll have to "plan accordingly"
for this "most unusual experience" – it has limited hours and it's a bit
"out of the way."

Design Museum   21 | 21 | 17 | M

Bermondsey | Shad Thames, SE1 (London Bridge/Tower Hill) |
0870-833 9955 | www.designmuseum.org

"Architecture and design lovers" will find a "paradise" at this museum
on the South Bank where "quirky, irreverent" displays related to modern design history include an "ingenious" look at "day-to-day items";
family days, scheduled talks and children's events (there's a kids'
summer animation school) are pluses, and though the interest for
some "depends on the exhibition", those who love the "A+ gift shop"
and the "great view of the Thames" find their time well spent.

Dickens House Museum

19 | 16 | 18 | I

Bloomsbury | 48 Doughty St., WC1 (Russell Sq.) | 020-7405 2127 |
www.dickensmuseum.com

"True Dickens lovers should not miss" this "small but cool" museum in
Bloomsbury, where the writer resided for a short while (long enough to
pen *Oliver Twist* and *Nicholas Nickleby*); "fantastic if you know the books
well" and like to look at rare editions and manuscripts, and "great for
true" fans of the author who find a "fascinating window" into his work it
has "limited appeal" for naysayers who niggle it's all a "bit of a yawn."

Dr. Johnson's House

▽ 14 | 10 | 14 | I

City | 17 Gough Sq., EC4 (Blackfriars/Chancery Ln.) | 020-7353 3745 |
www.drjohnsonshouse.org

Maybe you "need to be a big fan" of the author of the first English dictio-
nary (compiled here) or just interested in period furniture and portraits
to enjoy this "obscure but interesting" collection of artefacts in a "beautifully restored" Georgian House just off Fleet Street (one of the few residential houses of its age still surviving in the City); but most just stumble
onto it after drinking at the "great" Ye Olde Cheshire Cheese pub
nearby – look for the cute statue of Dr. Johnson's cat, Socks, fronting it.

Florence Nightingale Museum

▽ 23 | 17 | 19 | I

Waterloo | 2 Lambeth Palace Rd., SE1 (Waterloo/Westminster) |
020-7620 0374 | www.florence-nightingale.co.uk

An "overlooked treasure" at St Thomas's Hospital on the South Bank
opposite Parliament, this Waterloo museum of interest to "nurses or
historians" makes those in the former profession "swell with pride";
there's a "small, well-presented display" about the life of the world's
most famous nurse and her work in the Crimean War, and a "good
view of Big Ben" to boot.

Freud Museum

▽ 20 | 16 | 16 | I

Hampstead | 20 Maresfield Gdns., NW3 (Finchley Rd.) | 020-7435 2002 |
www.freud.org.uk

"The couch – not just any old couch, but the world-famous couch
where it all started" – is the main attraction at this Hampstead house
where Sigmund Freud and family lived after escaping Nazi annexation
of Austria in 1938; the office, a perfect re-creation of his Viennese
one, is "only for the idolatrous" say some, but others reckon that it's a
worthy "pilgrimage for any dedicated neurotic."

Geffrye Museum

24 | 20 | 21 | £0

Shoreditch | Kingsland Rd., E2 (Old St.) | 020-7739 9893 |
www.geffrye-museum.org.uk

Taking a look at middle-class house design from 1600 to the present, this
free Shoreditch museum lends "a fascinating insight" into the way "our
ancestors lived"; "lovely re-created rooms" have "correct period furnishings" and "the most interesting descriptive notes ever", but it's "off the
typical tourist beat" so at least try to "go when the garden is open."

Green Park

23 | 16 | 11 | £0

Mayfair | enter from Piccadilly, Constitution Hill or St. James's Park, SW1
(Green Park/Hyde Park Corner) | 020-7930 1793 | www.royalparks.gov.uk

A "tranquil and calming" piece of greenery in Mayfair "between
Buckingham Palace and Piccadilly", this "lovely respite from city life" is

as "emerald" "as its name" (except in spring when a "carpet of daffodils adds colour"); the "perfect place to take a rest from shopping", "watch the ducks" and enjoy a picnic, it nevertheless prompts picky sorts to posit it's just "a park to walk through on your way somewhere" else.

Greenwich Park
23 | 18 | 15 | £0

Greenwich | bordered by Crooms Hill & Maze Hill; Charlton Way & Park Vista, SE10 (Greenwich) | 020-8858 2608 | www.royalparks.gov.uk
"A vast, clean, green" Greenwich space that offers "a breath of fresh air" a few minutes from local tourist spots, this park boasts "amazing views at the top", especially of Canary Wharf; you can see the meridien line, "feed the squirrels", catch a glimpse of the deer in the enclosure at back or just "wander" around and watch the "natives at leisure."

Guildhall
23 | 19 | 16 | I

City | Milk St., EC2 (Bank) | 020-7332 1313 | www.cityoflondon.gov.uk
The site of the Roman amphitheatre ("check out the long-lost ruins" uncovered in 1987) and the centre of London's government since 1128, this "historic" building in the City boasts "beautiful interiors" including a "fantastic Titian ceiling", an "interesting print room", an art gallery and a great hall where notables and dignitaries have been entertained throughout the years; though it's one of those "hidden gems", some reviewers feel "only a few will find this interesting."

Hampstead Heath
25 | 17 | 14 | £0

Hampstead | enter from Hampstead, NW3 (Hampstead) | 020-7485 4491 | www.cityoflondon.gov.uk
To the uninitiated, this 320-hectare (790-acre) formal parkland is a "gigantic field", but to regulars it's a "truly special open space" where they can "get away from the hustle of town"; with a "wonderful view of London" (you can see St. Paul's on a clear day) and lots of spots to take a "wonderful stroll", fly a kite, picnic, swim and ramble ("don't be afraid to get your boots muddy"), it's "where locals go to relax" and "worth the Tube ride", especially when there's a staged opera or ballet at Waterloo Park; P.S. "after nightfall" it can get a little sketchy in some spots.

Hampton Court Palace
28 | 25 | 23 | M

Richmond | East Molesey, Surrey (Waterloo to Hampton Ct.) | 0870-751 5175 | www.hrp.org.uk
This "utterly wonderful Tudor building", developed by Cardinal Wolsey and later by Henry VIII, is worth the "day trip" (a "short train ride" 13 miles west of London) if you want to walk "in the footsteps of kings and queens" as you listen to "costumed guides" describe the "fascinating" environs; there are also "beautiful gardens" and an "amazing" shrubbery maze, and it gets "far fewer crowds" than many other sites.

Highgate Cemetery
24 | 11 | 12 | £0

Highgate | Swain's Ln., N6 (Archway) | 020-8340 1834 | www.highgate-cemetery.org
It might be "a bit run-down," but "the residents don't seem to mind" at this north London graveyard where you can see a "fantastic array of tombs and headstones", "from Karl Marx to Ralph Richardson"; it's a "long way to go" from the centre of town, so take one of the "wonderful" "guided tours" for a "fascinating insight into Victorian life" and then "combine it with a stroll through nearby Hampstead Heath."

ATTRACTIONS

| | APPEAL | FACIL. | SERVICE | COST |

HMS Belfast
Borough | Tooley St., SE1 (London Bridge) | 020-7940 6300 | www.iwm.org.uk

22 | 18 | 19 | M

Yes, it's a "warship" floating in the Thames between the Tower and London Bridges, but if you're a "naval buff" or have a "boy of any age", head here to "roam and poke around" a "great ship" and "imagine chasing subs in the North Sea"; too bad some ladies lament this is just a "guy thing" for men "bored with London's more sophisticated sights."

Holland Park
Kensington | enter from Abbotsbury Rd., Holland Park, Holland Walk, or Kensington High St., W8 (Holland Park) | 420-7471 9813

22 | 17 | 10 | £0

"Beautiful" flora, "wooded" areas, "tennis courts", a Japanese garden that is an "oasis of calm and beauty" and even an "orangerie" that gives "a taste of the place in Victorian times" come together at this Chelsea park that's "a London treasure"; it might be full of local "yummy mummies", but with the "lovely walking trails", it's like being "in a wooded country estate" – a real respite from "the bustle of nearby Kensington High Street"; P.S. there's a "lovely tearoom" too.

Horse Guards Parade
Westminster | Whitehall, SW1 (Westminster) | 017-5375 5297 | www.householdcavalry.co.uk

25 | 15 | 13 | £0

"You'll feel like a tourist" at this Whitehall sight, but "that's what you are", so check out the "pomp and circumstance for free", "get your picture taken" (if you get past the "huge" crowds) and then "check it off your list"; sure, the guard changing is "delightful" to some, "stuffy" and "cheesy" to others, but "you haven't been to London if you haven't seen it."

Houses of Parliament, The
Westminster | Parliament Sq., SW1 (Westminster) | 020-7219 3000 | www.parliament.uk

28 | 22 | 18 | £0

You'll have a "long wait" at this "must-see London experience", but it's "worth planning well ahead" to watch parliamentary debates, take a tour, climb Big Ben and just feel "history in every corridor"; it's all "pretty amazing" for political junkies and shutterbugs alike, since you "can't stop looking or taking photographs" of the "gorgeous", "stately" buildings.

Hyde Park
Mayfair | enter from Bayswater Rd., Knightsbridge, Park Ln., or W. Carriage Dr., W2 (Hyde Park Corner/Marble Arch) | 020-7298 2100 | www.royalparks.gov.uk

26 | 19 | 15 | £0

"One of the most beautiful parks in the world", this "truly lovely" central space (the former deer hunting ground of Henry VIII) within striking distance of Oxford Street, Mayfair and Knightsbridge is "an island of calm in this bustling city"; there's "always something going on" amid its "acres of greenery" full of people "sitting", "jogging", "sunbathing, strolling", "playing soccer" and "picnicking", plus you can take a "boat trip" on the Serpentine lake to pay a visit to the Princess Diana memorial.

Imperial War Museum
Southwark | Lambeth Rd., SE1 (Lambeth North) | 020-7416 5320 | www.iwm.org.uk

27 | 24 | 22 | £0

At this free "first-rate military museum" in south London, exhibits include a "mock-up of the city during the Blitz", "bullet-riddled tanks", a

	APPEAL	FACIL.	SERVICE	COST

"P51 Mustang suspended from the ceiling", "World War I trenches" and "an air-raid shelter"; it's a well-organised and "majestic" space that appeals to "war buffs" and "boys of any age", plus pacifists are relieved this "sobering" experience "doesn't glorify war"; N.B. there's a Royal Air Force annex near Oxford.

Institute of Contemporary Arts

-	-	-	M

Westminster | The Mall, SW1 (Charing Cross) | 020-7930 3647 | www.ica.org.uk

"As far as pizzazz goes, you can't beat this place" based in an unprepossessing Westminster building on the Mall, a minute from Trafalgar Square, where exhibitions of "cutting-edge contemporary art and culture" and the "latest" art-house films offer "an alternative" to most of central London's artistic offerings; it attracts a "young, trendy" crowd, who can be spotted pontificating in the appealing bar afterwards.

Jermyn St.

23	21	24	£0

Mayfair | Jermyn St., SW1 (Piccadilly Circus)

The "best men's shopping anywhere in the world" is the name of the game on this Mayfair street dedicated to "tailored suits", "bespoke shirts", "shaving brushes", "fine toiletries" and "other fripperies"; there's "style, sophistication and history" galore in the "ritzy" "traditionally English" shops, although the "top-notch quality" does mean you'll need to "bring you wallet" or stick to "window shopping"; P.S. "you won't find a more beautifully decorated street at Christmastime."

Kensington Gardens

25	19	15	£0

Kensington | enter from Hyde Park, Lancaster Gate, Queensway, or Royal Albert Hall, W2 (High St. Kensington/Queensway) | 020-7298 2100 | www.royalparks.gov.uk

These "beautiful traditional English gardens" in Kensington are a "good place to take a break from other attractions" and best when "the flowers are in bloom" (the spring tulips "get an honourable mention"); other highlights include "Peter Pan's statue", an Italian garden and a "playground for kids", but for many, it's all about Princess Di – you can stroll through here on a "pilgrimage to Kensington Palace" to "leave flowers at the gate."

Kensington Palace

24	22	20	M

Kensington | Kensington Palace State Apts., Kensington Gdns., W8 (High St. Kensington/Queensway) | 020-7937 9561 | www.hrp.org.uk

A "must-visit for Princess Diana fans", this house where she lived when in London now displays some of her "gorgeous gowns" as well as "historical items" related to its standing as Queen Victoria's birthplace; a few feel it's worth a "short visit", if only for Di's "aura", but others believe it's "just another palace" that's "not terribly interesting."

Kenwood House

23	20	19	I

Hampstead | Hampstead Ln., NW3 (Golders Green) | 020-8348 1286 | www.english-heritage.org.uk

A "beautiful country house and art collection" near Highgate and Hampstead, this museum boasts not only a "Vermeer and a show-stopping Reynolds", but it plays host to "lovely summer concert" performances too; it's a trek from town, so it's best to come on "a

beautiful sunny day to appreciate the grounds" and "combine it with a walk on Hampstead Heath."

Leadenhall Market   ▽ 18 | 16 | 16 | M

City | south of Leadenhall St., EC3 (Monument) | www.leadenhallmarket.co.uk

A "must for *Harry Potter* fans" since it was featured in one of the films, this "ornate", "beautiful Victorian arcade" filled with shops, bars and eateries near Monument is also worth seeing for the "gargoyles and gold leaf" alone; it can be filled with "braying City types", but if you want the "British banker pinstripe experience", go "on a weekday at lunchtime" and "enjoy the vibe"; N.B. there are now small farmer's markets and alfresco dining on some days, and if you're lucky you can catch one of the special festivals held during the year.

Legoland Windsor   21 | 21 | 17 | E

Windsor | Winkfield Rd., SL4 (Paddington/Waterloo to Windsor) | 0870-504 0404 | www.legoland.co.uk

"Getting there is a pain", but once on-site "it's wonderful" say loyalists of all things Lego; popular for the "under-eight" crowd, but wowing some adults as well, this Windsor attraction boasts "miniature cities" made of the blocks, which are "worth the admission alone"; but cranky critics cry it's "expensive for a whole family", you'll "queue for ages" during summer holidays and there's "terrible food" to boot ("pack a lunch").

Leicester Square   17 | 16 | 12 | £0

Soho | enter from Leicester Sq. station, WC2 (Leicester Sq.)

There's plenty of "chaos" at this "tatty" West End hub that reminds some of NYC's Times Square, but if you want "bargains at the half-price theatre ticket booth" or "if you're lucky enough to see a movie premier", you'll find yourself here surrounded by theatres, music stores, souvenir shops and "intoxicated teenagers"; sure, it's good for "people-watching", but "most of those people are tourists" because "there ain't no local anywhere near the place."

Lloyds Building, The   17 | 10 | 12 | £0

City | 1 Lime St., EC3 (Monument) | 020-7327 6586 | www.lloyds.com

"Lovers of modern architecture" and "insurance geeks" alike head to this "stunning" City building to marvel at "what Renzo Piano could do" (he and Richard Rogers co-designed it); see it "from the outside as part of a tour" or head to the much "cleaner" inside where there's a "Lord Nelson exhibition" (you'll have to book ahead for a tour).

London Aquarium   21 | 21 | 18 | M

South Bank | County Hall | Riverside Bldg., Westminster Bridge Rd., SE1 (Waterloo/Westminster) | 020-7967 8000 | www.londonaquarium.co.uk

Opened for about a year, this "new experience" in the South Bank that the "children will love" (there's a special Kids Zone) is a "nice way to spend an hour or two on a wet day" say fish fans fond of the "impressive displays", including 350 species from sharks to stingrays to moray eels; others, citing "dark corridors", "poor information" and "too-crowded" spaces are "disappointed" it's "not a world-class contender."

London Dungeon, The
16 16 17 M

Southwark | 28-34 Tooley St., SE1 (London Bridge) | 020-7403 7221 |
www.thedungeons.com

Sure, this Southwark venue is a "tourist trap", but the "torture and
dungeon-themed wax museum" with "ghoulish" "scenes" and "gore"
from London's history played out by "live actors" packs them in; "too
intense" for tots and just an "elaborate circus fun house" to sophisti-
cates, it's perfect for "macabre kids" and "teenagers", as well as those
who can chuckle at the "campness."

☑ London Eye, The
26 22 19 E

South Bank | County Hall | Riverside Bldg., Westminster Bridge Rd.,
SE1 (Waterloo/Westminster) | 0870-990 8883 |
www.londoneye.com

Get a "bird's-eye view" of Big Ben, Parliament, St. Paul's and a good
chunk of the city from the world's largest observation wheel – an
"icon" of modern London opened by British Airways in 2000 and already
in many "films and TV shows"; "bring a map" since the 30-minute
flight overlooks a vista that goes on "for miles" and gives you plenty of
time to "identify all the landmarks", but you'll have to first look past
the "expensive" admission, "long queue" and jaded types who jeer "if
you like it, you're definitely a tourist from Omaha" ("save your money
and walk across Waterloo Bridge instead").

London Zoo
23 19 19 M

Camden Town | Regent's Pk. | Outer Circle, NW1 (Baker St./Camden Town) |
020-7722 3333 | www.zsl.org

"Fun for the whole family" but "expensive" and requiring "a full day
out", this "fine" zoo in Camden Town offers a "nice range of wildlife"
say fans who especially like the kimodo dragon, the "great monkeys"
and "oh those giraffes"; even if a few find it "small" and the experience
"outdated", most enjoy it all – from the live animal demonstrations to
the early morning walks to the special summer nighttime visits.

Lord's
21 19 17 M

St. John's Wood | Marylebone Cricket Club | Lord's Cricket Ground,
St. John's Wood Rd., NW8 (St. John's Wood) | 020-7616 8500 |
www.lords.org

The "holy grail" "for anyone who cares a whit for cricket", this
Marylebone site is considered the spiritual headquarters for the sport
and hosts some of the biggest international games (there's also a state-
of-the-art cricket academy here); "when the sun is shining, it's hard to
think of a better place to be" say fans, but if you don't fancy watching
a five-day game, you might find "inspiration" in the on-site museum
housing historic artifacts from the 19th century to the present.

Madame Tussauds Wax Museum
21 20 17 E

Marylebone | Marylebone Rd., NW1 (Baker St.) | 0870-400 3000 |
www.madame-tussauds.co.uk

It may be "hokey and silly" yet it's "such fun" find fans of this
Marylebone wax-works museum where you can take your photo
alongside the "replicas of famous people" from "Marie Antoinette
to Louis XVI" and from Churchill to Madonna; even upper-crusts
who cringe over this "cheesy", "absurdly expensive" "tourist trap" for

"10-year-olds" with "queues that are a never-ending story" can't help but exclaim "wow", the "likenesses are amazing"; P.S. "book online to avoid waiting in line."

Monument, The

| 19 | 9 | 11 | £0 |

City | Monument St., EC3 (Monument) | 020-7626 2717

A "monument to the Great Fire" of 1666 that "almost destroyed London" in a "fascinating" part of the City, this "spiral staircase" is "only for the fit and healthy" – there are "a zillion steps" up; even so, it's a "worthwhile"enterprise since the "views at the top are spectacular", the Wren-designed column is "incredible" and they'll give you a certificate to prove you climbed it.

Museum of London, The

| 25 | 22 | 22 | £0 |

City | London Wall, EC2 (Barbican/Moorgate/St. Paul's) | 0870-444 3851 | www.museumoflondon.org.uk

The "excellent history of London going back to Roman days" is "brought to life through interactive displays" at this free, "wonderful", though "small", primer "for anyone who wants to understand the city"; fans say "the Great Fire exhibit is a must-see", and "fascinating exhibits" like a history of the Thames Valley before the city's founding in AD50 make it "highly recommended", but tot-toters tsk it "needs to be more child-friendly."

⊠ National Gallery, The

| 28 | 26 | 22 | £0 |

Westminster | Trafalgar Sq., WC2 (Charing Cross/Leicester Sq.) | 020-7747 2885 | www.nationalgallery.org.uk

An "amazing collection of paintings" from "every major artist of the past 600 years" makes this free West Ender "one of the great collections of the world"; a central location in Trafalgar Square, "outstanding gift shops" and a "good restaurant" further propel this museum up the ranks, but "overwhelmed" patrons say all this "mind-blowing" art is "impossible to view in one visit", especially given some "crowded" exhibitions.

National Portrait Gallery

| 26 | 24 | 21 | £0 |

Westminster | St. Martin's Pl., WC2 (Charing Cross/Leicester Sq.) | 020-7306 0055 | www.npg.org.uk

"Often overlooked" because of the proximity to the National Gallery, this "fascinating" museum is a "who's who of British history"; the "royal portraits" get a thumbs-up, and the likenesses of "contemporary folks" also attract, but modernists moan it's "a bit stodgy" and "oh-so British"; P.S. make reservations at the restaurant on top – it has a "great view."

National Theatre, The

| 25 | 24 | 22 | M |

South Bank | South Bank, SE1 (Embankment/Southwark/Waterloo) | 020-7452 3400 | www.nationaltheatre.org.uk

"The play's the thing" at this South Bank venue with "three marvellous theatres" hosting "some of the greatest English-language actors" performing "classic and new" works that are almost always "a thrill"; sure, the "dreadful" '60s cement building is an "eyesore" to some, but focus instead on the "gorgeous view" of the illuminated Savoy and St. Paul's from the lobby (which often hosts free entertainment); P.S. take one of the "fascinating" backstage tours.

ATTRACTIONS

	APPEAL	FACIL.	SERVICE	COST

Natural History Museum `26` `23` `21` `£0`

South Kensington | Cromwell Rd., SW7 (South Kensington) | 020-7942 5000 | www.nhm.ac.uk

"Stunning and breathtaking" for "anyone with an interest in wildlife" and the natural world, this free South Ken "classic" in a "beautiful" Victorian building" is an "old-fashioned" museum with "magnificent" exhibits (the "first and last stop is the dinosaurs"), plus plenty of "interactive" displays; the "lobby alone is exquisite", as are "special outdoor" displays, it's just "unfortunate" that "certain sections are crowded" at certain times; N.B. a new alfresco eatery is open in summer.

NEW O2, The `-` `-` `-` `M`

Greenwich | Arena | Greenwich Peninsula, SE1 (North Greenwich) | 020 8463 2000 | www.theo2.co.uk

Formerly known as the Millennium Dome, this massive complex on the north Greenwich riverside has finally reopened offering a vast array of facilities, from a 20,000-seat auditorium, to a smaller more intimate live music spot called Indigo02 to a sporting arena to an Entertainment Avenue featuring restaurants, bars, clubs and an 11-screen cinema; tot-toters will love the Beach, made up of 1,000 tons of sand that's a kids' play area during the day and a deluxe bar by night.

Oxford St. `17` `17` `15` `£0`

Westminster | Oxford St., W1 (Marble Arch/Oxford Circus/Tottenham Court Rd.) | www.oxfordstreet.co.uk

"Retail-hungry summer tourists" and Christmas gift-hunters keep the West End's (and Europe's) largest "shop-till-you-drop street" "extraordinarily crowded"; home to over 300 "landmark department stores", "upscale" "boutiques", "bargain basements", "tacky souvenir" purveyors and everything in between, it should be walked at least "once", for the "exhilarating, exhausting" "experience" – although a few opine with so many "unique things to do in London", it's a "waste of time."

Portobello Market `23` `15` `16` `£0`

Notting Hill | Portobello Rd., W11 (Ladbroke Grove/Notting Hill Gate) | 020-7229 8354 | www.portobelloroad.co.uk

"Great" for a Saturday morning "ramble", "London's (arguably) most famous street market" is jammed with "high-priced antiques", "collectibles", "fascinating knickknacks", "vintage clothes", "T-shirts" and "junk" "galore"; "bustling" with "massive crowds", it's "fun", "funky" and "colourful" whether you want to "buy or browse"; P.S. the *Notting Hill* connection makes the "many American tourists" "feel like Hugh Grant and Julia Roberts."

Regent's Park `26` `20` `15` `£0`

Marylebone | enter from Baker St. or Regent's Pk. stations, NW1 (Baker St./Regent's Park) | 020-7486 7905 | www.royalparks.gov.uk

You can take a "row on the lake", "have tea" in the inner circle (home to "some of the most wonderful rose gardens in the country") or just watch the "beautiful swans", "ducks, geese and other birdies" in this "marvellous" Marylebone park; originally a hunting ground for the Prince Regent, today it's London's largest outdoor sports area; P.S. "don't miss" "outdoor theatre" "on summer evenings" or the "zoo on the north side."

	APPEAL	FACIL.	SERVICE	COST

Royal Academy of Arts
25 | 22 | 20 | M

Mayfair | Burlington Hse. | Piccadilly, W1 (Green Park/Piccadilly Circus) | 020-7300 8000 | www.royalacademy.org.uk

"Extraordinarily fine special exhibits", including "blockbuster" "summer shows" and "smaller, more scholarly ones", are the stock and trade of this "glorious" art venue in a "wonderfully preserved", "stunningly beautiful" setting featuring an "impressive" "18th-century courtyard" and "gorgeous galleries"; for the most worthwhile trip, "base your visit" on whether "what's on view that month" interests you.

Royal Albert Hall
25 | 22 | 19 | M

South Kensington | Kensington Gore, SW7 (High St. Kensington/ Knightsbridge) | 020-7589 8212 | www.royalalberthall.com

"Stunning" "inside and out", this concert hall/"national treasure" in South Kensington is a "titan" among Britain's "Victorian splendours" – but it can only be truly "appreciated by attending a show" and experiencing its "fabulously plush" auditorium and "generally fine acoustics"; indeed, "see anything" you can here, be it "classical masterworks" or "rock concerts", but "don't miss" the annual Proms summer concert series – the "tickets are a true bargain" and the "last night" is "simply unforgettable."

Royal Botanic Gardens, Kew
28 | 24 | 20 | M

Richmond | Richmond, Surrey, TW9 (Kew Gardens) | 020-8332 5655 | www.kew.org

"More than just botany nuts" "adore" this "stunning" 300-acre "oasis" of flowers, "trees and grass" in Richmond – there's "lots of hiking possibilities" too, and though "you might want to bring a picnic", you can "eat well at one of the restaurants"; whatever you do, "don't miss" the "amazing" "bluebell glades" in spring or the "well-done" "indoor conservatories" in the autumn (though it's all "beautiful any time of year"); P.S. "the boat from Westminster" is "an unmissable experience."

Royal Festival Hall
- | - | - | M

South Bank | Southbank Ctr. | Belvedere Rd., SE1 (Waterloo) | 020-7960 4242 | www.southbankcentre.co.uk

Built on the South Bank in 1951 for the Festival of Britain, this iconic love-it-or-hate-it concrete arts centre has undergone a massive renovation; it houses numerous venues for concerts, talks, dances and cultural events, and includes a space for free performances throughout the day (from avant-garde electronic music to tea dances); outdoor areas promise to be a hit too, as the views over the river make this one of London's more desireable alfresco spots.

Royal Observatory Greenwich
25 | 22 | 20 | £0

Greenwich | National Maritime Museum | Park Row, SE10 (Cutty Sark DLR) | 020-8858 4422 | www.rog.nmm.ac.uk

The place that "ticks all our tocks", this "important" observatory in the National Maritime Museum in Greenwich (the 'G' in 'GMT') is literally "where time begins"; while the biggest attraction may be "straddling the prime meridian" to "stand in the Eastern and Western hemispheres" at once, there are also "intriguing" "displays of navigational instrumentation", and "getting there" via boat down the Thames is

"half the fun"; N.B. a £15-million redevelopment, including a new planetarium, was completed post-Survey.

Science Museum, The
26 | 24 | 21 | £0

South Kensington | Exhibition Rd., SW7 (South Kensington) | 0870-870 4868 | www.sciencemuseum.org.uk

"You can easily spend the whole day" at this free "state-of-the-art" South Kensington paean to physics and invention, as there's "plenty" "for kids aged five to 99" to explore, from "hands-on exhibits" to "always special" displays (some features, like IMAX films, cost extra but are "often worth paying for"); since it's "great for the whole family", the queue "runs deep into the bowels of the subway on school breaks, so start early."

Serpentine Gallery
22 | 18 | 14 | £0

Kensington | Kensington Gdns., W2 (Knightsbridge/ Lancaster Gate/South Kensington) | 020-7402 6075 | www.serpentinegallery.org

It's "always worth visiting" this "refreshing" "haven" for contemporary art, which enjoys a "stunning" setting in Kensington Gardens "in the middle" of Hyde Park; not only is the quality of the oft-changing exhibitions "high", but the fact that "it's free" makes it nearly "unbeatable."

Shakespeare's Globe Theatre
26 | 23 | 22 | M

Borough | 21 New Globe Walk, SE1 (London Bridge) | 020-7902 1400 | www.shakespeares-globe.org

"Spend a summer evening enjoying Shakespeare as it was meant to be" seen at this "amazing" Borough reconstruction of the "open-roof" original, a "very special experience" with galleries filled with "backless benches" ("schedule a massage for the next day") and a "groundling" "pit" (if you "don't mind standing for a couple hours", its five-quid price tag is one of the "best deals in London"); "even if you hate" the Bard, it's "definitely worth" taking the "enlightening" tour.

Sherlock Holmes Museum
19 | 15 | 18 | M

Marylebone | 221B Baker St., NW1 (Baker St.) | 020-7935 8866 | www.sherlock-holmes.co.uk

For "aficionados" of the "famous" "make-believe" sleuth, it's an "elementary" decision to "hold a pipe and take a photo outside" this "small" ode to all things Holmesian in Marylebone before heading into the "fun", "interesting" re-creation of his lodging house, as described in Sir Arthur Conan Doyle's stories (Holmes himself "would approve of the detail work"); non-"mystery buffs", however, find it a "dusty, musty, cheesy" "tourist trap."

Soane Museum, The
25 | 20 | 20 | £0

City | 13 Lincoln's Inn Fields, WC2 (Holborn) | 020-7405 2107 | www.soane.org

Bank of England architect Sir John Soane "collected everything and sold nothing", which is lucky for art lovers with "eclectic" tastes, because today his City home is this "quirky little museum" where "every room is a treasure" filled with "varied" works – "eccentric Egyptian antiquities", "Victoriana", a "famous Hogarth series" – and "it's free!"; just "don't go if there's a collector in your family – it'll scare you to death", as the man was "clearly crazy."

Somerset House

| | 24 | 23 | 22 | I |

Covent Garden | Strand, WC2 (Temple) | 020-7845 4600 |
www.somersethouse.org.uk

Home to the "outstanding" Courtauld Institute Galleries, this "staggeringly handsome" neoclassical palace "upon the river" in Westminster also houses other collections of "wonderful 19th- and 20th-century art", "top-notch artefacts", "photography", a "strong silver collection" and "small but excellent shows from the Russian Hermitage"; it's a "charming" "place to go in summer when you can sit in the courtyard" and watch the fountains, or "in the winter", when "ice-skating on the rink" makes for "a wonderful outing."

Southwark Cathedral

| | 24 | 20 | 18 | I |

Borough | London Bridge, SE1 (London Bridge) | 020-7367 6700 |
www.southwark.anglican.org

"Often overlooked" in favour of bigger churches, this "colorful" cathedral overlooking Borough Market is "well worth a visit", as it's just as "steeped in British history" (it's almost 800 years old), there's a "lack of crowds" and "explanatory placards" make learning easy; "beautiful memorials" to famous parishioners (like William Shakespeare) are always on view, but if you "visit on an afternoon when an evening service is scheduled", "you may hear the choir practising" its Evensong.

Speakers' Corner

| | 19 | 9 | 7 | £0 |

Mayfair | Cumberland Gate, Park Ln., NE corner of Hyde Pk., W2 (Marble Arch) | www.speakerscorner.net

Witness "what free speech is all about" at this "unique" "part of U.K. heritage" in the northeast corner of Hyde Park in Mayfair, where "varied" orators "harangue" "on any subject under the sun" (traditionally on Sunday mornings, although speakers can often be found throughout the week); if it seems "taken over" by "bigots, homophobes and religious extremists", most find it "worth" at least "a few minutes" for "free-entertainment" value; P.S. "due to a bit of anti-Americanism", Yanks should "have thick skins."

Spencer House

| | 25 | 24 | 21 | M |

St. James's | 27 St. James's Pl., SW1 (Green Park) | 020-7499 8620 |
www.spencerhouse.co.uk

"One of the great private homes of London", this "impressive", "elegant" St. James's mansion built by ancestors of Princess Diana in the 18th century offers "insight" as to "how the other half lived"; "beautiful decorations" strewn throughout the "exquisite rooms" are shown on "private tours only" on Sundays; N.B. it's closed in January and August.

Spitalfields Market

| | 22 | 17 | 18 | £0 |

Shoreditch | 105A Commercial St., E1 (Aldgate East/Liverpool St.) |
www.visitspitalfields.com

"High-end chains" juxtapose a "cornucopia" of stalls at this "funky" "reincarnation" of the old Shoreditch market, where an "arty feel" is fostered with "unique creations from new designers" and "vintage fashion and textile dealers" ("not at thrift store prices" though); the "mostly covered area" ("manageable even on a cold January day") also hosts "home-decor" purveyors, craftsmen

and "a number of eateries" – no wonder "it gets very packed", especially on Sundays.

St. James's Park

| 26 | 18 | 13 | £0 |

Westminster | enter from Green Park, The Mall, Birdcage Walk or Horse Guards Rd., SW1 (St. James's Park/Westminster) | 020-7930 1793 | www.royalparks.gov.uk

"Feed the royal swans and ducks" as you "walk from House of Parliament" to Buckingham Palace in this "utterly beautiful", even "magical", Westminster park; indeed, "the fauna is abundant and the views are breathtaking", and since it's "not as big as others in London", it's quite "manageable" even "in a short amount of time" – but if you've got an afternoon to spare, rent a "comfy" deck chair, breathe the scents of "gorgeous flora" and let your "sense of well-being" be "restored."

St. Paul's Cathedral

| 27 | 22 | 18 | I |

City | Chapter Hse. | St. Paul's Churchyard, EC4 (St. Paul's) | 020-7236 4128 | www.stpauls.co.uk

Since the "renovation" cleared away the grime and returned Christopher Wren's English baroque cathedral to something approaching its former state, this City site is once again an "amazing" and "overwhelming" attraction; from the "awesome interiors" to the crypt, "a resting place for many heroes", to the "whispering gallery" to the top of the dome that offers "breathtaking views" that "never get stale", it's a "must-see" on any visit; sheepish sorts admit they just want to walk "where Charles and Diana got married", but whatever brings you here, you'll be "wrapped in history."

Tate Britain

| 26 | 24 | 21 | £0 |

Pimlico | Millbank, SW1 (Pimlico) | 020-7887 8888 | www.tate.org.uk

This "magnificent" free collection of British art from the 16th-century to the present, housed in a facility built by Henry Tate of Tate & Lyle fame in a "great location on the river" in Pimlico, "packs 'em in" for "first-class paintings" – "go for the breathtaking Turners" and the Constables, "stay for everything else"; even if a few snobs sneer that the building is "far more interesting than its contents", the majority consider it a "wonderful exploration of the Masters"; N.B. the Tate family of galleries also includes the Modern in London along with sites in Liverpool and St. Ives.

Z Tate Modern

| 25 | 25 | 21 | £0 |

Southwark | Bankside, SE1 (Southwark/St. Paul's) | 020-7887 8888 | www.tate.org.uk

A "glorious space" filled with "extraordinary modern art", this converted power-station-turned-museum is literally an "architectural coup"; the Turbine Hall with its massive installations, the "views of St. Paul's" from the upper floors, the "interesting" collections of minimalism, surrealism, post-war abstractionism and cubism, the daily tours (including sign language versions) and the "first-class restaurant" on the top floor all combine to make this the "favourite museum in the world" for many; P.S. reviewers recommend you "take the ferry between the two Tates" and make a day of it.

	APPEAL	FACIL.	SERVICE	COST

Temple Church
 23 | 17 | 16 | I

City | The Temple, King's Bench Walk, EC4 (Blackfriars/Temple) |
020-7353 3470 | www.templechurch.com

"*Da Vinci Code* fans will love" this round Wren church built by the
Knights Templar in 1185 that lies just off Fleet Street "near the Courts
of Justice"; but others say "even before Dan Brown" this was a "wonderfully historic" and "beautiful" spot to hear an organ recital, listen to
the choir or simply get "away from" the maddening bustle nearby.

10 Downing St.
 18 | 8 | 6 | I

Westminster | 10 Downing St., SW1 (Westminster) | www.pm.gov.uk
True, "you might get a glimpse of the prime minister" coming out of his
Westminster residence, but even if you do, it'll be "from afar through
a huge gate" that stands at the end of Downing Street since "you can't
get near" this attraction anymore; finding a "lesson in the government's lack of openness", some snap "who wants to see a door?",
while others insist "if you're in the area", it's "thrilling" to stand in
front of this "historic" entrance.

Thames Barrier, The
 ▽ 19 | 13 | 13 | I

Greenwich | 1 Unity Way, SE1 (North Greenwich) |
www.environment-agency.gov.uk
You'll want to see the 11 sail-like floodgates of this "remarkable",
"lovely piece of architecture" in Greenwich "when they're being raised or
lowered" claim "engineering devotees" who head out past Woolwich to
catch the action before stopping into the "interesting" on-site museum; sure, there's "limited appeal" here and smart alecks snap "see it
before global warming makes it obsolete", but others say it's "worth"
getting on a riverboat for an "excellent" view from the water.

30 St. Mary Axe (The Gherkin)
 21 | 9 | 8 | £0

City | 30 St. Mary Axe, EC3 (Liverpool St.) | www.30stmaryaxe.com
Modern-architecture mavens gasp this "unique" office building, a
bullet-shaped tower of swirling light and dark glass known informally
as the Gherkin, is "quite stunning" and an essential site on any tour of
the Square Mile – but perhaps "more interesting from a distance",
which is just as well since "they won't let you inside" anyway; meanwhile, traditionalists wonder "why bother" with this "silly" "eyesore"?

Tower Bridge
 25 | 17 | 15 | £0

Bermondsey | Tower Bridge Exhibition, SE1 (London Bridge/Tower Hill) |
020-7403 3761 | www.towerbridge.org.uk
This "quintessential London" landmark since 1894 "high above the
Thames" with "views up and down the river" is a "romantic, historic"
spot and a "really fine photo-op", especially if you're walking across "à
la *Bridget Jones*"; you can't beat the "breathtaking" "picture-postcard"
view or the "impressive" architecture, and though you can pay to visit
the on-site history exhibit and Victorian engine rooms, some maintain
a "drive-by is sufficient" to avoid "too many tourists."

☒ Tower of London, The
 28 | 25 | 24 | M

City | HM Tower of London, EC3 (Tower Hill) | 0870-756 6060 |
www.hrp.org.uk
"The crown jewels are the highlight" of any visit to this City venue
"built by William the Conquerer", where you get a taste of "medieval

London" while the "friendly Beefeaters" "in Tudor garb" guide you through the "gory, gruesome", "turbulent history"; it's "chilling" to hear how the "mischievous were treated" back in the day (note the "prisoner writings scratched into the walls"), but it's "well worth the price of admission" since the "macabre" can also be "fun."

Trafalgar Square

22 | 14 | 10 | £0

Westminster | Charing Cross, WC2 (Charing Cross) | www.london.gov.uk

"Pigeons, pigeons, pigeons", plus "fountains" and "Nelson's column" are the enduring memories of this symbol of "imperial London" in the "heart" of Westminster; "climb the lions", "snap your photo" and enjoy the "glory" of a scene some consider "quitessential" even as others who "don't get the appeal" shrug that it's no more than a huge, "noisy" "plaza" that only "looks good from a distance."

Victoria and Albert Museum

27 | 25 | 22 | £0

South Kensington | Cromwell Rd., SW7 (South Kensington) | 020-7942 2000 | www.vam.ac.uk

With a "little bit of everything" (art, furniture, glass, fashion, textiles, jewellery, mulitmedia), this free South Ken classic "feeds the souls" of its fans with a "huge variety of fascinating displays" ("can't stay away from the costumes – real clothing from the late Elizabethan period forward"); the "scale is exhausting" and modernists moan about an overall "shabby elegance", but when you need a break, go to the "A+ gift shops" or the "great" V&A Café.

Wallace Collection, The

25 | 23 | 21 | £0

Fitzrovia | Hertford Hse., Manchester Sq., W1 (Baker St./Bond St.) | 020-7563 9500 | www.wallacecollection.org

"Tucked away" in a square just north of Oxford Street, this free, "refined" Fitzrovia private collection is simply a "beautiful house" full of "beautiful things"; with such an "eclectic" "treasure trove", including sculpture, armour, miniatures and paintings by Rembrandt, Titian, Velasquez and Franz Hals, "delighted" fans are surprised it's "grossly undervisited"; P.S. stop in the "wonderful tearoom" afterward.

Wellington Museum

24 | 20 | 18 | M

Mayfair | 149 Piccadilly, W1 (Hyde Park Corner) | 020-7499 5676 | www.english-heritage.org.uk

Military history buffs head to this "fine" Hyde Park Corner museum for "a fascinating introduction" to the life of The Iron Duke, who defeated Napoleon at Waterloo; it's "worth the time" to see lots of his memorabilia ("don't miss the boots"), plenty of "relics from Napoleon" and a "significant" art collection, all displayed in Wellington's former home – although "it's difficult to imagine anyone actually living here."

⊿ Westminster Abbey

28 | 23 | 20 | I

Westminster | 20 Dean's Yard, SW1 (St. James's Park/Westminster) | 020-7222 5152 | www.westminster-abbey.org

"You can't get any closer to heaven" than this "awe-inspiring" masterpiece that sits opposite the Houses of Parliament and leaves some visitors "humbled" and "close to tears"; the site of every coronation since 1066, numerous royal occasions and daily services, it's a "mind-boggling" journey through "a thousand years of English history", with the graves of lots of "famous dead people", including royals, scien-

tists, explorers and writers in the 'Poets' Corner' (Geoffrey Chaucer, Robert Browning, Lord Alfred Tennyson); add the "fabulous architecture" from the 13th to 16th centuries, and you'll "spend hours" here despite the "big crowds."

Westminster Cathedral

26 | 22 | 19 | £0

Westminster | 42 Francis St., SW1 (Victoria) | 020-7798 9055 | www.westminstercathedral.org.uk

A "stunning" Gothic and Byzantine-style Catholic cathedral "with lots of history" just down the road from the Abbey, this "memorable" spot might not be as "imposing" from the outside, but the (unfinished) "dark" interior boasts impressive "mosaics", hundreds of types of marble and distinguished artworks; head to the top for "one of the best views" of the city, and if you're a film buff, recall its appearance in Hitchcock's *Foreign Correspondent*.

☑ Windsor Castle

28 | 26 | 24 | M

Windsor | Windsor Castle (Paddington/Waterloo to Windsor) | 020-7321 2233 | www.royalcollection.org.uk

A "must-do" day trip from London, this "properly atmospheric" "jewel" in Windsor (one of the Queen's official residences) is, appropriately, a right "royal affair" where you can watch the "changing of the guard" (it "outguns Buckingham Palace's"), take a look at "Queen Mary's dolls' house" and visit the semi-state rooms when open to the public; though the air of "arrogant opulence" at this largest inhabited castle in the world is enough for some, others prefer to add a "stroll" in the "charming" town to their visit.

HOTELS

Hotels

RATES A'RISIN': With room rates rising in the capital, London remains an expensive proposition for most visitors. Flexible travellers can often find better rates by using an online booking site or calling the hotel directly and asking about promotions. Look for better deals or value-added amenities (included breakfast, dinner, theatre tickets) on weekends (especially if you stay in the Financial District) or during off-peak months such as January and February. Rates increase by up to 25% during the peak summer season. It's always best to ask when making a reservation if there are any special offers.

LOCATION, LOCATION: Even if you snag a good lodging at a great rate, if it's too far from where you'll spend most of your time, it may not end up saving you anything. Traffic is notoriously congested, eating up time and money. If you plan to visit many parts of town, look for hotels near direct Tube lines or bus stops.

WHAT'S YOUR TYPE? As with any major metropolitan city, there's a wide range of lodgings in London – from chains to cutting-edge business-friendly hotels to funky spots to designer boutiques to bed-and-breakfasts. This Survey's top spots are chain-affiliated, yet small in size. The Top Overall hotel (and No. 1 for Service and Dining) is Knightsbridge's St. Regis-affiliated Lanesborough, while the Marriott-run 47 Park Street, an elegant Edwardian-style residence-hotel in Mayfair, earned the Top Room score. Suffice it to say, ask as much as you can beforehand so that your choice suits your particular needs.

ROOM WITH A VIEW: Make sure you know what you're getting when you book. There's a tremendous difference in room type, so ask where yours is located, what floor it's on, when it was last updated and what kind of view it has. Also inquire about renovations and any planned events that may disrupt your stay.

TO EAT OR NOT TO EAT: The room price quoted by a London hotel may include a continental breakfast, a full English breakfast or no breakfast at all. Sometimes the rate includes the hotel tax – currently 17½% – sometimes it doesn't. Be sure to check what's included to avoid surprises.

CONFIRM THAT REZ: Call the hotel at least a day before you arrive to confirm your reservation and the spelling of your name. Hotels often overbook, and reservations made internationally can be 'lost' in the process. Take a copy of any e-mail booking confirmation with you, and if you reserve by phone, have a copy of the confirmation faxed to you.

TELLY TROUBLE: Ask about the markup on in-room telephone calls and if there is a charge for using a phone card or receiving a fax. Phone charges can add significantly to your bill, so figure out the least expensive option before calling home.

Top Room Ratings

Ratings are to the left of names. Lists exclude places with low votes.

27 47 Park Street
   Lanesborough
26 Soho Hotel
   Four Seasons Canary Wharf
25 Wyndham London

   Dorchester, The
   Claridge's
   Covent Garden Hotel
24 Ritz, The
   51 Buckingham Gate

Top Service Ratings

Ratings are to the left of names.

28 Lanesborough
27 47 Park Street
   Connaught, The
26 Halkin, The
   Four Seasons

   Stafford, The
   Goring, The
   Claridge's
   Milestone Hotel
   Ritz, The

Top Dining Ratings

Ratings are to the left of names.

25 Lanesborough
   Goring, The
   Connaught, The
24 Claridge's
   Berkeley, The

   Savoy
   Dorchester, The
23 Mandarin Oriental
   Four Seasons
   Metropolitan

Top Facilities Ratings

Ratings are to the left of names.

24 Four Seasons Canary Wharf
   One Aldwych
   Lanesborough
   Ritz, The
   Claridge's

23 Mandarin Oriental
   Dorchester, The
   Berkeley, The
   Covent Garden Hotel
   Savoy

Hotels

Ratings & Symbols

Rooms, Service, Dining and **Facilities** are rated on a 0 to 30 scale.

Cost reflects the hotel's high-season rate for a standard double room. It does not reflect seasonal changes.

†† children's programs   **♫♫** views
✕ exceptional restaurant   **Ⓢ** notable spa facilities
Ⓗ historic interest   **≋** swimming pools
☞ kitchens   **✎** tennis
✄ allows pets

▽ low response | less reliable

Athenaeum | 21 | 23 | 17 | 18 | £295 |
Hotel & Apartments ☞ ✄ ♫♫ Ⓢ
Piccadilly | 116 Piccadilly | 020-7499 3464 | fax 7493 1860 | 800-335-3300 | www.athenaeumhotel.com | 112 rooms, 12 suites, 33 apartments
Fans of this staple rave about its "perfect location on Piccadilly" – "across from Green Park" and near "the shopping district of Knightsbridge" – as well as the "top-of-the-line service", "24-hour" health club with Jacuzzi and a whisky bar that's among the "best in London"; less popular are the rooms, which, while "quiet", "modern" and outfitted with "chic bathrooms", can be "tiny"; for more space, stay in one of the apartments located in several Edwardian townhouses.

Beaufort, The | - | - | - | - | £195 |
Knightsbridge | 33 Beaufort Gdns. | 020-7584 5252 | fax 7589 2834 | www.thebeaufort.co.uk | 22 rooms, 7 suites
Not far from Harrods and Harvey Nichols, this privately owned non-smoking boutique hotel in Knightsbridge offers contemporary decor featuring English watercolour paintings, rooms with maple furnishings and fresh flowers, and free WiFi throughout; there's room service available until 10 PM, plus daily free afternoon tea and evening cocktails.

Berkeley, The ✕ ☞ ♫♫ Ⓢ ≋ | 23 | 24 | 24 | 23 | £459 |
Knightsbridge | Wilton Pl. | 020-7235 6000 | fax 7235 4330 | 800-637-2869 | www.the-berkeley.co.uk | 152 rooms, 62 suites
A "very traditional" and "proper" Knightsbridge "haven", this veteran overlooking Hyde Park wins the "best of breed" nod from fervent fans for its "attentive" service, rooms with "plush beds" and "luxury marble bathrooms", and "gorgeous" top-floor pool; with "exquisite" French dining at chef Marcus Wareing's Pétrus, a "rich and famous" scene at Blue Bar and proximity to Harrods, it "doesn't come cheap."

Blakes Hotel ✕ ☞ ✄ ♫♫ | 22 | 24 | 21 | 17 | £205 |
South Kensington | 33 Roland Gdns. | 020-7370 6701 | fax 7373 0442 | 800-926-3173 | www.blakeshotels.com | 36 rooms, 9 suites
Blokes love this "discreet", "super-cool, super-chic, super-expensive" boutique hotel in residential South Kensington that some consider the

"sexiest, most romantic" in London; "exotic" (though "small") rooms designed by owner Anouska Hempel are individually decorated, there's a "creative" Pacific Rim fusion restaurant via chef Neville Campbell and the "helpful" staff brings it all together; a few, however, find "too much attitude."

Brown's Hotel ⊕♨Ⓢ

22	24	22	19	£285

Mayfair | 30 Albemarle St. | 020-7493 6020 | fax 7493 9381 | www.brownshotel.com | 102 rooms, 15 suites

"After being closed for over a year", this "remodeled and rejuvenated London classic" – now part of the Rocco Forte group – is back and "better than ever", offering spacious rooms and bathrooms with "modern amenities" like "plasma TVs", "impeccable" service from staff that, "when they know you, treat you like family" and a "posh"-but-not-pretentious vibe; along with its "great shopping and walking location", pluses include the notable restaurant, "fabulous", trendy bar and a rave-worthy "high tea" that "is like something out of a Merchant Ivory film."

Cadogan, The ⊕⧖♨

19	21	16	16	£335

Knightsbridge | 75 Sloane St. | 020-7235 7141 | fax 7245 0994 | 877-783-4600 | www.cadogan.com | 55 rooms, 10 suites

Transformed by hotel designer Grace Leo-Andrieu (Montalembert in Paris), this 1887 landmark offers an "understated" and "sexy" option in an "amazing" Knightsbridge location for "seeing all of London"; the spot where Oscar Wilde was arrested for indecent acts now offers "distinctive" rooms with either contemporary or classic English decor, "gracious service" and a "wonderful low-key afternoon tea", plus a British restaurant and a fun red-glass bar sporting ostrich-leather chairs.

Capital Hotel

-	-	-	-	£195

Knightsbridge | 22 Basil St. | 020-7589 5171 | fax 7255 0011 | www.capitalhotel.co.uk | 41 rooms, 8 suites

Located in the Knightsbridge area, steps from Harrods, Harvey Nichols and the designer boutiques of Sloane Street, this family-run hotel draws particular notice for its legendary New French restaurant, under the auspices of chef Eric Chavot; but the classical rooms, with Egyptian cotton bedding and marble baths, plus the attached serviced apartments, are solid options for short- and long-term stays as well.

Charlotte Street Hotel ♨

23	23	22	22	£205

Bloomsbury | 15 Charlotte St. | 020-7806 2000 | fax 7806 2002 | 800-553-6674 | www.charlottestreethotel.com | 39 rooms, 13 suites

"Perfectly" located for "the British Museum, Chinatown and a night out", this Bloomsbury spot manages to be both "very hip" and "cozy and comfortable", offering a "home-on-the-road" atmosphere that makes guests feel like they "really live in London"; "first-class" rooms designed by Kit Kemp, "great amenities" and "professional service" earn traveler raves, while local "media and film types" come for the "screening room" and "cool bar."

⧖ Claridge's ✕⊕Ⓢ

25	26	24	24	£509

Mayfair | Brook St. | 020-7629 8860 | fax 7499 2210 | 800-637-2869 | www.theclaridgeshotellondon.com | 143 rooms, 60 suites

"Gorgeous, darling, gorgeous" gush guests of this "old-line" Mayfair "legend" voted the London Survey's Most Popular Hotel; service that's

"second to none" includes an "old-fashioned" elevator operator, and each room is "quirkily but luxuriously decorated" – beds are "made in heaven" and "the showerheads alone are worth the stay"; foodies recommend booking "well in advance" to experience chef Gordon Ramsay's "world-class" Modern European fare.

⚡ Connaught, The ✕⊕♨⑤ 　　24 | 27 | 25 | 22 | £459

Mayfair | Carlos Pl. | 020-7499 7070 | fax 7495 3262 | 800-637-2869 | www.theconnaughthotellondon.com | 69 rooms, 23 suites

You half expect James Bond to appear at this "clubby", "top-flight" Mayfair "treasure" that's the kind of place "you imagine spies meet at to trade secrets"; an ongoing renovation means the hotel is shuttered until December 2007, but fans expect it to keep the same nearly "perfect" service, "outstanding" dining and antiques-filled rooms as it has always had.

Covent Garden Hotel ⑤ 　　25 | 25 | 20 | 23 | £195

Covent Garden | 10 Monmouth St. | 020-7806 1000 | fax 7806 1100 | 800-553-6674 | www.coventgardenhotel.co.uk | 51 rooms, 7 suites

A "small", "tranquil hotel in a raucous location" near the shops and theatres of Covent Garden, this "trendy" but "charming" boutique features "beautifully appointed" quarters and "outstanding" service (the "best concierge experience I've ever had"); it also boasts a beauty room and gym, and though a few dis the dining as "subpar", there's a "world of food and entertainment" nearby.

⚡ Dorchester, The ⊕♨⑤ 　　25 | 26 | 24 | 23 | £525

Mayfair | Park Ln. | 020-7629 8888 | fax 7629 8080 | 800-727-9820 | www.dorchesterhotel.com | 194 rooms, 56 suites

It's "tops, tops, tops", old bean, at this "star-studded" landmark in Mayfair where the "luxurious" rooms have "fat, plushy beds" that you "can't wait to get back to", and the "kind" staff "know what you want before you do"; try a Thai massage in the spa, then dine at China Tang and "all will be well with the world"; N.B. Alain Ducasse plans a new restaurant here soon.

Dorset Square Hotel 　　22 | 22 | 18 | 18 | £150

Marylebone | 39 Dorset Sq. | 020-7723 7874 | fax 7724 3328 | www.dorsetsquare.co.uk | 34 rooms, 3 suites

For travellers who want to escape the "large business hotels" in London, this boutique option with unique rooms that "vary in size" but are "charming", "cosy and comfortable" offers "great value"; "very private and personal" service, a restaurant that features produce from Dorset County farmers and an "excellent location" close to intriguing shops on Marylebone High Street (as well as the Sherlock Holmes Museum) are further draws.

Dukes Hotel ♨⑤ 　　21 | 26 | 19 | 21 | £335

St. James's | 35 St. James's Pl. | 020-7491 4840 | fax 7493 1264 | 800-381-4702 | www.dukeshotel.com | 78 rooms, 12 suites

"Tucked away in a charming cul-de-sac", this "fabulous", "homey", "clublike" hotel is "worth the trip" to the St. James's area; the "first-rate staff" supplies a "warm welcome to weary travellers" who enjoy the "small" but "comfortable", "lovely" rooms, and no one should leave without repairing to the wood-panelled bar for what may be the "best martini in town."

	ROOMS	SERVICE	DINING	FACIL.	COST

51 Buckingham Gate ⏏ 👓 Ⓢ

| 24 | 26 | 18 | 21 | £360 |

Westminster | 51 Buckingham Gate | 020-7769 7766 | fax 7233 5014 | 877-528-2503 | www.51-buckinghamgate.com | 12 suites, 74 apartments

"Homey and inviting" apartments within "walking distance to the palace" lure travellers to this "stylish" "jewel" managed by Taj Hotels in Westminster where guests knock around "spacious kitchens" and enjoy "extremely helpful" service (which can include a personal butler); there's a "must-try" spa and French, British and Indian restaurants, and connoisseurs appreciate the discreet off-street entrance apparently favored by "stars and VIPs."

47 Park Street ⏏

| 27 | 27 | 19 | 21 | £363 |

Mayfair | 47 Park St. | 020-7491 7282 | fax 7491 7281 | 800-228-9290 | www.47parkstreet.com | 49 suites

Kick back and spread out in this "oasis in Mayfair", an elegant Edwardian residence-hotel that's a real "home away from home"; it's no wonder it has the No. 1 rated Rooms in the London Survey since they offer "plenty of space" – basically a full "London apartment to accommodate the family"– while superior service and "excellent" dining at Le Gavroche restaurant are further draws; although this Marriott club may subject you to a "time-share" sales pitch, at least it's "not pushy."

Four Seasons 👫 ✕ 🍴 👓

| 24 | 26 | 23 | 22 | £376 |

Mayfair | Hamilton Pl., Park Ln. | 020-7499 0888 | fax 7493 1895 | 800-332-3442 | www.fourseasons.com | 219 rooms, 26 suites

For a "slice of heaven" in Mayfair head to this "spectacular" spot boasting "unbelievable service" "with a smile but without the arrogance" and a concierge who "can arrange anything"; kudos go to the "great tearoom", Lanes Restaurant and "well-appointed" rooms with baths like "mini-spas", but a few find this outpost "somewhat ordinary" for the luxury hotel group, citing "dated decor" that "needs to be redone."

Four Seasons Canary Wharf 👫 ✕ 🍴 Ⓢ 🏊 🔍

| 26 | 26 | 22 | 24 | £318 |

Canary Wharf | 46 Westferry Circus | 020-7510 1999 | fax 7510 1998 | www.fourseasons.com | 128 rooms, 14 suites

"Sleek" and sassy, this "modern" Canary Wharf outpost offers "perfect comfort on a business trip"; it earns the London Survey's No. 1 ranking for Facilities, including a "top-notch gym" and a "spectacular" infinity pool "overlooking the Thames", while "huge" rooms with views, a "warm, wonderful staff" and a "very convenient" location near London's Financial Centre round out the offerings; the only negative, say a few, is a restaurant that leaves "something to be desired."

Gallery, The

| - | - | - | - | £170 |

South Kensington | 8-10 Queensberry Pl. | 020-7915 0000 | fax 7915 4400 | 800-270-9206 | www.galleryhotellondon.co.uk | 34 rooms, 2 suites

Close enough for a stroll in the gardens or a spot of retail therapy on High Street, this smart, stylish boutique hotel in South Kensington offers rooms decorated in subtle colors and rich fabrics, with satellite TVs, tea/coffeemakers and 24-hour room service plus executive suites with separate living areas suitable for longer stays; there's also an on-site breakfast buffet, and a bar and lounge.

HOTELS

	ROOMS	SERVICE	DINING	FACIL.	COST

Goring, The ⓗ

| 23 | 26 | 25 | 22 | £325 |

Victoria | Beeston Pl., Grosvenor Gdns. | 020-7396 9000 | fax 7834 4393 | www.goringhotel.co.uk | 61 rooms, 6 suites

Since 1910, this family-owned "wonderful sleeper" with a "brilliant location" in Victoria has served as a "home away from home" for staunch supporters of its "cheerful" but "polished" staff's "staggering attention to detail" as well as its "warm atmosphere" embodied in "elegant" rooms; the eponymous restaurant serves "fantastic" Traditional British fare, adding to the "old English charm" of the experience.

Great Eastern Hotel ⚄

| - | - | - | - | £265 |

City | 40 Liverpool St. | 020-7618 5000 | fax 7618 5001 | 800-822-4200 | www.hyatt.com | 206 rooms, 61 suites

A new City entrant from Hyatt, this Financial District hotel offers lots of modern business-friendly amenities in loft-style rooms with ergonomic work stations, Eames chairs, iPod docking stations, WiFi access and bathrooms with quick-draw tubs and hot towel rails; there's a full-service fitness facility and a business centre, and among the five on-site restaurants are a sushi eatery, a champagne bar and the dramatic stained-glass domed Aurora with its constantly changing seasonal eclectic menu.

Halkin, The ⚄

| 24 | 26 | 21 | 21 | £350 |

Belgravia | 5 Halkin St. | 020-7235 7141 | fax 7333 1100 | 800-223-6800 | www.halkin.como.bz | 30 rooms, 11 suites

"Chic" and "high-tech", this Belgravia boutique hotel near Hyde Park offers "immaculate" accommodations that have what may be the "largest bathrooms in London", "brilliant, cheerful" staff that "go out of their way to help" and Thai cuisine served up by chef David Thompson at Nahm restaurant; though it's tucked away in a residential nabe where there's "not much activity", it's right near a Tube stop.

NEW Haymarket Hotel ⚄

| - | - | - | - | £245 |

Piccadilly | 1 Suffolk Pl. | 020-7470 4000 | fax 7470 4004 | www.haymarkethotel.com | 46 rooms, 3 suites, 1 townhouse

Fans of the stage feel at home in this newly opened lodging in the heart of the Theatre District and surrounded by bars and restaurants, where the individually designed rooms feature contemporary English decor, minibars, personal safes, writing desks and baths with double basins and TVs; other highlights include an on-site Northern Italian restaurant serving breakfast, lunch and dinner, public sitting areas that display original British paintings and sculpture, and a pool and fully equipped fitness center.

Hempel, The ✗⊗⚄

| 23 | 20 | 19 | 21 | £265 |

Bayswater | 31-35 Craven Hill Gdns. | 020-7298 9000 | fax 7402 4666 | www.the-hempel.co.uk | 37 rooms, 5 suites, 5 apartments

"Zen" before Zen was hip, this "serene" "sleeper" in residential Bayswater was crafted by Brit designer Anouska Hempel and features "lovely, bright", "extremely white" "minimalist rooms", complemented by a "beautiful" geometric garden setting; despite the "inconvenient location", it's an "escape" for "young", savvy types, who appreciate the "chichi" design, the "killer", coolly sophisticated I-Thai restaurant (fusing Thai, Italian and Japanese) and the overall "good value."

Jumeirah Carlton Tower ♨Ⓢ≋ ▽ 22 | 21 | 20 | 24 | £479

Knightsbridge | 1 Cadogan Pl. | 020-7235 1234 | fax 7235 9129 |
877-854-8051 | www.jumeirah.com | 161 rooms, 59 suites
"Well-located" in Knightsbridge, with "Harrods and Harvey Nichols
nearby", this "elegant" spot has enjoyed ongoing upgrades since joining the Jumeirah family; new Garden Rooms and meeting spaces, a
Gilt Champagne Lounge, redone public spaces and a "world-class
gym" with spa and "huge stainless-steel swimming pool" are overseen
by "attentive and competent" staff, while business travellers appreciate the "great" Rib Room & Oyster Bar.

NEW Jumeirah Lowndes, The Ⓢ – | – | – | – | £325

Knightsbridge | 21 Lowndes St. | 020-7823 1234 | fax 7235 1154 |
877-854-8051 | www.jumeirah.com | 87 rooms, 14 suites
Some visitors find a "great boutique-style" hotel with "top-notch"
service when they stay at this small spot near Harvey Nichols
and Harrods in Knightsbridge; it closed briefly for renovations last
year, so you'll find a fresher look to the "well-appointed" rooms
and public areas.

K West Hotel & Spa ♨Ⓢ ▽ 20 | 19 | 17 | 22 | £250

Kensington | Richmond Way | 020-7674 1000 | fax 0811 2612 |
www.k-west.co.uk | 208 rooms, 12 suites
Admirers of this "low-key hotel in residential" West Kensington cite its
"quiet", "ultramodern" accommodations with "fabulous beds", "great
amenities" including "all the Internet you can eat" and "impressive
spa" as well as "yummy breakfasts" in an "elegant" dining room; the
"disappointed", however, deem the chambers "dark", the location "inconvenient" and the "dot-com boutique concept a bit passé."

Landmark London, The ⑪☕♨Ⓢ≋ 23 | 22 | 20 | 22 | £445

Marylebone | 222 Marylebone Rd. | 020-7631 8000 | fax 7631 8080 |
800-323-7500 | www.landmarklondon.co.uk | 252 rooms, 47 suites
Set in a "beautifully restored building", this "revived" Marylebone
classic boasts an "old-world feel" and "fantastically large rooms" –
particularly for "central London" – as well as a "convenient" location
for business with "close proximity to Paddington Station" and
Regent's Park; though the food "is nothing to write home about", the
"perfect execution" of the atrium "Winter Garden" and service
that's "the epitome of British" help create "a welcome refuge from
the outside world."

☑ Lanesborough, a St. Regis Hotel ⑪⛾♨Ⓢ 27 | 28 | 25 | 24 | £397

Knightsbridge | 1 Lanesborough Pl. | 020-7259 5599 | fax 7259 5606 |
800-999-1828 | www.lanesborough.com | 50 rooms, 46 suites
"You've really arrived when you arrive" at this "utter delight" in
Knightsbridge across from Hyde Park, voted the London Survey's No. 1
Hotel and garnering top rankings for Service and Dining as well; "outrageously helpful" staffers who "know their business" "set the standard"
for service "beyond belief", while "antiques-filled" rooms with "cutting-
edge technology" are worth leaving only for "lovely" breakfasts and high
tea (a "required stop") in the "beautiful" conservatory, and for the
Library Bar's "fantastic atmosphere"; if only it weren't "so expensive."

	ROOMS	SERVICE	DINING	FACIL.	COST

Leonard, The 🖉 🏻 | - | - | - | - | £220 |

Marylebone | 15 Seymour St. | 020-7935 2010 | fax 7935 6700 |
www.theleonard.com | 25 rooms, 21 suites

Set in four 19th-century townhouses off Portman Square, a two-minute walk from shopping at Oxford and Bond streets, this unique hotel offers rooms, suites and serviced apartments for extended stays, done up in contemporary English decor with Frette linens and Penhaligon amenities; you can enjoy traditional fare like fish 'n' chips and bangers and mash at the on-site Seymours.

Lincoln House Hotel | - | - | - | - | £69 |

Marylebone | 33 Gloucester Pl., Marble Arch | 020-7486 7630 |
fax 7486 0166 | www.lincolnhousehotel.co.uk | 25 rooms

For an intimate bed-and-breakfast experience, this 18th-century West End lodging set in a Georgian townhouse is a solid choice; a five-minute walk from Marble Arch Underground and a stroll away from Madame Tussaud's and the Wallace Collection, it features rooms with satellite TVs, direct-dial telephones, free WiFi and unlimited tea and coffee, and, of course, breakfast is included.

Mandarin Oriental Hyde Park ✗ 🏻ⓢ | 24 | 25 | 23 | 23 | £381 |

Knightsbridge | 66 Knightsbridge | 020-7235 2000 |
fax 7235 2001 | 800-526-6566 | www.mandarinoriental.com |
174 rooms, 24 suites

Be "treated like an emperor" at this "opulent jewel", a remade 1889 gentlemen's club a "two-minute walk" from Harrods, where "attention to detail is incredible" and a "truly memorable stay" can be had; regulars recommend the "excellent park view rooms" (avoid facing "noisy" Knightsbridge), the "outrageously priced" spa ("worth it"), the "very cool" Adam Tihany–designed bar ("be seen in the scene") and chef Chris Staines' "fantastic" French–Modern European Foliage restaurant.

Metropolitan ✗ 🏻🏻ⓢ | 21 | 19 | 23 | 19 | £320 |

Mayfair | Old Park Ln. | 020-7447 1000 | fax 7447 1100 | 800-337-4685 |
www.metropolitan.co.uk | 132 rooms, 18 suites, 19 apartments

"Über-modern" design is "applied in a thick paste" at this "slightly too hip" Mayfair boutique whose "big plus" is the "awesome" Nobu restaurant and a "super" location "next to the Tube"; but some say the "stylishly dressed" staff has "too much attitude" and "spartan" rooms "can be loud on lower floors" near the "noisy" lobby, so although it may "work for some" it "doesn't work" for others.

Milestone | 23 | 26 | 21 | 22 | £250 |
Hotel & Apartments 🖉 🏻🏻🏊

Kensington | 1 Kensington Ct. | 020-7917 1000 | fax 7917 1010 |
800-223-6800 | www.milestonehotel.com | 45 rooms, 12 suites,
6 apartments

A Victorian building in a "fabulous location" opposite Kensington Palace, one of London's "best" small hotels "treats you like returning royalty" with "flawless", "personalized" service that "never wavers"; "tasteful" and "different" rooms with "all the little extras" are "over-stuffed with stuff" and equipped with "Rube Goldberg" bathrooms, though some are "a bit snug" ("bigger rooms are in back"); families find "a welcome haven" in the apartments, and there's "a nice English bar."

HOTELS

	ROOMS	SERVICE	DINING	FACIL.	COST
Number Eleven	-	-	-	-	£117

Chelsea | 11 Cadogan Gdns. | 020-7730 7000 | fax 7730 5217 |
www.number-eleven.co.uk | 55 rooms, 5 suites

Set on Lord Chelsea's estate between Buckingham Palace and Harrods in
the heart of Chelsea, this cosy lodging occupies century-old Victorian
townhouses; traditionally styled rooms and suites boast Colefax and
Fowler fabrics and marble baths with extra-deep tubs and Molton
Brown products, while the public sitting area features panelled wood and
ancient portrait paintings; the Continental restaurant is open all day.

	ROOMS	SERVICE	DINING	FACIL.	COST
Number Sixteen 👣	-	-	-	-	£150

South Kensington | 16 Sumner Pl. | 020-7589 5232 | fax 7584 8615 |
www.numbersixteenhotel.co.uk | 42 rooms

Set in a Victorian white stucco building, this South Kensington hotel
sits within an easy stroll of the Natural History and Victoria and Albert
museums; individually designed rooms, with views of the gardens or
Sumner Place, feature minibars, 24-hour room service, Internet access and writing desks; guests can dine, drink or just relax in the on-
site private garden, the conservatory or in the two drawing rooms that
offer fully stocked honour bars.

	ROOMS	SERVICE	DINING	FACIL.	COST
One Aldwych 🕐👣Ⓢ🌊	22	24	23	24	£360

Covent Garden | 1 Aldwych | 020-7300 1000 | fax 7300 1001 |
800-223-6800 | www.onealdwych.com | 93 rooms, 12 suites

"Even if you're not staying" at this "swank" property with an "excellent
Covent Garden" location, the "see-and-be-seen" lobby bar is "not to
be missed" and the restaurants are "outstanding"; the "stylish" rooms
are "small but fantastically comfortable", service is "fabulous" and
"unpretentious" and the "beautiful" pool with its underwater
soundtrack is "recommended for stressed travellers"; naturally, it's a
"bit pricey", but this "grand duke of 'cool Britannia' sets the standard."

	ROOMS	SERVICE	DINING	FACIL.	COST
🔢 Ritz, The 👬✕🕐👣	24	26	22	24	£340

St. James's | 150 Piccadilly | 020-7493 8181 | fax 7493 2687 |
877-748-9536 | www.theritzlondon.com | 135 rooms, 46 suites

"Don't forget your jacket and tie" when you stay at this "classic"
"ideal" in Piccadilly – definitely a "tradition" you should try "before
you die"; if you can't afford an overnight at this "set of *Lifestyles of the
Rich and Famous*", "at least have the decency to take your mother to
tea" to "be seen", or to dinner in the "magnificent" "formal" Ritz restaurant; while a few are "put off" by the "stiff upper lips" among the
"pompous staff" and the overall "stuffy" air, the majority find it "lives
up to its reputation" so "what else need be said?"

	ROOMS	SERVICE	DINING	FACIL.	COST
Sanderson ✕🖼Ⓢ	23	18	22	21	£240

Soho | 50 Berners St. | 020-7300 1400 | fax 7300 1401 | 800-634-1444 |
www.morganshotelgroup.com | 136 rooms, 12 suites, 1 penthouse,
1 apartment

"Life's a party" at this "spectacular" West End/Soho Morgans Hotel, due
in part to the "tragically hip" Long and Purple bars "frequented by the
fashion and media crowds", "surreal" Philippe Starck–designed rooms
and the "transporting" Agua spa; too bad the "disorganised", "slow" service mars the overall effect; N.B. post-Survey, Alain Ducasse's Spoon
restaurant was replaced by Zak Pelaccio's Malaysian eatery, Suka.

	ROOMS	SERVICE	DINING	FACIL.	COST

Savoy, a Fairmont Hotel ✕ ⊕ 🎎 ⑤ 🏊

| | 22 | 24 | 24 | 23 | £199 |

Covent Garden | Strand | 020-7950 5492 | fax 7950 5487 | 888-590-9900 |
www.fairmont.com | 218 rooms, 45 suites

Go soon for an enjoyable stay at this "slightly funky" "grande dame" (circa 1889) since it plans to close at the end of 2007 for up to 16 months to complete a massive renovation; the Strand location of this veteran is "brilliant" if you're a theatre buff, and the service is "exemplary", plus you'll "never forget" dinner at Marcus Wareing's Savoy Grill.

Sheraton Park Tower 🎎

| | 22 | 20 | 18 | 20 | £400 |

Knightsbridge | 101 Knightsbridge | 020-7235 8050 | fax 7235 8231 |
800-325-3589 | www.luxurycollection.com | 242 rooms, 38 suites

The Knightsbridge location near "excellent shopping and transportation" and "incredible staff" "saves" this otherwise "forgettable" Sheraton; though the "dependable" rooms "seem bigger than they are" (some have "almost a 180-degree view of London"), a few say the food's "pitiful" and the decor "very plain."

Sofitel St. James ⊕ 🎎 🎎

| | 24 | 22 | 18 | 20 | £305 |

Piccadilly | 6 Waterloo Pl. | 020-7747 2200 | fax 7747 2210 | 800-763-4835 |
www.sofitelstjames.com | 166 rooms, 20 suites

With its "gorgeous, well-appointed rooms" featuring "fancy" bath fixtures, "excellent" Piccadilly location near the cultural and tourist attractions and "accommodating" service, this hotel in a "grand building" (formerly a bank) is a solid choice; there's also "delicious" French fare in the Brasserie Roux and a "trendy" bar.

Soho Hotel, The 🐾 🎎 ⑤

| | 26 | 22 | 19 | 21 | £265 |

Soho | 4 Richmond Mews | 020-7559 3000 | fax 7559 3003 | 800-553-6674 |
www.sohohotel.com | 85 rooms, 6 apartments

Best known for their Charlotte Street and Covent Garden hotels, the Firmdale group (aka Tim and Kit Kemp) has miraculously transformed a former car park in a quiet corner of central Soho into "the most stylish hotel in London" with "funky, large bedrooms", a "bar heaving with Soho media types" and "witty" decor "from the giant bronze cat in the lobby to the clever details throughout"; sure, the staff can be "too cool to acknowledge your presence" and the food just "so-so", but in such a "gorgeous" venue you can't help but have a "great time."

Stafford, The ⊕ 🎎

| | 23 | 26 | 22 | 21 | £305 |

St. James's | St. James's Pl. | 020-7493 0111 | fax 7493 7121 |
800-525-4800 | www.thestaffordhotel.co.uk | 69 rooms, 12 suites

"Incredible", "highly personalised service" from the "excellent porters" to the "best concierge in the world" is the hallmark of this "clubby" "home away from home" just off Green Park; the "posh" yet "cosy" accommodations are "individually decorated", and the "American Bar is a wonderful gathering place" (the 350-year-old wine cellar merits a tour).

St. Martins Lane 🐾 ⑤

| | 20 | 18 | 20 | 18 | £220 |

Covent Garden | 45 St. Martin's Ln. | 020-7300 5500 | fax 7300 5501 |
800-634-5500 | www.morganshotelgroup.com | 200 rooms, 2 suites,
1 penthouse, 1 apartment

"Light, airy and modern", this "Ian Schrager classic" (part of the Morgans Hotel Group and sister to the Sanderson) "continues to

please the cool crowd" with its "great" Asia de Cuba restaurant, "popular bar" and Covent Garden location in the "smack-center of the theatre district"; "designed by Philippe Starck", the lobby is "a playground for adults", while the "stylish but tiny" rooms feature the "best showers in London" and "multicolor" lighting that's changeable "to reflect your mood"; still, that "groovier-than-thou service" and an in-room setup that's "not functional for working" leaves some surveyors snapping "style over substance."

Threadneedles ⑪

| 21 | 23 | 15 | 18 | £285 |

City | 5 Threadneedle St. | 020-7657 8080 | fax 7657 8100 | www.theetoncollection.com | 58 rooms, 8 suites, 3 studios

Set in a converted 1865 bank right near the Tower of London and St. Paul's Cathedral, this "great little niche hotel" scores points for "excellent" service, a "central location" and rooms with "immensely comfortable beds" and "positively luxurious" limestone bathrooms; but guests give middling ratings to the European-Med restaurant, and warn "if you're looking for nightlife, stay elsewhere."

Trafalgar, The ♨

| 19 | 20 | 16 | 17 | £207 |

St. James's | 2 Spring Gdns. | 020-7870 2900 | fax 7870 2911 | 800-445-8667 | www.hilton.co.uk | 127 rooms, 2 suites

"Decent but lacks the final touch" is the word on this Trafalgar Square property with "nice-sized", "minimalist" rooms, "at least by London's standards", and "very modern decor" with the "attendant attitude from the chic staff"; a "popular" rooftop bar with "fantastic" views lends to the scene of the "young and hip who mingle to music in the lobby", but faultfinders fret that it has "not lived up to its promise."

22 Jermyn Street ♨♨

| 22 | 22 | – | 16 | £220 |

St. James's | 22 Jermyn St. | 020-7734 2353 | fax 7734 0750 | 800-682-7808 | www.22jermyn.com | 5 rooms, 13 suites

"Location, location, location" along with "lovely", "small" rooms" are part of the "charm" of this "small" but "cosy" "gem" of a townhouse in the St. James's area near Piccadilly, right in the "middle of the action" (which means it can get a little "noisy"); the "superb" staff that "will do anything to help" makes it "tough to say cheerio", unless it's to go out for dinner, since there's no bar or restaurant on-site.

NEW Wyndham London ♨♨♨ (fka Conrad)

| 25 | 23 | 19 | 22 | £189 |

Chelsea | Chelsea Harbour | 020-7823 3000 | fax 7351 6525 | www.wyndham.com | 154 suites, 6 penthouses

If you "ask for a room overlooking the harbour", you won't mind the "out-of-the-way location" in Chelsea of this "large, American-size" property with "comfortable suites" and "crisp, modern and posh British style"; just a few report "distant" service from "staff shipped from Madame Tussaud's", but that may soon change with the Wyndham reflagging.

INDEXES

LOCATION MAPS

Dining Cuisines

Includes restaurant names, locations and Food ratings. ☑ indicates places with the highest ratings, popularity and importance.

AMERICAN

Ed's Easy Diner	**multi. loc.**	15
Hard Rock	**W1**	13
𝐍𝐄𝐖 Kobe Jones	**WC1**	18
Lucky 7	**W2**	20
Sophie's Steak	**SW10**	23

ARGENTINEAN

☑ Gaucho Grill	**multi. loc.**	22

ASIAN FUSION

Asia de Cuba	**WC2**	22
Great Eastern	**EC2**	22
L'Etranger	**SW7**	24

BAKERIES

Baker & Spice	**multi. loc.**	22
La Fromagerie	**W1**	24
Le Pain Quotidien	**multi. loc.**	19
Ottolenghi	**multi. loc.**	24

BELGIAN

Belgo	**multi. loc.**	19
Le Pain Quotidien	**multi. loc.**	19

BRAZILIAN

𝐍𝐄𝐖 Mocotó	**SW1**	22

BRITISH (MODERN)

𝐍𝐄𝐖 Acorn House	**WC1**	19
Alastair Little	**W1**	24
Anchor & Hope	**SE1**	24
Anglesea Arms	**W6**	23
Boxwood Café	**SW1**	21
𝐍𝐄𝐖 Bumpkin	**W11**	21
☑ Chez Bruce	**SW17**	28
Clarke's	**W8**	25
Cow Dining Rm.	**W2**	21
𝐍𝐄𝐖 Empress of India	**E9**	-
𝐍𝐄𝐖 Fat Badger	**W10**	15
Glasshouse, The	**TW9**	24
☑ Gravetye Manor	**W. Sussex**	24
𝐍𝐄𝐖 Great Queen St.	**WC2**	-
Home House	**W1**	20
☑ Ivy, The	**WC2**	23

☑ Le Caprice	**SW1**	24
𝐍𝐄𝐖 Mews of Mayfair	**W1**	22
𝐍𝐄𝐖 Narrow, The	**E14**	-
Rhodes W1 Rest.	**W1**	-
Richard Corrigan	**W1**	23
Savoy Grill	**WC2**	24
St. John	**EC1**	25
St. John Bread/Wine	**E1**	22
𝐍𝐄𝐖 Tom's Kitchen	**SW3**	19
Vineyard/Stockcross	**Berks**	24

BRITISH (TRADITIONAL)

𝐍𝐄𝐖 Albion, The	**N1**	-
Annabel's	**W1**	22
Bentley's	**W1**	24
Bleeding Heart	**EC1**	22
Brown's/The Grill	**W1**	22
𝐍𝐄𝐖 Butcher & Grill	**SW11**	15
Canteen	**multi. loc.**	22
Chelsea Bun	**SW10**	18
Dorchester/The Grill	**W1**	24
ffiona's	**W8**	24
Goring	**SW1**	23
Green's	**SW1**	22
Guinea Grill	**W1**	22
Hinds Head	**Berks**	23
Maggie Jones's	**W8**	21
Mark's Club	**W1**	24
Pig's Ear	**SW3**	22
Rhodes 24	**EC2**	23
Rib Rm.	**SW1**	24
☑ Ritz, The	**W1**	23
☑ Rules	**WC2**	23
𝐍𝐄𝐖 1707 Wine Bar	**W1**	22
Sweetings	**EC4**	24
Wilton's	**SW1**	24

BURMESE

Mandalay	**W2**	23

CHINESE

(* dim sum specialist)

Bar Shu	**W1**	22
Eight Over Eight*	**SW3**	23

Four Seasons | **W2**	22
Fung Shing | **WC2**	22
☑ Hakkasan* | **W1**	24
☑ Hunan | **SW1**	28
Jenny Lo's Tea | **SW1**	20
Kai Mayfair | **W1**	25
Mandarin Kitchen | **W2**	23
Mao Tai* | **SW6**	22
Phoenix Palace* | **NW1**	23
Royal China* | **multi. loc.**	24
Royal China Club* | **W1**	24
☑ Yauatcha* | **W1**	25

CHOPHOUSE

☑ Gaucho Grill | **multi. loc.**	22
Guinea Grill | **W1**	22
NEW Hawksmoor | **E1**	28
Rib Rm. | **SW1**	24
☑ Rules | **WC2**	23
Sophie's Steak | **SW10**	23

CUBAN

Asia de Cuba | **WC2**	22

DANISH

Lundum's | **SW7**	22

ECLECTIC

Archipelago | **W1**	21
NEW Bacchus | **N1**	21
Banquette | **WC2**	22
Books for Cooks | **W11**	24
NEW Club, The | **W1**	-
NEW Hoxton Grille | **EC2**	-
☑ Lanes | **W1**	24
Lanesborough | **SW1**	21
Michael Moore | **W1**	22
Mosimann's | **SW1**	26
Providores, The | **W1**	22

EUROPEAN (MODERN)

Abingdon, The | **W8**	22
Andrew Edmunds | **W1**	22
Arbutus | **W1**	24
Chapter Two | **SE3**	24
NEW Cookbook Cafe | **W1**	-
Don | **EC4**	22
☑ Fat Duck | **Berks**	27
Flaneur | **EC1**	22

Foliage | **SW1**	26
NEW Forge, The | **WC2**	-
Gate, The | **W6**	25
George | **W1**	22
☑ Gordon Ramsay/Claridge's | **W1**	25
NEW Hat/Feathers | **EC1**	-
NEW High Road Brass. | **W4**	20
Home House | **W1**	20
Indigo | **WC2**	22
☑ Ivy, The | **WC2**	23
La Fromagerie | **W1**	24
☑ La Trompette | **W4**	27
☑ Le Caprice | **SW1**	24
Little Bay | **multi. loc.**	21
NEW Magdalen | **SE1**	-
Notting Hill Brass. | **W11**	24
Patterson's | **W1**	22
Salt Yard | **W1**	22
Sketch/Gallery | **W1**	19
☑ Sketch/Lecture Rm. | **W1**	21
NEW Skylon | **SE1**	-
NEW St. Alban | **SW1**	21
NEW Trinity | **SW4**	24
Vivat Bacchus | **EC4**	23
☑ Wolseley, The | **W1**	21

FISH 'N' CHIPS

North Sea | **WC1**	23
Sweetings | **EC4**	24
Two Brothers Fish | **N3**	24

FRENCH (BISTRO)

Bibendum Oyster | **SW3**	22
Galvin Bistrot | **W1**	24
La Poule au Pot | **SW1**	22
Le Boudin Blanc | **W1**	22
Le Café/Marché | **EC1**	23
Patisserie Valerie | **multi. loc.**	20
Racine | **SW3**	22
Truc Vert | **W1**	22

FRENCH (BRASSERIE)

NEW Chelsea Brass. | **SW1**	16
Cheyne Walk | **SW3**	23
Chez Gérard | **multi. loc.**	18
NEW St. Germain | **EC1**	21

FRENCH (CLASSIC)

Annabel's | **W1**	22
Chez Gérard | **multi. loc.**	18
Chez Kristof | **W6**	22
Foliage | **SW1**	26
French Horn | **Berks**	23
Ladurée | **SW1**	23
La Poule au Pot | **SW1**	22
L'Aventure | **NW8**	22
Le Café/Marché | **EC1**	23
☑ Le Gavroche | **W1**	27
Le Pont/Tour | **SE1**	22
L'Escargot | **W1**	22
☑ Les Trois Garçons | **E1**	19
Le Suquet | **SW3**	23
L'Oranger | **SW1**	24
Mark's Club | **W1**	24
Mirabelle | **W1**	22
Oslo Court | **NW8**	22
Papillon | **SW3**	23
Racine | **SW3**	22
☑ Ritz, The | **W1**	23
Vineyard/Stockcross | **Berks**	24
NEW Wallace, The | **W1**	20
☑ Waterside Inn | **Berks**	27

FRENCH (NEW)

Aubergine | **SW10**	26
Bibendum | **SW3**	24
Bleeding Heart | **EC1**	22
☑ Capital Rest. | **SW3**	27
☑ Cliveden House | **Berks**	24
Clos Maggiore | **WC2**	24
Club Gascon | **EC1**	26
Galvin/Windows | **W1**	22
☑ Gordon Ramsay/68 Royal | **SW3**	28
Greenhouse, The | **W1**	25
NEW ☑ L'Atelier/Robuchon | **WC2**	26
☑ La Trompette | **W4**	27
Le Cercle | **SW1**	24
Ledbury | **W11**	25
☑ Le Manoir/Quat | Oxfordshire	28
L'Etranger | **SW7**	24
Maze | **W1**	25

☑ Morgan M | **N7**	27
Morton's | **W1**	24
1 Lombard St. | **EC3**	22
One-O-One | **SW1**	23
Orrery | **W1**	25
Pearl | **WC1**	24
☑ Pétrus | **SW1**	28
☑ Pied à Terre | **W1**	28
Pig's Ear | **SW3**	22
Roussillon | **SW1**	26
NEW Spread Eagle | **SE10**	21
☑ Square, The | **W1**	28
Tom Aikens | **SW3**	26
☑ Waterside Inn | **Berks**	27

GASTROPUB

Anchor & Hope | British | **SE1**	24
Anglesea Arms | British | **W6**	23
NEW Bacchus | Eclectic | **N1**	21
Churchill Arms | Thai | **W8**	22
Cow Dining Rm. | British | **W2**	21
NEW Great Queen St. | British | **WC2**	—
NEW Hat/Feathers | Euro. | **EC1**	—
NEW Narrow, The | British | **E14**	—
Pig's Ear | British/French | **SW3**	22

GREEK

Halepi | **W2**	24

HAMBURGERS

Babes 'n' Burgers | **W11**	17
Ed's Easy Diner | **multi. loc.**	15
Gourmet Burger | **multi. loc.**	21
Hard Rock | **W1**	13
Lucky 7 | **W2**	20
Sophie's Steak | **SW10**	23

INDIAN

☑ Amaya | **SW1**	25
Benares | **W1**	23
Bombay Brass. | **SW7**	22
Café Spice Namasté | **E1**	23
Chutney Mary | **SW10**	23
Cinnamon Club | **SW1**	24
Khan's of Kensington | **SW7**	22
La Porte des Indes | **W1**	21
Ma Goa | **multi. loc.**	23

Malabar Junction	**WC1**	23
Mela	**WC2**	23
Painted Heron	**SW10**	22
Quilon	**SW1**	25
Rasa	**multi. loc.**	24
⊡ Rasoi Vineet Bhatia	**SW3**	27
Red Fort	**W1**	23
Star of India	**SW5**	24
⊡ Tamarind	**W1**	25
Vama	**SW10**	24
Veeraswamy	**W1**	22
Zaika	**W8**	25

IRISH

Richard Corrigan	**W1**	23

ITALIAN

(N=Northern; S=Southern)

Alloro	**W1**	22
Assaggi	**W2**	26
Buona Sera	**multi. loc.**	23
Caldesi	N	**W1**	22
Carluccio's	**multi. loc.**	17
NEW C Garden	**SW3**	18
Cipriani	**W1**	20
Da Mario	**SW7**	22
Delfino	**W1**	23
⊡ Enoteca Turi	**SW15**	27
Harry's Bar	**W1**	24
Il Bordello	**E1**	23
Il Convivio	**SW1**	23
Il Portico	**W8**	22
La Famiglia	**SW10**	21
La Genova	**W1**	23
La Porchetta	**multi. loc.**	19
Latium	**W1**	25
Locanda Locatelli	N	**W1**	25
Locanda Ottoemezzo	**W8**	24
Made in Italy	S	**SW3**	21
Mediterraneo	**W11**	22
Oliveto	**SW1**	23
NEW Olivomare	**SW1**	-
Osteria Basilico	**W11**	24
Passione	**W1**	23
⊡ Pizza Express	**multi. loc.**	17
Quadrato	N	**E14**	24
Quirinale	**SW1**	25
NEW Raviolo	**SW12**	-

NEW Rist. Semplice	N	**W1**	-
⊡ River Café	**W6**	27
Santini	**SW1**	22
Sardo	**W1**	23
Scalini	**SW3**	23
Signor Sassi	**SW1**	22
NEW Theo Randall	**W1**	26
Timo	**W8**	22
Toto's	**SW3**	24
NEW Via Condotti	S	**W1**	18
⊡ Zafferano	**SW1**	26
Ziani	N	**SW3**	25

JAPANESE

(* sushi specialist)

NEW Atami	**SW1**	24
Café Japan*	**NW11**	26
⊡ Defune*	**W1**	27
NEW Dinings*	**W1**	-
Jin Kichi*	**NW3**	26
Kiku*	**W1**	24
NEW Kobe Jones	**WC1**	18
Koi*	**W8**	22
Miyama*	**W1**	26
Nobu Berkeley St.*	**W1**	26
⊡ Nobu London*	**W1**	27
Roka*	**W1**	25
Sakura*	**W1**	23
Tokyo Diner	**WC2**	20
Tsunami	**SW4**	24
Ubon*	**E14**	24
Umu*	**W1**	26
⊡ Wagamama	**multi. loc.**	19
Yoshino*	**W1**	24
⊡ Zuma*	**SW7**	26

LEBANESE

Al Hamra	**W1**	22
Al Sultan	**W1**	22
Al Waha	**W2**	22
Fairuz	**multi. loc.**	22
Ishbilia	**SW1**	24

MALAYSIAN

NEW Suka	**W1**	-

MEDITERRANEAN

Baker & Spice	**multi. loc.**	22
⊡ Cliveden House	**Berks**	24

Fifteen | **N1**	23
Leon | **multi. loc.**	19
Little Bay | **multi. loc.**	21
Moro | **EC1**	25
Ottolenghi | **multi. loc.**	24
Pescatori | **W1**	22

MOROCCAN

NEW Bouga | **N8**	-
Pasha | **SW7**	18

NORTH AFRICAN

Momo | **W1**	19

PAKISTANI

New Tayyabs | **E1**	24
Original Lahore | **multi. loc.**	24
Salloos | **SW1**	23

PAN-ASIAN

Cocoon | **W1**	21
e&o | **W11**	22
Eight Over Eight | **SW3**	23
NEW Haiku | **W1**	-
Mao Tai | **SW6**	22
Park, The | **SW1**	24
Taman Gang | **W1**	22
NEW Tamarai | **WC2**	-
NEW XO | **NW3**	16

PERSIAN

Alounak | **multi. loc.**	23

PIZZA

Buona Sera | **multi. loc.**	23
Delfino | **W1**	23
Il Bordello | **E1**	23
La Porchetta | **multi. loc.**	19
Made in Italy | **SW3**	21
Oliveto | **SW1**	23
Osteria Basilico | **W11**	24
☑ Pizza Express | **multi. loc.**	17

POLISH

Baltic | **SE1**	21

PORTUGUESE

Eyre Brothers | **EC2**	22

SEAFOOD

Belgo | **multi. loc.**	19
Bentley's | **W1**	24

Bibendum Oyster | **SW3**	22
Cow Dining Rm. | **W2**	21
Green's | **SW1**	22
☑ J. Sheekey | **WC2**	25
Le Pont/Tour | **SE1**	22
Le Suquet | **SW3**	23
North Sea | **WC1**	23
NEW Olivomare | **SW1**	-
One-O-One | **SW1**	23
Pescatori | **W1**	22
NEW Scott's | **W1**	22
Sweetings | **EC4**	24
Two Brothers Fish | **N3**	24
Wilton's | **SW1**	24

SMALL PLATES

(See also Spanish tapas specialist)

☑ Amaya | Indian | **SW1**	25
NEW Burlington Club | French | **W1**	-
Club Gascon | French | **EC1**	26
NEW Dinings | Jap. | **W1**	-
☑ Hunan | Chinese | **SW1**	28
Il Convivio | Italian | **SW1**	23
Le Cercle | French | **SW1**	24
Maze | French | **W1**	25
Providores, The | Eclectic | **W1**	22
NEW Trinity | Euro. | **SW4**	24

SPANISH

(* tapas specialist)

NEW Barrafina* | **W1**	24
NEW Burlington Club | **W1**	-
Cambio de Tercio | **SW5**	24
Cigala* | **WC1**	22
El Pirata* | **W1**	23
Eyre Brothers | **EC2**	22
Fino* | **W1**	23
Salt Yard* | **W1**	22
Tapas Brindisa* | **SE1**	22

THAI

NEW Benja | **W1**	-
Blue Elephant | **SW6**	20
Busaba Eathai | **multi. loc.**	21
Churchill Arms | **W8**	22
Nahm | **SW1**	26
Patara | **multi. loc.**	23
Pepper Tree | **SW4**	19

TURKISH

Haz | **E1** 25

Pasha | **N1** 20

VEGETARIAN

(* vegan)

Food for Thought | **WC2** 24

Gate, The | **W6** 25

Lanesborough | **SW1** 21

Mildreds* | **W1** 22

Z Morgan M | **N7** 27

Rasa | **multi. loc.** 24

Roussillon | **SW1** 26

VIETNAMESE

Viet Hoa | **E2** 23

Dining Locations

Includes restaurant names, cuisines and Food ratings. ⚋ indicates places with the highest ratings, popularity and importance.

Central London

BELGRAVIA

⚋ Amaya	*Indian*	25
Baker & Spice	*Med.*	22
Boxwood Café	*British*	21
Il Convivio	*Italian*	23
Ishbilia	*Lebanese*	24
Jenny Lo's Tea	*Chinese*	20
Mosimann's	*Eclectic*	26
Nahm	*Thai*	26
Oliveto	*Italian*	23
NEW Olivomare	*Italian/Seafood*	-
Patisserie Valerie	*French*	20
⚋ Pétrus	*French*	28
Rib Rm.	*British/Chops*	24
Salloos	*Pakistani*	23
Santini	*Italian*	22
⚋ Zafferano	*Italian*	26

BLOOMSBURY/ FITZROVIA

Archipelago	*Eclectic*	21
Busaba Eathai	*Thai*	21
Carluccio's	*Italian*	17
Chez Gérard	*French*	18
Cigala	*Spanish*	22
Fino	*Spanish*	23
⚋ Hakkasan	*Chinese*	24
NEW Kobe Jones	*Jap.*	18
Latium	*Italian*	25
Malabar Junction	*Indian*	23
North Sea	*Seafood*	23
Passione	*Italian*	23
Pescatori	*Med.*	22
⚋ Pied à Terre	*French*	28
Rasa	*Indian*	24
Roka	*Jap.*	25
Salt Yard	*Euro.*	22
Sardo	*Italian*	23
NEW Suka	*Malaysian*	-
⚋ Wagamama	*Jap.*	19

CHINATOWN

Fung Shing	*Chinese*	22
Tokyo Diner	*Jap.*	20

COVENT GARDEN

Asia de Cuba	*Asian/Cuban*	22
Banquette	*Eclectic*	22
Belgo	*Belgian*	19
Chez Gérard	*French*	18
Clos Maggiore	*French*	24
Ed's Easy Diner	*Hamburgers*	15
Food for Thought	*Veg.*	24
NEW Forge, The	*Euro.*	-
Gourmet Burger	*Hamburgers*	21
NEW Great Queen St.	*British*	-
Indigo	*Euro.*	22
⚋ Ivy, The	*British/Euro.*	23
⚋ J. Sheekey	*Seafood*	25
NEW ⚋ L'Atelier/Robuchon	*French*	26
Leon	*Med.*	19
Mela	*Indian*	23
Patisserie Valerie	*French*	20
⚋ Pizza Express	*Pizza*	17
⚋ Rules	*British/Chops*	23
Savoy Grill	*British*	24
NEW Tamarai	*Pan-Asian*	-
⚋ Wagamama	*Jap.*	19

HOLBORN

Chez Gérard	*French*	18
⚋ Gaucho Grill	*Argent./Chops*	22
La Porchetta	*Pizza*	19
Pearl	*French*	24

KNIGHTSBRIDGE

⚋ Capital Rest.	*French*	27
Foliage	*Euro./French*	26
Ishbilia	*Lebanese*	24
Ladurée	*French*	23
Lanesborough	*Eclectic*	21
Leon	*Med.*	19
NEW Mocotó	*Brazilian*	22
One-O-One	*French/Seafood*	23

Park, The | *Pan-Asian*	24
Patara | *Thai*	23
Patisserie Valerie | *French*	20
☑ Pizza Express | *Pizza*	17
Racine | *French*	22
Signor Sassi | *Italian*	22
☑ Wagamama | *Jap.*	19
☑ Zuma | *Jap.*	26

MARYLEBONE

Busaba Eathai | *Thai*	21
Caldesi | *Italian*	22
Carluccio's | *Italian*	17
☑ Defune | *Jap.*	27
NEW Dinings | *Jap.*	-
Fairuz | *Lebanese*	22
Galvin Bistrot | *French*	24
Home House | *British/Euro.*	20
La Fromagerie | *Euro.*	24
La Porte des Indes | *Indian*	21
Leon | *Med.*	19
Le Pain Quotidien | *Bakery/Belgian*	19
Locanda Locatelli | *Italian*	25
Mandalay | *Burmese*	23
Michael Moore | *Eclectic*	22
Orrery | *French*	25
Patisserie Valerie | *French*	20
Phoenix Palace | *Chinese*	23
Providores, The | *Eclectic*	22
Rhodes W1 Rest. | *British*	-
Royal China | *Chinese*	24
Royal China Club | *Chinese*	24
☑ Wagamama | *Jap.*	19
NEW Wallace, The | *French*	20

MAYFAIR

Al Hamra | *Lebanese*	22
Alloro | *Italian*	22
Al Sultan | *Lebanese*	22
Annabel's | *British/French*	22
Benares | *Indian*	23
Brown's/The Grill | *British*	22
NEW Burlington Club | *Spanish*	-
Carluccio's | *Italian*	17
Chez Gérard | *French*	18
Cipriani | *Italian*	20
NEW Cookbook Cafe | *Euro.*	-

Delfino | *Italian*	23
Dorchester/The Grill | *British*	24
El Pirata | *Spanish*	23
Galvin/Windows | *French*	22
George | *Euro.*	22
☑ Gordon Ramsay/Claridge's | *Euro.*	25
Greenhouse, The | *French*	25
Guinea Grill | *British/Chops*	22
NEW Haiku | *Pan-Asian*	-
Harry's Bar | *Italian*	24
Kai Mayfair | *Chinese*	25
Kiku | *Jap.*	24
La Genova | *Italian*	23
☑ Lanes | *Eclectic*	24
Le Boudin Blanc | *French*	22
☑ Le Gavroche | *French*	27
Mark's Club | *British/French*	24
Maze | *French*	25
NEW Mews of Mayfair | *British*	22
Mirabelle | *French*	22
Miyama | *Jap.*	26
Morton's | *French*	24
Nobu Berkeley St. | *Jap./Peruvian*	26
☑ Nobu London | *Jap./Peruvian*	27
Patara | *Thai*	23
Patterson's | *Euro.*	22
Pescatori | *Med.*	22
Rasa | *Indian*	24
NEW Rist. Semplice | *Italian*	-
Sakura | *Jap.*	23
NEW Scott's | *Seafood*	22
Sketch/Gallery | *Euro.*	19
☑ Sketch/Lecture Rm. | *Euro.*	21
☑ Square, The | *French*	28
Taman Gang | *Pan-Asian*	22
☑ Tamarind | *Indian*	25
NEW Theo Randall | *Italian*	26
Truc Vert | *French*	22
Umu | *Jap.*	26
Veeraswamy | *Indian*	22
NEW Via Condotti | *Italian*	18

PICCADILLY

Bentley's | *British/Seafood*	24
Cocoon | *Pan-Asian*	21

Ed's Easy Diner	*Hamburgers*	15
🅩 Gaucho Grill	*Argent./Chops*	22
Hard Rock	*Amer.*	13
Momo	*African*	19
Patisserie Valerie	*French*	20
NEW 1707 Wine Bar	*British*	22
NEW St. Alban	*Euro.*	21
🅩 Wolseley, The	*Euro.*	21
Yoshino	*Jap.*	24

SOHO

Alastair Little	*British*	24
Andrew Edmunds	*Euro.*	22
Arbutus	*Euro.*	24
NEW Barrafina	*Spanish*	24
Bar Shu	*Chinese*	22
NEW Benja	*Thai*	–
Busaba Eathai	*Thai*	21
NEW Club, The	*Eclectic*	–
Ed's Easy Diner	*Hamburgers*	15
Leon	*Med.*	19
Le Pain Quotidien	*Bakery/Belgian*	19
L'Escargot	*French*	22
Mildreds	*Veg.*	22
Patara	*Thai*	23
Patisserie Valerie	*French*	20
🅩 Pizza Express	*Pizza*	17
Red Fort	*Indian*	23
Richard Corrigan	*British/Irish*	23
🅩 Wagamama	*Jap.*	19
🅩 Yauatcha	*Chinese*	25

ST. JAMES'S

Green's	*British/Seafood*	22
🅩 Le Caprice	*British/Euro.*	24
L'Oranger	*French*	24
🅩 Ritz, The	*British/French*	23
Wilton's	*British/Seafood*	24

VICTORIA

Chez Gérard	*French*	18
Goring	*British*	23
Quilon	*Indian*	25

WESTMINSTER

NEW Atami	*Jap.*	24
Cinnamon Club	*Indian*	24
Quirinale	*Italian*	25

East/South East London

BLACKFRIARS

🅩 Pizza Express	*Pizza*	17
🅩 Wagamama	*Jap.*	19

BOW/MILE END/ HACKNEY/ BETHNAL GREEN

NEW Empress of India	*British*	–

BROADGATE

🅩 Gaucho Grill	*Argent./Chops*	22

CANARY WHARF/ DOCKLANDS

Carluccio's	*Italian*	17
🅩 Gaucho Grill	*Argent./Chops*	22
Quadrato	*Italian*	24
Royal China	*Chinese*	24
Ubon	*Jap./Peruvian*	24

CITY

Café Spice Namasté	*Indian*	23
Chez Gérard	*French*	18
Don	*Euro.*	22
🅩 Gaucho Grill	*Argent./Chops*	22
Haz	*Turkish*	25
Leon	*Med.*	19
1 Lombard St.	*French*	22
Patisserie Valerie	*French*	20
Rhodes 24	*British*	23
Sweetings	*British/Seafood*	24
Vivat Bacchus	*Euro.*	23
🅩 Wagamama	*Jap.*	19

CLERKENWELL/ SMITHFIELD/ FARRINGDON

Bleeding Heart	*British/French*	22
Carluccio's	*Italian*	17
Club Gascon	*French*	26
Flaneur	*Euro.*	22
NEW Hat/Feathers	*Euro.*	–
La Porchetta	*Pizza*	19
Le Café/Marché	*French*	23
Little Bay	*Euro./Med.*	21
Moro	*Med.*	25
NEW St. Germain	*French*	21
St. John	*British*	25

GREENWICH/ BLACKHEATH

Chapter Two | *Euro.* — 24

NEW Spread Eagle | *French* — 21

SHOREDITCH/ SPITALFIELDS/ HOXTON/WHITECHAPEL

NEW Bacchus | *Eclectic* — 21

Canteen | *British* — 22

Eyre Brothers | *Portug./Spanish* — 22

Fifteen | *Med.* — 23

Great Eastern | *Asian* — 22

NEW Hawksmoor | *Chops* — 28

NEW Hoxton Grille | *Eclectic* — –

Leon | *Med.* — 19

Z Les Trois Garçons | *French* — 19

New Tayyabs | *Pakistani* — 24

Original Lahore | *Pakistani* — 24

St. John Bread/Wine | *British* — 22

Viet Hoa | *Vietnamese* — 23

SOUTH BANK/BOROUGH

Canteen | *British* — 22

Le Pain Quotidien | — 19
Bakery/Belgian

NEW Magdalen | *Euro.* — –

NEW Skylon | *Euro.* — –

Tapas Brindisa | *Spanish* — 22

TOWER BRIDGE/ LIMEHOUSE/WAPPING

Il Bordello | *Italian* — 23

Le Pont/Tour | *French/Seafood* — 22

NEW Narrow, The | *British* — –

WATERLOO/ SOUTHWARK/ KENNINGTON

Anchor & Hope | *British* — 24

Baltic | *Polish* — 21

Chez Gérard | *French* — 18

North/ North West London

CAMDEN TOWN/CHALK FARM/KENTISH TOWN/ PRIMROSE HILL

Belgo | *Belgian* — 19

Z Wagamama | *Jap.* — 19

GOLDERS GREEN/ FINCHLEY

Café Japan | *Jap.* — 26

Two Brothers Fish | *Seafood* — 24

HAMPSTEAD/KILBURN/ SWISS COTTAGE

Baker & Spice | *Med.* — 22

Z Gaucho Grill | *Argent./Chops* — 22

Gourmet Burger | *Hamburgers* — 21

Jin Kichi | *Jap.* — 26

Little Bay | *Euro./Med.* — 21

NEW XO | *Pan-Asian* — 16

HIGHGATE/MUSWELL HILL/CROUCH END/ TUFNELL PARK

NEW Bouga | *Moroccan* — –

La Porchetta | *Pizza* — 19

Original Lahore | *Pakistani* — 24

ISLINGTON

NEW Albion, The | *British* — –

Carluccio's | *Italian* — 17

La Porchetta | *Pizza* — 19

Z Morgan M | *French* — 27

Ottolenghi | *Med.* — 24

Pasha | *Moroccan* — 20

Rasa | *Indian* — 24

Z Wagamama | *Jap.* — 19

KING'S CROSS

NEW Acorn House | *British* — 19

ST. JOHN'S WOOD

Baker & Spice | *Med.* — 22

L'Aventure | *French* — 22

Oslo Court | *French* — 22

Royal China | *Chinese* — 24

STOKE NEWINGTON

La Porchetta | *Pizza* — 19

Rasa | *Indian* — 24

South/ South West London

BARNES

NEW Barnes Grill | *British* — –

BATTERSEA

Buona Sera | *Italian* — 23

NEW Butcher & Grill | *British* — 15

Gourmet Burger | *Hamburgers* 21
Little Bay | *Euro./Med.* 21
☑ Pizza Express | *Pizza* 17

BRIXTON/CLAPHAM

Pepper Tree | *Thai* 19
NEW Trinity | *Euro.* 24
Tsunami | *Jap.* 24

CHELSEA

Aubergine | *French* 26
Baker & Spice | *Med.* 22
Buona Sera | *Italian* 23
NEW C Garden | *Italian* 18
NEW Chelsea Brass. | *French* 16
Chelsea Bun | *British* 18
Cheyne Walk | *French* 23
Chutney Mary | *Indian* 23
Eight Over Eight | *Pan-Asian* 23
☑ Gaucho Grill | *Argent./Chops* 22
☑ Gordon Ramsay/68 Royal | *French* 28
La Famiglia | *Italian* 21
Le Cercle | *French* 24
Le Suquet | *French/Seafood* 23
Made in Italy | *Italian* 21
Painted Heron | *Indian* 22
Patisserie Valerie | *French* 20
Pig's Ear | *British/French* 22
☑ Pizza Express | *Pizza* 17
☑ Rasoi Vineet Bhatia | *Indian* 27
Scalini | *Italian* 23
Sophie's Steak | *Amer./Chops* 23
Tom Aikens | *French* 26
NEW Tom's Kitchen | *British* 19
Toto's | *Italian* 24
Vama | *Indian* 24
Ziani | *Italian* 25

FULHAM

Blue Elephant | *Thai* 20
Carluccio's | *Italian* 17
Gourmet Burger | *Hamburgers* 21
Little Bay | *Euro./Med.* 21
Ma Goa | *Indian* 23
Mao Tai | *Chinese* 22
☑ Pizza Express | *Pizza* 17
Royal China | *Chinese* 24

PIMLICO

☑ Hunan | *Chinese* 28
La Poule au Pot | *French* 22
Roussillon | *French* 26

PUTNEY/RICHMOND

Carluccio's | *Italian* 17
☑ Enoteca Turi | *Italian* 27
☑ Gaucho Grill | *Argent./Chops* 24
Glasshouse, The | *British* 24
Gourmet Burger | *Hamburgers* 21
Ma Goa | *Indian* 23

SOUTH KENSINGTON

Bibendum | *French* 24
Bibendum Oyster | *French/Seafood* 22
Bombay Brass. | *Indian* 22
Cambio de Tercio | *Spanish* 24
Khan's of Kensington | *Indian* 22
L'Etranger | *French* 24
Lundum's | *Danish* 22
Papillon | *French* 23
Pasha | *Moroccan* 18
Patara | *Thai* 23
Star of India | *Indian* 24

WANDSWORTH/ BALHAM/WIMBLEDON

☑ Chez Bruce | *British* 28
Gourmet Burger | *Hamburgers* 21
NEW Raviolo | *Italian* -

West London

BAYSWATER

Al Waha | *Lebanese* 22
Fairuz | *Lebanese* 22
Four Seasons | *Chinese* 22
Gourmet Burger | *Hamburgers* 21
Halepi | *Greek* 24
Mandarin Kitchen | *Chinese* 23
Royal China | *Chinese* 24

CHISWICK

Gourmet Burger | *Hamburgers* 21
NEW High Road Brass. | *Euro.* 20
☑ La Trompette | *Euro./French* 27

DINING

LOCATIONS

Dining Special Features

Listings cover the best in each category and include restaurant names, locations and Food ratings. Multi-location restaurants' features may vary by branch. ⚊ indicates places with the highest ratings, popularity and importance.

ALL-DAY DINING

NEW Acorn House | **WC1**	19
Baker & Spice | **multi. loc.**	22
Banquette | **WC2**	22
Bar Shu | **W1**	22
Belgo | **WC2**	19
Bibendum Oyster | **SW3**	22
Busaba Eathai | **multi. loc.**	21
Canteen | **multi. loc.**	22
Carluccio's | **multi. loc.**	17
NEW Chelsea Brass. | **SW1**	16
Chelsea Bun | **SW10**	18
Chez Gérard | **multi. loc.**	18
NEW Cookbook Cafe | **W1**	–
Ed's Easy Diner | **multi. loc.**	15
Flaneur | **EC1**	22
Food for Thought | **WC2**	24
Four Seasons | **W2**	22
⚊ Gaucho Grill | **multi. loc.**	22
Gourmet Burger | **multi. loc.**	21
Halepi | **W2**	24
Hard Rock | **W1**	13
Haz | **E1**	25
NEW High Road Brass. | **W4**	20
Hinds Head | **Berks**	23
Ladurée | **SW1**	23
La Fromagerie | **W1**	24
Leon | **multi. loc.**	19
Le Pain Quotidien | **multi. loc.**	19
Lucky 7 | **W2**	20
Mildreds | **W1**	22
Original Lahore | **NW4**	24
Ottolenghi | **multi. loc.**	24
Pasha | **N1**	20
Patisserie Valerie | **multi. loc.**	20
⚊ Pizza Express | **multi. loc.**	17
Royal China | **multi. loc.**	24
Royal China Club | **W1**	24
⚊ Rules | **WC2**	23
Salt Yard | **W1**	22
Sophie's Steak | **SW10**	23

St. John Bread/Wine | **E1**	22
Truc Vert | **W1**	22
⚊ Wagamama | **multi. loc.**	19
NEW Wallace, The | **W1**	20
⚊ Wolseley, The | **W1**	21

BREAKFAST
(See also Hotel Dining)

Baker & Spice | **multi. loc.**	22
Books for Cooks | **W11**	24
Carluccio's | **multi. loc.**	17
Cinnamon Club | **SW1**	24
NEW Empress of India | **E9**	–
Ladurée | **SW1**	23
La Fromagerie | **W1**	24
Lucky 7 | **W2**	20
Lundum's | **SW7**	22
Ottolenghi | **multi. loc.**	24
Patisserie Valerie | **multi. loc.**	20
Providores, The | **W1**	22
St. John Bread/Wine | **E1**	22
⚊ Wolseley, The | **W1**	21

BRUNCH

Abingdon, The | **W8**	22
Blue Elephant | **SW6**	20
Clarke's | **W8**	25
Lanesborough | **SW1**	21
⚊ Le Caprice | **SW1**	24
Lucky 7 | **W2**	20
Lundum's | **SW7**	22
Providores, The | **W1**	22
Quadrato | **E14**	24
Sophie's Steak | **SW10**	23
NEW St. Germain | **EC1**	21
NEW Tom's Kitchen | **SW3**	19
Vama | **SW10**	24

BUSINESS DINING

Alloro | **W1**	22
⚊ Amaya | **SW1**	25
Arbutus | **W1**	24
NEW Atami | **SW1**	24

DINING

SPECIAL FEATURES

Square, The | **W1** — 28

NEW St. Alban | **SW1** — 21

NEW Suka | **W1** — -

Tamarind | **W1** — 25

NEW Theo Randall | **W1** — 26

Tom Aikens | **SW3** — 26

NEW Tom's Kitchen | **SW3** — 19

NEW Trinity | **SW4** — 24

Ubon | **E14** — 24

Umu | **W1** — 26

NEW Via Condotti | **W1** — 18

Vineyard/Stockcross | **Berks** — 24

NEW Wallace, The | **W1** — 20

Waterside Inn | **Berks** — 27

Wilton's | **SW1** — 24

Zafferano | **SW1** — 26

Zaika | **W8** — 25

Zuma | **SW7** — 26

CELEBRITY CHEFS

Banquette | *Marcus Wareing* | **WC2** — 22

NEW Barnes Grill | *Antony Worrall Thompson* | **SW13** — -

Benares | *Atul Kochhar* | **W1** — 23

Bentley's | *Richard Corrigan* | **W1** — 24

Boxwood Café | *Gordon Ramsay & Stuart Gillies* | **SW1** — 21

Café Spice Namasté | *Cyrus Todiwala* | **E1** — 23

Capital Rest. | *Eric Chavot* | **SW3** — 27

Carluccio's | *Antonio Carluccio* | **multi. loc.** — 17

Chez Bruce | *Bruce Poole* | **SW17** — 28

Cinnamon Club | *Vivek Singh* | **SW1** — 24

Clarke's | *Sally Clarke* | **W8** — 25

Club Gascon | *Pascal Aussignac* | **EC1** — 26

Fat Duck | *Heston Blumenthal* | **Berks** — 27

Fifteen | *Jamie Oliver* | **N1** — 23

Galvin/Windows | *Chris Galvin* | **W1** — 22

Galvin Bistrot | *Chris Galvin* | **W1** — 24

Gordon Ramsay/Claridge's | *Gordon Ramsay & Mark Sargeant* | **W1** — 25

Gordon Ramsay/68 Royal | *Gordon Ramsay & Mark Askew* | **SW3** — 28

Hinds Head | *Heston Blumenthal* | **Berks** — 23

Ivy, The | *Mark Hix* | **WC2** — 23

J. Sheekey | *Mark Hix* | **WC2** — 25

NEW L'Atelier/Robuchon | *Joël Robuchon* | **WC2** — 26

Le Caprice | *Mark Hix* | **SW1** — 24

Le Cercle | *Pascal Aussignac* | **SW1** — 24

Le Gavroche | *Michel Roux Jr.* | **W1** — 27

Le Manoir/Quat | *Raymond Blanc* | **Oxfordshire** — 28

Locanda Locatelli | *Giorgio Locatelli* | **W1** — 25

Maze | *Gordon Ramsay & Jason Atherton* | **W1** — 25

Moro | *Sam & Sam Clark* | **EC1** — 25

Nahm | *David Thompson* | **SW1** — 26

NEW Narrow, The | *Gordon Ramsay* | **E14** — -

Nobu Berkeley St. | *Nobu Matsuhisa & Mark Edwards* | **W1** — 26

Nobu London | *Nobu Matsuhisa & Mark Edwards* | **W1** — 27

Pearl | *Jun Tanaka* | **WC1** — 24

Pétrus | *Marcus Wareing* | **SW1** — 28

Providores, The | *Peter Gordon* | **W1** — 22

Racine | *Henry Harris* | **SW3** — 22

Rasoi Vineet Bhatia | *Vineet Bhatia* | **SW3** — 27

Rhodes 24 | *Gary Rhodes* | **EC2** — 23

Rhodes W1 Rest. | *Gary Rhodes* | **W1** — -

Richard Corrigan | *Richard Corrigan* | **W1** — 23

River Café | *Rose Gray & Ruth Rodgers* | **W6** — 27

Roka | *Rainer Becker* | **W1** — 25

DINING

SPECIAL FEATURES

☑ Rasoi Vineet Bhatia | **SW3** 27	Mandalay | T | **W2** 23
☑ Ritz, The* | **W1** 23	Mao Tai | D, T | **SW6** 22
☑ River Café | **W6** 27	Mela | T | **WC2** 23
Roussillon* | **SW1** 26	North Sea | T | **WC1** 23
Royal China | **multi. loc.** 24	Oliveto | T | **SW1** 23
☑ Rules | **WC2** 23	Original Lahore | T | **multi. loc.** 24
Santini | **SW1** 22	Ottolenghi | T | **multi. loc.** 24
Sophie's Steak* | **SW10** 23	Painted Heron | T | **SW10** 22
NEW Tom's Kitchen | **SW3** 19	Patara | T | **multi. loc.** 23
Truc Vert | **W1** 22	☑ Pizza Express | T | **multi. loc.** 17
Two Brothers Fish* | **N3** 24	Rasa | T | **multi. loc.** 24
Ubon | **E14** 24	Royal China | T | **multi. loc.** 24
Vama | **SW10** 24	Salloos | T | **SW1** 23
☑ Wagamama* | **multi. loc.** 19	Star of India | T | **SW5** 24
☑ Waterside Inn* | **Berks** 27	St. John Bread/Wine | T | **E1** 22
☑ Wolseley, The | **W1** 21	☑ Tamarind | D, T | **W1** 25
☑ Yauatcha | **W1** 25	Truc Vert | D, T | **W1** 22
Yoshino | **W1** 24	Two Brothers Fish | T | **N3** 24
☑ Zafferano | **SW1** 26	Ubon | T | **E14** 24
☑ Zuma | **SW7** 26	Vama | D, T | **SW10** 24
	Veeraswamy | T | **W1** 22
	Yoshino | T | **W1** 24

DELIVERY/TAKEAWAY

(D=delivery, T=takeaway)

Alounak | D, T | **multi. loc.** 23	**DINING ALONE**
Baker & Spice | T | **multi. loc.** 22	(Other than hotels and places with counter service)
Blue Elephant | D, T | **SW6** 20	☑ Amaya | **SW1** 25
Café Spice Namasté | D, T | **E1** 23	Baker & Spice | **multi. loc.** 22
Carluccio's | T | **multi. loc.** 17	NEW Barrafina | **W1** 24
Churchill Arms | T | **W8** 22	Bibendum Oyster | **SW3** 22
Chutney Mary | T | **SW10** 23	Books for Cooks | **W11** 24
☑ Defune | T | **W1** 27	Busaba Eathai | **multi. loc.** 21
Ed's Easy Diner | T | **W1** 15	Carluccio's | **multi. loc.** 17
Fairuz | D, T | **multi. loc.** 22	Ed's Easy Diner | **W1** 15
☑ Gaucho Grill | T | **multi. loc.** 22	Fino | **W1** 23
Halepi | T | **W2** 24	☑ Hakkasan | **W1** 24
Ishbilia | D, T | **SW1** 24	Jenny Lo's Tea | **SW1** 20
Jenny Lo's Tea | D, T | **SW1** 20	Ladurée | **SW1** 23
Jin Kichi | T | **NW3** 26	La Fromagerie | **W1** 24
Khan's of Kensington | D, T | **SW7** 22	Leon | **multi. loc.** 19
Kiku | T | **W1** 24	Maze | **W1** 25
Koi | D, T | **W8** 22	Mildreds | **W1** 22
La Fromagerie | D, T | **W1** 24	Ottolenghi | **multi. loc.** 24
La Porchetta | T | **multi. loc.** 19	Patisserie Valerie | **multi. loc.** 20
La Porte des Indes | T | **W1** 21	Providores, The | **W1** 22
Lucky 7 | T | **W2** 20	NEW 1707 Wine Bar | **W1** 22
Ma Goa | T | **SW15** 23	St. John Bread/Wine | **E1** 22

Tapas Brindisa | **SE1** 22

NEW Tom's Kitchen | **SW3** 19

Truc Vert | **W1** 22

Z Wagamama | **multi. loc.** 19

Z Wolseley, The | **W1** 21

Z Yauatcha | **W1** 25

ENTERTAINMENT

(Call for days and
times of performances)

Bentley's | piano | **W1** 24

Cheyne Walk | jazz | **SW3** 23

Chutney Mary | jazz | **SW10** 23

Z Hakkasan | DJ | **W1** 24

Ishbilia | belly dancing | **SW1** 24

Lanesborough | jazz | **SW1** 21

Le Café/Marché | jazz | **EC1** 23

Z Le Caprice | piano | **SW1** 24

Le Pont/Tour | piano | **SE1** 22

Mirabelle | piano | **W1** 22

Rib Rm. | piano | **SW1** 24

Z Ritz, The | piano | **W1** 23

Vineyard/Stockcross | piano |
Berks 24

FIREPLACES

Anglesea Arms | **W6** 23

Belgo | **NW1** 19

Cambio de Tercio | **SW5** 24

Cheyne Walk | **SW3** 23

Churchill Arms | **W8** 22

Z Cliveden House | **Berks** 24

Clos Maggiore | **WC2** 24

French Horn | **Berks** 23

Goring | **SW1** 23

Z Gravetye Manor | **W. Sussex** 24

NEW Hoxton Grille | **EC2** -

La Poule au Pot | **SW1** 22

Le Cercle | **SW1** 24

Z Le Manoir/Quat |
Oxfordshire 28

L'Escargot | **W1** 22

Lundum's | **SW7** 22

Richard Corrigan | **W1** 23

Z Rules | **WC2** 23

NEW Spread Eagle | **SE10** 21

Tsunami | **SW4** 24

Z Waterside Inn | **Berks** 27

GAME IN SEASON

NEW Albion, The | **N1** -

Anchor & Hope | **SE1** 24

Andrew Edmunds | **W1** 22

Arbutus | **W1** 24

Bibendum | **SW3** 24

Bleeding Heart | **EC1** 22

Boxwood Café | **SW1** 21

Brown's/The Grill | **W1** 22

NEW Bumpkin | **W11** 21

Z Capital Rest. | **SW3** 27

Z Chez Bruce | **SW17** 28

Chutney Mary | **SW10** 23

Cinnamon Club | **SW1** 24

Cipriani | **W1** 20

Z Cliveden House | **Berks** 24

Clos Maggiore | **WC2** 24

Club Gascon | **EC1** 26

NEW Cookbook Cafe | **W1** -

Dorchester/The Grill | **W1** 24

Z Enoteca Turi | **SW15** 27

Z Fat Duck | **Berks** 27

ffiona's | **W8** 24

Fifteen | **N1** 23

Fino | **W1** 23

Foliage | **SW1** 26

NEW Forge, The | **WC2** -

French Horn | **Berks** 23

Glasshouse, The | **TW9** 24

Z Gordon Ramsay/Claridge's |
W1 25

Z Gordon Ramsay/68 Royal |
SW3 28

Goring | **SW1** 23

Z Gravetye Manor | **W. Sussex** 24

NEW Great Queen St. | **WC2** -

Greenhouse, The | **W1** 25

Green's | **SW1** 22

NEW Hat/Feathers | **EC1** -

Il Convivio | **SW1** 23

La Famiglia | **SW10** 21

Lanesborough | **SW1** 21

La Poule au Pot | **SW1** 22

Z La Trompette | **W4** 27

L'Aventure | **NW8** 22

Z Le Caprice | **SW1** 24

DINING

SPECIAL FEATURES

Le Cercle | **SW1**	24
Ledbury | **W11**	25
🗷 Le Gavroche | **W1**	27
🗷 Le Manoir/Quat | **Oxfordshire**	28
Le Pont/Tour | **SE1**	22
L'Escargot | **W1**	22
🗷 Les Trois Garçons | **E1**	19
L'Etranger | **SW7**	24
Locanda Locatelli | **W1**	25
Michael Moore | **W1**	22
Mirabelle | **W1**	22
🗷 Morgan M | **N7**	27
Moro | **EC1**	25
Notting Hill Brass. | **W11**	24
1 Lombard St. | **EC3**	22
Orrery | **W1**	25
Papillon | **SW3**	23
Passione | **W1**	23
Pearl | **WC1**	24
🗷 Pétrus | **SW1**	28
Pig's Ear | **SW3**	22
Providores, The | **W1**	22
Quadrato | **E14**	24
Quirinale | **SW1**	25
Racine | **SW3**	22
Rhodes 24 | **EC2**	23
Rhodes W1 Rest. | **W1**	–
Rib Rm. | **SW1**	24
Richard Corrigan | **W1**	23
🆕 Rist. Semplice | **W1**	–
🗷 Ritz, The | **W1**	23
🗷 River Café | **W6**	27
Roussillon | **SW1**	26
🗷 Rules | **WC2**	23
Santini | **SW1**	22
Sardo | **W1**	23
Savoy Grill | **WC2**	24
Sketch/Gallery | **W1**	19
🗷 Sketch/Lecture Rm. | **W1**	21
🆕 Spread Eagle | **SE10**	21
🗷 Square, The | **W1**	28
🆕 St. Alban | **SW1**	21
St. John | **EC1**	25
St. John Bread/Wine | **E1**	22
🆕 Theo Randall | **W1**	26

Timo | **W8**	22
Tom Aikens | **SW3**	26
🆕 Tom's Kitchen | **SW3**	19
🆕 Trinity | **SW4**	24
Veeraswamy | **W1**	22
Vineyard/Stockcross | **Berks**	24
Vivat Bacchus | **EC4**	23
🗷 Waterside Inn | **Berks**	27
Wilton's | **SW1**	24
🗷 Wolseley, The | **W1**	21
🗷 Zafferano | **SW1**	26
Zaika | **W8**	25

GASTROPUB

Anchor & Hope | **SE1**	24
Anglesea Arms | **W6**	23
🆕 Bacchus | **N1**	21
Churchill Arms | **W8**	22
Cow Dining Rm. | **W2**	21
🆕 Great Queen St. | **WC2**	–
🆕 Hat/Feathers | **EC1**	–
🆕 Narrow, The | **E14**	–
Pig's Ear | **SW3**	22

HISTORIC PLACES

(Year opened; * building)

1550 | Fat Duck* | **Berks**	27
1598 | Gravetye Manor* | **W. Sussex**	24
1662 | Bleeding Heart* | **EC1**	22
1680 | French Horn* | **Berks**	23
1690 | Hinds Head | **Berks**	23
1700 | Lanesborough* | **SW1**	21
1725 | Patisserie Valerie* | **WC2**	20
1740 | Richard Corrigan* | **W1**	23
1742 | Wilton's | **SW1**	24
1750 | Food for Thought* | **WC2**	24
1780 | Andrew Edmunds* | **W1**	22
1790 | Carluccio's* | **EC1**	17
1790 | Chez Gérard* | **EC2**	18
1798 | Don* | **EC4**	22
1798 | Rules* | **WC2**	23
1800 | Anglesea Arms* | **W6**	23
1800 | Churchill Arms* | **W8**	22
1810 | Pig's Ear* | **SW3**	22
1834 | Albion, The* | **N1**	–
1837 | Brown's/The Grill* | **W1**	22

DINING

SPECIAL FEATURES

Sheraton Park Tower		Tokyo Diner | 12 AM | **WC2**	20
One-O-One | **SW1**	23	**NEW** Tom's Kitchen | 12 AM |	19
Sloane Square Hotel		**SW3**	
NEW Chelsea Brass. | **SW1**	16	**Z** Wolseley, The | 12 AM | **W1**	21
St. Giles Hotel			

St. Giles Hotel	
NEW Kobe Jones | **WC1**	18
St. Martins Lane Hotel	
Asia de Cuba | **WC2**	22
Thistle Hotel	
Chez Gérard | **SW1**	18
Vineyard at Stockcross	
Vineyard/Stockcross | **Berks**	24
Waterside Inn	
Z Waterside Inn | **Berks**	27

LATE DINING

(Weekday closing hour)

Alounak | varies | **W14**	23
Asia de Cuba | varies | **WC2**	22
Blue Elephant | 12 AM | **SW6**	20
Boxwood Café | 12 AM | **SW1**	21
NEW Bumpkin | varies | **W11**	21
Buona Sera | 12 AM | **multi. loc.**	23
Chelsea Bun | 12 AM | **SW10**	18
Cocoon | varies | **W1**	21
NEW Forge, The | 12 AM | **WC2**	-
Z Gaucho Grill | 12 AM | **NW3**	22
Z Hakkasan | 12 AM | **W1**	24
Halepi | 12 AM | **W2**	24
Hard Rock | 12:30 AM | **W1**	13
Haz | 12 AM | **E1**	25
Ishbilia | 12 AM | **SW1**	24
Z Ivy, The | 12 AM | **WC2**	23
Z J. Sheekey | 12 AM | **WC2**	25
La Porchetta | 12 AM | **multi. loc.**	19
NEW Z L'Atelier/Robuchon | varies | **WC2**	26
Z Le Caprice | 12 AM | **SW1**	24
Little Bay | 12 AM | **multi. loc.**	21
Original Lahore | 12 AM | **multi. loc.**	24
Pasha | 12 AM | **SW7**	18
Z Pizza Express | varies | **multi. loc.**	17
NEW St. Alban | 12 AM | **SW1**	21
NEW St. Germain | varies | **EC1**	21
NEW Suka | varies | **W1**	-

NOTEWORTHY NEWCOMERS

Acorn House | **WC1**	19
Albion, The | **N1**	-
Atami | **SW1**	24
Bacchus | **N1**	21
Barnes Grill | **SW13**	-
Barrafina | **W1**	24
Benja | **W1**	-
Bouga | **N8**	-
Bumpkin | **W11**	21
Burlington Club | **W1**	-
Butcher & Grill | **SW11**	15
C Garden | **SW3**	18
Chelsea Brass. | **SW1**	16
Club, The | **W1**	-
Cookbook Cafe | **W1**	-
Dinings | **W1**	-
Empress of India | **E9**	-
Fat Badger | **W10**	15
Forge, The | **WC2**	-
Great Queen St. | **WC2**	-
Haiku | **W1**	-
Hat/Feathers | **EC1**	-
Hawksmoor | **E1**	28
High Road Brass. | **W4**	20
Hoxton Grille | **EC2**	-
Kobe Jones | **WC1**	18
Z L'Atelier/Robuchon | **WC2**	26
Magdalen | **SE1**	-
Mews of Mayfair | **W1**	22
Mocotó | **SW1**	22
Narrow, The | **E14**	-
Olivomare | **SW1**	-
Raviolo | **SW12**	-
Rhodes W1 Rest. | **W1**	-
Rist. Semplice | **W1**	-
Scott's | **W1**	22
1707 Wine Bar | **W1**	22
Skylon | **SE1**	-
Spread Eagle | **SE10**	21
St. Alban | **SW1**	21

St. Germain | **EC1**	21
Suka | **W1**	-
Tamarai | **WC2**	-
Theo Randall | **W1**	26
Tom's Kitchen | **SW3**	19
Trinity | **SW4**	24
Via Condotti | **W1**	18
Wallace, The | **W1**	20
XO | **NW3**	16

OFFBEAT

NEW Acorn House | **WC1**	19
Alounak | **multi. loc.**	23
Archipelago | **W1**	21
Asia de Cuba | **WC2**	22
Baker & Spice | **multi. loc.**	22
Belgo | **multi. loc.**	19
Blue Elephant | **SW6**	20
Books for Cooks | **W11**	24
Cambio de Tercio | **SW5**	24
Club Gascon | **EC1**	26
Cocoon | **W1**	21
NEW Dinings | **W1**	-
☑ Fat Duck | **Berks**	27
ffiona's | **W8**	24
Fifteen | **N1**	23
Flaneur | **EC1**	22
Food for Thought | **WC2**	24
Jenny Lo's Tea | **SW1**	20
La Fromagerie | **W1**	24
La Porte des Indes | **W1**	21
Le Cercle | **SW1**	24
☑ Les Trois Garçons | **E1**	19
Lucky 7 | **W2**	20
Maggie Jones's | **W8**	21
Momo | **W1**	19
Moro | **EC1**	25
Nahm | **SW1**	26
Ottolenghi | **multi. loc.**	24
Providores, The | **W1**	22
☑ Rasoi Vineet Bhatia | **SW3**	27
Richard Corrigan | **W1**	23
Sketch/Gallery | **W1**	19
St. John | **EC1**	25
St. John Bread/Wine | **E1**	22
Tapas Brindisa | **SE1**	22
Truc Vert | **W1**	22

Tsunami | **SW4**	24
☑ Wagamama | **multi. loc.**	19

OUTDOOR DINING

(G=garden; P=patio; PV=pavement;
T=terrace; W=waterside)

Abingdon, The | PV | **W8**	22
NEW Albion, The | G | **N1**	-
Al Hamra | P | **W1**	22
Anglesea Arms | P | **W6**	23
Archipelago | P | **W1**	21
NEW Barrafina | PV | **W1**	24
NEW C Garden | P | **SW3**	18
Chez Kristof | T | **W6**	22
e&o | PV | **W11**	22
Hard Rock | T | **W1**	13
Ishbilia | PV | **SW1**	24
La Famiglia | G | **SW10**	21
La Poule au Pot | P | **SW1**	22
☑ La Trompette | T | **W4**	27
L'Aventure | T | **NW8**	22
Ledbury | P | **W11**	25
Le Pont/Tour | P, W | **SE1**	22
Locanda Ottoemezzo | PV | **W8**	24
L'Oranger | P | **SW1**	24
Lundum's | T | **SW7**	22
Made in Italy | T | **SW3**	21
Mediterraneo | PV | **W11**	22
Mildreds | PV | **W1**	22
Mirabelle | P | **W1**	22
Momo | T | **W1**	19
Moro | PV | **EC1**	25
NEW Olivomare | PV | **SW1**	-
Orrery | T | **W1**	25
Osteria Basilico | P | **W11**	24
Painted Heron | G | **SW10**	22
Passione | P | **W1**	23
Quadrato | T | **E14**	24
☑ Ritz, The | T | **W1**	23
☑ River Café | P, W | **W6**	27
Roka | PV | **W1**	25
Santini | T | **SW1**	22
NEW Suka | G, T | **W1**	-
Toto's | G | **SW3**	24
Vama | P | **SW10**	24
Vineyard/Stockcross | T, W | **Berks**	24

PEOPLE-WATCHING

NEW Albion, The	N1	-
Z Amaya	SW1	25
Asia de Cuba	WC2	22
NEW Atami	SW1	24
NEW Barrafina	W1	24
Bar Shu	W1	22
Bibendum	SW3	24
Bibendum Oyster	SW3	22
Boxwood Café	SW1	21
Brown's/The Grill	W1	22
NEW Bumpkin	W11	21
NEW Butcher & Grill	SW11	15
NEW C Garden	SW3	18
Cinnamon Club	SW1	24
Cipriani	W1	20
NEW Club, The	W1	-
Club Gascon	EC1	26
e&o	W11	22
Eight Over Eight	SW3	23
Fifteen	N1	23
Fino	W1	23
Galvin/Windows	W1	22
Galvin Bistrot	W1	24
Z Gordon Ramsay/Claridge's	W1	25
Z Gordon Ramsay/68 Royal	SW3	28
NEW Great Queen St.	WC2	-
Z Hakkasan	W1	24
NEW High Road Brass.	W4	20
Z Ivy, The	WC2	23
Z J. Sheekey	WC2	25
La Famiglia	SW10	21
NEW Z L'Atelier/Robuchon	WC2	26
Z La Trompette	W4	27
Z Le Caprice	SW1	24
Le Cercle	SW1	24
Ledbury	W11	25
Locanda Locatelli	W1	25
Maze	W1	25
NEW Mews of Mayfair	W1	22
Mirabelle	W1	22
NEW Mocotó	SW1	22
Momo	W1	19
NEW Narrow, The	E14	-

Nobu Berkeley St.	W1	26
Z Nobu London	W1	27
NEW Olivomare	SW1	-
Papillon	SW3	23
Z Pétrus	SW1	28
Racine	SW3	22
NEW Rist. Semplice	W1	-
Z River Café	W6	27
Roka	W1	25
Santini	SW1	22
Savoy Grill	WC2	24
NEW Scott's	W1	22
Sketch/Gallery	W1	19
Z Sketch/Lecture Rm.	W1	21
Sophie's Steak	SW10	23
NEW St. Alban	SW1	21
NEW Suka	W1	-
NEW Theo Randall	W1	26
Tom Aikens	SW3	26
NEW Tom's Kitchen	SW3	19
Ubon	E14	24
Z Waterside Inn	Berks	27
Wilton's	SW1	24
Z Wolseley, The	W1	21
NEW XO	NW3	16
Z Yauatcha	W1	25
Z Zafferano	SW1	26
Z Zuma	SW7	26

POWER SCENES

NEW Acorn House	WC1	19
Bentley's	W1	24
Boxwood Café	SW1	21
Brown's/The Grill	W1	22
Cinnamon Club	SW1	24
Cipriani	W1	20
Club Gascon	EC1	26
Z Gordon Ramsay/Claridge's	W1	25
Z Gordon Ramsay/68 Royal	SW3	28
Goring	SW1	23
Greenhouse, The	W1	25
Green's	SW1	22
NEW Hat/Feathers	EC1	-
Z Ivy, The	WC2	23
Z J. Sheekey	WC2	25

🛛 Lanes | **W1**	24	
NEW 🛛 L'Atelier/Robuchon | **WC2**	26	
🛛 Le Caprice | **SW1**	24	
Ledbury | **W11**	25	
🛛 Le Gavroche | **W1**	27	
🛛 Le Manoir/Quat | **Oxfordshire**	28	
Le Pont/Tour | **SE1**	22	
Maze | **W1**	25	
Mirabelle | **W1**	22	
Nahm | **SW1**	26	
Nobu Berkeley St. | **W1**	26	
🛛 Nobu London | **W1**	27	
1 Lombard St. | **EC3**	22	
🛛 Pétrus | **SW1**	28	
Quirinale | **SW1**	25	
Rhodes 24 | **EC2**	23	
🛛 Ritz, The | **W1**	23	
Savoy Grill | **WC2**	24	
🛛 Sketch/Lecture Rm. | **W1**	21	
🛛 Square, The | **W1**	28	
NEW St. Alban | **SW1**	21	
NEW St. Germain | **EC1**	21	
Tom Aikens | **SW3**	26	
Umu | **W1**	26	
NEW Via Condotti | **W1**	18	
🛛 Waterside Inn | **Berks**	27	
Wilton's | **SW1**	24	
🛛 Wolseley, The | **W1**	21	
🛛 Zafferano | **SW1**	26	
🛛 Zuma | **SW7**	26	

PRE-THEATRE MENUS

(Call for prices and times)

Arbutus | **W1**	24	
Asia de Cuba | **WC2**	22	
Baltic | **SE1**	21	
Benares | **W1**	23	
Brown's/The Grill | **W1**	22	
Cinnamon Club | **SW1**	24	
NEW Empress of India | **E9**	–	
🛛 Gordon Ramsay/Claridge's | **W1**	25	
Goring | **SW1**	23	
Indigo | **WC2**	22	
L'Escargot | **W1**	22	

Racine | **SW3**	22	
Red Fort | **W1**	23	
Richard Corrigan | **W1**	23	
🛛 Ritz, The | **W1**	23	
Savoy Grill | **WC2**	24	
Veeraswamy | **W1**	22	
Zaika | **W8**	25	

PUDDING SPECIALISTS

Alastair Little | **W1**	24	
🛛 Amaya | **SW1**	25	
Asia de Cuba | **WC2**	22	
Aubergine | **SW10**	26	
Baker & Spice | **multi. loc.**	22	
Bibendum Oyster | **SW3**	22	
Boxwood Café | **SW1**	21	
🛛 Capital Rest. | **SW3**	27	
🛛 Chez Bruce | **SW17**	28	
Cipriani | **W1**	20	
Clarke's | **W8**	25	
Club Gascon | **EC1**	26	
🛛 Fat Duck | **Berks**	27	
Foliage | **SW1**	26	
Galvin/Windows | **W1**	22	
Galvin Bistrot | **W1**	24	
Glasshouse, The | **TW9**	24	
🛛 Gordon Ramsay/Claridge's | **W1**	25	
🛛 Gordon Ramsay/68 Royal | **SW3**	28	
Greenhouse, The | **W1**	25	
Ladurée | **SW1**	23	
🛛 Lanes | **W1**	24	
Lanesborough | **SW1**	21	
NEW 🛛 L'Atelier/Robuchon | **WC2**	26	
🛛 La Trompette | **W4**	27	
Le Cercle | **SW1**	24	
Ledbury | **W11**	25	
🛛 Le Gavroche | **W1**	27	
🛛 Le Manoir/Quat | **Oxfordshire**	28	
Locanda Locatelli | **W1**	25	
L'Oranger | **SW1**	24	
Maze | **W1**	25	
Mirabelle | **W1**	22	
Nobu Berkeley St. | **W1**	26	

DINING

SPECIAL FEATURES

🗹 Nobu London | **W1**	27
Orrery | **W1**	25
Ottolenghi | **multi. loc.**	24
Patisserie Valerie | **multi. loc.**	20
🗹 Pétrus | **SW1**	28
🗹 Pied à Terre | **W1**	28
Providores, The | **W1**	22
🗹 Rasoi Vineet Bhatia | **SW3**	27
Rhodes W1 Rest. | **W1**	-
Richard Corrigan | **W1**	23
NEW Rist. Semplice | **W1**	-
🗹 Ritz, The | **W1**	23
🗹 River Café | **W6**	27
Savoy Grill | **WC2**	24
Sketch/Gallery | **W1**	19
🗹 Sketch/Lecture Rm. | **W1**	21
🗹 Square, The | **W1**	28
NEW St. Alban | **SW1**	21
NEW Theo Randall | **W1**	26
Tom Aikens | **SW3**	26
Ubon | **E14**	24
🗹 Waterside Inn | **Berks**	27
🗹 Wolseley, The | **W1**	21
🗹 Yauatcha | **W1**	25
🗹 Zafferano | **SW1**	26
🗹 Zuma | **SW7**	26

QUIET CONVERSATION

Al Sultan | **W1**	22
Arbutus | **W1**	24
Aubergine | **SW10**	26
Banquette | **WC2**	22
Benares | **W1**	23
NEW Benja | **W1**	-
🗹 Capital Rest. | **SW3**	27
NEW C Garden | **SW3**	18
NEW Chelsea Brass. | **SW1**	16
NEW Cookbook Cafe | **W1**	-
Foliage | **SW1**	26
Goring | **SW1**	23
Green's | **SW1**	22
Il Convivio | **SW1**	23
Indigo | **WC2**	22
La Genova | **W1**	23
🗹 Lanes | **W1**	24
Lanesborough | **SW1**	21
🗹 Le Gavroche | **W1**	27

🗹 Le Manoir/Quat | **Oxfordshire**	28
L'Oranger | **SW1**	24
Lundum's | **SW7**	22
NEW Magdalen | **SE1**	-
Nahm | **SW1**	26
One-O-One | **SW1**	23
Orrery | **W1**	25
Park, The | **SW1**	24
🗹 Pied à Terre | **W1**	28
Quadrato | **E14**	24
Quirinale | **SW1**	25
🗹 Rasoi Vineet Bhatia | **SW3**	27
Rhodes W1 Rest. | **W1**	-
🗹 Ritz, The | **W1**	23
Roussillon | **SW1**	26
Salloos | **SW1**	23
🗹 Sketch/Lecture Rm. | **W1**	21
NEW Theo Randall | **W1**	26
NEW Via Condotti | **W1**	18
🗹 Waterside Inn | **Berks**	27
Wilton's | **SW1**	24

ROMANTIC PLACES

NEW Albion, The | **N1**	-
🗹 Amaya | **SW1**	25
Andrew Edmunds | **W1**	22
Archipelago | **W1**	21
NEW Benja | **W1**	-
Blue Elephant | **SW6**	20
🗹 Capital Rest. | **SW3**	27
NEW C Garden | **SW3**	18
🗹 Chez Bruce | **SW17**	28
Chutney Mary | **SW10**	23
Cipriani | **W1**	20
Clarke's | **W8**	25
Club Gascon | **EC1**	26
French Horn | **Berks**	23
Galvin/Windows | **W1**	22
Glasshouse, The | **TW9**	24
🗹 Gordon Ramsay/Claridge's | **W1**	25
🗹 Gordon Ramsay/68 Royal | **SW3**	28
🗹 Gravetye Manor | **W. Sussex**	24
Greenhouse, The | **W1**	25
🗹 Hakkasan | **W1**	24

DINING

SPECIAL FEATURES

Restaurant	Location	Rating
Papillon	SW3	23
Park, The	SW1	24
Patisserie Valerie	multi. loc.	20
Z Pétrus	SW1	28
Quadrato	E14	24
Quirinale	SW1	25
Racine	SW3	22
Red Fort	W1	23
Rhodes W1 Rest.	W1	-
Rib Rm.	SW1	24
NEW Rist. Semplice	W1	-
Z Ritz, The	W1	23
Z Rules	WC2	23
Santini	SW1	22
Savoy Grill	WC2	24
Scalini	SW3	23
NEW Scott's	W1	22
Z Sketch/Lecture Rm.	W1	21
Z Square, The	W1	28
NEW St. Alban	SW1	21
NEW Theo Randall	W1	26
Tom Aikens	SW3	26
Toto's	SW3	24
NEW Via Condotti	W1	18
NEW Wallace, The	W1	20
Z Waterside Inn	Berks	27
Wilton's	SW1	24
Z Wolseley, The	W1	21
Z Zafferano	SW1	26

SET-PRICE MENUS

(Call for prices and times)

Restaurant	Location	Rating
Abingdon, The	W8	22
Alastair Little	W1	24
Alloro	W1	22
Al Waha	W2	22
Z Amaya	SW1	25
Arbutus	W1	24
Asia de Cuba	WC2	22
Aubergine	SW10	26
NEW Bacchus	N1	21
Baltic	SE1	21
Banquette	WC2	22
Belgo	multi. loc.	19
Benares	W1	23
Bibendum	SW3	24
Blue Elephant	SW6	20
NEW Bouga	N8	-
Boxwood Café	SW1	21
Brown's/The Grill	W1	22
Café Japan	NW11	26
Café Spice Namasté	E1	23
Z Capital Rest.	SW3	27
NEW C Garden	SW3	18
Chapter Two	SE3	24
Cheyne Walk	SW3	23
Z Chez Bruce	SW17	28
Chez Gérard	multi. loc.	18
Chez Kristof	W6	22
Chutney Mary	SW10	23
Cigala	WC1	22
Cinnamon Club	SW1	24
Cipriani	W1	20
Clarke's	W8	25
Z Cliveden House	Berks	24
Clos Maggiore	WC2	24
Club Gascon	EC1	26
NEW Cookbook Cafe	W1	-
Cow Dining Rm.	W2	21
Z Defune	W1	27
Dorchester/The Grill	W1	24
Eight Over Eight	SW3	23
El Pirata	W1	23
Z Enoteca Turi	SW15	27
Fairuz	multi. loc.	22
NEW Fat Badger	W10	15
Z Fat Duck	Berks	27
Fifteen	N1	23
Foliage	SW1	26
Four Seasons	W2	22
French Horn	Berks	23
Fung Shing	WC2	22
Galvin Bistrot	W1	24
Z Gaucho Grill	multi. loc.	22
Glasshouse, The	TW9	24
Z Gordon Ramsay/Claridge's	W1	25
Z Gordon Ramsay/68 Royal	SW3	28
Goring	SW1	23
Z Gravetye Manor	W. Sussex	24
Greenhouse, The	W1	25
Haz	E1	25

subscribe to zagat.com

DINING

SPECIAL FEATURES

Restaurant		Score
Tsunami	SW4	24
Ubon	E14	24
Umu	W1	26
Vama	SW10	24
Veeraswamy	W1	22
NEW Via Condotti	W1	18
Vineyard/Stockcross	Berks	24
Z Waterside Inn	Berks	27
NEW XO	NW3	16
Yoshino	W1	24
Z Zafferano	SW1	26
Zaika	W8	25
Ziani	SW3	25
Z Zuma	SW7	26

SINGLES SCENES

Restaurant		Score
Z Amaya	SW1	25
Asia de Cuba	WC2	22
Belgo	multi. loc.	19
Buona Sera	SW3	23
Cocoon	W1	21
e&o	W11	22
Eight Over Eight	SW3	23
Fifteen	N1	23
Fino	W1	23
Z Hakkasan	W1	24
Le Cercle	SW1	24
Maze	W1	25
NEW Mews of Mayfair	W1	22
NEW Mocotó	SW1	22
Momo	W1	19
Moro	EC1	25
Nobu Berkeley St.	W1	26
Z Nobu London	W1	27
Roka	W1	25
Sketch/Gallery	W1	19
Sophie's Steak	SW10	23
NEW Suka	W1	–
NEW XO	NW3	16
Z Zuma	SW7	26

SLEEPERS

(Good to excellent food, but little known)

Restaurant		Score
NEW Atami	SW1	24
NEW Barrafina	W1	24
Café Japan	NW11	26
Chapter Two	SE3	24
ffiona's	W8	24
Gate, The	W6	25
Halepi	W2	24
NEW Hawksmoor	E1	28
Haz	E1	25
Kiku	W1	24
Latium	W1	25
Locanda Ottoemezzo	W8	24
Miyama	W1	26
New Tayyabs	E1	24
Pearl	WC1	24
Quadrato	E14	24
Quilon	SW1	25
Quirinale	SW1	25
Royal China Club	W1	24
Sweetings	EC4	24
NEW Theo Randall	W1	26
NEW Trinity	SW4	24
Tsunami	SW4	24
Two Brothers Fish	N3	24
Vineyard/Stockcross	Berks	24
Yoshino	W1	24

SPECIAL OCCASIONS

Restaurant		Score
Z Amaya	SW1	25
Asia de Cuba	WC2	22
Aubergine	SW10	26
NEW Benja	W1	–
Bentley's	W1	24
Bibendum	SW3	24
Blue Elephant	SW6	20
Boxwood Café	SW1	21
Brown's/The Grill	W1	22
Z Capital Rest.	SW3	27
Z Chez Bruce	SW17	28
Chutney Mary	SW10	23
Cinnamon Club	SW1	24
Cipriani	W1	20
Clarke's	W8	25
Club Gascon	EC1	26
Dorchester/The Grill	W1	24
Z Fat Duck	Berks	27
Fifteen	N1	23
Fino	W1	23
Foliage	SW1	26
French Horn	Berks	23
Galvin/Windows	W1	22

TEA SERVICE

TRENDY

DINING

SPECIAL FEATURES

Busaba Eathai	multi. loc.	21	Nobu London	W1	27
Canteen	E1	22	Oliveto	SW1	23
Carluccio's	multi. loc.	17	NEW Olivomare	SW1	-
Cheyne Walk	SW3	23	Ottolenghi	multi. loc.	24
Z Chez Bruce	SW17	28	Papillon	SW3	23
Cinnamon Club	SW1	24	Pasha	SW7	18
Cipriani	W1	20	Providores, The	W1	22
Clarke's	W8	25	Racine	SW3	22
NEW Club, The	W1	-	Z Rasoi Vineet Bhatia	SW3	27
Club Gascon	EC1	26	Z River Café	W6	27
Cocoon	W1	21	Roka	W1	25
e&o	W11	22	Salt Yard	W1	22
Eight Over Eight	SW3	23	NEW Scott's	W1	22
Fifteen	N1	23	Sketch/Gallery	W1	19
Fino	W1	23	Sophie's Steak	SW10	23
Galvin/Windows	W1	22	NEW St. Alban	SW1	21
Galvin Bistrot	W1	24	NEW St. Germain	EC1	21
Z Gordon Ramsay/Claridge's	W1	25	St. John	EC1	25
Z Gordon Ramsay/68 Royal	SW3	28	St. John Bread/Wine	E1	22
			NEW Suka	W1	-
NEW Great Queen St.	WC2	-	NEW Tamarai	WC2	-
NEW Haiku	W1	-	Tapas Brindisa	SE1	22
Z Hakkasan	W1	24	Tom Aikens	SW3	26
NEW Hawksmoor	E1	28	NEW Tom's Kitchen	SW3	19
NEW High Road Brass.	W4	20	Tsunami	SW4	24
NEW Hoxton Grille	EC2	-	Ubon	E14	24
Z Ivy, The	WC2	23	Vama	SW10	24
Z J. Sheekey	WC2	25	Z Wagamama	multi. loc.	19
La Fromagerie	W1	24	Z Wolseley, The	W1	21
NEW Z L'Atelier/Robuchon	WC2	26	NEW XO	NW3	16
Z La Trompette	W4	27	Z Yauatcha	W1	25
Z Le Caprice	SW1	24	Z Zafferano	SW1	26
Le Cercle	SW1	24	Ziani	SW3	25
Ledbury	W11	25	Z Zuma	SW7	26
Z Les Trois Garçons	E1	19			

VIEWS

L'Etranger	SW7	24	NEW Butcher & Grill	SW11	15
Locanda Locatelli	W1	25	Café Spice Namasté	E1	23
Lucky 7	W2	20	Cheyne Walk	SW3	23
Maze	W1	25	Cocoon	W1	21
NEW Mews of Mayfair	W1	22	Foliage	SW1	26
Mirabelle	W1	22	French Horn	Berks	23
Momo	W1	19	Galvin/Windows	W1	22
Moro	EC1	25	Z Gaucho Grill	E14	22
Nobu Berkeley St.	W1	26	Z Gravetye Manor	W. Sussex	24
			Greenhouse, The	W1	25
			Z Lanes	W1	24

VISITORS ON EXPENSE ACCOUNT

DINING

SPECIAL FEATURES

NEW Skylon | **SE1**	—
Z Square, The | **W1**	28
NEW St. Alban | **SW1**	21
NEW Suka | **W1**	—
Z Tamarind | **W1**	25
NEW Theo Randall | **W1**	26
Tom Aikens | **SW3**	26
NEW Trinity | **SW4**	24
Ubon | **E14**	24
Umu | **W1**	26
NEW Via Condotti | **W1**	18
Vineyard/Stockcross | **Berks**	24
Z Waterside Inn | **Berks**	27
Wilton's | **SW1**	24
Z Zafferano | **SW1**	26
Zaika | **W8**	25
Z Zuma | **SW7**	26

WINNING WINE LISTS

Andrew Edmunds | **W1**	22
Aubergine | **SW10**	26
Bibendum | **SW3**	24
Bleeding Heart | **EC1**	22
Brown's/The Grill | **W1**	22
Z Capital Rest. | **SW3**	27
Z Chez Bruce | **SW17**	28
Chutney Mary | **SW10**	23
Cinnamon Club | **SW1**	24
Cipriani | **W1**	20
Clarke's | **W8**	25
Z Cliveden House | **Berks**	24
Club Gascon | **EC1**	26
Dorchester/The Grill | **W1**	24
Z Enoteca Turi | **SW15**	27
Z Fat Duck | **Berks**	27
Fifteen | **N1**	23
Fino | **W1**	23
Foliage | **SW1**	26
NEW Forge, The | **WC2**	—
Glasshouse, The | **TW9**	24
Z Gordon Ramsay/Claridge's | **W1**	25
Z Gordon Ramsay/68 Royal | **SW3**	28

Z Gravetye Manor | **W. Sussex**	24
Greenhouse, The | **W1**	25
Z Hakkasan | **W1**	24
Il Convivio | **SW1**	23
Z Lanes | **W1**	24
Lanesborough | **SW1**	21
Latium | **W1**	25
Z La Trompette | **W4**	27
Le Cercle | **SW1**	24
Ledbury | **W11**	25
Z Le Gavroche | **W1**	27
Z Le Manoir/Quat | **Oxfordshire**	28
Le Pont/Tour | **SE1**	22
L'Escargot | **W1**	22
L'Etranger | **SW7**	24
Locanda Locatelli | **W1**	25
L'Oranger | **SW1**	24
NEW Magdalen | **SE1**	—
Maze | **W1**	25
Mirabelle | **W1**	22
Z Morgan M | **N7**	27
Nahm | **SW1**	26
1 Lombard St. | **EC3**	22
Orrery | **W1**	25
Papillon | **SW3**	23
Z Pétrus | **SW1**	28
Z Pied à Terre | **W1**	28
Rib Rm. | **SW1**	24
Richard Corrigan | **W1**	23
Z Ritz, The | **W1**	23
Savoy Grill | **WC2**	24
Z Sketch/Lecture Rm. | **W1**	21
Z Square, The | **W1**	28
NEW Theo Randall | **W1**	26
Tom Aikens | **SW3**	26
Umu | **W1**	26
Vineyard/Stockcross | **Berks**	24
Vivat Bacchus | **EC4**	23
Z Waterside Inn | **Berks**	27
Wilton's | **SW1**	24
Z Zafferano | **SW1**	26
Z Zuma | **SW7**	26

Nightlife Locations

Includes venue names and Appeal ratings. ☑ indicates places with the highest ratings, popularity and importance.

Central London

BELGRAVIA

☑ Grenadier	24

BLOOMSBURY/FITZROVIA

All Star Lanes	22
Bloomsbury Bowling	19
Bradley's	18
Fitzroy	15
Jamies	17
☑ Ling Ling	26
Long Bar	20
Market Place	14
☑ O'Neill's	16
Perseverance	15
Princess Louise	20
Purple Bar	22
Queen's Larder	18
Shochu Lounge	21
Social	18
Toucan	16

CHINATOWN

De Hems	16

COVENT GARDEN

☑ American Bar	22
Bar des Amis	16
NEW Bedford & Strand	-
☑ Belgo	19
Coach & Horses	19
Davy's	16
☑ End, The	24
Light Bar	22
Lowlander	-
☑ O'Neill's	16
Porterhouse	19
☑ Smollensky's	17
Stringfellows	19
Tup	16
Walkabout	12

HOLBORN

Bierodrome	14
☑ Pitcher & Piano	15
Seven Stars	20

KNIGHTSBRIDGE

Blue Bar	-
☑ Fifth Floor	19
NEW Gilt Champagne	21
☑ Library	23
NEW Mocotó	22

MARYLEBONE

Salt Whisky Bar	17
Tup	16

MAYFAIR

Absolut Icebar	23
☑ Annabel's	24
Balls Brothers	17
☑ Claridge's Bar	25
☑ Dorchester	24
43	19
NEW Galvin/Windows	-
NEW Mahiki	18
NEW Mews of Mayfair	19
NEW Moose, The	-
Mulligans Mayfair	19
☑ Nobu Berkeley	24
Red Bar	21
☑ Sketch	22
☑ Slug & Lettuce	16
Taman Gang	19
Trader Vic's	18
☑ Whisky Bar	23

PICCADILLY

☑ All Bar One	16
Café de Paris	18
Comedy Store	20
Cork & Bottle	22
Gordon's	23
Mint Leaf	18
Rockwell	21

NEW 1707 Wine Bar	20	
Sherlock Holmes	22	
Z Slug & Lettuce	16	
Z Tiger Tiger	15	
NEW Volstead	24	
Waxy O'Connor's	21	

SOHO

Admiral Duncan	16
Ain't Nothin' But	15
Z All Bar One	16
Astoria	18
Café Boheme	19
Z Chinawhite	22
Coach & Horses	21
Comptons of Soho	17
Cuckoo Club	23
Dog & Duck	18
Floridita	21
Freedom	15
French House	19
G-A-Y	20
Heaven	23
100 Club	15
John Snow	12
Kabaret's Prophecy	16
Kettners	20
Lab	21
Lucky Voice	–
Madame JoJo's	16
Z Milk & Honey	27
Mo*vida	20
Paper	17
Z Pitcher & Piano	15
Player	21
Revolution	14
Z Ronnie Scott's	25
Z Slug & Lettuce	16
Stringfellows	19
Toucan	16
Z Yauatcha	24
Zebrano	15

ST. JAMES'S

Balls Brothers	17
Z Dukes Hotel Bar	24
Z Rivoli Bar	25

VICTORIA

Balls Brothers	17
Boisdale	19

WESTMINSTER

Chandos	15
ICA Bar	19

East/South East London

BLACKFRIARS

Z All Bar One	16
Black Friar	–
Corney & Barrow	18
El Vino	17
Jamies	17
Old Bank	15
Z O'Neill's	16
Ye Olde Cheshire	24

CANARY WHARF/DOCKLANDS

Corney & Barrow	18
Davy's	16
1802	18
Jamies	17
Z Slug & Lettuce	16
Z Smollensky's	17

CITY

Z All Bar One	16
Balls Brothers	17
Cittie of Yorke	22
Corney & Barrow	18
Davy's	16
El Vino	17
Fishmarket	20
Jamaica Wine	24
Jamies	17
La Grande Marque	–
Lamb Tavern	17
Lowlander	–
Z O'Neill's	16
Z Pitcher & Piano	15
Z Slug & Lettuce	16
Tup	16
Vertigo 42	23
Ye Olde Mitre	26

NIGHTLIFE

LOCATIONS

South/
South West London

BRIXTON/CLAPHAM

Bierodrome ___14___
Plan B ___17___
Revolution ___14___
Z Slug & Lettuce ___16___

CHELSEA

Apartment 195 ___21___
NEW Kitts ___17___

EARL'S COURT

Nam Long-Le Shaker ___16___
Z O'Neill's ___16___

FULHAM

Z Pitcher & Piano ___15___
Z Slug & Lettuce ___16___
Tup ___16___

PIMLICO

Davy's ___16___
Morpeth Arms ___14___

PUTNEY/RICHMOND

Duke's Head ___19___
Z Pitcher & Piano ___15___

SOUTH KENSINGTON

NEW Amika ___21___
Boujis ___22___

WANDSWORTH/
BALHAM/WIMBLEDON

Z O'Neill's ___16___
Tup ___16___

West London

BAYSWATER

Cow ___23___

CHISWICK

Z All Bar One ___16___
Davy's ___16___
Sam's Brasserie & Bar ___20___

HAMMERSMITH

Dove ___21___
Z Smollensky's ___17___

NOTTING HILL

NEW Bumpkin ___18___
Z e&o ___22___
Elbow Room ___19___
NEW Montgomery Pl. ___19___

SHEPHERD'S BUSH

Z O'Neill's ___16___
Walkabout ___12___

Nightlife Special Appeals

Listings cover the best in each category and include venue names, locations and Appeal ratings. Multi-location nightspots' features may vary by branch. ⦿ indicates places with the highest ratings, popularity and importance.

AFTER WORK

⦿ All Bar One	**multi. loc.**	16
Apartment 195	**SW3**	21
Balls Brothers	**multi. loc.**	17
Baltic	**SE1**	20
⦿ Belgo	**WC2**	19
Bierodrome	**multi. loc.**	14
Black Friar	**EC4**	–
Bleeding Heart Tavern	**EC1**	22
Boisdale	**SW1**	19
Bradley's	**W1**	18
Chandos	**WC2**	15
Cittie of Yorke	**WC1**	22
Coach & Horses	**W1**	21
Cork & Bottle	**WC2**	22
Corney & Barrow	**multi. loc.**	18
Davy's	**multi. loc.**	16
De Hems	**W1**	16
Dog & Duck	**W1**	18
1802	**E14**	18
Fishmarket	**EC2**	20
Fitzroy	**W1**	15
Flask, The	**NW3**	17
Gordon's	**WC2**	23
Hoop & Grapes	**EC3**	–
Jamaica Wine	**EC3**	24
Jamies	**multi. loc.**	17
Jerusalem	**EC1**	22
John Snow	**W1**	12
Kick	**multi. loc.**	19
La Grande Marque	**EC4**	–
Lamb Tavern	**EC3**	17
⦿ Ling Ling	**W1**	26
Lowlander	**WC2**	–
Market Place	**W1**	14
Morpeth Arms	**SW1**	14
Mulligans Mayfair	**W1**	19
Old Bank	**EC4**	15
Old Thameside	**SE1**	–
⦿ O'Neill's	**multi. loc.**	16

⦿ Pitcher & Piano	**multi. loc.**	15
Porterhouse	**WC2**	19
Princess Louise	**WC1**	20
Revolution	**multi. loc.**	14
Seven Stars	**WC2**	20
⦿ Slug & Lettuce	**multi. loc.**	16
Smiths/Smithfield	**EC1**	20
⦿ Smollensky's	**multi. loc.**	17
Ten Bells	**E1**	19
Toucan	**W1**	16
Tup	**multi. loc.**	16
Walkabout	**multi. loc.**	12
Ye Olde Cheshire	**EC4**	24
Zebrano	**W1**	15

BEAUTIFUL PEOPLE

⦿ American Bar	**WC2**	22
⦿ Annabel's	**W1**	24
Apartment 195	**SW3**	21
Baltic	**SE1**	20
Café de Paris	**W1**	18
⦿ Chinawhite	**W1**	22
⦿ Dukes Hotel Bar	**SW1**	24
⦿ e&o	**W11**	22
⦿ Fifth Floor	**SW1**	19
G-A-Y	**W1**	20
Heaven	**WC2**	23
ICA Bar	**SW1**	19
Light Bar	**WC2**	22
⦿ Ling Ling	**W1**	26
Long Bar	**W1**	20
⦿ Milk & Honey	**W1**	27
Mint Leaf	**SW1**	18
Nam Long-Le Shaker	**SW5**	16
Purple Bar	**W1**	22
Rockwell	**SW1**	21
Salt Whisky Bar	**W2**	17
⦿ Sketch	**W1**	22
Taman Gang	**W1**	19
Vibe Bar	**E1**	17

BLUES

Ain't Nothin' But | **W1** — 15
100 Club | **W1** — 15
Wenlock Arms | **N1** — 22

BOTTLE SERVICE

(Bottle purchase sometimes required to secure a table)

NEW Amika | **W8** — 21
Boujis | **SW7** — 22
Café de Paris | **W1** — 18
Z Chinawhite | **W1** — 22
Cuckoo Club | **W1** — 23
Floridita | **W1** — 21
Kabaret's Prophecy | **W1** — 16
NEW Kitts | **SW1** — 17
NEW Moose, The | **W1** — –
Red Bar | **W1** — 21
Taman Gang | **W1** — 19
Turnmills | **EC1** — 15

CABARET

Black Cap | **NW1** — 13

CELEB-SIGHTINGS

Absolut Icebar | **W1** — 23
All Star Lanes | **WC1** — 22
NEW Amika | **W8** — 21
Z Annabel's | **W1** — 24
Z Dorchester | **W1** — 24
Z e&o | **W11** — 22
Floridita | **W1** — 21
Z Ling Ling | **W1** — 26
NEW Mahiki | **W1** — 18
NEW Mocotó | **SW1** — 22
Mo*vida | **W1** — 20
Nam Long-Le Shaker | **SW5** — 16
Paper | **W1** — 17
Purple Bar | **W1** — 22
Stringfellows | **WC2** — 19

CHEAP DRINKS

Bloomsbury Bowling | **WC1** — 19
Chandos | **WC2** — 15
Fitzroy | **W1** — 15
John Snow | **W1** — 12
Princess Louise | **WC1** — 20
Prospect Whitby | **E1** — 22

COFFEEHOUSES

Z Yauatcha | **W1** — 24

COMEDY CLUBS

(Call ahead to check nights, times, performers and covers)

Comedy Store | **SW1** — 20
Tup | **N16** — 16

COOL LOOS

Absolut Icebar | **W1** — 23
Z Belgo | **multi. loc.** — 19
Lab | **W1** — 21
Mo*vida | **W1** — 20
Z Nobu Berkeley | **W1** — 24
Princess Louise | **WC1** — 20
Purple Bar | **W1** — 22
Z Sketch | **W1** — 22

DANCE CLUBS

Astoria | **WC2** — 18
Boujis | **SW7** — 22
Z Chinawhite | **W1** — 22
Cuckoo Club | **W1** — 23
Dragon | **EC2** — 23
Elbow Room | **N1** — 19
Electric Ballroom | **NW1** — 15
Z End, The | **WC1** — 24
Fabric | **EC1** — 22
43 | **W1** — 19
Freedom | **W1** — 15
G-A-Y | **W1** — 20
Heaven | **WC2** — 23
NEW Hideaway, The | **N19** — –
Kabaret's Prophecy | **W1** — 16
NEW Kitts | **SW1** — 17
Market Place | **W1** — 14
Mo*vida | **W1** — 20
Paper | **W1** — 17
Plan B | **SW9** — 17
Revolution | **SW4** — 14
Taman Gang | **W1** — 19
333 Mother Bar | **EC1** — 15
Z Tiger Tiger | **SW1** — 15
Turnmills | **EC1** — 15
Vibe Bar | **E1** — 17

DANCING

NEW Amika | **W8** — 21
Z Annabel's | **W1** — 24

Astoria | **WC2**	18
Black Cap | **NW1**	13
Boujis | **SW7**	22
Café Boheme | **W1**	19
Café de Paris | **W1**	18
☒ Chinawhite | **W1**	22
Comptons of Soho | **W1**	17
Cuckoo Club | **W1**	23
Dragon | **EC2**	23
Dublin Castle | **NW1**	16
Elbow Room | **N1**	19
Electric Ballroom | **NW1**	15
☒ End, The | **WC1**	24
Fabric | **EC1**	22
Floridita | **W1**	21
43 | **W1**	19
Freedom | **W1**	15
G-A-Y | **W1**	20
Heaven | **WC2**	23
NEW Hideaway, The | **N19**	-
100 Club | **W1**	15
Kabaret's Prophecy | **W1**	16
NEW Kitts | **SW1**	17
Koko | **NW1**	17
Lab | **W1**	21
Madame JoJo's | **W1**	16
NEW Mahiki | **W1**	18
Market Place | **W1**	14
NEW Mocotó | **SW1**	22
NEW Moose, The | **W1**	-
Mo*vida | **W1**	20
93 Feet East | **E1**	16
Paper | **W1**	17
Plan B | **SW9**	17
Player | **W1**	21
Revolution | **SW4**	14
☒ Ronnie Scott's | **W1**	25
☒ Sketch | **W1**	22
☒ Slug & Lettuce | **SW6**	16
☒ Smollensky's | **WC2**	17
Taman Gang | **W1**	19
333 Mother Bar | **EC1**	15
☒ Tiger Tiger | **SW1**	15
Trafalgar Tavern | **SE10**	20
Turnmills | **EC1**	15
Vibe Bar | **E1**	17

DIVES

Bradley's | **W1**	18
Chandos | **WC2**	15
Coach & Horses | **W1**	21
Comptons of Soho | **W1**	17
Dog & Duck | **W1**	18
Dublin Castle | **NW1**	16
Electric Ballroom | **NW1**	15
100 Club | **W1**	15
John Snow | **W1**	12
Kick | **EC1**	19

DJS

Astoria | **WC2**	18
Boujis | **SW7**	22
☒ Chinawhite | **W1**	22
Comptons of Soho | **W1**	17
Cuckoo Club | **W1**	23
Dragon | **EC2**	23
Elbow Room | **multi. loc.**	19
Electric Ballroom | **NW1**	15
☒ End, The | **WC1**	24
Fabric | **EC1**	22
43 | **W1**	19
Freedom | **W1**	15
G-A-Y | **W1**	20
Heaven | **WC2**	23
NEW Hideaway, The | **N19**	-
Hoxton Sq. | **N1**	19
Kabaret's Prophecy | **W1**	16
NEW Kitts | **SW1**	17
Madame JoJo's | **W1**	16
Market Place | **W1**	14
Mo*vida | **W1**	20
93 Feet East | **E1**	16
Paper | **W1**	17
Plan B | **SW9**	17
Player | **W1**	21
Revolution | **SW4**	14
☒ Sketch | **W1**	22
Social | **W1**	18
Taman Gang | **W1**	19
Ten Bells | **E1**	19
333 Mother Bar | **EC1**	15
☒ Tiger Tiger | **SW1**	15
Turnmills | **EC1**	15

Vibe Bar | **E1** — 17

☑ Yauatcha | **W1** — 24

DRAG SHOWS

Black Cap | **NW1** — 13

DRINK SPECIALISTS

BEER SPECIALIST

Anchor & Hope | **SE1** — 21

☑ Belgo | **multi. loc.** — 19

Bierodrome | **multi. loc.** — 14

Cittie of Yorke | **WC1** — 22

Coach & Horses | **WC2** — 19

Cow | **W2** — 23

De Hems | **W1** — 16

Dog & Duck | **W1** — 18

Dove | **W6** — 21

Duke of Cambridge | **N1** — 20

1802 | **E14** — 18

Filthy MacNasty's | **EC1** — 19

Flask | **N6** — 21

George Inn | **SE1** — 21

Greenwich Union | **SE1** — –

Jerusalem | **EC1** — 22

Kick | **E1** — 19

Lamb Tavern | **EC3** — 17

Lowlander | **multi. loc.** — –

Market Porter | **SE1** — 18

Morpeth Arms | **SW1** — 14

Mulligans Mayfair | **W1** — 19

NEW Narrow, The | **E14** — –

Perseverance | **WC1** — 15

Porterhouse | **WC2** — 19

NEW Rake, The | **SE1** — –

☑ Royal Oak | **SE1** — –

Toucan | **W1** — 16

Well | **EC1** — 18

Wenlock Arms | **N1** — 22

CHAMPAGNE

☑ American Bar | **WC2** — 22

NEW Amika | **W8** — 21

☑ Annabel's | **W1** — 24

NEW Bedford & Strand | **WC2** — –

☑ Claridge's Bar | **W1** — 25

Cutty Sark | **SE10** — 19

Davy's | **multi. loc.** — 16

☑ Dorchester | **W1** — 24

☑ Dukes Hotel Bar | **SW1** — 24

☑ Fifth Floor | **SW1** — 19

Fishmarket | **EC2** — 20

Floridita | **W1** — 21

NEW Gilt Champagne | **SW1** — 21

Gordon's | **WC2** — 23

Kettners | **W1** — 20

La Grande Marque | **EC4** — –

NEW Mews of Mayfair | **W1** — 19

☑ Rivoli Bar | **W1** — 25

Rockwell | **SW1** — 21

Smiths/Smithfield | **EC1** — 20

Vertigo 42 | **EC2** — 23

COCKTAILS

All Star Lanes | **WC1** — 22

☑ American Bar | **WC2** — 22

☑ Annabel's | **W1** — 24

Apartment 195 | **SW3** — 21

Baltic | **SE1** — 20

NEW Bar, The | **SE10** — –

Café Boheme | **W1** — 19

Café de Paris | **W1** — 18

☑ Chinawhite | **W1** — 22

☑ Claridge's Bar | **W1** — 25

Cuckoo Club | **W1** — 23

☑ Dorchester | **W1** — 24

☑ Dukes Hotel Bar | **SW1** — 24

☑ e&o | **W11** — 22

☑ Fifth Floor | **SW1** — 19

Floridita | **W1** — 21

43 | **W1** — 19

Freedom | **W1** — 15

NEW Hawksmoor | **E1** — 20

ICA Bar | **SW1** — 19

Lab | **W1** — 21

☑ Library | **SW1** — 23

Light Bar | **WC2** — 22

☑ Ling Ling | **W1** — 26

Long Bar | **W1** — 20

NEW Mahiki | **W1** — 18

NEW Mews of Mayfair | **W1** — 19

☑ Milk & Honey | **W1** — 27

Mint Leaf | **SW1** — 18

NEW Mocotó | **SW1** — 22

NEW Montgomery Pl. | **W11** — 19

Mo*vida | **W1** — 20

Nam Long-Le Shaker | **SW5** | 16
Nobu Berkeley | W1 | 24
Paper | **W1** | 17
Player | **W1** | 21
Purple Bar | **W1** | 22
NEW Raan | **SE10** | -
Red Bar | **W1** | 21
Revolution | **multi. loc.** | 14
Rivoli Bar | W1 | 25
Rockwell | **SW1** | 21
Salt Whisky Bar | **W2** | 17
Shochu Lounge | **W1** | 21
Sketch | W1 | 22
NEW Skylon | **SE1** | -
Smiths/Smithfield | **EC1** | 20
Taman Gang | **W1** | 19
Trader Vic's | **W1** | 18
Zebrano | **W1** | 15

MARTINIS

NEW Montgomery Pl. | **W11** | 19
NEW Skylon | **SE1** | -

SCOTCH/SINGLE MALTS

NEW Bumpkin | **W11** | 18

VODKA

Absolut Icebar | **W1** | 23

WINE BARS

Balls Brothers | **multi. loc.** | 17
Bar des Amis | **WC2** | 16
NEW Bedford & Strand | **WC2** | -
Bleeding Heart Tavern | **EC1** | 22
Cork & Bottle | **WC2** | 22
Corney & Barrow | **multi. loc.** | 18
Davy's | **multi. loc.** | 16
El Vino | **multi. loc.** | 17
Gordon's | **WC2** | 23
Jamaica Wine | **EC3** | 24
Jamies | **multi. loc.** | 17
Kettners | **W1** | 20
La Grande Marque | **EC4** | -
Mulligans Mayfair | **W1** | 19
NEW 1707 Wine Bar | **W1** | 20
Vertigo 42 | **EC2** | 23

WINE BY THE GLASS

American Bar | WC2 | 22
Annabel's | W1 | 24

Balls Brothers | **multi. loc.** | 17
Bar des Amis | **WC2** | 16
Bleeding Heart Tavern | **EC1** | 22
Boisdale | **SW1** | 19
Claridge's Bar | W1 | 25
Cork & Bottle | **WC2** | 22
Corney & Barrow | **multi. loc.** | 18
Cow | **W2** | 23
Davy's | **multi. loc.** | 16
Duke of Cambridge | **N1** | 20
1802 | **E14** | 18
El Vino | **multi. loc.** | 17
Engineer | **NW1** | 22
French House | **W1** | 19
Gordon's | **WC2** | 23
Jamaica Wine | **EC3** | 24
Jamies | **multi. loc.** | 17
Kettners | **W1** | 20
Mulligans Mayfair | **W1** | 19
Sam's Brasserie & Bar | **W4** | 20
Seven Stars | **WC2** | 20
Well | **EC1** | 18

EXPENSE-ACCOUNTERS

American Bar | WC2 | 22
Annabel's | W1 | 24
Apartment 195 | **SW3** | 21
Baltic | **SE1** | 20
Café de Paris | **W1** | 18
Chinawhite | W1 | 22
Claridge's Bar | W1 | 25
Cuckoo Club | **W1** | 23
Dorchester | W1 | 24
Dukes Hotel Bar | SW1 | 24
Fifth Floor | SW1 | 19
Fishmarket | **EC2** | 20
Floridita | **W1** | 21
NEW Gilt Champagne | **SW1** | 21
Kettners | **W1** | 20
Library | SW1 | 23
Ling Ling | W1 | 26
Long Bar | **W1** | 20
NEW Mews of Mayfair | **W1** | 19
NEW Mocotó | **SW1** | 22
Mo*vida | **W1** | 20
Nobu Berkeley | W1 | 24
Paper | **W1** | 17

Purple Bar | **W1**	22
Red Bar | **W1**	21
Rockwell | **SW1**	21
Z Sketch | **W1**	22
Stringfellows | **WC2**	19
Taman Gang | **W1**	19
Trader Vic's | **W1**	18
NEW Volstead | **W1**	24

FINE FOOD TOO

Anchor & Hope | **SE1**	21
Baltic | **SE1**	20
NEW Bedford & Strand | **WC2**	–
Z Belgo | **multi. loc.**	19
Bleeding Heart Tavern | **EC1**	22
Café Boheme | **W1**	19
Z Claridge's Bar | **W1**	25
Cork & Bottle | **WC2**	22
Cow | **W2**	23
Davy's | **multi. loc.**	16
Dove | **W6**	21
Duke of Cambridge | **N1**	20
Z e&o | **W11**	22
1802 | **E14**	18
El Vino | **multi. loc.**	17
Engineer | **NW1**	22
Flask | **N6**	21
Floridita | **W1**	21
43 | **W1**	19
French House | **W1**	19
Gordon's | **WC2**	23
NEW Hawksmoor | **E1**	20
Z Ling Ling | **W1**	26
Lowlander | **WC2**	–
Medcalf | **EC1**	–
NEW Mews of Mayfair | **W1**	19
NEW Mocotó | **SW1**	22
Mulligans Mayfair | **W1**	19
NEW Narrow, The | **E14**	–
Z Nobu Berkeley | **W1**	24
Perseverance | **WC1**	15
Queen's Larder | **WC1**	18
Salt Whisky Bar | **W2**	17
NEW 1707 Wine Bar | **W1**	20
Shochu Lounge | **W1**	21
Z Sketch | **W1**	22
Smiths/Smithfield | **EC1**	20

Trafalgar Tavern | **SE10**	20
NEW Volstead | **W1**	24
Well | **EC1**	18
Z Yauatcha | **W1**	24

FIREPLACES

Z Annabel's | **W1**	24
Apartment 195 | **SW3**	21
Bierodrome | **multi. loc.**	14
Bleeding Heart Tavern | **EC1**	22
Cittie of Yorke | **WC1**	22
Z Claridge's Bar | **W1**	25
Coach & Horses | **W1**	21
Cork & Bottle | **WC2**	22
Cow | **W2**	23
Cutty Sark | **SE10**	19
De Hems | **W1**	16
Dog & Duck | **W1**	18
Dove | **W6**	21
Dragon | **EC2**	23
Filthy MacNasty's | **EC1**	19
Flask, The | **NW3**	17
Z Grenadier | **SW1**	24
Z Holly Bush | **NW3**	25
Jerusalem | **EC1**	22
John Snow | **W1**	12
Z Library | **SW1**	23
NEW Narrow, The | **E14**	–
Prospect Whitby | **E1**	22
Seven Stars | **WC2**	20
Z Slug & Lettuce | **SE1**	16
Z Spaniard's Inn | **NW3**	23
Stringfellows | **WC2**	19
Ten Bells | **E1**	19
Wenlock Arms | **N1**	22
Ye Olde Mitre | **EC1**	26

FIRST DATE

Z American Bar | **WC2**	22
Apartment 195 | **SW3**	21
Bleeding Heart Tavern | **EC1**	22
Z Claridge's Bar | **W1**	25
Cork & Bottle | **WC2**	22
Z Dorchester | **W1**	24
Z Holly Bush | **NW3**	25
Kettners | **W1**	20
Light Bar | **WC2**	22

subscribe to zagat.com

NIGHTLIFE

SPECIAL APPEALS

Black Cap | **NW1**	13
Comptons of Soho | **W1**	17
Freedom | **W1**	15
G-A-Y | **W1**	20
Heaven* | **WC2**	23

HEN NIGHT

Madame JoJo's | **W1**	16
Nam Long-Le Shaker | **SW5**	16
☑ Pitcher & Piano | **multi. loc.**	15
Player | **W1**	21
Revolution | **multi. loc.**	14
☑ Slug & Lettuce | **multi. loc.**	16
☑ Smollensky's | **multi. loc.**	17
☑ Tiger Tiger | **SW1**	15
Waxy O'Connor's | **W1**	21

HOTEL BARS

Athenaeum Hotel	
☑ Whisky Bar | **W1**	23
Berkeley	
Blue Bar | **SW1**	–
Claridge's Hotel	
☑ Claridge's Bar | **W1**	25
Dorchester Hotel	
☑ Dorchester | **W1**	24
Dukes Hotel	
☑ Dukes Hotel Bar | **SW1**	24
Great Eastern Hotel	
Fishmarket | **EC2**	20
Grosvenor House Hotel	
Red Bar | **W1**	21
Hilton Park Ln.	
NEW Galvin/Windows | **W1**	–
Trader Vic's | **W1**	18
Jumeirah Carlton Tower	
NEW Gilt Champagne | **SW1**	21
Lanesborough	
☑ Library | **SW1**	23
Ritz Hotel	
☑ Rivoli Bar | **W1**	25
Sanderson Hotel	
Long Bar | **W1**	20
Purple Bar | **W1**	22
Savoy Hotel	
☑ American Bar | **WC2**	22

Tavistock Hotel	
Bloomsbury Bowling | **WC1**	19
Trafalgar Hilton	
Rockwell | **SW1**	21

JACKET REQUIRED

☑ Annabel's | **W1**	24
☑ Rivoli Bar | **W1**	25

JAZZ CLUBS

☑ Ronnie Scott's | **W1**	25

KARAOKE BARS

(Call to check nights,
times and prices)

Lucky Voice | **W1**	–

LIVE ENTERTAINMENT

(See also Blues, Cabaret,
Comedy Clubs, Drag Shows,
Jazz Clubs, Karaoke Bars, Music
Clubs, Strip Clubs)

Baltic | jazz | **SE1**	20
Café de Paris | cabaret | **W1**	18
Dragon | varies | **EC2**	23
Electric Ballroom | rock | **NW1**	15
☑ End, The | rock | **WC1**	24
Fabric | hip-hop/rock | **EC1**	22
Filthy MacNasty's | varies | **EC1**	19
Kettners | varies | **W1**	20
☑ Library | piano | **SW1**	23
333 Mother Bar | rock | **EC1**	15
Trader Vic's | Latin | **W1**	18
Turnmills | rock | **EC1**	15
Vibe Bar | dance music | **E1**	17
Walkabout | rock | **multi. loc.**	12
Waxy O'Connor's | rock/folk | **W1**	21

LOUNGES

Apartment 195 | **SW3**	21
NEW Gilt Champagne | **SW1**	21
☑ Loungelover | **E1**	25
NEW Mews of Mayfair | **W1**	19
Nam Long-Le Shaker | **SW5**	16
Player | **W1**	21
Purple Bar | **W1**	22
Shochu Lounge | **W1**	21
Taman Gang | **W1**	19
Turnmills | **EC1**	15

MATURE CROWDS

Absolut Icebar | **W1**	23
☑ American Bar | **WC2**	22

Anchor & Hope | **SE1**	21
Ⓩ Annabel's | **W1**	24
Bar des Amis | **WC2**	16
NEW Bedford & Strand | **WC2**	-
NEW Bumpkin | **W11**	18
Ⓩ Claridge's Bar | **W1**	25
Cuckoo Club | **W1**	23
Davy's | **multi. loc.**	16
Ⓩ Dorchester | **W1**	24
Dove | **W6**	21
Ⓩ Dukes Hotel Bar | **SW1**	24
El Vino | **multi. loc.**	17
Floridita | **W1**	21
French House | **W1**	19
George Inn | **SE1**	21
NEW Gilt Champagne | **SW1**	21
Gordon's | **WC2**	23
Kettners | **W1**	20
Ⓩ Ling Ling | **W1**	26
NEW Mews of Mayfair | **W1**	19
Ⓩ Milk & Honey | **W1**	27
NEW Montgomery Pl. | **W11**	19
Ⓩ Ronnie Scott's | **W1**	25
NEW 1707 Wine Bar | **W1**	20
Shochu Lounge | **W1**	21
Ⓩ Sketch | **W1**	22
NEW Skylon | **SE1**	-
Taman Gang | **W1**	19
NEW Volstead | **W1**	24
Wenlock Arms | **N1**	22
Ⓩ Yauatcha | **W1**	24
Ye Olde Cheshire | **EC4**	24
Ye Olde Mitre | **EC1**	26

MEAT MARKETS

Ⓩ All Bar One | **multi. loc.**	16
NEW Amika | **W8**	21
Astoria | **WC2**	18
Ⓩ Chinawhite | **W1**	22
Comptons of Soho | **W1**	17
Freedom | **W1**	15
G-A-Y | **W1**	20
Heaven | **WC2**	23
Jamies | **multi. loc.**	17
NEW Mocotó | **SW1**	22
NEW Moose, The | **W1**	-
Paper | **W1**	17

Player | **W1**	21
Ⓩ Tiger Tiger | **SW1**	15

MUSIC CLUBS

(See also Blues & Jazz Clubs)

Astoria | **WC2**	18
Dublin Castle | **NW1**	16
Koko | **NW1**	17
93 Feet East | **E1**	16

NOTEWORTHY NEWCOMERS

Amika | **W8**	21
Bar, The | **SE10**	-
Bedford & Strand | **WC2**	-
Bumpkin | **W11**	18
Galvin/Windows | **W1**	-
Gilt Champagne | **SW1**	21
Hawksmoor | **E1**	20
Hideaway, The | **N19**	-
Kitts | **SW1**	17
Mahiki | **W1**	18
Mews of Mayfair | **W1**	19
Mocotó | **SW1**	22
Montgomery Pl. | **W11**	19
Moose, The | **W1**	-
Narrow, The | **E14**	-
Raan | **SE10**	-
Rake, The | **SE1**	-
1707 Wine Bar | **W1**	20
Skylon | **SE1**	-
Taman Gang | **W1**	19
Volstead | **W1**	24
Ⓩ Yauatcha | **W1**	24

OUTDOOR SPACES

GARDEN DINING

Black Cap | **NW1**	13
Cutty Sark | **SE10**	19
Engineer | **NW1**	22
Flask | **N6**	21
George Inn | **SE1**	21
Greenwich Union | **SE1**	-
NEW Hideaway, The | **N19**	-
La Grande Marque | **EC4**	-
93 Feet East | **E1**	16
Old Bank | **EC4**	15
Prospect Whitby | **E1**	22

Slug & Lettuce | **SW6**
Spaniard's Inn | **NW3**
Tup | **multi. loc.**

PATIO/TERRACE

All Bar One	**WC2**	16
Anchor & Hope	**SE1**	21
Bar des Amis	**WC2**	16
Belgo	**NW1**	19
Bierodrome	**SW4**	14
Café Boheme	**W1**	19
Corney & Barrow	**multi. loc.**	18
Cutty Sark	**SE10**	19
Davy's	**multi. loc.**	16
Dove	**W6**	21
Duke of Cambridge	**N1**	20
Duke's Head	**SW15**	19
1802	**E14**	18
El Vino	**EC4**	17
43	**W1**	19
Gordon's	**WC2**	23
Hoxton Sq.	**N1**	19
Jamies	**multi. loc.**	17
Kick	**EC1**	19
Long Bar	**W1**	20
Market Place	**W1**	14
Medcalf	**EC1**	–
Morpeth Arms	**SW1**	14
NEW Narrow, The	**E14**	–
93 Feet East	**E1**	16
Old Thameside	**SE1**	–
Pitcher & Piano	**TW9**	15
Porterhouse	**WC2**	19
Prospect Whitby	**E1**	22
Purple Bar	**W1**	22
NEW Rake, The	**SE1**	–
Rockwell	**SW1**	21
Slug & Lettuce	**multi. loc.**	16
Smollensky's	**E14**	17
Vibe Bar	**E1**	17
Ye Olde Mitre	**EC1**	26

SIDEWALK

All Bar One	**multi. loc.**	16
Balls Brothers	**multi. loc.**	17
Bierodrome	**WC2**	14
Black Friar	**EC4**	–
Coach & Horses	**W1**	21

De Hems	**W1**	16
Duke of Cambridge	**N1**	20
e&o	**W11**	22
Filthy MacNasty's	**EC1**	19
Fitzroy	**W1**	15
Grenadier	**SW1**	24
Jerusalem	**EC1**	22
Lowlander	**WC2**	–
Market Place	**W1**	14
NEW Mews of Mayfair	**W1**	19
NEW Montgomery Pl.	**W11**	19
NEW Moose, The	**W1**	–
O'Neill's	**NW1**	16
Perseverance	**WC1**	15
Pitcher & Piano	**multi. loc.**	15
Queen's Larder	**WC1**	18
Salt Whisky Bar	**W2**	17
Sherlock Holmes	**WC2**	22
Ten Bells	**E1**	19
Trafalgar Tavern	**SE10**	20
Tup	**multi. loc.**	16
Well	**EC1**	18

WATER VIEWS

Cutty Sark	**SE10**	19
Dove	**W6**	21
Duke's Head	**SW15**	19
1802	**E14**	18
NEW Narrow, The	**E14**	–
Old Thameside	**SE1**	–
Pitcher & Piano	**TW9**	15
Prospect Whitby	**E1**	22
Trafalgar Tavern	**SE10**	20

PEOPLE-WATCHING

American Bar	**WC2**	22
Annabel's	**W1**	24
Apartment 195	**SW3**	21
Astoria	**WC2**	18
Café de Paris	**W1**	18
Chinawhite	**W1**	22
Claridge's Bar	**W1**	25
Coach & Horses	**W1**	21
e&o	**W11**	22
Fifth Floor	**SW1**	19
Freedom	**W1**	15
Hoxton Sq.	**N1**	19
ICA Bar	**SW1**	19

Kabaret's Prophecy | **W1**	16
Ⓩ Ling Ling | **W1**	26
Long Bar | **W1**	20
Nam Long-Le Shaker | **SW5**	16
Purple Bar | **W1**	22
Ⓩ Sketch | **W1**	22
Taman Gang | **W1**	19
Vibe Bar | **E1**	17

PUB GRUB

Admiral Duncan | **W1**	16
Black Friar | **EC4**	-
Chandos | **WC2**	15
Cittie of Yorke | **WC1**	22
Coach & Horses | **W1**	21
Coach & Horses | **WC2**	19
Comptons of Soho | **W1**	17
Cutty Sark | **SE10**	19
Dog & Duck | **W1**	18
Dove | **W6**	21
Duke's Head | **SW15**	19
Engineer | **NW1**	22
Filthy MacNasty's | **EC1**	19
Fitzroy | **W1**	15
Flask | **N6**	21
Flask, The | **NW3**	17
George Inn | **SE1**	21
Greenwich Union | **SE1**	-
Ⓩ Grenadier | **SW1**	24
Ⓩ Holly Bush | **NW3**	25
Hoop & Grapes | **EC3**	-
Jamaica Wine | **EC3**	24
Jerusalem | **EC1**	22
John Snow | **W1**	12
Lamb Tavern | **EC3**	17
Market Porter | **SE1**	18
Morpeth Arms | **SW1**	14
Mulligans Mayfair | **W1**	19
Old Bank | **EC4**	15
Old Thameside | **SE1**	-
Ⓩ O'Neill's | **multi. loc.**	16
Perseverance | **WC1**	15
Porterhouse | **WC2**	19
Princess Louise | **WC1**	20
Prospect Whitby | **E1**	22
Queen's Larder | **WC1**	18

Ⓩ Royal Oak | **SE1**	-
Seven Stars | **WC2**	20
Sherlock Holmes | **WC2**	22
Social | **W1**	18
Ⓩ Spaniard's Inn | **NW3**	23
Ten Bells | **E1**	19
Tup | **multi. loc.**	16
Walkabout | **multi. loc.**	12
Waxy O'Connor's | **W1**	21
Well | **EC1**	18
Wenlock Arms | **N1**	22
Ye Olde Cheshire | **EC4**	24
Ye Olde Mitre | **EC1**	26

QUIET CONVERSATION

Ⓩ American Bar | **WC2**	22
Ⓩ Annabel's | **W1**	24
Bar des Amis | **WC2**	16
NEW Bedford & Strand | **WC2**	-
Boisdale | **SW1**	19
Ⓩ Claridge's Bar | **W1**	25
Coach & Horses | **WC2**	19
Cork & Bottle | **WC2**	22
Dog & Duck | **W1**	18
Ⓩ Dorchester | **W1**	24
Dove | **W6**	21
El Vino | **multi. loc.**	17
Flask, The | **NW3**	17
George Inn | **SE1**	21
Ⓩ Grenadier | **SW1**	24
Ⓩ Holly Bush | **NW3**	25
Hoop & Grapes | **EC3**	-
Jamaica Wine | **EC3**	24
Jerusalem | **EC1**	22
Ⓩ Library | **SW1**	23
NEW Mews of Mayfair | **W1**	19
Ⓩ Milk & Honey | **W1**	27
NEW Montgomery Pl. | **W11**	19
Perseverance | **WC1**	15
Prospect Whitby | **E1**	22
Ⓩ Royal Oak | **SE1**	-
NEW 1707 Wine Bar | **W1**	20
Ye Olde Cheshire | **EC4**	24

ROMANTIC

Ⓩ American Bar | **WC2**	22
Bleeding Heart Tavern | **EC1**	22

☒ Claridge's Bar	**W1**	25
☒ Dorchester	**W1**	24
Dove	**W6**	21
Flask	**N6**	21
George Inn	**SE1**	21
Gordon's	**WC2**	23
☒ Holly Bush	**NW3**	25
☒ Library	**SW1**	23
☒ Ling Ling	**W1**	26
NEW Mocotó	**SW1**	22
Queen's Larder	**WC1**	18
☒ Rivoli Bar	**W1**	25
Taman Gang	**W1**	19
Vertigo 42	**EC2**	23
Ye Olde Cheshire	**EC4**	24

SLEEPERS

(Good to excellent ratings,
but little known)

All Star Lanes	**WC1**	22
Cittie of Yorke	**WC1**	22
Dragon	**EC2**	23
Jamaica Wine	**EC3**	24
Prospect Whitby	**E1**	22
Vertigo 42	**EC2**	23
NEW Volstead	**W1**	24
Wenlock Arms	**N1**	22
Ye Olde Mitre	**EC1**	26

SPORTS VIEWING

☒ Slug & Lettuce	**SW6**	16

STAG NIGHT

☒ Belgo	**WC2**	19
Comedy Store	**SW1**	20
☒ Pitcher & Piano	**multi. loc.**	15
Player	**W1**	21
Porterhouse	**WC2**	19
Revolution	**multi. loc.**	14
☒ Slug & Lettuce	**multi. loc.**	16
Stringfellows	**WC2**	19
☒ Tiger Tiger	**SW1**	15
Walkabout	**multi. loc.**	12
Waxy O'Connor's	**W1**	21

STRIP CLUBS

Stringfellows	**WC2**	19

TRENDY

NEW Amika	**W8**	21
Apartment 195	**SW3**	21
NEW Bumpkin	**W11**	18
Cuckoo Club	**W1**	23
Dragon	**EC2**	23
☒ e&o	**W11**	22
Elbow Room	**multi. loc.**	19
☒ End, The	**WC1**	24
Fabric	**EC1**	22
NEW Hawksmoor	**E1**	20
NEW Hideaway, The	**N19**	-
Hoxton Sq.	**N1**	19
Kabaret's Prophecy	**W1**	16
Kick	**EC1**	19
Lab	**W1**	21
Light Bar	**WC2**	22
☒ Ling Ling	**W1**	26
Lucky Voice	**W1**	-
NEW Mahiki	**W1**	18
Market Place	**W1**	14
☒ Milk & Honey	**W1**	27
Mo*vida	**W1**	20
Paper	**W1**	17
Plan B	**SW9**	17
Player	**W1**	21
Salt Whisky Bar	**W2**	17
☒ Sketch	**W1**	22
Social	**W1**	18
Taman Gang	**W1**	19
333 Mother Bar	**EC1**	15
Turnmills	**EC1**	15
Vibe Bar	**E1**	17
☒ Yauatcha	**W1**	24

VIEWS OF LONDON

☒ American Bar	**WC2**	22
Balls Brothers	**SW1**	17
Duke's Head	**SW15**	19
1802	**E14**	18
NEW Narrow, The	**E14**	-
Rockwell	**SW1**	21
Smiths/Smithfield	**EC1**	20
333 Mother Bar	**EC1**	15
Trafalgar Tavern	**SE10**	20
Vertigo 42	**EC2**	23

Shopping Merchandise

Includes store names, locations and Quality ratings. ☒ indicates a top-rated or otherwise important place.

ACCESSORIES

Accessorize | **W1**	16
☒ Burberry | **multi. loc.**	26
Claire's | **W1**	12
Diverse | **N1**	-
☒ Hermes | **multi. loc.**	29
Kilgour/Stanbury | **W1**	26
Mulberry | **multi. loc.**	24
☒ Smythson | **multi. loc.**	28

ACTIVEWEAR

Adidas | **multi. loc.**	21
American Apparel | **multi. loc.**	16
Foot Locker | **multi. loc.**	17
Niketown | **W1**	21

BABY GEAR

NEW Mamas & Papas | **W1**	21

CLOTHING: CHILDREN'S

Bumpsville | **multi. loc.**	-
Catimini | **multi. loc.**	26
Daisy & Tom | **SW3**	25
Disney | **multi. loc.**	18
Gap Kids & Baby Gap | **W1**	21
Jigsaw Junior | **multi. loc.**	21
Marie-Chantal | **SW3**	-
Petit Bateau | **multi. loc.**	25
Tartine Chocolat | **W1**	26

CLOTHING: DESIGNER

Alberta Ferretti | **SW1**	27
Alexander McQueen | **W1**	26
Aquascutum | **W1**	25
NEW Armani Collezioni | **W1**	26
☒ Bottega Veneta | **SW1**	28
☒ Burberry | **multi. loc.**	26
Canali | **W1**	26
Celine | **W1**	23
☒ Chanel | **multi. loc.**	29
Christian Dior | **SW1**	25
D & G | **W1**	22
Diane/Furstenberg | **multi. loc.**	25
Dolce & Gabbana | **multi. loc.**	-

NEW Donna Karan | **W1**	24
Emilio Pucci | **SW1**	-
Emporio Armani | **multi. loc.**	23
☒ Ermenegildo Zegna | **W1**	28
Etro | **W1**	26
Fendi | **SW1**	26
☒ Giorgio Armani | **SW1**	28
Gucci | **multi. loc.**	26
☒ Hermes | **multi. loc.**	29
Hugo Boss | **SW1**	23
Issey Miyake | **multi. loc.**	27
Kenzo | **SW3**	23
☒ Louis Vuitton | **multi. loc.**	27
NEW Marc Jacobs | **W1**	23
Matthew Williamson | **W1**	-
MaxMara | **W1**	27
Miu Miu | **W1**	23
Moschino | **W1**	22
NEW Nanette Lepore | **W11**	24
Nicole Farhi | **multi. loc.**	21
Ozwald Boateng | **W1**	-
☒ Prada | **multi. loc.**	28
Stella McCartney | **W1**	22
Valentino | **SW1**	27
Versace | **SW1**	21
Vivienne Westwood | **multi. loc.**	27
Yves Saint Laurent | **multi. loc.**	28

CLOTHING: MEN'S

Bamford | **multi. loc.**	-
Canali | **W1**	26
Daks | **SW1**	22
Diverse | **N1**	-
Duffer/St. George | **WC2**	19
☒ Dunhill | **SW1**	28
Energie | **multi. loc.**	19
☒ Ermenegildo Zegna | **W1**	28
☒ Gieves & Hawkes | **multi. loc.**	26
Hackett | **multi. loc.**	21
Kilgour/Stanbury | **W1**	26
Library, The | **SW3**	20
☒ Loro Piana | **W1**	29

Matches | **multi. loc.**	22
Moss Bros | **WC2**	16
Nicole Farhi | **WC2**	21
Nigel Hall | **WC2**	20
Ozwald Boateng | **W1**	-
Topman | **W1**	14

CLOTHING: MEN'S/ WOMEN'S

(Stores carrying both)

🆕 Abercrombie | **W1**	18
Alexander McQueen | **W1**	26
All Saints | **multi. loc.**	-
American Apparel | **multi. loc.**	16
Aquascutum | **W1**	25
Ballantyne | **multi. loc.**	25
⚡ Bottega Veneta | **SW1**	28
⚡ Brioni | **W1**	29
Brora | **multi. loc.**	20
Browns | **multi. loc.**	27
Daks | **W1**	22
D & G | **W1**	22
Diesel | **multi. loc.**	22
Dispensary, The | **W11**	-
DKNY | **W1**	18
Dolce & Gabbana | **multi. loc.**	-
🆕 Donna Karan | **W1**	24
Dover St. Mkt. | **W1**	24
Emporio Armani | **multi. loc.**	23
Etro | **W1**	26
French Connection | **W1**	19
Gap | **W1**	17
⚡ Giorgio Armani | **SW1**	28
H & M | **multi. loc.**	13
Hugo Boss | **SW1**	23
Issey Miyake | **W1**	27
John Smedley | **W1**	25
Joseph | **SW3**	22
Kenzo | **SW3**	23
Lacoste | **multi. loc.**	21
⚡ Loro Piana | **SW1**	29
🆕 Marc Jacobs | **W1**	23
Massimo Dutti | **multi. loc.**	19
Matches | **W11**	22
Next | **W1**	17
Nicole Farhi | **multi. loc.**	21
⚡ N.Peal | **W1**	27

Paul & Joe | **WC2**	22
Paul Smith | **multi. loc.**	23
⚡ Prada | **multi. loc.**	28
Primark | **W1K**	-
Pringle/Scotland | **multi. loc.**	26
Ralph Lauren | **multi. loc.**	22
Reiss | **W1**	21
River Is. | **W1**	16
Ted Baker | **multi. loc.**	24
⚡ Thomas Pink | **SW1**	26
Tommy Hilfiger | **multi. loc.**	20
Uniqlo | **multi. loc.**	16
United Colors/Benetton | **multi. loc.**	18
Urban Outfitters | **multi. loc.**	16
Valentino | **SW1**	27
Versace | **SW1**	21
Yves Saint Laurent | **multi. loc.**	28
⚡ Zara | **W1**	17

CLOTHING: WOMEN'S

Anne Fontaine | **multi. loc.**	27
Bamford | **SW3**	-
🆕 Betsey Johnson | **WC2**	20
Celine | **W1**	23
Christian Dior | **SW1**	25
Coco Ribbon | **W11**	16
Debenhams | **W1**	17
Diane/Furstenberg | **multi. loc.**	25
Dispensary, The | **W1**	-
Diverse | **N1**	-
Emilio Pucci | **SW1**	-
J & M Davidson | **W11**	-
Jigsaw | **W1**	20
🆕 Karen Millen | **W1**	23
Kew | **multi. loc.**	-
Koh Samui | **WC2**	-
L.K. Bennett | **WC2**	19
⚡ Loro Piana | **W1**	29
Mango | **multi. loc.**	17
Marni | **SW1**	-
Matches | **multi. loc.**	22
Matthew Williamson | **W1**	-
MaxMara | **W1**	27
Miss Selfridge | **W1**	18
Miss Sixty | **multi. loc.**	20
Miu Miu | **W1**	23

SHOPPING

MERCHANDISE

Theo Fennell | **multi. loc.**	‒
Tiffany & Co. | **multi. loc.**	26
Van Cleef & Arpels | **W1**	‒

LUGGAGE

Connolly | **W1**	‒
☒ Dunhill | **SW1**	28
☒ Louis Vuitton | **multi. loc.**	27
Pickett | **multi. loc.**	24
Tanner Krolle | **multi. loc.**	25

MATERNITY

Blossom | **SW3**	‒
Bumpsville | **multi. loc.**	‒
Formes | **multi. loc.**	25

SHOES: MEN'S

Bally | **W1**	24
Canali | **W1**	26
Church's | **W1**	27
Daks | **SW1**	22
Duffer/St. George | **WC2**	19
Fratelli Rossetti | **SW1**	26
☒ Gieves & Hawkes | **multi. loc.**	26
Hogan | **SW1**	‒
Jones | **SW3**	20
Kurt Geiger | **multi. loc.**	22
Office | **W1**	17
Oliver Sweeney | **multi. loc.**	‒
Patrick Cox | **SW1**	‒
Poste | **W1**	‒
Russell & Bromley | **multi. loc.**	22
Salvatore Ferragamo | **multi. loc.**	27

Shellys | **multi. loc.**	15
Size? | **multi. loc.**	‒

SHOES: WOMEN'S

Bally | **W1**	24
☒ Christian Louboutin | **SW1**	28
Church's | **W1**	27
Fratelli Rossetti | **SW1**	26
French Sole | **SW1**	21
Furla | **multi. loc.**	26
Gina | **multi. loc.**	26
Hogan | **SW1**	‒
☒ Jimmy Choo | **multi. loc.**	28
Jones | **SW3**	20
Kurt Geiger | **multi. loc.**	22
☒ Manolo Blahnik | **SW3**	29
Office | **W1**	17
Patrick Cox | **SW1**	‒
Russell & Bromley | **multi. loc.**	22
Salvatore Ferragamo | **multi. loc.**	27
Shellys | **multi. loc.**	15

SNEAKERS

Adidas | **multi. loc.**	21
Foot Locker | **multi. loc.**	17
Niketown | **W1**	21
Puma | **W1**	22

SPORTING GOODS

Holland & Holland | **W1**	28

TOYS

Daisy & Tom | **SW3**	25
Disney | **multi. loc.**	18
☒ Hamleys | **W1**	25

subscribe to zagat.com

Shopping Locations

Includes store names, merchandise type (where necessary) and Quality ratings. ☑ indicates a top-rated or otherwise important place.

Central London

BELGRAVIA

Erickson Beamon | *Jewellery* — |

Little White Co. | 23 |
   Children's Furniture

BLOOMSBURY/FITZROVIA

Habitat | *Home* 20 |

H & M | *Men's & Women's* 13 |
   Clothing

Muji | *Home* 21 |

Planet Organic | *Food* — |

Shellys | *Shoes* 15 |

Swarovski | *Jewellery* 24 |

Uniqlo | *Men's & Women's* 16 |
   Clothing

COVENT GARDEN

Adidas | *Activewear/Sneakers* 21 |

All Saints | *Men's & Women's* — |
   Clothing

NEW Betsey Johnson | *Designer* 20 |

Diesel | *Men's & Women's* 22 |
   Clothing

Disney | *Toys* 18 |

Duffer/St. George | 19 |
   Men's Clothing

Energie | *Men's Clothing* 19 |

Foot Locker | *Sneakers* 17 |

Formes | *Maternity* 25 |

Hackett | *Men's Clothing* 21 |

H & M | *Men's & Women's* 13 |
   Clothing

Kiehl's | *Cosmetics/Toiletries* 26 |

Koh Samui | *Women's Clothing* — |

L.K. Bennett | *Shoes* 19 |

MAC Cosmetics 25 |

Mango | *Women's Clothing* 17 |

Miss Sixty | *Women's Clothing* 20 |

Moss Bros | *Men's Clothing* 16 |

Muji | *Home* 21 |

Nat'l Portrait Gallery | 23 |
   Museum Shop

Neal's Yard Remedies | 25 |
   Cosmetics/Toiletries

Nicole Farhi | *Designer* 21 |

Nigel Hall | *Men's Clothing* 20 |

Original Levi's | *Men's &* 22 |
   Women's Clothing

Paul & Joe | *Men's & Women's* 22 |
   Clothing

Paul Smith | *Designer* 23 |

Penhaligon's | 27 |
   Cosmetics/Toiletries

Pepe Jeans | *Men's & Women's* — |
   Clothing

Russell & Bromley | *Shoes* 22 |

Shellys | *Shoes* 15 |

Size? | *Shoes* — |

Swarovski | *Jewellery* 24 |

Ted Baker | *Men's & Women's* 24 |
   Clothing

☑ Topshop | *Women's Clothing* 17 |

Urban Outfitters | *Men's &* 16 |
   Women's Clothing

West Village | *Women's Clothing* — |

HOLBORN

Hackett | *Men's Clothing* 21 |

KNIGHTSBRIDGE

Agent Provocateur | — |
   Hosiery/Lingerie

Alberta Ferretti | *Designer* 27 |

Anya Hindmarch | *Accessories* 23 |

☑ Bottega Veneta | *Designer* 28 |

Browns | *Men's & Women's* 27 |
   Clothing

☑ Burberry | *Designer* 26 |

☑ Chanel | *Designer* 29 |

Christian Dior | *Designer* 25 |

☑ Christian Louboutin | *Shoes* 28 |

Divertimenti | *Cookware* 24 |

Dolce & Gabbana | *Designer* — |

Emilio Pucci | *Designer* — |

Emporio Armani | *Designer* 23 |

Fendi | *Designer* 26 |

Fratelli Rossetti | *Shoes* 26 |

Gina | *Shoes* | 26

☑ Giorgio Armani | *Designer* | 28

Gucci | *Designer* | 26

H & M | *Men's & Women's Clothing* | 13

☑ Harrods | *Dept. Store* | 26

Harrods Food Hall | -

☑ Harvey Nichols | *Dept. Store* | 26

Harvey Nichols Food Mkt. | -

☑ Hermes | *Designer* | 29

Hogan | *Shoes* | -

☑ Jimmy Choo | *Shoes* | 28

Lacoste | *Men's & Women's Clothing* | 21

☑ Loro Piana | *Men's & Women's Clothing* | 29

☑ Louis Vuitton | *Designer* | 27

Marni | *Designer* | -

Massimo Dutti | *Men's & Women's Clothing* | 19

Mulberry | *Accessories* | 24

Nicole Farhi | *Designer* | 21

Philip Treacy | *Accessories* | -

☑ Prada | *Designer* | 28

Russell & Bromley | *Shoes* | 22

Salvatore Ferragamo | *Shoes* | 27

Swarovski | *Jewellery* | 24

Tanner Krolle | *Accessories* | 25

Tod's | *Accessories* | 27

Tommy Hilfiger | *Men's & Women's Clothing* | 20

United Colors/Benetton | *Men's & Women's Clothing* | 18

Valentino | *Designer* | 27

Versace | *Designer* | 21

Yves Saint Laurent | *Designer* | 28

MARYLEBONE

Accessorize | 16

Adidas | *Activewear/Sneakers* | 21

Alfies Antique Mkt. | -

All Saints | *Men's & Women's Clothing* | -

Body Shop | *Cosmetics/Toiletries* | 20

Brora | *Men's & Women's Clothing* | 20

Church St. Mkt. | *Antiques* | -

Claire's | *Accessories* | 12

☑ Conran Shop | *Home* | 23

Debenhams | *Dept. Store* | 17

Divertimenti | *Cookware* | 24

Foot Locker | *Sneakers* | 17

French Connection | *Men's & Women's Clothing* | 19

Gap | *Men's & Women's Clothing* | 17

Gap Kids & Baby Gap | *Children's* | 21

H & M | *Men's & Women's Clothing* | 13

House of Fraser | *Dept. Store* | 21

☑ John Lewis | *Dept. Store* | 23

NEW Karen Millen | *Women's Clothing* | 23

Kew | *Women's Clothing* | -

Kurt Geiger | *Shoes* | 22

La Fromagerie | *Food* | -

L'Artisan Parfumeur | *Cosmetics/Toiletries* | 25

Little White Co. | *Children's Furniture* | 23

Mango | *Women's Clothing* | 17

☑ Marks & Spencer | *Dept. Store* | 20

Miss Selfridge | *Women's Clothing* | 18

☑ Monsoon | *Women's Clothing* | 19

Mulberry | *Accessories* | 24

Neal's Yard Remedies | *Cosmetics/Toiletries* | 25

Niketown | *Activewear/Sneakers* | 21

Original Levi's | *Men's & Women's Clothing* | 22

Reiss | *Men's & Women's Clothing* | 21

River Is. | *Men's & Women's Clothing* | 16

Russell & Bromley | *Shoes* | 22

☑ Selfridges | *Dept. Store* | 25

Selfridges Food Hall | -

Shellys | *Shoes* | 15

Topman | *Men's Clothing* | 14

☑ Topshop | *Women's Clothing* | 17

United Colors/Benetton | *Men's & Women's Clothing* | 18

Urban Outfitters | *Men's & Women's Clothing* | 16

Warehouse | *Women's Clothing* | 16

Sonia Rykiel | *Designer* 25
Stella McCartney | *Designer* 22
Swarovski | *Jewellery* 24
Tartine Chocolat | *Children's* 26
Ted Baker | *Men's & Women's* 24
Clothing
🖸 Thomas Goode | *Home* 28
Tiffany & Co. | *Jewellery* 26
Tod's | *Accessories* 27
Van Cleef & Arpels | *Jewellery* ⌐
Vivienne Westwood | *Designer* 27
Yves Saint Laurent | *Designer* 28
🖸 Zara | *Men's & Women's* 17
Clothing

PICCADILLY

Aquascutum | *Designer* 25
🖸 Boots | *Cosmetics/Toiletries* 20
🖸 Burberry | *Designer* 26
🖸 Fortnum & Mason | *Dept. Store* 27
🖸 Gieves & Hawkes | 26
Men's Clothing
Habitat | *Home* 20
Hackett | *Men's Clothing* 21
Kilgour/Stanbury | 26
Men's Clothing
NEW Mamas & Papas | 21
Children's Furniture
Mango | *Women's Clothing* 17
Massimo Dutti | *Men's &* 19
Women's Clothing
Next | *Men's & Women's Clothing* 17
🖸 N.Peal | *Men's & Women's* 27
Clothing
Original Levi's | *Men's &* 22
Women's Clothing
Penhaligon's | 27
Cosmetics/Toiletries
Pickett | *Accessories* 24
Swarovski | *Jewellery* 24
Tanner Krolle | *Accessories* 25
Tommy Hilfiger | *Men's &* 20
Women's Clothing
Uniqlo | *Men's & Women's Clothing* 16

SOHO

Adidas | *Activewear/Sneakers* 21
Agent Provocateur | ⌐
Hosiery/Lingerie

All Saints | *Men's & Women's* ⌐
Clothing
American Apparel | *Men's &* 16
Women's Clothing
Church's | *Shoes* 27
Diesel | *Men's & Women's* 22
Clothing
Dispensary, The | *Men's &* ⌐
Women's Clothing
Energie | *Men's Clothing* 19
🖸 Hamleys | *Toys* 25
🖸 Liberty | *Dept. Store* 26
MAC Cosmetics 25
Miss Sixty | *Women's Clothing* 20
Muji | *Home* 21
Neal's Yard Remedies | 25
Cosmetics/Toiletries
Office | *Shoes* 17
Pepe Jeans | *Men's & Women's* ⌐
Clothing
Puma | *Shoes* 22
Size? | *Shoes* ⌐

ST. JAMES'S

Daks | *Designer* 22
🖸 Dunhill | *Designer* 28
Hackett | *Men's Clothing* 21
Russell & Bromley | *Shoes* 22
🖸 Thomas Pink | *Men's &* 26
Women's Clothing

VICTORIA

House of Fraser | *Dept. Store* 21
🖸 Topshop | 17
Women's Clothing

East/South East London

BROADGATE

All Saints | *Men's & Women's* ⌐
Clothing
Hackett | *Men's Clothing* 21
Oliver Sweeney | *Shoes* ⌐

CANARY WHARF/
DOCKLANDS

Hackett | *Men's Clothing* 21
Ted Baker | *Men's & Women's* 24
Clothing

North/
North West London

South/
South West London

SHOPPING

LOCATIONS

subscribe to zagat.com

Shopping Special Features

Listings cover the best in each category and include store names, locations and Quality ratings. ⊠ indicates a top-rated or otherwise important place.

AVANT-GARDE

Alexander McQueen	**W1**	26
Dover St. Mkt.	**W1**	24
⊠ Harvey Nichols	**SW1**	26
Issey Miyake	**SW3**	27
⊠ Liberty	**W1**	26
Library, The	**SW3**	20
Matches	**multi. loc.**	22
Muji	**W8**	21
Ozwald Boateng	**W1**	–
Patrick Cox	**SW1**	–
Philip Treacy	**SW1**	–
Shop at Bluebird	**SW3**	–
Vivienne Westwood	**W1**	27

CELEBRITY CLIENTELE

Alberta Ferretti	**SW1**	27
Alexander McQueen	**W1**	26
Anya Hindmarch	**W11**	23
NEW Armani Collezioni	**W1**	26
Blossom	**SW3**	–
⊠ Bottega Veneta	**SW1**	28
⊠ Brioni	**W1**	29
Browns	**SW1**	27
⊠ Burberry	**W1**	26
⊠ Chanel	**W1**	29
⊠ Christian Louboutin	**SW1**	28
Coco Ribbon	**W11**	16
Diane/Furstenberg	**SW19**	25
Diptyque	**W11**	24
NEW Donna Karan	**W1**	24
Dover St. Mkt.	**W1**	24
⊠ Ermenegildo Zegna	**W1**	28
Fendi	**SW1**	26
⊠ Garrard	**W1**	28
Gina	**SW1**	26
⊠ Giorgio Armani	**SW1**	28
Gucci	**SW1**	26
H & M	**WC2**	13
⊠ Harrods	**SW1**	26
NEW⊠ Harry Winston	**W1**	29
⊠ Harvey Nichols	**SW1**	26
⊠ Hermes	**W1**	29

⊠ Jimmy Choo	**SW1**	28
Jo Malone	**W1**	26
Kilgour/Stanbury	**W1**	26
Koh Samui	**WC2**	–
⊠ Louis Vuitton	**W1**	27
⊠ Manolo Blahnik	**SW3**	29
NEW Marc Jacobs	**W1**	23
Marie-Chantal	**SW3**	–
Matches	**W11**	22
Matthew Williamson	**W1**	–
Miu Miu	**W1**	23
Moschino	**W1**	22
Mulberry	**SW3**	24
Ozwald Boateng	**W1**	–
Paul & Joe	**SW3**	22
Pepe Jeans	**W10**	–
Philip Treacy	**SW1**	–
⊠ Prada	**SW1**	28
Ralph Lauren	**W1**	22
Rellik	**W10**	–
⊠ Selfridges	**W1**	25
Steinberg & Tolkien	**SW3**	23
Stella McCartney	**W1**	22
Temperley London	**W11**	–
Theo Fennell	**SW3**	–
Tod's	**SW1**	27
⊠ Topshop	**W1**	17
Valentino	**SW1**	27
Versace	**SW1**	21
Vivienne Westwood	**W1**	27
Yves Saint Laurent	**SW1**	28

CUSTOM-MADE GOODS

All Saints	**multi. loc.**	–
Andrew Martin	**SW3**	23
Blossom	**SW3**	–
⊠ Bottega Veneta	**multi. loc.**	28
⊠ Brioni	**W1**	29
Bulgari	**W1**	29
Canali	**W1**	26
⊠ Cartier	**multi. loc.**	27
Church's	**W1**	27

Connolly | **W1**	–
Divertimenti | **multi. loc.**	24
NEW Donna Karan | **W1**	24
Dover St. Mkt. | **W1**	24
Z Dunhill | **SW1**	28
Erickson Beamon | **SW1**	–
Z Ermenegildo Zegna | **W1**	28
Fendi | **SW1**	26
Z Garrard | **W1**	28
General Trading Co. | **SW3**	23
Z Gieves & Hawkes | **multi. loc.**	26
Gina | **multi. loc.**	26
Z Giorgio Armani | **SW1**	28
Graham & Green | **multi. loc.**	20
Gucci | **multi. loc.**	26
Habitat | **W1**	20
Hackett | **multi. loc.**	21
Z Harrods | **SW1**	26
NEW Z Harry Winston | **W1**	29
Z Harvey Nichols | **SW1**	26
Z Hermes | **multi. loc.**	29
Holland & Holland | **W1**	28
J & M Davidson | **W11**	–
Z Jimmy Choo | **multi. loc.**	28
Joseph | **SW3**	22
Kilgour/Stanbury | **W1**	26
Z Liberty | **W1**	26
Z Louis Vuitton | **multi. loc.**	27
Z Marks & Spencer | **W1**	20
Massimo Dutti | **W1**	19
Miller Harris | **multi. loc.**	–
Oliver Sweeney | **multi. loc.**	–
Ozwald Boateng | **W1**	–
Philip Treacy | **SW1**	–
Pickett | **multi. loc.**	24
Z Prada | **multi. loc.**	28
Rug Co. | **W1**	–
Z Selfridges | **W1**	25
Z Smythson | **multi. loc.**	28
Swarovski | **multi. loc.**	24
Tanner Krolle | **multi. loc.**	25
Temperley London | **W11**	–
Theo Fennell | **multi. loc.**	–
Z Thomas Goode | **W1**	28
Z Thomas Pink | **SW1**	26
Tiffany & Co. | **multi. loc.**	26

Tod's | **multi. loc.**	27
Van Cleef & Arpels | **W1**	–

HIP/HOT PLACES

NEW Abercrombie | **W1**	18
Adidas | **WC2**	21
Alexander McQueen | **W1**	26
All Saints | **WC2**	–
American Apparel | **W11**	16
Anya Hindmarch | **W11**	23
Ballantyne | **W1**	25
Bamford | **SW3**	–
B & B Italia | **SW3**	26
Blossom | **SW3**	–
Z Bottega Veneta | **SW1**	28
Z Brioni | **W1**	29
Browns | **SW1**	27
Z Burberry | **W1**	26
Z Chanel | **W1**	29
Z Christian Louboutin | **SW1**	28
Coco Ribbon | **W11**	16
Z Conran Shop | **SW3**	23
Diane/Furstenberg | **SW19**	25
Diesel | **W1**	22
Diptyque | **W11**	24
Dispensary, The | **W11**	–
DKNY | **W1**	18
NEW Donna Karan | **W1**	24
Dover St. Mkt. | **W1**	24
Emilio Pucci | **SW1**	–
Energie | **WC2**	19
Erickson Beamon | **SW1**	–
Z Ermenegildo Zegna | **W1**	28
Fenwick | **W1**	22
French Connection | **W1**	19
French Sole | **SW1**	21
Gina | **SW1**	26
Graham & Green | **SW3**	20
Gucci | **SW1**	26
H & M | **WC2**	13
Z Harvey Nichols | **SW1**	26
Z Jimmy Choo | **SW1**	28
Jo Malone | **W1**	26
Joseph | **SW3**	22
Kelly Hoppen | **SW3**	–
Kiehl's | **SW3**	26
Koh Samui | **WC2**	–

L'Artisan Parfumeur | **EC3** 25
🔲 Liberty | **W1** 26
Library, The | **SW3** 20
🔲 Manolo Blahnik | **SW3** 29
NEW Marc Jacobs | **W1** 23
Matches | **multi. loc.** 22
Matthew Williamson | **W1** -
Miu Miu | **W1** 23
Muji | **W8** 21
Mulberry | **SW3** 24
NEW Nanette Lepore | **W11** 24
Paul & Joe | **SW3** 22
🔲 Prada | **SW1** 28
Reiss | **W1** 21
Rellik | **W10** -
🔲 Selfridges | **W1** 25
Shop at Bluebird | **SW3** -
🔲 Smythson | **W1** 28
SPACE.NK | **W2** 26
Stella McCartney | **W1** 22
Temperley London | **W11** -
Tod's | **SW1** 27
Topman | **W1** 14
🔲 Topshop | **W1** 17
Urban Outfitters | **W1** 16
Vivienne Westwood | **W1** 27
Yves Saint Laurent | **SW1** 28
🔲 Zara | **W1** 17

LEGENDARY

(Date company founded)
1638 | Spitalfields Mkt. | **E16** -
1735 | Garrard | **W1** 28
1760 | Hamleys | **W1** 25
1771 | Gieves & Hawkes | **multi. loc.** 26
1781 | Asprey | **W1** 29
1794 | John Smedley | **W1** 25
1800 | Loro Piana | **multi. loc.** 29
1813 | Harvey Nichols | **SW1** 26
1815 | Pringle/Scotland | **multi. loc.** 26
1827 | Thomas Goode | **W1** 28
1835 | Holland & Holland | **W1** 28
1837 | Hermes | **multi. loc.** 29
1837 | Tiffany & Co. | **multi. loc.** 26
1846 | John Lewis | **W1** 23

1849 | Boots | **W1** 20
1849 | Harrods | **SW1** 26
1849 | Harrods Food Hall | **SW1** -
1849 | House of Fraser | **W1** 21
1851 | Aquascutum | **W1** 25
1851 | Bally | **W1** 24
1851 | Kiehl's | **multi. loc.** 26
1851 | Moss Bros | **WC2** 16
1854 | Louis Vuitton | **multi. loc.** 27
1856 | Burberry | **multi. loc.** 26
1856 | Nat'l Portrait Gallery | **WC2** 23
1856 | Tanner Krolle | **multi. loc.** 25
1857 | Jones | **SW3** 20
1857 | Science Museum | **SW7** 20
1870 | Penhaligon's | **multi. loc.** 27
1873 | Church's | **W1** 27
1873 | Original Levi's | **multi. loc.** 22
1875 | Liberty | **W1** 26
1877 | Peter Jones | **SW1** 23
1879 | Russell & Bromley | **multi. loc.** 22
1880 | Harvey Nichols Food Mkt. | **SW1** -
1882 | Fenwick | **W1** 22
1884 | Bulgari | **W1** 29
1884 | Marks & Spencer | **W1** 20
1887 | Smythson | **multi. loc.** 28
1892 | Abercrombie | **W1** 18
1893 | Petit Bateau | **multi. loc.** 25
1895 | Swarovski | **multi. loc.** 24
1896 | Dunhill | **SW1** 28
1897 | Sainsbury's | **NW3** -
1902 | Cartier | **W1** 27
1906 | Van Cleef & Arpels | **W1** -
1909 | Selfridges | **W1** 25
1909 | Selfridges Food Hall | **W1A** -
1910 | Chanel | **multi. loc.** 29
1910 | Ermenegildo Zegna | **W1** 28
1913 | Prada | **multi. loc.** 28
1914 | Salvatore Ferragamo | **multi. loc.** 27
1918 | Fendi | **SW1** 26
1920 | Adidas | **multi. loc.** 21

1920 | General Trading Co. | **SW3**	23
1920 | Harry Winston | **W1**	29
1921 | Ballantyne | **multi. loc.**	25
1921 | Gucci | **multi. loc.**	26
1923 | Disney | **multi. loc.**	18
1923 | Hugo Boss | **SW1**	23
1925 | Kilgour/Stanbury | **W1**	26
1927 | Furla | **multi. loc.**	26
1933 | Lacoste | **multi. loc.**	21
1934 | Canali | **W1**	26
1936 | Daks | **multi. loc.**	22
1945 | Brioni | **W1**	29
1946 | Shellys | **multi. loc.**	15
1947 | Celine | **W1**	23
1947 | Christian Dior | **SW1**	25
1947 | Emilio Pucci | **SW1**	-
1947 | H & M | **multi. loc.**	13
1948 | Puma | **W1**	22

ONLY IN LONDON

Bamford | **SW3**	-
Browns | **SW1**	27
Coco Ribbon | **W11**	16
Connolly | **W1**	-
Designers Guild | **SW3**	25
Design Museum | **SE1**	21
Dispensary, The | **W11**	-
Diverse | **N1**	-
Divertimenti | **SW3**	24
Erickson Beamon | **SW1**	-
☑ Fortnum & Mason | **W1**	27
Graham & Green | **SW3**	20
☑ Harrods | **SW1**	26
J & M Davidson | **W11**	-
Kilgour/Stanbury | **W1**	26
Koh Samui | **WC2**	-
☑ Liberty | **W1**	26
Library, The | **SW3**	20
Lulu Guiness | **SW1**	25
Matches | **multi. loc.**	22
Matthew Williamson | **W1**	-
Miller Harris | **W11**	-
Museum of London | **EC2**	20
Nat'l Portrait Gallery | **WC2**	23
Nigel Hall | **WC2**	20
Nina Campbell | **SW3**	29

☑ N.Peal | **W1**	27
Ozwald Boateng | **W1**	-
☑ Peter Jones | **SW1**	23
Philip Treacy | **SW1**	-
Pickett | **W1**	24
Rellik | **W10**	-
Science Museum | **SW7**	20
Shop at Bluebird | **SW3**	-
Steinberg & Tolkien | **SW3**	23
Tanner Krolle | **SW1**	25
☑ Tate Modern | **SE1**	23
Theo Fennell | **SW3**	-
☑ Thomas Goode | **W1**	28
☑ Victoria & Albert | **SW7**	24

STATUS GOODS

Alberta Ferretti | **SW1**	27
Alexander McQueen | **W1**	26
Anne Fontaine | **SW1**	27
Anya Hindmarch | **W11**	23
Aquascutum | **W1**	25
NEW Armani Collezioni | **W1**	26
☑ Asprey | **W1**	29
Ballantyne | **W1**	25
Bamford | **SW3**	-
B & B Italia | **SW3**	26
Blossom | **SW3**	-
☑ Bottega Veneta | **SW1**	28
☑ Brioni | **W1**	29
Brora | **SW19**	20
Browns | **SW1**	27
☑ Burberry | **W1**	26
Canali | **W1**	26
☑ Cartier | **EC3**	27
Catimini | **W1**	26
Celine | **W1**	23
☑ Chanel | **W1**	29
Christian Dior | **SW1**	25
☑ Christian Louboutin | **SW1**	28
Connolly | **W1**	-
☑ Conran Shop | **SW3**	23
Daks | **SW1**	22
D & G | **W1**	22
Diane/Furstenberg | **SW19**	25
Diptyque | **W11**	24
Diverse | **N1**	-
Divertimenti | **SW3**	24

Store	Location	
DKNY	W1	18
NEW Donna Karan	W1	24
Dover St. Mkt.	W1	24
Z Dunhill	SW1	28
Emilio Pucci	SW1	-
Emporio Armani	SW3	23
Z Ermenegildo Zegna	W1	28
Etro	W1	26
Fendi	SW1	26
Fenwick	W1	22
Z Fortnum & Mason	W1	27
Fratelli Rossetti	SW1	26
Furla	SW3	26
Z Garrard	W1	28
Z Gieves & Hawkes	SW1	26
Gina	SW1	26
Z Giorgio Armani	SW1	28
Gucci	SW1	26
Hackett	EC3	21
Z Hamleys	W1	25
Z Harrods	SW1	26
NEW Z Harry Winston	W1	29
Z Harvey Nichols	SW1	26
Z Hermes	W1	29
Hogan	SW1	-
Hugo Boss	SW1	23
Issey Miyake	SW3	27
J & M Davidson	W11	-
Z Jimmy Choo	SW1	28
John Smedley	W1	25
Jo Malone	W1	26
Joseph	SW3	22
Kelly Hoppen	SW3	-
Kenzo	SW3	23
Kilgour/Stanbury	W1	26
Koh Samui	WC2	-
Kurt Geiger	W8	22
Lacoste	SW3	21
L'Artisan Parfumeur	EC3	25
Z Liberty	W1	26
Library, The	SW3	20
Little White Co.	W1	23
Z Loro Piana	SW1	29
Z Louis Vuitton	W1	27
Lulu Guiness	SW1	25
Z Manolo Blahnik	SW3	29
NEW Marc Jacobs	W1	23
Marie-Chantal	SW3	-
Marni	SW1	-
Matches	multi. loc.	22
Matthew Williamson	W1	-
MaxMara	W1	27
Miu Miu	W1	23
Z Molton Brown	W1	26
Moschino	W1	22
Mulberry	SW3	24
Nicole Farhi	W11	21
Nicole Farhi Home	W1	-
Nina Campbell	SW3	29
Z N.Peal	W1	27
Ozwald Boateng	W1	-
Patrick Cox	SW1	-
Paul Smith	WC2	23
Philip Treacy	SW1	-
Pickett	W1	24
Z Prada	SW1	28
Pringle/Scotland	W1	26
Ralph Lauren	W1	22
Salvatore Ferragamo	W1	27
Science Museum	SW7	20
Z Selfridges	W1	25
Shop at Bluebird	SW3	-
Z Smythson	W1	28
Sonia Rykiel	W1	25
Stella McCartney	W1	22
Swarovski	W1	24
Tanner Krolle	SW1	25
Temperley London	W11	-
Theo Fennell	SW3	-
Z Thomas Goode	W1	28
Z Thomas Pink	SW1	26
Tiffany & Co.	SW1	26
Tod's	SW1	27
Tommy Hilfiger	SW1	20
Valentino	SW1	27
Van Cleef & Arpels	W1	-
Versace	SW1	21
Vivienne Westwood	W1	27
White Company	W1	21
Yves Saint Laurent	SW1	28

TWEEN/TEEN APPEAL

NEW Abercrombie | **W1**	18
Accessorize | **W1**	16
Adidas | **WC2**	21
American Apparel | **W11**	16
Body Shop | **W1**	20
Z Boots | **W1**	20
Claire's | **W1**	12
Energie | **WC2**	19
Foot Locker | **W1**	17
French Connection | **W1**	19
French Sole | **SW1**	21
Gap | **W1**	17
Graham & Green | **SW3**	20
H & M | **WC2**	13
Z Harrods | **SW1**	26
House of Fraser | **W1**	21
Jigsaw Junior | **W1**	21
MAC Cosmetics | **SW3**	25
Mango | **W1**	17
Miss Selfridge | **W1**	18
Miss Sixty | **WC2**	20
Muji | **W8**	21
Museum of London | **EC2**	20
Nat'l Portrait Gallery | **WC2**	23
Niketown | **W1**	21
Office | **W1**	17
Original Levi's | **WC2**	22
Pepe Jeans | **W10**	-
Poste | **W1**	-
Puma | **W1**	22
Reiss | **W1**	21
River Is. | **W1**	16
Z Selfridges | **W1**	25
Shellys | **SW3**	15
Size? | **WC2**	-
SPACE.NK | **W2**	26
Z Tate Modern | **SE1**	23
Topman | **W1**	14
Z Topshop | **W1**	17
Uniqlo | **W1**	16
United Colors/Benetton | **SW3**	18
Urban Outfitters | **W1**	16
Z Victoria & Albert | **SW7**	24
Warehouse | **W1**	16
Z Zara | **W1**	17

Attractions Types

Includes attraction names, locations and Appeal ratings. ☑ indicates places with the highest ratings, popularity and importance.

AQUARIUMS

London Aquarium	**SE1**	21

ARTS/PERFORMANCE CENTRES

Barbican, The	**EC2**	20
Institute/Contemp. Arts	**SW1**	–
National Theatre	**SE1**	25
NEW O2, The	**SE1**	–
Royal Albert Hall	**SW7**	25
Shakespeare's Globe	**SE1**	26

CEMETERIES

Highgate Cemetery	**N6**	24

FAMOUS BUILDINGS & LOCATIONS

Lloyds Building	**EC3**	17
☑ London Eye	**SE1**	26
Thames Barrier	**SE1**	19
30 St. Mary Axe (Gherkin)	**EC3**	21

GARDENS

Chelsea Physic Gdn.	**SW3**	21
Royal Botanic Gdns., Kew	**TW9**	28

HISTORIC LANDMARKS

☑ Buckingham Palace	**SW1**	27
Guildhall	**EC2**	23
Hampton Court Palace	**KT8**	28
Horse Guards Parade	**SW1**	25
Houses of Parliament	**SW1**	28
Kensington Palace	**W8**	24
Monument, The	**EC3**	19
St. Paul's Cathedral	**EC4**	27
10 Downing St.	**SW1**	18
Tower Bridge	**SE1**	25
☑ Tower of London	**EC3**	28
☑ Windsor Castle	**SL4**	28

HISTORICAL HOUSES

Dennis Severs' House	**E1**	27
Spencer House	**SW1**	25
Wellington Museum	**W1**	24

LIBRARIES

British Library	**NW1**	25

MUSEUMS: ART

Courtauld Institute	**WC2**	27
Institute/Contemp. Arts	**SW1**	–
Kenwood House	**NW3**	23
☑ National Gallery	**WC2**	28
National Portrait Gallery	**WC2**	26
Royal Academy/Arts	**W1**	25
Serpentine Gallery	**W2**	22
Somerset House	**WC2**	24
Tate Britain	**SW1**	26
☑ Tate Modern	**SE1**	25
Wallace Collection	**W1**	25

MUSEUMS: CULTURAL

Bank of England	**EC2**	19
☑ British Museum	**WC1**	28
Design Museum	**SE1**	21
Dr. Johnson's House	**EC4**	14
Freud Museum	**NW3**	20
Imperial War Museum	**SE1**	27
London Dungeon	**SE1**	16
Madame Tussauds	**NW1**	21
Museum of London	**EC2**	25
Royal Academy/Arts	**W1**	25
Sherlock Holmes Museum	**NW1**	19
Soane Museum	**WC2**	25
Victoria & Albert	**SW7**	27

MUSEUMS: HISTORY

Churchill Museum	**SW1**	27
Dickens House Museum	**WC1**	19
Flor. Nightingale Museum	**SE1**	23
Geffrye Museum	**E2**	24
HMS Belfast	**SE1**	22
Wellington Museum	**W1**	24

MUSEUMS: NATURAL HISTORY

Natural History Museum	**SW7**	26

Attractions Locations

Includes attraction names and Appeal ratings. ☑ indicates places with the highest ratings, popularity and importance.

ATTRACTIONS

LOCATIONS

SOUTH BANK/BOROUGH

Borough Mkt.	26
HMS Belfast	22
London Aquarium	21
⚡ London Eye	26
National Theatre	25
Royal Festival Hall	–
Shakespeare's Globe	26
Southwark Cathedral	24

WATERLOO/ SOUTHWARK/ KENNINGTON

Flor. Nightingale Museum	23
Imperial War Museum	27
London Dungeon	16
⚡ Tate Modern	25

North/ North West London

CAMDEN TOWN/CHALK FARM/KENTISH TOWN/ PRIMROSE HILL

Camden Market	20
London Zoo	23

HAMPSTEAD/KILBURN/ SWISS COTTAGE

Freud Museum	20
Hampstead Heath	25
Kenwood House	23

HIGHGATE/MUSWELL HILL/CROUCH END/ TUFNELL PARK

Highgate Cemetery	24

KING'S CROSS

British Library	25

ST. JOHN'S WOOD

Lord's	21

South/ South West London

CHELSEA

Chelsea Physic Gdn.	21

PIMLICO

Tate Britain	26

PUTNEY/RICHMOND

Hampton Court Palace	28
Royal Botanic Gdns., Kew	28

SOUTH KENSINGTON

Natural History Museum	26
Royal Albert Hall	25
Science Museum	26
Victoria & Albert	27

West London

KENSINGTON

Holland Park	22
Kensington Gdns.	25
Kensington Palace	24
Serpentine Gallery	22

NOTTING HILL

Portobello Mkt.	23

Outside London

WINDSOR

Legoland Windsor	21
⚡ Windsor Castle	28

Attractions Special Features

Listings cover the best in each category and include attraction names, locations and Appeal ratings. ☑ indicates places with the highest ratings, popularity and importance.

CITY VIEWS

Greenwich Park | **SE10**	23
Hampstead Heath | **NW3**	25
☑ London Eye | **SE1**	26
Monument, The | **EC3**	19
St. Paul's Cathedral | **EC4**	27
☑ Tate Modern | **SE1**	25
Tower Bridge | **SE1**	25
Trafalgar Square | **WC2**	22

DRAMATIC DESIGN

Bank of England | **EC2**	19
Barbican, The | **EC2**	20
Brick Lane | **E1**	18
British Library | **NW1**	25
☑ British Museum | **WC1**	28
☑ Buckingham Palace | **SW1**	27
Burlington Arcade | **W1**	21
Canary Wharf | **E1**	16
Guildhall | **EC2**	23
Houses of Parliament | **SW1**	28
Jermyn St. | **SW1**	23
Kenwood House | **NW3**	23
Leadenhall Mkt. | **EC3**	18
Lloyds Building | **EC3**	17
☑ London Eye | **SE1**	26
National Theatre | **SE1**	25
Natural History Museum | **SW7**	26
Royal Academy/Arts | **W1**	25
Royal Albert Hall | **SW7**	25
Shakespeare's Globe | **SE1**	26
Somerset House | **WC2**	24
Spencer House | **SW1**	25
St. Paul's Cathedral | **EC4**	27
☑ Tate Modern | **SE1**	25
Thames Barrier | **SE1**	19
30 St. Mary Axe (Gherkin) | **EC3**	21
Tower Bridge | **SE1**	25
☑ Tower of London | **EC3**	28
Trafalgar Square | **WC2**	22
Victoria & Albert | **SW7**	27
☑ Westminster Abbey | **SW1**	28

Westminster Cathedral | **SW1**	26
☑ Windsor Castle | **SL4**	28

EDUCATIONAL

Royal Academy/Arts | **W1**	25
Royal Botanic Gdns., Kew | **TW9**	28
Royal Observatory | **SE10**	25
Science Museum | **SW7**	26
Shakespeare's Globe | **SE1**	26
Soane Museum | **WC2**	25
Somerset House | **WC2**	24
Southwark Cathedral | **SE1**	24
St. Paul's Cathedral | **EC4**	27
Tate Britain | **SW1**	26
☑ Tate Modern | **SE1**	25
☑ Tower of London | **EC3**	28
Victoria & Albert | **SW7**	27
Wallace Collection | **W1**	25
Wellington Museum | **W1**	24
Westminster Cathedral | **SW1**	26
☑ Windsor Castle | **SL4**	28

GUIDED TOURS

Barbican, The | **EC2**	20
British Library | **NW1**	25
☑ British Museum | **WC1**	28
☑ Buckingham Palace | **SW1**	27
Churchill Museum | **SW1**	27
Courtauld Institute | **WC2**	27
Dickens House Museum | **WC1**	19
Dr. Johnson's House | **EC4**	14
Flor. Nightingale Museum | **SE1**	23
Freud Museum | **NW3**	20
Geffrye Museum | **E2**	24
Green Park | **SW1**	23
Greenwich Park | **SE10**	23
Hampton Court Palace | **KT8**	28
Highgate Cemetery | **N6**	24
HMS Belfast | **SE1**	22
Houses of Parliament | **SW1**	28
Hyde Park | **W2**	26
Imperial War Museum | **SE1**	27

Kensington Gdns.	**W2**	25
Kensington Palace	**W8**	24
Kenwood House	**NW3**	23
Lloyds Building	**EC3**	17
London Aquarium	**SE1**	21
London Dungeon	**SE1**	16
London Zoo	**NW1**	23
Lord's	**NW8**	21
Museum of London	**EC2**	25
☑ National Gallery	**WC2**	28
National Portrait Gallery	**WC2**	26
National Theatre	**SE1**	25
Royal Academy/Arts	**W1**	25
Royal Albert Hall	**SW7**	25
Royal Botanic Gdns., Kew	**TW9**	28
Royal Observatory	**SE10**	25
Serpentine Gallery	**W2**	22
Shakespeare's Globe	**SE1**	26
Sherlock Holmes Museum	**NW1**	19
Soane Museum	**WC2**	25
Somerset House	**WC2**	24
Southwark Cathedral	**SE1**	24
Spencer House	**SW1**	25
St. James's Park	**SW1**	26
St. Paul's Cathedral	**EC4**	27
Tate Britain	**SW1**	26
☑ Tate Modern	**SE1**	25
Tower Bridge	**SE1**	25
☑ Tower of London	**EC3**	28
Victoria & Albert	**SW7**	27
Wallace Collection	**W1**	25
Wellington Museum	**W1**	24
☑ Westminster Abbey	**SW1**	28
☑ Windsor Castle	**SL4**	28

MUST-SEES

Borough Mkt.	**SE1**	26
☑ British Museum	**WC1**	28
☑ Buckingham Palace	**SW1**	27
Covent Gdn.	**WC2**	23
Hampton Court Palace	**KT8**	28
Horse Guards Parade	**SW1**	25
Houses of Parliament	**SW1**	28
☑ London Eye	**SE1**	26
☑ National Gallery	**WC2**	28
Natural History Museum	**SW7**	26
St. Paul's Cathedral	**EC4**	27

☑ Tate Modern	**SE1**	25
10 Downing St.	**SW1**	18
Tower Bridge	**SE1**	25
☑ Tower of London	**EC3**	28
Victoria & Albert	**SW7**	27
☑ Westminster Abbey	**SW1**	28
☑ Windsor Castle	**SL4**	28

OFFBEAT/FUNKY

Barbican, The	**EC2**	20
Brick Lane	**E1**	18
Burlington Arcade	**W1**	21
Camden Market	**NW1**	20
Carnaby St.	**W1**	16
Chinatown	**WC2**	18
Dennis Severs' House	**E1**	27
Institute/Contemp. Arts	**SW1**	–
Portobello Mkt.	**W11**	23
Soane Museum	**WC2**	25
Speakers' Corner	**W2**	19
Spitalfields Mkt.	**E1**	22
30 St. Mary Axe (Gherkin)	**EC3**	21

TEENS TOO

(13 & Above)

☑ British Museum	**WC1**	28
Camden Market	**NW1**	20
Carnaby St.	**W1**	16
Covent Gdn.	**WC2**	23
HMS Belfast	**SE1**	22
Imperial War Museum	**SE1**	27
Leicester Square	**WC2**	17
London Aquarium	**SE1**	21
London Dungeon	**SE1**	16
Madame Tussauds	**NW1**	21
Natural History Museum	**SW7**	26
Oxford St.	**W1**	17
Portobello Mkt.	**W11**	23
Royal Observatory	**SE10**	25
Science Museum	**SW7**	26
Spitalfields Mkt.	**E1**	22
☑ Tate Modern	**SE1**	25
☑ Tower of London	**EC3**	28
Victoria & Albert	**SW7**	27

TODDLERS

(3 & Under)

Holland Park	**W8**	22
Hyde Park	**W2**	26

Kensington Gdns. | **W2** 25

Legoland Windsor | **SL4** 21

London Aquarium | **SE1** 21

London Zoo | **NW1** 23

Madame Tussauds | **NW1** 21

Regent's Park | **NW1** 26

St. James's Park | **SW1** 26

YOUNG CHILDREN

(4–7)

Holland Park | **W8** 22

Hyde Park | **W2** 26

Kensington Gdns. | **W2** 25

Legoland Windsor | **SL4** 21

London Aquarium | **SE1** 21

London Zoo | **NW1** 23

Regent's Park | **NW1** 26

Science Museum | **SW7** 26

St. James's Park | **SW1** 26

☑ Tower of London | **EC3** 28

ATTRACTIONS

SPECIAL FEATURES

Hotel Types

Listings cover the best in each category and include hotel names,
locations and Room ratings. ☑ indicates places with the highest ratings,
popularity and importance.

BED & BREAKFAST

Lincoln House	**W1**	-ㅣ
Number Eleven	**SW3**	-ㅣ
Number Sixteen	**SW7**	-ㅣ
22 Jermyn St.	**SW1**	22

BOUTIQUE

Beaufort, The	**SW3**	-ㅣ
Blakes	**SW7**	22
Capital Hotel	**SW3**	-ㅣ
Charlotte St.	**W1**	23
Covent Garden	**WC2**	25
Dorset Square	**NW1**	22
51 Buckingham Gate	**SW1**	24
Gallery, The	**SW7**	-ㅣ
Halkin	**SW1**	24
🆕 Haymarket Hotel	**SW1**	-ㅣ
Hempel	**W2**	23
🆕 Jumeirah Lowndes	**SW1**	-ㅣ
Milestone	**W8**	23
One Aldwych	**WC2**	22
Sanderson	**W1**	23

Soho Hotel	**W1**	26
Stafford	**SW1**	23
Threadneedles	**EC2**	21

BUSINESS-ORIENTED

Berkeley	**SW1**	23
☑ Claridge's	**W1**	25
☑ Dorchester	**W1**	25
51 Buckingham Gate	**SW1**	24
Four Seasons	**W1**	24
Four Seasons Canary Wharf	**E14**	26
Great Eastern Hotel	**EC2**	-ㅣ
Landmark	**NW1**	23
☑ Lanesborough	**SW1**	27
Mandarin Oriental	**SW1**	24
One Aldwych	**WC2**	22

CONVENTION

Four Seasons Canary Wharf	**E14**	26
Sheraton	**SW1**	22

subscribe to zagat.com

Hotel Locations

Includes hotel names and Room ratings.

Central London

BELGRAVIA
Halkin	24

BLOOMSBURY/ FITZROVIA
Charlotte St.	23

COVENT GARDEN
Covent Garden	25
One Aldwych	22
Savoy	22
St. Martins Lane	20

KNIGHTSBRIDGE
Beaufort, The	-
Berkeley	23
Cadogan	19
Capital Hotel	-
Jumeirah Carlton	22
NEW Jumeirah Lowndes	-
☑ Lanesborough	27
Mandarin Oriental	24
Sheraton	22

MARYLEBONE
Dorset Square	22
Landmark	23
Leonard, The	-
Lincoln House	-

MAYFAIR
Brown's	22
☑ Claridge's	25
☑ Connaught	24
☑ Dorchester	25
47 Park St.	27
Four Seasons	24
Metropolitan	21

PICCADILLY
Athenaeum	21
NEW Haymarket Hotel	-
Sofitel St. James	24

SOHO
Sanderson	23
Soho Hotel	26

ST. JAMES'S
Dukes	21
☑ Ritz	24
Stafford	23
Trafalgar	19
22 Jermyn St.	22

VICTORIA
Goring	23

WESTMINSTER
51 Buckingham Gate	24

East/South East London

CANARY WHARF/ DOCKLANDS
Four Seasons Canary Wharf	26

CITY
Great Eastern Hotel	-
Threadneedles	21

South/ South West London

CHELSEA
Number Eleven	-
NEW Wyndham	25

SOUTH KENSINGTON
Blakes	22
Gallery, The	-
Number Sixteen	-

West London

BAYSWATER
Hempel	23

KENSINGTON
K West	20
Milestone	23

HOTEL

LOCATIONS

Hotel Special Features

Listings cover the best in each category and include hotel names, locations and Room ratings. ⧉ indicates places with the highest ratings, popularity and importance.

CITY VIEWS

Athenaeum | **W1**	21
Berkeley | **SW1**	23
Blakes | **SW7**	22
Brown's | **W1**	22
Cadogan | **SW1**	19
Charlotte St. | **W1**	23
⧉ Connaught | **W1**	24
⧉ Dorchester | **W1**	25
Dukes | **SW1**	21
Four Seasons | **W1**	24
Four Seasons Canary Wharf | **E14**	26
Halkin | **SW1**	24
Jumeirah Carlton | **SW1**	22
⧉ Lanesborough | **SW1**	27
Leonard, The | **W1**	–
Mandarin Oriental | **SW1**	24
Metropolitan | **W1**	21
Milestone | **W8**	23
Number Sixteen | **SW7**	–
One Aldwych | **WC2**	22
⧉ Ritz | **W1**	24
Sheraton | **SW1**	22
Sofitel St. James | **SW1**	24
Stafford | **SW1**	23
Trafalgar | **SW1**	19
22 Jermyn St. | **SW1**	22

DRAMATIC DESIGN

Blakes | **SW7**	22
Cadogan | **SW1**	19
Metropolitan | **W1**	21
One Aldwych | **WC2**	22
Sanderson | **W1**	23

NOTEWORTHY NEWCOMERS

Haymarket Hotel | **SW1**	–
Jumeirah Lowndes | **SW1**	–
Wyndham | **SW10**	25

OFFBEAT/FUNKY

Charlotte St. | **W1**	23
Sanderson | **W1**	23
St. Martins Lane | **WC2**	20

POWER SCENES

⧉ Claridge's | **W1**	25
Four Seasons | **W1**	24
Mandarin Oriental | **SW1**	24

SPA FACILITIES

⧉ Claridge's | **W1**	25
Covent Garden | **WC2**	25
⧉ Dorchester | **W1**	25
Four Seasons Canary Wharf | **E14**	26
Great Eastern Hotel | **EC2**	–
Jumeirah Carlton | **SW1**	22
K West | **W14**	20
Mandarin Oriental | **SW1**	24
Metropolitan | **W1**	21
Sanderson | **W1**	23

TRENDY PLACES

Berkeley | **SW1**	23
Blakes | **SW7**	22
Charlotte St. | **W1**	23
⧉ Dorchester | **W1**	25
Metropolitan | **W1**	21
One Aldwych | **WC2**	22
Sanderson | **W1**	23
St. Martins Lane | **WC2**	20

WATER VIEWS

Four Seasons Canary Wharf | **E14**	26
One Aldwych | **WC2**	22
Savoy | **WC2**	22
NEW Wyndham | **SW10**	25

subscribe to zagat.com

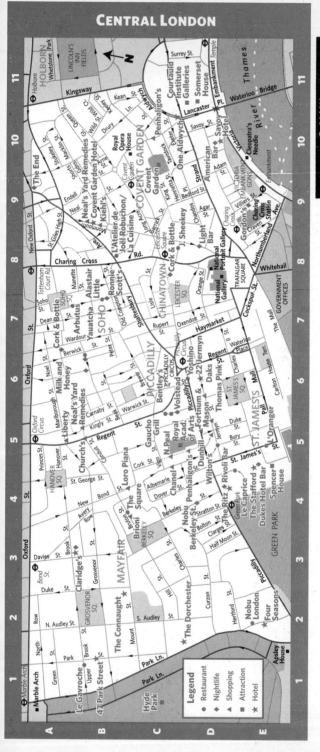

CENTRAL LONDON

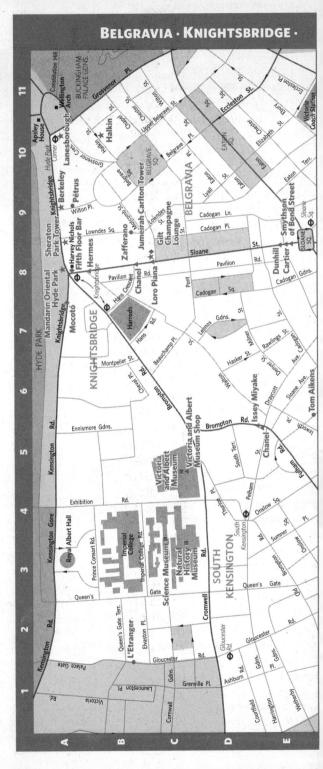

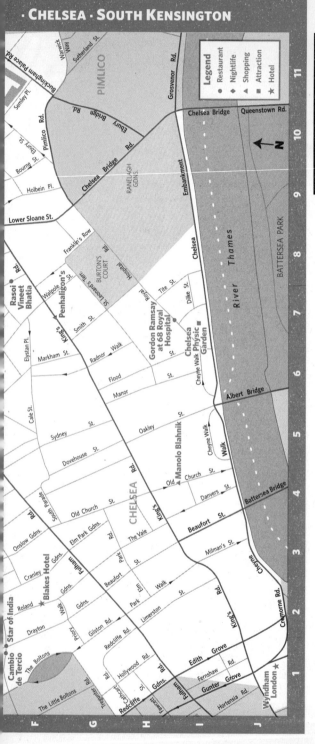

· CHELSEA · SOUTH KENSINGTON

Legend
- ● Restaurant
- ◆ Nightlife
- ▲ Shopping
- ■ Attraction
- ★ Hotel

MAPS

PIMLICO

Warwick Way

Sutherland St.

Semley Pl.

Buckingham Palace Rd.

Ebury St.

Pimlico Rd.

Ebury Bridge Rd.

Bourne St.

Chelsea Bridge Rd.

Holbein Pl.

Lower Sloane St.

Grosvenor Rd.

Chelsea Bridge

Queenstown Rd.

RANELAGH GDNS.

Embankment

Franklin's Row

BURTON'S COURT

Rasoi
Vineet Bhatia

Walpole's

Penhaligon's

St. Leonard's Terr.

Hospital Rd.

Chelsea

River Thames

BATTERSEA PARK

King's Rd.

Smith St.

Elystan Pl.

Markham St.

Radnor Walk

Flood St.

Manor St.

Cale St.

Sydney St.

Dovehouse St.

Oakley St.

Gordon Ramsay at 68 Royal Hospital

Chelsea Physic Garden

Cheyne Walk

Tite St.

Dilke St.

Royal

Albert Bridge

Cheyne Walk

Manolo Blahnik

Old Church St.

Church St.

Danvers St.

Battersea Bridge

CHELSEA

King's Rd.

Onslow Gdns.

South Parade

Old Church St.

Beaufort St.

Milman's St.

Cheyne

Blakes Hotel

Cranley Gdns.

Elm Park Gdns.

The Vale

Fulham Rd.

Park Rd.

Beaufort St.

Elm Park Rd.

Walk

Star of India

Roland Gdns.

Gilston Rd.

Limerston St.

King's Rd.

Cambio de Tercio

Drayton

Priory Walk

Redcliffe Rd.

Hollywood Rd.

Edith Grove

Fernshaw Rd.

Cremorne Rd.

The Boltons

The Little Boltons

Gilston Rd.

Redcliffe Gdns.

Fawcett St.

Fulham Rd.

Gunter Grove

Hortensia Rd.

Wyndham London ★

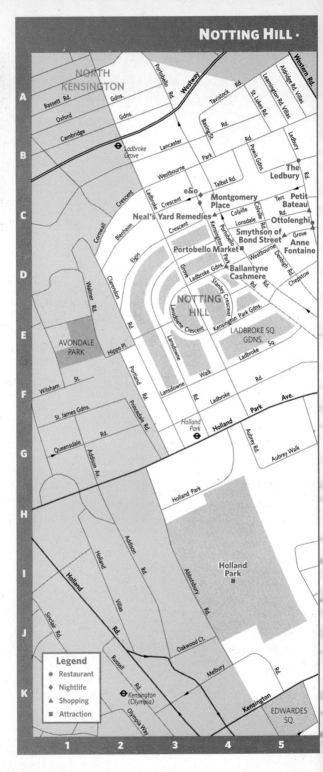

NORTH KENSINGTON

Bassett Rd.

Oxford Gdns.

Cambridge

Portobello Rd.

Westway

Ladbroke Grove

Lancaster

Tavistock Rd.

St. Lukes Rd.

Basing St.

Leamington Rd. Villas

Aldridge Rd. Villas

Western Rd.

Cornwall Crescent

Ladbroke Crescent

Blenheim Crescent

Elgin Crescent

Clarendon Rd.

Walmer Rd.

Westbourne

Powis Gdns.

Rd.

Talbot Rd.

e&o

Montgomery Place

Neal's Yard Remedies

Colville Terr.

Colville Rd.

Lonsdale Rd.

Portobello Rd.

Kensington Park Rd.

Portobello Market

Smythson of Bond Street

Ballantyne Cashmere

Ledbury Rd.

The Ledbury

Petit Bateau

Ottolenghi

Grove

Anne Fontaine

Westbourne

Denbigh Rd.

Chepstow

Ladbroke Gdns.

Grove

Stanley Crescent

NOTTING HILL

Kensington Park Gdns.

LADBROKE SQ. GDNS.

Lansdowne Crescent

Lansdowne

Ladbroke Sq.

AVONDALE PARK

Hippo Pl.

Portland Rd.

Walk

Ladbroke Rd.

Wilsham St.

Lansdowne Rd.

Ladbroke Rd.

Park Ave.

St. James Gdns.

Princedale Rd.

Holland Park

Holland

Aubrey Rd.

Queensdale Rd.

Addison Av.

Aubrey Walk

Holland

Sinclair Rd.

Holland Villas Rd.

Addison Rd.

Holland Park

Abbotsbury Rd.

Holland Park

Russell

Oakwood Ct.

Melbury Rd.

Rd.

Kensington (Olympia)

Olympia Way

Kensington Rd.

EDWARDES SQ.

Legend
- ● Restaurant
- ◆ Nightlife
- ▲ Shopping
- ■ Attraction

subscribe to zagat.com

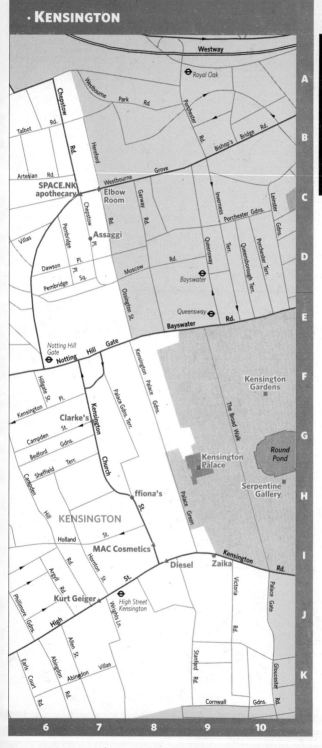

Westway

Royal Oak

Westbourne Park Rd.

Chepstow Rd.

Talbot Rd.

Hereford Rd.

Porchester Rd.

Bishop's Bridge Rd.

Artesian Rd.

Westbourne Grove

SPACE.NK apothecary

Elbow Room

Chepstow Rd.

Garway Rd.

Inverness Terr.

Porchester Gdns.

Leinster Gdns.

Villas

Pembridge Pl.

Assaggi

Queensway

Porchester Terr.

Queensborough Terr.

Dawson Pl.

Pembridge Sq.

Moscow Rd.

Ossington St.

Bayswater

Queensway

Bayswater Rd.

Notting Hill Gate

Notting Hill Gate

Kensington

Kensington Palace Gdns.

Kensington Gardens

Hillgate St.

Pl.

Palace Gdns. Terr.

Kensington Palace Gdns.

The Broad Walk

Kensington

Clarke's St.

Campden

Bedford Gdns.

Sheffield Terr.

Church St.

Round Pond

Kensington Palace

Campden Hill

ffiona's St.

KENSINGTON

Holland St.

Palace Green

Serpentine Gallery

MAC Cosmetics

Kensington Rd.

Argyll Rd.

Hornton St.

Diesel

Zaika

Kurt Geiger

High St.

Wrights Ln.

High Street Kensington

Victoria Rd.

Palace Gate

Phillimore Gdns.

Allen St.

Earls Court Rd.

Abingdon Rd.

Abingdon Villas

Stanford Rd.

Gloucester Rd.

Cornwall Gdns.

6 7 8 9 10

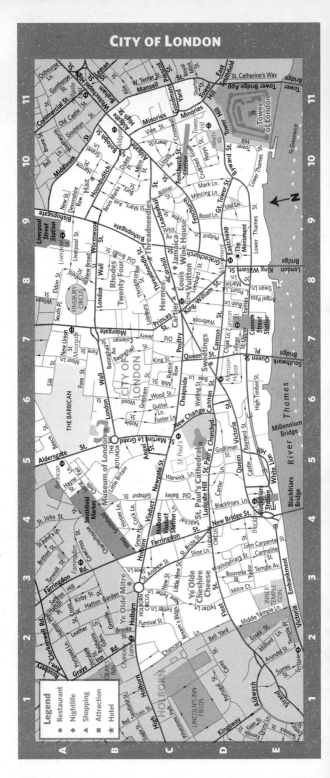

CITY OF LONDON

ALPHABETICAL
PAGE INDEX

☑ indicates places with the highest ratings, popularity and importance.

Wine Vintage Chart

This chart, based on our 0 to 30 scale, is designed to help you select wine. The ratings (by **Howard Stravitz**, a law professor at the University of South Carolina) reflect the vintage quality and the wine's readiness to drink. We exclude the 1987, 1991–1993 vintages because they are not that good. A dash indicates the wine is either past its peak or too young to rate.

Whites	86	88	89	90	94	95	96	97	98	99	00	01	02	03	04	05
French:																
Alsace	–	–	26	26	25	24	24	23	26	24	26	27	25	22	24	25
Burgundy	25	–	23	22	–	28	27	24	23	26	25	24	27	23	25	26
Loire Valley	–	–	–	–	–	–	–	–	–	–	24	25	26	23	24	25
Champagne	25	24	26	29	–	26	27	24	23	24	24	22	26	–	–	–
Sauternes	28	29	25	28	–	21	23	25	23	24	24	28	25	26	21	26
California:																
Chardonnay	–	–	–	–	–	–	–	–	24	23	26	26	27	28	29	
Sauvignon Blanc	–	–	–	–	–	–	–	–	–	–	27	28	26	27	26	
Austrian:																
Grüner Velt./ Riesling	–	–	–	–	–	25	21	28	28	27	22	23	24	26	26	26
German:	–	25	26	27	24	23	26	25	26	23	21	29	27	25	26	26

Reds	86	88	89	90	94	95	96	97	98	99	00	01	02	03	04	05
French:																
Bordeaux	25	23	25	29	22	26	25	23	25	24	29	26	24	25	23	27
Burgundy	–	–	24	26	–	26	27	26	22	27	22	24	27	24	24	25
Rhône	–	26	28	28	24	26	22	24	27	26	27	26	–	25	24	–
Beaujolais	–	–	–	–	–	–	–	–	–	–	24	–	23	27	23	28
California:																
Cab./Merlot	–	–	–	28	29	27	25	28	23	26	22	27	26	25	24	24
Pinot Noir	–	–	–	–	–	–	–	24	23	24	23	27	28	26	23	–
Zinfandel	–	–	–	–	–	–	–	–	–	–	–	25	23	27	22	–
Oregon:																
Pinot Noir	–	–	–	–	–	–	–	–	–	–	–	26	27	24	25	–
Italian:																
Tuscany	–	–	–	25	22	24	20	29	24	27	24	26	20	–	–	–
Piedmont	–	–	27	27	–	23	26	27	26	25	28	27	20	–	–	–
Spanish:																
Rioja	–	–	–	–	26	26	24	25	22	25	24	27	20	24	25	–
Ribera del Duero/Priorat	–	–	–	–	26	26	27	25	24	25	24	27	20	24	26	–
Australian:																
Shiraz/Cab.	–	–	–	–	24	26	23	26	28	24	24	27	27	25	26	–

subscribe to zagat.com

ON THE GO.
IN THE KNOW.

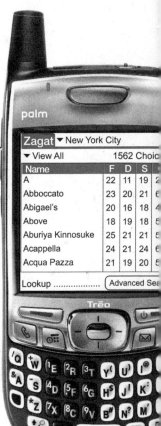

ZAGAT TO GO℠

Unlimited access
to Zagat dining &
travel content
in hundreds of
major cities.

Search by name,
location, ratings,
cuisine, special
features and Top Lists.

For BlackBerry,® Palm,®
Windows Mobile®
and mobile phones.

Get it now at **mobile.zagat.com**
or text* **ZAGAT** to **78247**

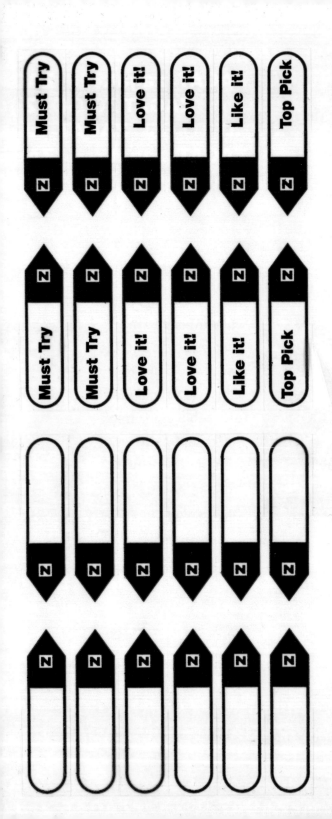

GW00492576